Captured Peace

Ohio University Research in International Studies

This series of publications on Africa, Latin America, Southeast Asia, and Global and Comparative Studies is designed to present significant research, translation, and opinion to area specialists and to a wide community of persons interested in world affairs. The editors seek manuscripts of quality on any subject and can usually make a decision regarding publication within three months of receipt of the original work. Production methods generally permit a work to appear within one year of acceptance. The editors work closely with authors to produce high-quality books. The series is distributed worldwide. For more information, consult the Ohio University Press website, ohioswallow.com.

Books in the Ohio University Research in International Studies series are published by Ohio University Press in association with the Center for International Studies. The views expressed in individual volumes are those of the authors and should not be considered to represent the policies or beliefs of the Center for International Studies, Ohio University Press, or Ohio University.

Captured Peace

Elites and Peacebuilding in El Salvador

Christine J. Wade

Ohio University Press
Research in International Studies
Latin America Series No. 52
Athens, Ohio

To obtain permission to quote, reprint, or otherwise reproduce or distribute material from
Ohio University Press publications, please contact our rights and permissions department at
(740) 593-1154 or (740) 593-4536 (fax).
www.ohioswallow.com

Printed in the United States of America

The books in the Ohio University Research in International Studies Series
are printed on acid-free paper ∞ ™

26 25 24 23 22 21 20 19 18 17 16   5 4 3 2 1

Library of Congress Cataloging-in-Publication Data

Names: Wade, Christine J.
Title: Captured peace : elites and peacebuilding in El Salvador / Christine
J. Wade.
Description: Athens, Ohio : Ohio University Press, 2016. | Series: Ohio
University research in international studies ; no. 52 | Includes
bibliographical references and index.
Identifiers: LCCN 2015038304| ISBN 9780896802971 (hardcover : acid-free
paper) | ISBN 9780896802988 (paperback : acid-free paper) | ISBN
9780896804913 (PDF)
Subjects: LCSH: El Salvador—Politics and government—1992- | Elite (Social
sciences)—Political activity—El Salvador—History. |
Peace-building—Social aspects—El Salvador—History. | Social control—El
Salvador—History. | Political violence—El Salvador—History. |
Violence—Economic aspects—El Salvador—History. | Alianza Republicana
Nacionalista (El Salvador) | Political parties—El Salvador—History. |
Political participation—El Salvador—History. | BISAC: POLITICAL SCIENCE
/ General. | SOCIAL SCIENCE / General. | POLITICAL SCIENCE / Peace.
Classification: LCC F1488.5 .W33 2016 | DDC 972.8405/3—dc23
LC record available at http://lccn.loc.gov/2015038304

For Greg

Contents

Illustrations

Figures

Tables

Acknowledgments

This book is based on field research conducted during visits to El Salvador in July 1999–March 2000, March 2004, October–November 2006, and March 2009. Over the course of that decade, I conducted interviews with more than one hundred government representatives, politicians, analysts, labor leaders, business leaders, and representatives of various nongovernmental organizations from across the political spectrum. These interviews were vital in shaping my understanding of how much El Salvador has achieved since the end of the war, and how far it has yet to go. As with most projects of this duration and scope, I could not have done it without the assistance of others. I received faculty enhancement and travel funds from Washington College for this project in 2004, 2006, and 2009. I was also the recipient of a Christian A. Johnson Fellowship, which generously provided me with a semester-long sabbatical in the fall of 2006 to work on this project. I have also benefited from funds from the Louis L. Goldstein '35 Program in Public Affairs.

I am particularly grateful to Tommie Sue Montgomery, Rubén Zamora, María Ester del Pilar Chamorro de Zamora, Salvador Sanabria, Alberto Arene, Francesca Jessup, David Holiday, Loly de Zuniga, Roberto Cañas, Graciela Villamariona, Gloria Pacas, Damian Alegria, Francisco Altschul, and Melinda Altschul for their assistance with various aspects of my research while in El Salvador. I would like to thank Michael Allison, John Booth, Héctor Lindo-Fuentes, Tommie Sue Montgomery, Scott Palmer, Bill Stanley, and an anonymous reviewer for their comments on all or parts of the draft manuscript. Their insights and suggestions were enormously helpful. Any errors are mine. I am especially thankful to Gillian Berchowitz and the editorial team at Ohio University Press for their support throughout this project. I also wish to acknowledge my student research assistants, David Hosey, Maureen Sentman, and Brittany Weaver, who assisted me with various parts of the manuscript preparation over the years. I also owe a debt of thanks to my long-suffering friends and colleagues who supported me on this project, including Melissa Deckman, Kathryn Moncrief, Andrew Oros, Daniel Premo, and John Taylor. I am indebted to my parents, who encouraged my interests and supported my research even though I know my far-flung adventures often scared them. Finally, my husband, Gregory Waddell, has been an endless well of love and support. Thank you, Greg, for always believing in me.

Abbreviations

ABC   American Baptist Churches

ABECAFE   Association of Coffee Processors and Exporters (Asociación
           Salvadoreña de Beneficiadores y Exportadores del Café)

ADC   Democratic Peasant Alliance (Alianza Democrática
           Campesina)

AFP   pension fund administrator (Administradora de Fondos de
           Pensiones)

AMPES   Association of Medium and Small Businesses (Asociación de
           Medianos y Pequeños Empresarios de El Salvador)

ANDA   National Administration of Aqueducts and Sewers
           (Administración Nacional de Acueductos y Alcantarillados)

ANDES   National Association of Salvadoran Educators (Asociación
           Nacional de Educadores Salvadoreños)

ANEP   National Association of Private Enterprise (Asociación
           Nacional de la Empresa Privada)

ANSP   National Academy for Public Security (Academia Nacional
           de Seguridad Pública)

ANTEL   National Telecommunications Company (Administración
           Nacional de Telecomunicaciones)

APROAS   Association of Salvadoran Agricultural Producers
           (Asociación de Productores Agricolas)

ARENA   Nationalist Republican Alliance (Alianza Republicana
           Nacionalista)

ASCAFE   Salvadoran Coffee Association (Asociación Salvadoreña de
           Café)

ASIC   Association of Friends of San Isidro Cabañas (Asociación
           Amigos de San Isidro Cabañas)

ATCA	U.S. Alien Tort Claims Act
BANAFI	National Industrial Development Bank (Banco Nacional de Fomento Industrial)
BIRI	Rapid-Deployment Infantry Battalion (Batallón Infantería Reacción Inmediata)
BPR	Popular Revolutionary Bloc (Bloque Popular Revolucionario)
BPS	Popular Social Bloc (Bloque Popular Social)
CAC	Cabañas Environmental Committee (Comité Ambiental de Cabañas)
CACIF	Coordinating Committee of Agricultural, Commercial, Industrial, and Financial Associations (Comité Coordinador de Asociaciones Agrícolas, Comerciales, Industriales y Financieras) (Guatemala)
CACM	Central American Common Market
CAFTA	Central America Free Trade Agreement
CAFTA-DR	Dominican Republic–Central America Free Trade Agreement
CARECEN	Central American Resource Center (Centro de Recursos Centroamericanos)
CCE	Central Election Council (Consejo Central de Elecciones)
CD	Democratic Convergence (Convergencia Democrática)
CDU	United Democratic Center (Centro Democrático Unido)
CEB	Christian base communities (*comunidades eclesiales de base*)
CEL	Executive Hydroelectric Commission of the Lempa River (Comisión Ejecutiva Hidroeléctrica del Río Lempa)
CELAM II	Second Latin American Episcopal Conference (Consejo Episcopal Latinoamericano)
CN	National Coalition (Concertación Nacional)
CND	National Development Commission (Comisión Nacional de Desarrollo)
COENA	National Executive Council (Consejo Ejecutivo Nacional)

COMURES Corporation of Municipalities of the Republic of El Salvador (Corporación de Municipalidades de la República de El Salvador)

CONASOL Committee for National Solidarity (Comité Nacional Solidario)

COPAZ National Commission for the Consolidation of Peace (Comisión Nacional para la Consolidación de la Paz)

CORSAIN Salvadoran Investment Corporation (Corporación Salvadoreña de Inversiones)

CREDISA Property Loans, SA (Crédito Inmobiliario Sociedad Anónima)

CRIPDES Association for the Development of El Salvador (Asociación de Comunidades Rurales para el Desarrollo de El Salvador)

CSJ Supreme Court of Justice (Corte Suprema de Justicia)

DGACE Directorate General of Attention for the Community Abroad (Dirección General De Atención a las Comunidades en el Exterior)

DRU United Revolutionary Directorate (Directorio Revolucionario Unido)

DUI universal identification card (*documento único de identidad*)

ENADE National Meeting of Private Enterprise (Encuentro Nacional de la Empresa Privada)

ERP People's Revolutionary Army (Ejército Revolucionario del Pueblo)

FAES Armed Forces of El Salvador (Fuerza Armada de El Salvador)

FAL Armed Forces of Liberation (Fuerzas Armadas de Liberación)

FALANGE Anticommunist Armed Forces of Liberation by Wars of Elimination (Fuerzas Armadas de Liberación Anticomunista de Guerras de Eliminación)

FAN Broad Nationalist Front (Frente Amplio Nacional)

FAPU United Popular Action Front (Frente de Acción Popular Unificada)

FARN — Armed Forces of National Resistance (Fuerzas Armadas de Resistencia Nacional)

FDR — Democratic Revolutionary Front (Frente Democrático Revolucionario)

FECCAS — Christian Federation of Salvadoran Campesinos (Federación Cristiana de Campesinos Salvadoreños)

FENASTRAS — National Trade Union Federation of Salvadoran Workers (Federación Nacional Sindical de Trabajadores Salvadoreños)

FESAL — National Family Health Survey (Encuesta Nacional de Salud Familiar)

FESPAD — Foundation for the Study of the Application of Law (Fundación de Estudios para la Aplicación del Derecho)

FGR — Public Prosecutor's Office (Fiscalía General de la República)

FISDL — Social Investment Fund for Local Development (Fondo Inversión Social para el Desarrollo Local)

FLACSO — Latin American School of Social Sciences (Facultad Latinoamericana de Ciencias Sociales)

FMLN — Farabundo Martí National Liberation Front (Frente Farabundo Martí para la Liberación Nacional)

Foro — Forum for Economic and Social Consultation (Foro de Concertación Económica y Social)

FOSALUD — Fund for Health Solidarity (Fondo Solidario para la Salud)

FPL — Popular Forces of Liberation (Fuerzas Populares de Liberación)

FUNDE — National Foundation for Development (Fundación Nacional para el Desarrollo)

FUSADES — Salvadoran Foundation for Economic and Social Development (Fundación Salvadoreña para el Desarrollo Económico y Social)

GANA — Grand Alliance for National Unity (Gran Alianza Nacional)

GDR	Democratic Revolutionary Government (Gobierno Democrático Revolucionario)
GOES	government of El Salvador
GTA	Antigang Task Forces (Grupos de Tarea Antipandillas)
IACHR	Inter-American Court of Human Rights
IDB	Inter-American Development Bank
IDHUCA	Human Rights Institute at the University of Central America (Instituto de Derechos Humanos de la UCA)
IIRAIRA	Illegal Immigration Reform and Immigrant Responsibility Act
ILO	International Labor Organization
IML	Institute of Forensic Medicine (Instituto de Medicina Legal)
INAZUCAR	National Sugar Institute (Instituto Nacional de Azúcar)
INCAFE	National Coffee Institute (Instituto Nacional del Café)
INS	Immigration and Naturalization Service
ISDEMU	Salvadoran Institute for the Advancement of Women (Instituto Salvadoreño para el Desarrollo de la Mujer)
ISI	import substitution industrialization
ISSS	Salvadoran Social Security Institute (Instituto Salvadoreño del Seguro Social)
IUDOP	University of Central America Institute for Public Opinion (Instituto Universitario de Opinión Pública Universidad Centroamericana, "José Simeón Cañas")
IVA	value-added tax (*impuesto al valor agregado*)
JVE	Electoral Review Board (Junta de Revisión Electoral)
LAR	ARENA League to the Rescue (Liga Arenera al Rescate)
MAC	Authentic Christian Movement (Movimiento Auténtico Cristiano)
MCC	Millennium Challenge Corporation
MINUSAL	United Nations Mission in El Salvador (Misión de las Naciones Unidas en El Salvador)

MIPLAN   Ministry of Planning and Coordination of Economic and Social Development (Ministerio de Planificación y Coordinación del Desarrollo Económico y Social)

MNR   National Revolutionary Movement (Movimiento Nacional Revolucionario)

MPR-12   Popular Resistance Movement of October 12 (Movimiento Popular de Resistencia 12 de Octubre)

MPSC   Popular Social Christian Movement (Movimiento Popular Social Cristiana)

MS-13   Mara Salvatrucha

NACLA   North American Congress on Latin America

NGO   nongovernmental organization

OAS   French Secret Army Organization (Organisation de l'Armée Secrète)

ONUCA   United Nations Observer Group in Central America

ONUSAL   United Nations Observer Mission in El Salvador

ORDEN   Nationalist Democratic Organization (Organización Democrática Nacionalista)

PARLACEN Central American Parliament (Parlamento Centroamericano)

PCN   National Conciliation Party (Partido de Conciliación Nacional)

PCS   Salvadoran Communist Party (Partido Comunista de El Salvador)

PD   Democratic Party (Partido Democrático)

PDC   Christian Democratic Party (Partido Demócrata Cristiana)

PDDH   National Counsel for the Defense of Human Rights (Procuraduría para la Defensa de los Derechos Humanos)

PES   Party of Hope (Partido de la Esperanza)

PFG   Partnership for Growth

PLD   Liberal Democratic Party (Partido Liberal Democráta)

PMR	Reformist Movement Party (Partido Movimiento Renovador)
PN	National Police (Policía Nacional)
PNC	National Civilian Police (Policía Nacional Civil)
PND	National Democratic Party (Partido Nacional Democrático)
PRI	Institutional Revolutionary Party (Partido Revolucionario Institucional) (Mexico)
PRN	National Reconstruction Plan (Plan de Reconstrucción Nacional)
PRTC	Revolutionary Party of Central American Workers (Partido Revolucionario de Trabajadores Centroamericanos)
PRUD	Revolutionary Party of Democratic Unification (Partido Revolucionario de Unificación Democrática)
PTT	Land Transfer Program (Programa de Transferencia de la Tierra)
RN	National Resistance (Resistencia Nacional)
RNPN	National Registry of Natural Persons (Registro Nacional de Personas Naturales)
SIF	Social Investment Fund (Fondo de Inversión Social)
SIMETRISSS	Medical Workers Union of the Salvadoran Social Security Institute (Sindicato de Médicos Trabajadores del Instituto Salvadoreño del Seguro Social)
SIU	Special Investigative Unit of the Commission to Investigate Criminal Acts
SRN	Secretariat for National Reconstruction
SRP	Social Rescue Plan
STISSS	Workers' Union Salvadoran Social Security Institute (Sindicato de Trabajadores del Instituto Salvadoreño del Seguro Social)
TPS	temporary protected status

TSE	Supreme Electoral Tribunal (Tribunal Supremo Electoral)
TVPA	U.S. Torture Victim Protection Act
UCA	University of Central America (Universidad Centroamericano, "Jose Simeón Cañas")
UDN	Nationalist Democratic Union (Unión Democráta Nacional)
UEA	Executive Anti–Drug Trafficking Unit of the National Police (Unidad Ejecutiva Antinarcotráfico)
UES	University of El Salvador (Universidad de El Salvador)
UNDP	United Nations Development Program
Unidos	United for Solidarity (Unidos por la Solidaridad)
UNO	National Opposition Union (Unión Oposición Nacional)
UNODC	United Nations Office on Drugs and Crime
USAID	U.S. Agency for International Development

Introduction

Peacebuilding, Elites, and the Problem of Capture

> The population does not value peace as a synonym for
> progress. Peace for most people does not make sense
> because it has no social content, or the content lacks
> justice. The impact of the neoliberal transition of the
> past fifteen years has laid a foundation for society that
> trends toward authoritarianism rather than democracy.
>
> —Salvador Sánchez Cerén, October 2006[1]

ON OCTOBER 15, 1979, a group of junior officers overthrew El Salvador's military government with the intent of forestalling a revolution. Decades of systematic repression, socioeconomic exclusion, and the collapse of legal political space in the early 1970s had resulted in the mobilization of guerrilla organizations and affiliated social groups that wished to dismantle the existing political and economic order in one of Central America's most unequal and violent societies. The subsequent juntas, composed of military officers and civilians, had hoped to loosen the military's grip on the state and the oligarchy's grip on the economy. The successive juntas failed to achieve the reforms it deemed necessary to prevent the escalation of violence, reforms that threatened the country's most powerful economic elites. The levels of state violence increased and, by 1980, El Salvador was a country at war with itself.

1

More than seventy-five thousand Salvadorans were killed and one million more displaced in the civil war, making it one of the most destructive in the region. Driven to the negotiating table by a military stalemate with the Farabundo-Martí National Liberation Front (FMLN) guerrillas, the Salvadoran government under President Alfredo Cristiani invited the United Nations to mediate a settlement that would end the war. El Salvador's civil war was to be the first in which the United Nations agreed to act as mediator in such negotiations. The negotiations began in April 1990 and continued for almost two years, during which the participation of the UN and mediation by the secretary general's office were crucial to the successful negotiation of sensitive issues, particularly military reform. On January 16, 1992, representatives for the government of El Salvador (GOES) and the FMLN signed the peace accords that aimed not only to end the civil war but to build lasting peace. The Chapúltepec Peace Accords, named after the castle where they were signed in Mexico City, promised a new beginning for El Salvador. Hailed as a success story of United Nations peacebuilding efforts, the peace process transformed the country's political landscape. The accords placed the military under civilian control for the first time in El Salvador's history. State-sponsored terrorism ceased to be the modus operandi of the country's various "security forces," which were eliminated and replaced with a new civilian police force. Opposition parties and their affiliated organizations were legalized and, over time, functioned without fear of recrimination. The FMLN transitioned from a guerrilla movement to political party, becoming the largest party in the legislature and governing more than 50 percent of the population following the 2000 legislative and municipal elections. The party later won presidential elections in 2009 and 2014. While implementation of the accords was not without its problems, the ceasefire has never been broken. According to a 1997 report of the United Nations secretary general, "the most notable development has been that the peace process has also allowed for the opening-up of political space for democratic participation. A climate of tolerance prevails today, unlike any the country has known before."[2] El Salvador was undoubtedly freer than it had ever been throughout its history.

But all was not well in El Salvador. A mere seven years later, another UN secretary general's report commented that the 2004 elections had "generated a wave of polarization that surpassed any seen since the signing of the Peace Agreement."[3] While the peace accords ended the armed conflict, numerous factors continued to undermine the quality of that peace. Democratic elections have become routinized, but Salvadoran voters are increasingly disenchanted with the political process. Political parties control the public discourse, and political polarization limits representation and political space. Corruption and impunity are pervasive, resulting in low levels of confidence in state institutions. Organized crime and social violence have replaced political violence, making El Salvador one of the most violent countries in the world. Successive administrations have failed to reduce the violence, and their authoritarian solutions to the problems have not only been in direct contradiction to the peace accords but have exacerbated the problem. Millions of Salvadorans still live in poverty and many are forced to supplement their families' incomes by making the dangerous journey to the United States in search of work. More Salvadorans have left the country since the end of the war than during it, and their remittances sustain the stagnant Salvadoran economy. Twenty years after the signing of the peace accords, 62 percent of Salvadorans said that things were the same or worse than during the war, and 57 percent expressed little to no satisfaction with the functioning of Salvadoran democracy.[4] While the peace accords ended the war, many Salvadorans remained dissatisfied with the quality of peace, as illustrated by the epigraph to this introduction from newly elected president Salvador Sánchez Cerén. One of the great ironies of El Salvador's peace process is that while outsiders consider it a success, Salvadorans do not.[5] All this begs the question, What happened to the peace in El Salvador?

UN Peacebuilding and the Liberal Peace

During the past two decades, the United Nations has become increasingly involved in the settlement of civil wars across the globe. Since 1989 more than a dozen civil wars have ended with UN-brokered peace agreements, including those in El Salvador, Cambodia, Mozambique, Bosnia, and Guatemala. In 1992 former UN secretary general Boutros Boutros-Ghali recognized that the needs of postconflict societies extended well beyond the bounds of traditional peacekeeping, which was generally limited to international conflicts and involved activities such as dispute settlement, monitoring ceasefires, and the separation of forces. In his book *An Agenda for Peace*, Boutros-Ghali pushes for an increase in international assistance to effectively rebuild these societies. Peacebuilding, he argues, requires that peace processes address the root causes of conflict in order to prevent any reversion to armed violence.[6] The creation of lasting peace entails moving beyond the mere cessation of war and toward creating a stable, just, and reconciled society. His thesis reflects work done in the field of peace and conflict studies by theorists such as Johan Galtung, who developed the concepts of positive (eliminations of the causes of violence) and negative peace (absence of war) in an attempt to more fully define the criteria for the consolidation of peace.[7] As such, peacebuilding efforts often comprised a wide variety of activities aimed at reconstructing postwar societies. These include conflict cessation (including disarmament, demobilization, and reintegration of ex-combatants), institutional reform, human rights and elections monitoring, provision and training of security forces, and the repatriation of refugees. While much of this work was conducted by the UN and its programs and specialized agencies, nongovernmental organizations (NGOs) also engaged in a vast array of humanitarian assistance and reconstruction activities. Among them were disarmament, education, health care, societal reconciliation, and infrastructure and development projects.

In practice, peacebuilding has often combined elements of traditional peacekeeping with statebuilding and economic development.[8] As such, "liberal" peacebuilding, as it is often referred to by critics, seeks to establish democratic governments and market economies as the chief means of delivering peace and prosperity. This approach has been largely informed by the democratic peace theory, the idea that democracy reduces prospects for war between democratic states.[9] While there has been increasing attention paid to the establishment of functioning state institutions, rule of law, and societal reconciliation or transitional justice, these elements have often been secondary to the dual processes of democratization and marketization.

Peacebuilding Outcomes

The results of UN peacebuilding efforts have been mixed, and measuring "success" has been difficult. Early peacebuilding missions tended to be overly broad and vague in purpose (prevention of the recurrence of conflict) and scope (extending to the many needs of postconflict societies). Moreover, there were no clear criteria for mission success beyond sustaining the cessation of armed conflict.[10] In that regard, the results are discouraging: as many as one-third of negotiated settlements collapse within five years and the resulting violence may eclipse preaccord violence.[11] Additionally, relatively few

4

peacebuilding efforts have resulted in liberal democracies. In an analysis of nineteen major peacebuilding operations, Christoph Zürcher has found that fewer than half could be considered liberal or electoral democracies.[12] Fewer still showed outward signs of established rule of law, societal reconciliation or economic development.[13] Virginia Page Fortna's study of the effect of peace-keeping missions on democratization demonstrates that while missions are generally effective at maintaining peace and security, they may serve to under-mine democracy in the long term.[14] It is worth noting, however, that this is not dissimilar from the broader experience of transitional countries that exist in what Thomas Carothers refers to as "the gray zone," wherein countries have some characteristics of democracy but suffer significant democratic deficits.[15] Dozens of countries remain trapped somewhere between dictatorship and lib-eral democracy, some with little prospect of making a complete transition any time soon. The modest, if not disappointing, peacebuilding outcomes resulted in the emergence of a wide-ranging critique of UN peacebuilding efforts. Critics of liberal peacebuilding argue that it has failed to deliver sus-tainable peace. Roland Paris, Michael Pugh, Oliver Richmond, and others argue that the application of neoliberal economic reforms, the imposition of Western values before institutional development (liberalization before institutionalization), the emphasis on stability over freedom, and the failure to incorporate civil society into peacebuilding efforts all may serve to under-mine and reduce the quality of peace.[16] Additionally, critics argue that this basic formula has been applied in countries as diverse as Bosnia, Cambodia, El Salvador, Guatemala, Mozambique, and Rwanda without respect to local cultures or realities. In each of these cases, the peace processes envisioned peace through democratization, focusing primarily on creating a climate con-ducive to holding free and fair elections as quickly as possible. The emphasis on elections was based on the underlying assumption that elections would create participatory democracy, which presumably would yield peace divi-dends. Given the failure of most transitions to produce liberal democracies, critics charge that electoral competition and neoliberal economic policies have undermined prospects for peace in most postconflict societies. Accord-ing to Paris, such "Wilsonianism" is potentially destabilizing and may even reproduce the sources of conflict in postconflict societies.[17] While the causes of recurrence of civil war (and peace failure) are more complicated than some of the critical literature suggests, it does succeed in highlighting the gaps between the stated intentions of peacebuilding and actual outcomes.[18]

The Importance of Local Actors in Peacebuilding

Both traditional peacebuilding literature and critical theory focus heavily on the ideologies, actions, and policies of outside actors (the peacebuilders). But peacebuilders do not bear the sole responsibility for the outcomes of peacebuilding. In his critique, Ole Jacob Sending argues that the focus on external actors largely ignores the extent to which these practices are shaped by the principle of sovereignty and the role of local actors.[19] In fact, local actors are integral to the outcomes of every aspect of the peace process, from agenda setting through implementation. Peacebuilders are involved at the will of local actors and, by necessity, must work within the constraints set forth by them. As noted by Miles Kahler, "their [peacebuilders'] programs become part of an intricate set of political calculations on the part of existing elites and their rivals. Whatever the asymmetries in power, local actors possess bargaining power and often use it effectively."[20] This bargaining power may occur through either formal or informal power at the negotiating table. As Roman Krznaric demonstrates in the case of Guatemala, the Coordinating Committee of Agricultural, Commercial, Industrial, and Financial Associations (CACIF), the country's most important business organization, wielded significant influence over the socioeconomic content of the accords despite not being a direct party to the negotiations.[21]

While local peacebuilding actors may include the state, armed opposition forces, civil society, and other political actors, elites often have the most influence on peacebuilding. Depending on the case, local elites may include economic elites, political elites, military elites, or some nexus of the three.[22] The preferences, or desired outcomes, and capacity of local elites engaged in peacemaking and peacebuilding have been long neglected in both peacebuilding literature and the critical responses to it. Yet local elite preferences have a significant impact on peace processes and peacebuilding, more specifically. The two most obvious ways that elite preferences shape peace processes are through their desire to maintain the status quo and their control of state resources and patronage networks. It is, perhaps, not surprising that elites seek to preserve their interests during peace processes, which often seek to alter the status quo. As David Roberts notes, elite entrenchment is a characteristic of many postconflict societies.[23] While one result of this entrenchment may be institutional reform, patterns of patronage and clientelism continue to dominate political culture in these countries. In its most benign form, elite entrenchment can result in increased polarization and may undermine democratic governance. At its worst, elite entrenchment may result in the resuscitation of conflict, as elites attempt to retain power and fight proposed reforms.[24]

Far from being impotent actors at the mercy of international institutions, local elites often find ways to use the peacebuilding process to (re)consolidate or establish their control. Elites may feign interest in reforms to appease peacebuilders in order to gain or maintain access to resources without ever intending to undertake liberalizing reforms or by undermining reforms through informal structures.[25] Michael Barnett and Christoph Zürcher argue that the interactions between state elites, who seek to maximize their own interests, and peacebuilders shape the content of negotiations and determine the outcomes of peacebuilding.[26] The authors describe a range of potential outcomes of this interaction, as defined by the extent of the antagonistic relationship between peacebuilders and local elites. The authors argue that most cases result in "compromised peacebuilding," where "state elites accept the legitimacy of the peacebuilders' reforms in exchange for international assistance and legitimacy but seek to preserve their self-interest."[27] Under this model, state elites work with peacebuilders to jointly determine policies. The result is an outcome that promotes reform while protecting the interests of the status quo.[28] In a more recent work, Barnett, Songying Fang, and Zürcher elaborate on compromised peacebuilding by employing a game-theoretic model to examine the outcome of bargaining between peacebuilders, elites, and secondary elites. Not surprisingly, divergence between the peacebuilders' ideal outcome and elites' preference toward the status quo leads to compromised peacebuilding and, as such, contributes to illiberal democracy.[29] That said, the authors do not argue that compromised peacebuilding is necessarily detrimental to future democratic development but may create the basis for it.

One result of this bargaining between local elites and peacebuilders may be hybridity, a condition "where liberal and illiberal norms, institutions, and actors coexist, interact, and even clash."[30] The literature on hybridity and hybrid governance seeks to explain peacebuilding outcomes as the by-product of the liberal peacebuilding agenda and local actors and culture.[31] It can also, as Richmond demonstrates, serve as a critique about peacebuilding's failure to engage the local.[32] Hybridity is useful in explaining the wide variety of outcomes seen in postconflict peacebuilding, as most cases exist on the continuum between liberal and illiberal.[33] In its most illiberal form, hybrid governance may result in state capture by economic elites while still possessing some features of democracy.

Elites and Capture

The literature on state capture yields interesting insights for our understanding of the role of elites in peacebuilding. Derived from the literature on regulatory capture, which deals with the influence of firms (or interest groups) on policy outcomes, capture theory has recently been applied by theorists to examine corruption in transitional states and economies.[34] State capture occurs when powerful individuals or firms are able to influence the content and application of public policy in accordance with their own interests in exchange for bribes to public officials.[35] It is a system of corruption characterized by a "perversion of the rules of the game, through corruption, to the benefit of the captors, rather than for society as a whole."[36] Recent studies on state capture indicate that it can affect a wide range of institutions, including the legislature, executive judiciary, ministries, and security. But elites do not just capture the state through bribes or special-interest groups; they occupy positions within the government. This capture may be facilitated by the overlapping economic and political interests of elites, or when "preexisting networks and new economic elites have secured positions of dominance in the transition environment creating a new fusion of economic and political power."[37] Because states in transition and newly democratic states may be particularly vulnerable to capture, it may also help to illuminate obstacles in peacebuilding.[38]

There is relatively little literature exploring elite capture in peacebuilding, though recent scholarship on corruption and peacebuilding helps illuminate many of the same challenges.[39] In addition to compromised peacebuilding, "captured peacebuilding" is one of the outcomes identified by Barnett and Zürcher. In captured peacebuilding, state and local elites are able to redirect the distribution of assistance so that it maximizes their interests.[40] Beyond merely protecting the status quo, this scenario allows elites to direct resources brought in by the peace process to reinforce those interests for years to come. In her work on decentralization and peacebuilding in Sierra Leone, Melissa Labonte explores the problem of elite capture and its effects on peacebuilding. According to Labonte, elite capture occurs "when elites control, shape or manipulate decision-making processes, institutions, or structures in ways that serve their self-interests and priorities."[41] Elite capture is made possible by a variety of factors, including institutional design and enduring structures and power relations, that may transcend or limit prospects for peacebuilding and democratization. Daron Acemoglu and James Robinson also find that some structures (particularly economic institutions) persist even in the face of radical change. In their explanation of "captured democracy," de jure power (by right) is offset by de facto power (in fact) of elites, resulting in "captured democracy."[42] These findings reinforce the importance of path dependence and the legacies of deeply rooted institutions.[43] As old networks merge with new elites during the transition, it is not only the preferences of elites during the peacebuilding processes that influence outcomes but the cumulative effect of past preferences that have shaped structures within which peacebuilding occurs. As such, elites may adopt the language of peacebuilding and liberalism while retaining a political culture of patronage and clientelism. As David Roberts puts it, "the norm trumps the nomenclature."[44]

I would add that elite capture need not be the result of a transition but may actually precede it. In the case of El Salvador, elites captured the state through a political party before the negotiation and implementation of peace accords. As Ho-Won Jeong notes, incumbent governments that remained in power through the transitions enjoyed significant advantages by controlling state institutions and resources. Relatively few incumbent governments have lost elections in the immediate aftermath of conflict, giving them significant leverage over the peacebuilding process.[45] Miles Kahler finds that "control of the state provides a key resource to local actors," and may ultimately diminish the influence of peacebuilders.[46] Thus, incumbents (and those who support them) can use the state to wield significant influence over peace processes.

Argument and Structure of the Book

This is a book about politics—it shows how those in power seek to preserve their own interests at the expense of their professed commitment to peacebuilding, how an incumbent party wields this political advantage throughout the peace process (in terms of both negotiations and implementation), and the consequences of that advantage to the quality of peace that results.[47]

Incumbents may leverage such benefits as the control of state institutions and resources, perceptions of experience, access to resources (such as the media), and international recognition and legitimacy to obtain desired outcomes, namely protecting their own self-interest. Drawing on Labonte's definition of *capture,* I use the term to describe the system by which elites controlled and manipulated institutions (whether formal or informal) and policy outcomes to preserve and advance their own interests.

The case of El Salvador presents a unique opportunity to investigate the impact of local actors, particularly incumbent elites, on peacebuilding. The incumbent party the Nationalist Republican Alliance (ARENA), held the presidency for twenty years (1989–2009). Those twenty years spanned the final months of the war, peace negotiations, the implementation of the accords, and four presidential election cycles that culminated in ARENA's loss of the presidency, in 2009. The structure of the Salvadoran political system, alliances with smaller parties, and U.S. assistance gave the party near complete dominance over policymaking during that period. I argue that ARENA's incumbency gave it significant political advantages in determining the content of negotiations, overseeing the implementation of the peace accords, and directing economic policy. This control enabled ARENA to minimize its losses in the negotiated settlement—at least in the short term.

The primary goal of the Alfredo Cristiani administration (1989–94) was to end the war in order to restore economic stability without sacrificing political power. Unlike elites in other conflicts and even some factions among the Salvadoran right, ARENA did not need to be convinced of the benefits of democracy. Salvadoran elites had a long tradition of electoral politics, which it used to protect its own interests. Moreover, as Elizabeth Wood so convincingly argues, elites had determined that they could preserve and even promote their economic interests while supporting democratic reforms.[48] Cristiani envisioned El Salvador as the financial capital of Latin America, something that could only be accomplished with the end of the war. To that end, his administration was willing to sacrifice the apparatus responsible for carrying out the violence and to agree to basic reforms that would create the minimal climate necessary for democratic elections. Cristiani made it clear to the FMLN at the beginning of negotiations that there would be no discussion of the neoliberal economic policies that ARENA was implementing. The FMLN, despite its opposition to the neoliberal model, accepted these terms as a price of the negotiated peace.[49] Both Cristiani's terms and the

10

FMLN's acquiescence diverged from popular opinion about the fundamental objectives of the peace process. In a 1991 poll, 30 percent of respondents said that the most important issue to be addressed in the peace negotiations was economic reform. Additionally, it was agreed that the 1983 constitution, written during the civil war without the participation of the full spectrum of Salvadoran political society, would serve as the basic political instrument for the new democracy. Any institutional reforms negotiated by the parties would be implemented by amending that constitution. These factors gave ARENA a significant political advantage by establishing the basic framework of the state and limiting the scope of possible reforms.

In addition to limiting the scope of negotiations, ARENA also leveraged significant control over the implementation process.[50] The responsibility for key reforms that supported the peace accords was assigned to domestic authorities, most of which were highly politicized and controlled by ARENA. Not surprisingly, successive ARENA administrations either stalled or failed to implement necessary reforms or offer meaningful solutions to El Salvador's most pressing problems because they conflicted with their own interests—often to the detriment of building peace. Little more than a year after the signing of the accords, David Holiday and William Stanley noted the lack of political will of the government to purge the officers' corps, as well as delays and funding shortages in the start-up of the new National Civilian Police (PNC) and the human rights ombudsman's office.[51] According to Larry Ladutke, this lack of will "increased the ability of authoritarian forces within both state and society to take back the concessions which the government had made at the negotiating table."[52] The failure to fully support these new, accord-mandated structures has had a significant impact on the credibility of these institutions, as well as serious consequences for civilian security.[53] The National Commission for the Consolidation of Peace (COPAZ) also suffered from serious deficiencies and lacked the ability to enforce compliance, even though it was the national body created to verify implementation of the accords.[54] Other reforms that threatened elite interests stalled or were diluted under ARENA leadership. Having the ARENA-dominated Supreme Electoral Tribunal (TSE) in charge of electoral reform set the foxes to guard the hen house. The tribunal failed to enact many reforms mandated by the accords, including depoliticization of the institution. The sole economic body created by the peace accords, the Forum for Economic and Social Consultation (Foro), failed due to a lack of support from ARENA and the business community. The Cristiani administration developed the National Reconstruction Plan (PRN) with very little input from either the FMLN or the United Nations Development Program (UNDP). Finally, the very public rejection of the findings of the Truth Commission by President Cristiani and the sweeping amnesty law that passed mere days later were indicative of the impunity that long characterized Salvadoran politics. As stated by Antonio Cañas and Héctor Dada, "within the forces and authorities charged with leading state institutions, interests and powers persist that have found it more beneficial to operate by the old system of unwritten, undemocratic rules of the game than to cultivate respect for and adherence to the rule of law."[55] Such practices and thinking continued during the Armando Calderón Sol, Francisco Flores, and Antonio Saca administrations and, it would appear, influenced various aspects of the Mauricio Funes administration. The peace accords may have restructured some of the country's most notorious institutions, but it did little to change the preferences or interests of elites.

The consequences of this incumbency can be felt throughout Salvadoran society and extend well beyond the implementation of the accords. For two decades, ARENA and its allies dominated the country's political, economic, and social agenda. In the political sphere, institutions became highly politicized and limited the scope of representation. Political parties, not citizens, became the primary political actors in El Salvador's new democracy. Moreover, the lack of reconciliation between the wartime adversaries limited prospects for societal reconciliation. Neoliberal economic reforms failed to generate long-term sustainable growth, and Salvadorans increasingly came to rely on remittances to sustain their households. The delays and difficulties associated with the restructuring of the armed forces and the creation of the new civilian police force resulted in a security gap that has had profound consequences for every aspect of Salvadoran society. This book investigates the political, economic, and social aftermath of the peace accords in an effort to illuminate the serious limitations of peacebuilding in what might otherwise be considered a successful peace process.

Chapter 1 identifies patterns of elite behavior and interests that have characterized the Salvadoran state, with the intention of identifying patterns and structures that made captured peacebuilding possible. As demonstrated herein, Salvadoran elites have historically used state resources to consolidate control and advance their own interests. This tendency is evident in the political and economic foundations of the independent Salvadoran state, as demonstrated by the consolidation of power by the Salvadoran oligarchy in the late nineteenth century. I seek to identify critical junctures in El Salvador's past that underscored elite preferences and shaped the context of negotiations and implementation of the accords. As such, I examine the 1881 and 1882 land reforms; the resulting socioeconomic and political tensions of the early twentieth century sparked by the 1931 coup and 1932 peasant rebellion led by Farabundo Martí (and the crushing response to it) that resulted in the a precarious arrangement between the oligarchy and the military; the succession of reactionary and reformist military governments in the 1960s and 1970s that culminated in heightened repression and the overthrow of the military regime in October 1979; and the consequences of U.S. support for the military and democracy promotion in the 1980s.

Chapter 2 examines the structures and dynamics of the peace process that made captured peace possible. I begin with an overview of the peace negotiations and the contents of the agreements that made up the peace accords, examining the extent to which local actors were able to shape the scope and the contents of the agreements. I then address the implementation of the accords, with particular emphasis on the gap between the content of peace accords and their actual implementation. I also examine the extent to which the incumbent government undermined societal reconciliation through the 1993 amnesty law, which has had significant implications for peacebuilding. The chapter concludes with a discussion of the 1994 "elections of the century" that mark El Salvador's transition to democracy, as well as the return of the incumbent ARENA party to power.

Chapters 3 through 5 offer an empirical analysis of postwar peacebuilding in El Salvador by exploring the political, economic, and social dynamics of a captured peace. Chapter 3 assesses postwar politics, including the challenges of democratization and increasing polarization. I review the electoral reforms implemented during and after the peace accords in order to highlight systematic barriers to participation that may have benefited the incumbent party. The chapter then focuses on the monopolization of political discourse by political parties, as well as the extent to which parties provide a meaningful conduit for popular representation. I also provide a discussion of the internal development of political parties and examine how party polarization affects representation and the quality of democracy. This is followed by an analysis of the postwar election cycles after 1994 for presidential elections (1999, 2004, 2009, 2014) and legislative and municipal elections (1997, 2000, 2003, 2006, 2009, 2012, 2015).

Chapter 4 examines the postwar economy, which has been characterized by deepening economic exclusion through the application of the neoliberal model across four successive ARENA administrations. The policies implemented under the administration of Alfredo Cristiani were concurrent with the negotiation of the peace accords and the early phases of their implementation. The continued application of the model by the Calderón Sol and Flores administrations deepened the reforms, which resulted in increased political and social opposition. The popular dissatisfaction with the economy under Flores led to a change in discourse under the Saca administration, which was instead imbued with populist language and social programs while continuing neoliberal policies. ARENA's policies did little to alleviate socioeconomic exclusion, and the economy became overly dependent on remittances sent back from Salvadorans living abroad. The failure of these policies was exposed by the global financial crisis, from which the country has yet to recover. I also assess the extent to which the Funes administration was able to diverge from the model established by the ARENA governments and the conflicts that arose as a result of policies that threatened elite interests. Additionally, various corruption scandals exposed the extent to which those in power used the state for their own benefit.

Chapter 5 addresses three dominant problems of postwar society: migration, crime, and the limitation of political space for civil society. Social exclusion and marginalization have both political and economic roots that precede the peace accords, although the impact of neoliberalism and the retraction of the state from public spheres have contributed greatly to these problems. The failure to deal with these issues has resulted in the mass emigration of Salvadorans in the postwar era, which has resulted in the deterioration of families and society and has helped fuel a wave of crime and violence of epic proportions, for which El Salvador has now become notorious. The multifaceted causes of this crime and violence are examined, which includes a discussion of state complicity and failures during the implementation of security reforms. This chapter also explores policy responses to crime and highlights how ARENA used social exclusion and authoritarianism as instruments of the state to maintain the status quo.

In the final chapter I summarize the book's major findings and discuss the extent to which it is possible to reclaim the captured peace. I also discuss the lessons that El Salvador's captured peace holds for peacebuilders and seek to identify mechanisms that might limit the advantage of incumbent elites.

Chapter 1

Elites and the Salvadoran State

> The main bequest of the nineteenth century was a
> small elite, entrenched in power and virtually closed
> to newcomers, that was to shape the twentieth
> century. . . . Upon those weak foundations they built
> a structure heavy with injustices, inconsistencies,
> and political ineptitude.
>
> —Héctor Lindo-Fuentes, 1990[1]

EL SALVADOR WAS a backwater colony of the Spanish empire in Latin America, which lacked the natural resources and labor pool that were so plentiful in countries such as Mexico and Peru. As a consequence, little investment in the basic infrastructure of the country took place before independence. While an independent El Salvador inherited the poverty of its colonial past, much of the extreme inequality of Salvadoran society is often attributed to the development of the coffee oligarchy known as Las Catorce (the Fourteen Families).[2] The country's oligarchy ruled El Salvador by itself for the first century after independence, then through the military for a sixty-year period beginning in the 1930s, using force to quell any real or perceived challenge to the status quo. Even modest attempts to alter the social order were resisted by elites, who relied on an intricate nexus of political patronage, the military,

15

and state and financial institutions to protect their interests. As Elisabeth Wood has so astutely noted, "Salvadoran history is thus characterized by elite resistance to change."[3] This resistance ultimately culminated in a violent civil war during the 1980s. This chapter focuses on the historical efforts of the oligarchy, in alliance with the military, to preserve power, extend economic dominance, and control the population. In doing so, it highlights the sources and structures of elite entrenchment that would make the captured peace possible.

El Salvador's "Radical Liberalism"

At the time of Central American independence[4] in 1823, the Salvadoran economy was largely dedicated to the production of indigo.[5] By the mid-nineteenth century, however, El Salvador's once booming trade in indigo declined significantly due to the manufacture of cheaper dyes in Germany. Additionally, the U.S. Civil War resulted in a decreased demand for the Salvadoran export, and shipping the crop was complicated by a naval blockade. Recognizing that the indigo market was shrinking, exporters began searching for a replacement crop.

Coffee and the State

El Salvador's rich volcanic soil and mountainous terrain were ideal for the cultivation of coffee, which grows at altitudes higher than 750 meters above sea level. The introduction of coffee in the mid-nineteenth century coincided with the expansion of the state apparatus at a time when the country's Conservatives and Liberals were fighting for political dominance. Coffee and land were at the heart of the dispute. In the mid-nineteenth century, El Salvador's land system was divided into private, communal, public, and communal lands (*ejidos*).[6] As coffee cultivation spread, the desire for land ownership increased and coffee growers increasingly pressured local governments to sell town lands. After several municipalities conceded, coffee growers began to pressure the national government.[7] In 1847 the Salvadoran legislature passed its first law supporting coffee, offering service exemptions and tax benefits to those who had more than fifteen thousand coffee trees.[8] In 1859 and again in 1863, Gen. Gerardo Barrios, often credited with introducing coffee to El Salvador, offered to transfer public land to private hands

16

on the condition that the land be used for coffee production.[9] Much of the infrastructure that developed during the mid- to late nineteenth century was designed to benefit the export of coffee.

El Salvador's Liberals believed that coffee held the key to the country's modernization and prosperity. The Liberals were able to consolidate power by using the state to create policies directly benefiting coffee production. The liberal land reforms of 1881 and 1882 abolished communal lands, which were considered an "impediment to agricultural production and economic growth" by the oligarchy.[10] Opposition to the ejido system was not limited to the oligarchy. As Aldo Lauria-Santiago demonstrates, other social groups opposed the ejido system as well.[11] While the reforms did create an opportunity for other groups, the vast majority of the land was claimed by the agrarian class.[12] Under the 1881–82 reforms, thousands of campesinos were made landless and were subsequently forced to work on haciendas. The "land reform" strengthened the Liberals' control of the economy and the state by further concentrating wealth in the hands of a select few. Seventy-three percent of the land confiscated by the reforms was distributed to 5.6 percent of the new owners, while 50 percent of the owners received 3.45 percent of the land.[13] Banks were created to facilitate the purchase of new lands. In 1880 Banco Internacional was established as El Salvador's first commercial bank. Banco Occidental was founded in 1890 and Banco Agricola Comercial in 1895. By the end of the century, there were more than half a dozen banks dedicated to financing the agricultural sector. The availability of land and financing enabled both large and small growers to expand coffee cultivation. It also increased the power of coffee growers vis-à-vis the state. Thus, coffee, the state, and finance became entangled early in El Salvador's history.

One noteworthy characteristic of the Salvadoran elites was their espousal of the virtues of liberalism alongside mechanisms, policies, and practices that were distinctly illiberal. From very early on, there was a rhetorical commitment to liberal political ideas. The constitution of 1886 reaffirmed Liberal values by creating a secular state, providing for the popular election of municipal authorities, and protecting private property.[14] Elections helped create the façade of liberal democracy, though the actual practice was quite deficient. Erik Ching explains that elites developed sophisticated patronage networks at the municipal and national levels, which allowed them to subvert individual liberties for their own gain.[15] He describes these networks as "highly personalistic, typically hierarchical units designed to monopolize voting, control public office, and militarily resist rival networks when necessary."[16] Political bosses bargained with voters for their votes, which were known because voting was conducted orally and in public until 1950. This bargaining enabled elites to use public offices for their own enrichment. Coffee growers occupied the presidency for seventeen years between 1856 and 1898, and eight of the ten presidents from 1898 to 1927 were from coffee families.[17] By 1895 well over 90 percent of the members in the Salvadoran legislature were coffee planters.[18] This dominance continued well into the twentieth century, as growers consolidated their hold on the state. One notable example was the Meléndez-Quiñónez family (1913–29), which used a combination of party patronage through the National Democratic Party (PND) coupled with a repressive intelligence apparatus known as the Ligas Rojas.

Coffee growers and producers used various instruments of the state to protect their own interests. The unpopularity of the land reforms, especially among the Indian communities, resulted in several revolts during the 1880s. Municipalities reacted by imposing a tax on coffee growers to fund the rural police (1884) and the mounted police (1889), which Robert Williams notes were "under the growers' direct control."[19] The desire to maintain order and stability in the countryside resulted in a close relationship between the landed elites and the military. For the oligarchy, stability was paramount to other freedoms commonly associated with liberal politics in the European tradition. The National Guard was established in 1912 and paid for by the coffee elite itself to maintain internal security by policing rural areas.[20] Peasant conscripts were also used throughout the countryside to maintain order and provide information on "suspicious" activities. The use of peasant conscripts also disrupted communal relations, further strengthening the oligarchy.[21] By 1930 much of the Salvadoran countryside was under military control.[22] Thus, the Liberals' proclamations of democracy were undermined by authoritarian tendencies.

The coffee elites were also responsible for the growth of the financial and commercial industries.[23] The Salvadoran Coffee Association (ASCAFE), the organization of coffee growers, was formed in 1929 to consolidate elite interests.[24] The Cafetalera, as it came to be known, has been likened to a "second state" or an "invisible government, often making policy decisions associated with government bureaucracies."[25] As a result, coffee production continued to expand well into the twentieth century. From 1919 to 1932 the amount of land devoted to coffee cultivation grew from 70,000 to 106,000 hectares.[26]

By 1931 coffee accounted for 96 percent of El Salvador's exports.[27] This dependence left the country vulnerable to the Great Depression, during the first six months of which the price of coffee fell 45 percent; it would later tumble another 12 percent.[28] From 1930 to 1932, export earnings from coffee were cut in half, dropping from 34 million colones to 13 million colones.[29] Additionally, many of the smaller producers were driven out of business and the wealth from coffee became increasingly concentrated in the hands of a select few.[30] Smaller producers were unable to pay their debts to the banks, and, as a result, several banks came to own portions of the coffee industry.[31]

La Matanza

Working conditions on coffee fincas deteriorated with the Depression. Income in 1931 was one-half that in 1928 and the daily wages of plantation workers were slashed in half, from 30 to 15 centavos.[32] Declining economic conditions resulted in increasing tensions throughout the countryside. Peasant uprisings, which had been sporadic throughout the countryside for the past century, were becoming more dangerous for elite interests.

President Pío Romero Bosque, a reformer who had been critical of the civil-rights violations of previous administrations, promoted labor unions and allowed competitive presidential elections. The growing strength of labor unions and peasant activism, coupled with the founding of the Salvadoran Communist Party (PCS), in 1930, raised concerns among the elites. In 1931, Labor Party candidate Arturo Araujo, a sugar and coffee producer, was elected president. Araujo's campaign promised land reform and labor rights, both of which were in direct conflict with the interests of the coffee elites. In December 1931, Araujo was overthrown by the military and replaced by his vice president, Gen. Maximiliano Hernández Martínez. Tensions were exacerbated by the electoral fraud of the January 1932 municipal elections, in which the government suspended elections in strongholds of the PCS and refused to certify results in areas where the PCS claimed victory.[33] Days later a peasant uprising led by Communist Party founder Augustín Farabundo Martí would dramatically alter the future of El Salvador. The military acted swiftly and ruthlessly. In the end, as many as thirty thousand peasants, most of whom were not actual participants the rebellion, were dead, including Martí.[34] La Matanza (the Massacre), as it came to be known, resulted in the implementation of a military-oligarchy coalition that would rule El Salvador for another five decades. Whether the threat of mass rebellion was real or perceived, the oligarchy reached an agreement with the military to maintain stability and protect elite economic interests. William Stanley suggests that the military may have exaggerated the extent of the "Communist threat" in order to gain control of the state apparatus.[35] Martínez, who initially had very little support among elites or the armed forces, consolidated power through the centralization of decision making, public works, and services; replacing civilians with officers at the municipal and local level; discouraging labor unions, and prohibiting peasant organizations.[36] Martínez also established the National Party of the Fatherland (Pro Patria), an extensive hierarchical party network, to guarantee his victory in the 1935 presidential and municipal elections. The party's success (and the consolidation of broader powers) relied on the incorporation of workers and peasants into the party's corporatist structure, offering modest protection from elites in exchange for support.[37]

Martínez and the coffee elites had differing interpretations of the causes of the 1932 rebellion. While Martínez seemed to have a general understanding of the structural causes of the rebellion, elites believed the uprising was the result of naïve peasants (mostly Indians) who were influenced by imported communism. They denied that there was any exploitation present, and argued that class stratification was an inevitable feature of any society.[38] The narrative developed by elites to explain the 1932 uprising shaped elite policy preferences and alliances for the next five decades—longer among some of the more recalcitrant elements. They viewed themselves the driving force behind El Salvador's development, nationalists threatened by nefarious communist forces.[39] Thus, while elites disagreed with Martínez's social reforms, they were willing to support him (at least initially) because they approved of his crushing response to the massacre and economic policies in the midst of the Great Depression. The development of what Stanley describes as "quasi-statal financial institutions" during the period demonstrates the depth of the relationship between the state and coffee elites.[40] The Central Bank and Banco Hipotecario, an agricultural bank, were established in 1934, and the Salvadoran Coffee Company (Compañía Salvadoreña de Café) was established in 1942 to provide loans and regulate coffee prices. The relationship between the banking and coffee sectors was rather incestuous—the Cafetelera owned 75 percent of Hipotacario.[41]

Martínez was overthrown in 1944 for attempting to seek a third term in office and was succeeded by Gen. Salvador Castañeda Castro in May 1945.[42]

20

Castañeda Castro represented the old guard of the Salvadoran armed forces and was relatively isolated from the junior officers. In an attempt to keep the junior officers in check and reduce the possibility of another coup, he sent many overseas for further military training.[45] Those officers returned in 1948, on the eve of a hastily arranged presidential election. When Castañeda Castro attempted to extend his term as president, he was summarily overthrown in what was referred to as the 1948 "revolution."[44] The 1948 coup summarily ended the caudillo state in El Salvador and paved the way for significant institutional change.

Institutional Military Rule

For nearly a century, elites had maintained power through coercive mechanisms designed to protect them from the socioeconomic exclusion produced by their policies. By the mid-nineteenth century, cracks were beginning to emerge in the model. The 1948 "revolution," which effectively ended caudillo rule, was primarily the result of a fissure between junior officers and older generals.[45] Junior officers were mostly of working-class backgrounds who did not benefit from the spoils system that had enriched the generals.[46] Because of their socioeconomic background, junior officers tended to favor policies that benefited the poor.[47] This is not to suggest that their beliefs were entirely altruistic. While some junior officers favored reforms on their own merit, others simply believed them necessary to ensure political stability.[48] They agreed, however, on the importance of democratic governance and economic reform for creating growth and stability.[49] The Revolutionary Council of Government, composed of three military and two civilian representatives, sought to institutionalize democracy and modernize the Salvadoran state. The platform of the Revolutionary Council was embodied in the "fourteen points," a platform expressing a commitment to a democratic regime with free and fair elections, a professionalized military, and universal suffrage.[50] Despite the noted commitment to democracy, the Revolutionary Council banned political parties affiliated with religious groups, those receiving foreign aid, and the Communist Party. The economic components of the platform focused on increased social services and, more significantly, increased state intervention in the economy to promote industrialization.[51] The period from 1948 through 1979 is punctuated by a succession of reformist coups encouraging political liberalization followed by increasingly repressive coups.[52] Philip J. Williams and Knut Walter describe this phenomenon as "a state of continuous tension between those lines of thought that would try to prevent crisis by promoting change of varying degrees and those who would seek to prevent even expressions of the need for change."[53] While regime change during this period was frequent (sixteen different governments between 1944 and 1979), there are certain characteristics that define this period as a whole. First, the regime type is best described as a procedural democracy in which the military held elections and ruled through official parties.[54] With the exception of the PCS, the party system in El Salvador was developed after Martínez's departure and was used to consolidate the oligarchy's rule through "official" military parties, such as the Revolutionary Party of Democratic Unification (PRUD). Elections were frequently organized around "mini-parties" created to promote various candidates representative of the different strains of thought within the military.[55] Much like their predecessors, political parties of this era were ill-equipped, at best, to perform the typical functions of a party system—channeling the demands of the population—and, in fact, functioned solely for the purpose of elections. To that end, the party system merely served as a means by which the oligarchy could reassert its control through military regimes. In fact, despite encouraging opposition parties to participate, from 1952 to 1961 the opposition never held a seat in the Legislative Assembly.[56] Second, these regimes often pledged varying degrees of socioeconomic reform, though never enough to redress the country's inequalities or affect the interests of the oligarchy. Finally, when liberalization went too far—that is, encroached upon the interests of the oligarchy—repression increased and the state used force to maintain order.[57]

Mobilization and Electoral Competition

The 1960s in El Salvador witnessed unprecedented political and economic change. The decade was characterized by relatively competitive elections, albeit far from open, and the growth of popular organizations, including Christian base communities (CEB), unions, and other popular organizations. The opening of political space, however limited, was accompanied by changing economic policy and respectable levels of growth. By the mid-1970s, however, this political opening would give way to repression, and the fallacy behind economic growth was revealed.

The political system opened significantly in the 1960s. Following a reformist coup—and three months later, a countercoup in late 1960 and early 1961—the PRUD reorganized itself to create the National Conciliation Party (PCN), modeled after the PRI in Mexico, in anticipation of the 1962 elections.[58] Opposition parties, including the newly formed Christian Democratic Party (PDC), abstained from participating in those elections due to questionable behavior by the PCN. After soundly defeating a donkey—the only opposition candidate—in the 1962 presidential elections, PCN president Julio Adalberto Rivera called for open elections and established a system of proportional representation.[59] As such, opposition parties were allowed to participate in the 1964 municipal elections. The PDC fared well and even won the mayoral race in San Salvador. The PDC emerged as a significant opposition force during the 1960s, more than doubling the number of municipalities it controlled from 1964 to 1966 (37 to 83). Much of this success can be attributed to the PDC's emphasis on developing a relationship with the working class. During his tenure as mayor of San Salvador, José Napoleón Duarte developed Acción Comunitaria, a neighborhood action program that encouraged community development.[60] This strategy of developing a middle-class and urban working class–constituency also benefited the PDC in the 1967 presidential elections. While the PCN won handily, the PDC garnered 21.6 percent of the vote.[61] In Salvadoran terms, the PDC was becoming a well-organized opposition party.

The period from 1972 to 1979 was a major turning point in Salvadoran politics. Throughout the 1960s the military government had permitted the participation of opposition political parties, such as the PDC, and had even tolerated their expansion. By the early 1970s, however, the increasing success of the opposition became too close for comfort. The rise of the PDC was also accompanied by increasing mobilization among labor, peasant organizations, and Christian base communities, which made the military increasingly nervous. Rather than permit the further expansion of the opposition, the military regime sought to diminish the power of the opposition, first through electoral fraud and later through repression. This seizure of political space resulted in a severe deterioration of the sociopolitical environment and eventually led to the breakdown of Salvadoran society as a whole.

In September 1971 the PDC joined a coalition with two other left-wing parties, the National Revolutionary Movement (MNR) and the Nationalist Democratic Union (UDN). Together the three parties formed the National

Opposition Union (UNO) to participate in the 1972 elections, selecting José Napoleón Duarte, the popular mayor of San Salvador, as their presidential candidate. Even though Duarte was leading in the polls when radio election coverage was terminated, the final tally favored the PCN. According to official reports, the PCN won 334,600 votes to UNO's 324,756, while UNO's tally attributed 317,535 to the PCN and 326, 968 votes to UNO.[62] Protests followed and attempts were made to nullify the election. In the end, PCN candidate Col. Arturo Molina assumed the presidency and Duarte was forced into exile.

The 1972 presidential elections were a critical juncture in Salvadoran politics. For more than a decade, various regimes had tolerated the growth of the PDC and other opposition parties, and the opposition had shown its growing organizational and electoral capacity. The growth and success of the PDC and other opposition parties was alarming to elites, who feared that a win by the opposition would result in land reform and threaten their very livelihood.[63] The victory of Marxist Popular Unity presidential candidate, Salvador Allende, in Chile following a Christian Democratic president, fueled fears among the Salvadoran elites and the more conservative members of the military that a victory by the PDC would "serve as a bridge for the left to take power."[64] Thus, while the Salvadoran Christian Democrats served a valuable role in legitimizing the electoral process, they were not allowed to ascend to power. The 1972 elections demonstrated that reform through elections was unattainable.[65] It was in this environment that popular mobilization and repression intensified.

Repression as a Response to Mobilization

Popular mobilization and repression intensified following the 1972 elections. While anticommunist military and paramilitary organizations were not new to El Salvador, their activities increased significantly following the 1972 elections. The Nationalist Democratic Organization (ORDEN) was formed in 1966 by the military for thwarting communism by way of indoctrination—or murder, if deemed necessary. ORDEN soon was followed by the emergence of more ruthless and ubiquitous "death squads." By 1975 paramilitary organizations and death squads, such as the Anticommunist Wars of Elimination Liberation Armed Forces (FALANGE) and Mano Blanca (White Hand), patrolled the countryside with the explicit goal of exterminating

24

"communists," whether they were priests, students, union leaders, peasants, or progressive politicians." Maj. Roberto D'Aubuisson, former chief of intelligence, was instrumental in the development of these groups. D'Aubuisson was the head of the White Warriors' Union (Unión Guerrera Blanca), a death squad that targeted priests. His relationship with a group of wealthy businessmen, collectively known as the Broad Nationalist Front (FAN), ensured their financing.[67] The motto "Be a Patriot, Kill a Priest," was more than just bravado. D'Aubuisson's group threatened to kill forty-six Jesuits unless they left the country. During the late 1970s and early 1980s, priests and layworkers were increasingly the victims of death squads. The assassination of Father Rutilio Grande of Aguilares, in March 1977, just one month after the elections, was intended to deliver a clear message to the church about its "political activism."

The 1977 presidential election took place amid increasing protest and social violence. Throughout the 1970s, both sides had become increasingly radicalized. The 1977 elections were further testament that reform via elections did not exist. The electoral fraud of 1972 was repeated in 1977 when PCN candidate Carlos Humberto Romero defeated the UNO candidate, retired Col. Ernesto Claramount. Not surprisingly, voting irregularities were rampant. To protest, Claramount and his supporters (a crowd that grew to fifty thousand in a few days) gathered in the Plaza Libertad in San Salvador. National police opened fire on the crowd, killing dozens.[68] Claramount fled into exile and Romero assumed the presidency, as planned. While the 1977 election results merely reinforced the fraud of the 1972 elections, the ending was a decidedly more violent demonstration of what was to come.

Descent into War

In October 1979, junior officers of the armed forces carried out a reformist coup against the Romero government. The first junta consisted of two officers and three civilians; members of the political opposition served in various administrative positions. The objectives of the junta included support for the fundamental elements of citizen participation, guarantees of human rights, dissolution of ORDEN and other death squads, and the more equitable distribution of economic resources.[69] In short, the intended goal of the coup was to establish an environment for free elections by curtailing violence and providing an agrarian reform program aimed at easing tensions

25

created by the inequitable distribution of wealth and land. Ultimately, the coup failed to redefine the role of the military vis-à-vis the state, and the oligarchy remained in control of the economy.[70]

The reforms proposed by the junta included agrarian reform and the nationalization of the banks and the coffee sector. In December 1979 the junta passed Decree 75, which nationalized the coffee export process and created the National Coffee Institute (INCAFE) to manage those exports.[71] Elites viewed these programs as radical and interpreted them and the mass mobilization of the 1970s through the lens of the 1932 uprising. The solution was to unleash a repressive response akin to La Matanza, relying on increasing, albeit inconsistent, levels of violence.[72] The first junta collapsed in January 1980 when the three civilian members of the junta resigned to protest the violence. Under pressure from the United States, the military extended junta leadership to the PDC in January 1980, a tactical move to ensure legitimacy at home and military funds from the United States. The PDC agreed to join the junta on the condition that human rights violations would lessen and that the reforms proffered by the junta, including agrarian reform, would proceed. As a result, José Napoleón Duarte, who had been denied the presidency eight years earlier, joined the junta and became its president in December 1980.

Rather than subside, however, the levels of violence increased. Death squads and right-wing paramilitary groups began "disappearing"[73] those associated with labor unions, peasant groups, the church, and students. Between 1980 and 1982, approximately forty-two thousand people were killed by police, military, and paramilitary death squads.[74] More than thirteen thousand people were murdered or disappeared in 1980 alone, most of them peasants, workers, and students.[75] Innocent civilians, including children, were frequently caught in the military's "low-intensity," counterinsurgency strategy. Numerous massacres of civilians, including those at the Sumpul River, El Mozote, the Lempa River, El Calabozo, and the Gualsinga River, demonstrated the brutality of government forces. At El Mozote, more than seven hundred unarmed civilians, including infants and children, were summarily executed.[76] One of the most frequent perpetrators of the massacres was the "elite" U.S.-trained Atlacatl Battalion, which was widely regarded as "the most efficient killing machine that the Salvadoran army had to offer."[77]

A series of high-profile assassinations in 1980 effectively ended any prospect for a peaceful settlement to the conflict. Archbishop Óscar Arnulfo

Romero was assassinated while celebrating mass on March 24, 1980. Although initially thought to be a conservative Vatican appointment, Romero was radicalized by the overwhelming violence in El Salvador, particularly the attacks on priests and the murder of his good friend Rutilio Grande. During the three years that Romero was the archbishop of San Salvador, he implored government forces, paramilitary death squads, and revolutionaries to lay down their weapons. His powerful sermons on themes of social justice, impunity, repression, and poverty made him the "voice of the voiceless." They also made him a threat to elites. The month before his assassination, Romero wrote a letter to U.S. president Jimmy Carter asking him to prohibit military aid. So compelling was his presence that many combatants would later say that his assassination drove them to join the revolution.[78] Six leaders of the opposition Democratic Revolutionary Front (FDR), including the organization's president, Enrique Álvarez Córdova, were abducted, tortured, and murdered in November 1980 by security forces as they gathered for a press conference.[79] The remaining leadership was forced into exile. Weeks later, in December 1980, three American nuns and a layworker were abducted, raped, and murdered by members of the National Guard. Three days later the bodies of Maura Clarke, Ita Ford, Dorothy Kazel, and Jean Donovan, who served as a pallbearer at Romero's funeral, were found buried in a single shallow grave. These deaths shocked Salvadorans and the international community and convinced many that the space for political settlements had closed.

With all avenues for nonviolent protest eliminated, increasing repression drove once divided opposition groups together. The Democratic Revolutionary Front was established in April 1980 by three center-left parties, members of which had participated in the junta. During the summer of 1980 the FDR organized several general strikes designed to demonstrate the popular support for the group.[80] The public nature of the FDR's activities naturally drew the attention of the military. The murders of one organization's leadership later that year had a dramatic impact on the group's organizational capacity within the country. The FDR gained international prominence through the establishment of diplomatic missions abroad and was recognized as the Salvadoran representative to the Socialist International. In 1981 the FDR was recognized by the governments of France and Mexico as a "representative political force."[81] In October 1980 five guerrilla organizations formed the Farabundo Martí National Liberation Front (FMLN).[82] The FDR, which had an open alliance with the FMLN's predecessor, the United Revolutionary Directorate (DRU), then aligned with the FMLN.[83] The polarizing events and heightened repression of 1979–82 provided ample opportunity for recruitment. The FMLN peaked in 1983 with some twelve thousand troops, making it one of the largest, most disciplined guerrilla movements in the hemisphere. Almost one-third of FMLN combatants and 20 percent of commanders were women. The FMLN derived much of its strength from the grassroots and peasant organizations, both in terms of recruitment and general support.

U.S. Policy and the Emergence of ARENA

U.S. interest in El Salvador, which had been fairly negligible compared to other countries in the region before 1979, rose sharply with the victory of the Sandinistas in Nicaragua and the emergence of the FMLN. The goal of the Carter administration was to prevent the accession of a leftist regime in El Salvador while promoting human rights, a policy it sought to promote throughout Latin America. Believing that the 1979 junta offered the best solution to the political violence, the Carter administration approved the reprogramming of $5.7 million in nonlethal military aid to the junta in March 1980.[84] In an effort to support the junta and diminish support for the guerrillas, the administration developed a policy that included agrarian reform and the nationalization of banks and coffee.[85] These policies, which many elites characterized as socialist, were deeply at odds with the interests of most elites and their policy preferences at the time. Despite efforts by some in the Carter administration to tie human rights to aid, abuses increased and aid continued to flow in an effort to combat the encroaching "communist threat" posed by the FMLN rebels.[86]

But elites found a much more suitable partner in the Reagan administration.[87] The attitudes and policy preference of hardliners within the administration coincided with those of El Salvador's elites. Salvadoran elites and the military successfully resurrected the 1932 narrative, which was also echoed by the administration: the situation in El Salvador was the result of Soviet encroachment into the hemisphere and a consequence of Carter's permissive policy environment in the region.[88] The FMLN's failed January 1981 offensive fueled speculation in Washington that the guerrillas were receiving significant assistance from Cuba and Nicaragua.[89] The Reagan administration, eager to use El Salvador as a showcase in its efforts to combat communism in the hemisphere, developed a strategy to undercut support for the guerrillas while also supporting democracy.[90] The Reagan Doctrine, as it came to be known, and the fear of communist expansion in the hemisphere dominated U.S. policy in the region for almost a decade.[91]

The dominant narrative about the FMLN's military weakness and lack of popular appeal undermined attempts for political resolution of the conflict throughout the decade. The military, many elites, and the Reagan adminis-tration believed that the FMLN could be defeated on the battlefield. Dur-ing the 1980s the United States spent $4.35 billion, $1.035 billion of that in military aid, to defeat the FMLN.[92] As a result, there was little support for a negotiated end to the conflict during much of the 1980s. Failed talks between the Duarte administration and FDR-FMLN at La Palma, Chalatenango, in October 1984, Ayagualo in November 1984, and numerous overtures in 1985–86 received no support from the military or the Reagan administration.

While the support of a military victory was clearly one of the defining fea-tures of Reagan's policy, elections were paramount for achieving the admin-istration's overall goal. Not only would elections provide legitimacy for the Salvadoran government and guarantee continued aid from a highly critical, Democrat-controlled Congress, but they would also undermine guerrilla ef-forts by providing a democratic alternative.[93] Elections were held in 1982 for a Constituent Assembly, which would, in turn, elect a provisional president and replace the junta. The primary goal of the assembly was to draft a new constitution to create a new framework for a more inclusive electoral democ-racy. These elections, and the subsequent elections in 1984, were touted as "free elections" by the United States despite obvious deficiencies—not the least of which was that they were held against the backdrop of the war.[94] Seven parties registered with the new Central Elections Council (CCE), including the PCN and the PDC.

In 1981 a new party, the Nationalist Republican Alliance (ARENA), emerged as the political expression of right-wing extremism. In some re-spects, ARENA mirrored past patronage party networks, combining repres-sion with tightly controlled political participation. The party grew out of FAN, uniting the oligarchy, military, and death squads in the anticommunist cause. The ORDEN organizational network served as the "foundation" for the party.[95] Among the party's founders was former intelligence chief Maj. Roberto D'Aubuisson, who combined ultranationalist and anticommunist rhetoric to galvanize support for the new party. His charismatic persona and fiery speeches fueled U.S. fears that the election could deliver a "slow-motion right-wing coup" rather than victory for the center-right PDC.[96] The Reagan administration reacted to the growing strength of ARENA by channeling financial support to Duarte in hopes of ensuring a PDC victory, which was seen as vital to approval for continued military aid.

While the PDC won a plurality of the votes (40.27 percent, twenty-four seats) in the 1982 elections, ARENA (29.32 percent, nineteen seats) joined in coalition with the PCN (19.03 percent, fourteen seats) to ensure control of the assembly. As a result, D'Aubuisson, who had been described by former U.S. ambassador Robert White (1977–80) as a "pathological killer" was poised to be elected as provisional president. The Reagan administration sent the message via a congressional delegation that U.S. aid was contingent on the election of a moderate government. In a conciliatory move, Salvadoran banker Dr. Álvaro Magaña was named president. Unhappy with Washington's influence and manipulation, D'Aubuisson was named assembly president.[97] There were deep divisions between the PDC, ARENA, and the PCN, which had a general mistrust of one another. Under pressure from the United States, the parties signed the Pact of Apaneca in an attempt to end the infighting between parties. Though its strength was somewhat diminished following the pact, ARENA was able to use its position in the transitional government to limit the size of land expropriated in the land reforms, protecting some of the larger estates and also overseeing the ministries charged with land reform, which enabled ARENA to essentially halt the reforms.[98] Thus, the oligarchy was establishing a foothold in politics once again thanks, in part, to the electoral process.

"Demonstration" Democracy and the Making of a New Right

The March 1984 elections were supposed to signify the transition away from the political uncertainty that had plagued El Salvador since the 1979 coup. Still concerned that a victory by ARENA would threaten the flow of military aid to defeat the FMLN, the United States spent $6 million on the elections, including $2 million in covert aid to Duarte and the PCN.[99] No parties from the Left participated in the elections, based on both principle and security concerns. Despite a number of significant irregularities and much confusion at polling stations, voter turnout was higher than predicted. Approximately

1.4 million Salvadorans voted in the 1984 elections. Duarte won 43 percent of the vote, followed by 30 percent for D'Aubuisson. Duarte's failure to win a majority of the vote necessitated a runoff in May. Duarte defeated ARENA's D'Aubuisson for president in the runoff with almost 54 percent of the vote. Duarte's presidential victory was also buoyed by PDC victories in the 1985 legislative and municipal elections, which gave the party a majority in the Legislative Assembly.

The Duarte government embarked on a program of reforms to undercut the popular support for the FMLN in an effort to stem the effect of the war on the economy.[100] Such reforms included wage increases for public-sector employees, a minimum wage for urban workers, and increased access to credit and price controls.[101] Many of Duarte's policies were made possible by the influx of economic and military assistance from the United States after his election. But these policies were increasingly at odds with the new economic prescription being encouraged by the United States: liberal economic reforms, including devaluation, privatization, and trade liberalization. Duarte resisted, believing that such policies would be unpopular and would generate support for the FMLN. But his policies had become unsustainable. In 1985, 50 percent of the national budget was dedicated to the war.[102] Rising inflation, capital flight, and an expanding budget deficit required action. Inflation increased from 11.7 percent in 1984 to 31.9 percent in 1986.[103] In 1986 the Salvadoran government was forced to launch a new stabilization policy, which included a 100 percent nominal devaluation of the Salvadoran colón.[104]

While the austerity measures weren't popular with the traditional elites, they were well received by the Salvadoran Foundation for Economic and Social Development (FUSADES). FUSADES was created with funding from the United States Agency for International Development (USAID) in 1983 in response to Duarte's hesitance at Washington's new economic direction.[105] The Salvadoran think tank, which was designed to promote the Reagan administration's commitment to neoliberal reform in the country, served as a key instrument for the elites in advancing their economic policies. The positions and policies of FUSADES closely mirrored the sentiments of the elites espoused during the late nineteenth century: unfettered economic liberalism. That said, there was also the recognition of the need to break from export agriculture in the increasingly globalized economy. This aspect was clearly at odds with some of the agricultural elites and came to symbolize a growing rupture within elites—the traditional agrarian elites versus the emerging agro-industrialists.[106] Not surprisingly, the key founders of FUSADES were also members of the Association of Coffee Processors and Exporters (ABECAFE), founded in 1961 to represent the interests of coffee processors and exporters (as distinct from the growers). From 1984 to 1992, USAID contributed $100 million to FUSADES alone.[107] Recognizing that the United States would never support ARENA with D'Aubuisson as the head of the party, he was replaced by Alfredo "Fredy" Cristiani in 1985. Cristiani, a wealthy coffee grower, businessman, former president of ABECAFE, and member of the board of directors of FUSADES, represented a new, more moderate (and electable) right. By 1988, ARENA was the dominant electoral force in Salvadoran politics. Aided by allegations of egregious corruption by the Duarte administration, ARENA won thirty-one seats in the Assembly and 178 mayoralties (including all departmental capitals) in the 1988 elections. Together with the PCN, which won seven seats and four mayoralties, ARENA controlled the assembly. By the late 1980s, ARENA no longer represented the interests of the landed oligarchy to the extent that it had earlier in the decade.[108] It was becoming a powerful extension of the new right, and it was willing to sacrifice former allies to achieve its vision for El Salvador's future.

The Rocky Road to Peace

By 1989 there was a significant shift in both the domestic and international context. The beginning of the collapse of the Soviet Union and the discrediting of communist ideology together with the election of George H. W. Bush as president, in 1988, resulted in a change in U.S. foreign policy in the region. Latin American insurgencies were not solely in the context of an international communist threat, but rather as domestic issues. The decline of the Soviet Union also had an impact on the FMLN's willingness to seek a negotiated settlement to the war.[109] In 1989, FMLN commander Joaquín Villalobos wrote an article in *Foreign Policy* detailing the FMLN's ideological position and preference for democracy.[110] The regional commitment made to peace and democracy by the Central American presidents in the Esquipulas I and II peace accords, in 1986–87, as well as changing dynamics in Cuba and Nicaragua, also created an environment conducive to a negotiated settlement.[111] These changes, combined with ARENA's seeming transformation from extremist to pragmatic also helped pave the way for a political settlement to the war.

In early 1989 the FMLN offered to lay down their weapons and participate in the presidential elections provided that the government postpone the elections for six months, and other criteria, to ensure safeguards for its participation. While the FMLN ultimately did not participate in the elections, the Democratic Convergence (CD), a coalition of center-left parties affiliated with the FDR, did. Guillermo Ungo, who returned from exile along with Rubén Zamora in 1987, was the CD's presidential candidate. The elections confirmed ARENA's new political dominance and the PDC's precipitous decline. ARENA candidate Alfredo Cristiani won by a comfortable margin in the first round of voting with 54 percent of the vote; PDC candidate Fidel Chávez Mena won 36 percent.[112] Cristiani assumed the presidency in June, pledging economic recovery and peace talks. Cristiani's plans for economic recovery were largely based on the recommendations of FUSADES. The plan sought a strict adherence to the neoliberal model through the implementation of structural-adjustment policies, including the privatization of the financial sector and other state-owned entities, significant reduction in tariffs, and other policies designed to favor foreign investment. The war was incompatible with Cristiani's vision for the Salvadoran economy, as was ARENA's increasingly uneasy alliance with the military. As Wood demonstrates, changes to the Salvadoran economy during the war had a profound impact on elite interests. The decline of the agro-export sector was altering the orientation of the Salvadoran economy, and many elites were changing in response to the fluctuations in the economy. The war had resulted in the diversification of their economic holdings, which made the repressive apparatus long used to maintain their interests unnecessary. Additionally, the growing electoral power of ARENA convinced many elites that their interests could be preserved through electoral politics.[113] This is not to say that the far right had been vanquished by Cristiani, merely displaced by the face of moderation.[114] While Cristiani proceeded with peace talks in September 1989, the military (which opposed the talks) sought to flex its muscle through a series of bombings the following month against allies of the FMLN, including FENASTRAS headquarters and the home of FDR leader Rubén Zamora, causing the FMLN to abruptly terminate them. On November 11, 1989, the FMLN staged its first offensive in the capital city, eventually occupying areas of elite neighborhoods to the shock of many residents.

Indeed, the offensive took the Salvadoran government and army by total surprise.[115] Both entities had spent years minimizing the size, effectiveness, and popular support of the guerrillas. Now it was overwhelmingly clear that the FMLN was not the poorly coordinated, rogue band of rebels the military had made them out to be. While the primary objective of the offensive (the overthrow of the government) failed, it succeeded in exposing the failure of U.S. and Salvadoran intelligence, the incompetence of the Salvadoran army, and the exposure of the failure of nine years of U.S. policy.[116] But it was the military's response to the offensive that would ultimately bring about the end of the war.

In the early morning hours of November 16, 1989, members of the U.S.-trained Atlacatl Battalion, the same one responsible for the El Mozote and other massacres, entered the grounds of the Universidad Centroamericana "José Simeón Cañas" (UCA), and murdered six Jesuit priests, their housekeeper, and her daughter.[117] There were numerous attempts to deflect responsibility and conceal the military's role in the crime. Soldiers attempted to frame the FMLN by scrawling FMLN propaganda at the scene, indicating that the Jesuits had been considered traitors by the organization. But a more insidious institutional cover-up by the High Command of the armed forces followed. Botched investigations—including the destruction and withholding of evidence, perjured testimony, and the refusal to testify—impeded the judicial process.[118] The murders captured world attention and drew heightened scrutiny to the Salvadoran military and the inability of the new Cristiani government to control it. The murders clearly demonstrated that vast amounts of aid had failed to reform the military, which had operated with impunity throughout the war. The U.S. government, in turn, withheld $42.5 million in military aid promised to El Salvador, signaling its unwillingness to tolerate continuing egregious abuses.[119] Without aid from the United States, the Salvadoran military could not defeat the FMLN. Both sides recognized that a military victory was no longer a possibility and agreed to pursue a negotiated settlement to end the war.[120]

Preserving Power:
The Foundations and Legacy of a Century of Capture

El Salvador's history has been defined by exclusionary politics, inequities, and military rule. To some extent, the phenomenon of capture has been omnipresent in El Salvador's history as the country's elites routinely combined the rhetoric of liberal democracy with distinctly illiberal practices to advance their own interests. The expansion of the coffee sector in the mid- to late nineteenth century resulted in a series of policies that concentrated wealth in the hands of an increasingly powerful coffee oligarchy in which the economic and political liberties of elites were often guaranteed by force. When those interests were challenged, as in the case of the 1932 uprising, elites supported highly repressive measures to curtail popular mobilization. As we have seen, the narrative to explain La Matanza was key to shaping how elites interpreted subsequent events and justified their responses to those events. The subsequent alliance between landed elites and the military defined the Salvadoran state for decades. Even when elites did not formally hold power, they were able to advance their interests through the creation and control of various financial institutions.

Political participation was allowed, even encouraged, so long as it did not threaten elite interests. When political reforms in the 1960s resulted in the rising popularity of parties beyond the control of the oligarchy, most notably the PDC, elites and their partners in the military responded by closing avenues for mass participation and enforcing those closures through unrelenting violence. The 1979 reformist coup sought to forestall a bloody civil war by implementing social and economic programs to alleviate socioeconomic inequality and undercut support for guerrilla forces, but elites opposed those programs and continued to support repression by the military and by paramilitary death squads. The country soon descended into a civil war that would take the lives of more than seventy-five thousand Salvadorans, force 1 million (20 percent of the population) to flee the country, and displace an additional three-quarter million. While elites found a willing partner in the United States, assistance from the superpower was conditioned upon stemming abuses and the development of a democratic process. As they had done before, elites created a political party in the 1980s to serve as a vehicle for protecting their interests. Borne of an alliance between the oligarchy and the death squads, ARENA demonstrated itself to be particularly adept at evolving throughout the decade. The replacement of highly controversial D'Aubuisson with Cristiani reflected not only a growing rift within the Right but also signaled a changing philosophy within the Right and positioned ARENA to dominate the electoral system. With the continuation of the war at odds with ARENA's new economic agenda, Cristiani proceeded with talks with the FMLN to end the war. As demonstrated in the next chapter, the historical patterns, networks, and institutions established by Salvadoran elites enabled them to exercise significant control over the peace negotiations and peacebuilding outcomes.

Chapter 2

Making the Captured Peace

People go [to the table] to negotiate, not to sacrifice themselves.

—Rubén Zamora, 1999[1]

BY LATE 1989 it appeared that El Salvador's decade-long civil war was ripe for negotiations. A mutually hurting stalemate coincided with the end of the Cold War, which contributed to an environment conducive for negotiations. For two years, the Cristiani administration and the FMLN hammered out the details on a plan to end the war and bring peace to El Salvador. The outcome of those negotiations, the Chapúltepec Accords, provided the foundation to dramatically transform the political landscape of the country while also preserving the interests of elites. As one of the United Nations' first forays into postwar peacebuilding, the Salvadoran peace process was unprecedented in scope. Not only did the accords dismantle and redefine the country's most notorious security organizations, but they also addressed electoral and judicial reforms, guarantees for human rights, and some socioeconomic issues. They also provided the basis for the FMLN's incorporation into the country's political life, which was realized in the 1994 elections. While the peace process in El Salvador is widely considered a success, it was certainly not without its problems. As detailed below, elite

37

control over content and implementation of the peace accords facilitated a captured peace by undermining reforms set forth in the accords. Moreover, the lack of transitional justice and a controversial amnesty law, which was designed to protect elites, undermined prospects for reconciliation and sustained a war narrative that would come to define postwar society.

The Broker of Peace: The Participation of the United Nations

The peace process in El Salvador represents one of the United Nations' first peacebuilding missions. While the UN had little prior experience in the region, changing international conditions and a renewed regional commitment to peace made an entrée into the region more feasible. The United Nations first became involved in El Salvador in 1981 to report on the human rights situation. The installation of the UN's first Latin American secretary general, Javier Pérez de Cuéllar in the same year brought a slow but increasing attention to the region. In 1983 the UN formally supported the actions of the Contadora Group, consisting of Colombia, Mexico, Panama, and Venezuela, in its efforts to promote peace in the region. However, it was 1989 before the UN became involved in more than a supporting role. At a summit of Central American presidents in February 1989, leaders of the five Central American countries called on the United Nations to take a more active role in the verification of the security aspects of the Esquipulas agreements.[2] In essence, they invited the participation of the United Nations in the region, and the UN responded favorably. In July 1989 the United Nations Security Council published Resolution 637, commending the Central American leaders for their continued commitment to the Esquipulas agreements and pledging to take any steps necessary to support the secretary general in promoting peace in the region. Resolution 637 opened the door for unprecedented UN involvement in Central America.

In an effort to salvage the peace process and the reputation of his administration—both of which were badly damaged following the October 1989 FENESTRAS bombings and the November 16, 1989, Jesuit murders—Cristiani personally solicited Secretary General Pérez de Cuéllar to mediate peace talks between the government of El Salvador and the FMLN following a similar request by the FMLN in late 1989.[4] In an unprecedented decision, the secretary general agreed to aid in peace negotiations between the two parties.[5] The Salvadoran peace process was the first in which the United Nations had acted as mediator in a civil war.

As other works have described in great detail, the United Nations played an indispensible role as mediator during the negotiations.[6] The use of good offices and the personal commitment of Pérez de Cuéllar demonstrated the importance of third parties in resolving this seemingly intractable conflict. By most accounts, the government of El Salvador (GOES), the FMLN, and the UN worked together to resolve most disputes. That said, the UN and the United Nations Observer Mission in El Salvador (ONUSAL) occasionally experienced great difficulty in overcoming ARENA's resistance to the implementation of various elements of the accords. This was particularly true with regard to police and judicial reform.

The Contents of the Negotiations and the Accords

As with most other UN-mediated settlements, the content of the peace accords focused on conflict resolution (moving the conflict from the battle-field to the ballot box) as opposed to conflict transformation (addressing the underlying causes of the conflict as well as changing the relationships between and attitudes of the parties).[7] As such, negotiations focused on structural changes to formal institutions. The framework for the peace accords developed through a series of six agreements over a two-year period. The Geneva Agreement (April 1990) established the parties' commitment to negotiations, as well as an agreement for secret, continuous negotiations with the support of the secretary general's office. As stated in the Geneva Agreement, the purpose of the peace negotiations was "to end armed conflict by political means as speedily as possible, promote the democratization of the country, guarantee unrestricted respect for human rights and reunify Salvadoran society."[8] This language provides not only for the end of the war but extends to cover sociopolitical issues aimed at restructuring Salvadoran society. Although the terms of the agreement mandated that the negotiation process was confidential, there was also an acknowledgment that civil-society organizations "have an important role to play in achieving peace."[9] As such, the parties were permitted to consult these organizations "when it is deemed appropriate and on the basis of mutual agreement."[10] However, the agreement did not establish any official channel for consultation. This established a pattern of popular exclusion that would characterize not only the peace process but extend well beyond the implementation phase. The following month in Caracas, the parties agreed to an agenda and timetable, albeit vague, for future talks. Issues on the agenda included the armed forces, human rights, judicial and electoral reform, economic and social issues, and the reintegration of the FMLN. It also affirmed that a ceasefire would be postponed until the political agreements had been reached.[11] The postponement of the ceasefire was vital to the participation of the FMLN, as the FMLN (with the backing of the secretary general) claimed that they would lose any leverage if the ceasefire was imposed before the agreements.

Military reform had become a quagmire in the negotiations early on, a testament to both its controversy and its immense importance to the proceedings. In an effort to advance negotiations, the parties agreed to focus on human rights in the San José Agreement (July 1990). This agreement assured the parties' commitment to human rights as they existed under both Salvadoran law and in accordance with international standards and treaties. The most significant agreement, however, was the verification of the accords by the UN through the creation of ONUSAL.[12] The mission's main purpose was to verify the observance of human rights by both sides and to promote respect for human rights. It would be the first and most extensive of its kind, conducting in situ verification of human rights following the ceasefire. Furthermore, the parties agreed to the "full guarantee of the freedom and integrity of the person," prohibiting the arrest of persons for political reasons and "torture and other cruel, inhumane or degrading treatment or punishment."[13] The San José Agreement also provided for support of habeas corpus and freedom of expression and association, including trade union freedom and enjoyment of labor rights.

The Mexico Agreement (April 1991) reflected agreements on constitutional reforms to the armed forces, judiciary, and electoral system. The agreement laid the groundwork for the restructuring of the military. The reforms included the subordination of the armed forces to civilian authorities and a redefinition of mission to defend the sovereignty of the state, creation of a new civilian police force, placing the military and police under different ministries, and dismantling paramilitary forces. Building on the agreements reached in the San José Agreement, the parties also agreed to the creation of the National Counsel for the Defense of Human Rights (PDDH), whose purpose was to "promote and ensure respect for human rights" (and which was to be elected by a two-thirds majority of the Legislative Assembly), as well as to the creation of a Truth Commission to investigate "serious acts of violence that have occurred since 1980 and whose impact on society urgently requires that the public should know the truth."[14] The main element of electoral reform was the creation of the Supreme Electoral Tribunal (TSE) as the ruling administrative authority. Wary of the politicization that had characterized its predecessor, the Central Election Council (CCE), the agreement stipulated that "the composition of the Tribunal shall be determined by secondary legislation, making sure that no party or coalition of parties predominates it. It has also been agreed that the Supreme Electoral Tribunal shall include members without any party affiliation, elected by a majority of the Legislative Assembly."[15] A special commission would later suggest changes to the electoral code.

The agreement provided for the separation of the judiciary and executive through the reorganization of the Supreme Court and established a new procedure for the elections of Supreme Court judges, requiring a two-thirds majority of deputies in the Legislative Assembly. This same formula was applied to the election of the attorney general and the PDDH. The parties also agreed to a set allocation of the national budget for the judiciary at 6 percent. The restructuring of the National Judiciary Council made it responsible for nominating judges and running the judicial training school.[16] The government did not agree to FMLN proposals for replacing the Supreme Court, evaluating and purging the judiciary, or a number of other reforms of criminal procedure.[17] The proposed reforms were insufficient to modernize El Salvador's judiciary, but the FMLN was not equipped to advance the agenda. As Margaret Popkin has observed, "a guerrilla insurgency with minimal experience in the legal system is not the ideal protagonist for profound judicial reform."[18]

The stalemate on the reduction of the armed forces was finally broken when the FMLN agreed to drop the demand that FMLN forces be incorporated into the armed forces in exchange for its members participation in the new civilian police force and an oversight commission for the implementation of the accords. The New York Agreement (September 1991) stipulated the purification of the armed forces based on a review of personnel conducted by the Ad Hoc Commission and the reduction of the armed forces, the specifics of which were to be determined. Additionally, the agreement provided for the creation of the National Commission for the Consolidation of Peace (COPAZ) as the party responsible for ensuring the implementation of all political agreements.[19] COPAZ was to be composed of two government representatives, including a member of the armed forces, two FMLN representatives, and one representative of each party or coalition in the Legislative Assembly, while the archbishop of San Salvador was given observer status.

Although COPAZ was given no executive powers, the agreement did require that the commission be consulted on all matters relating to the implementation and oversight of the peace agreements. COPAZ was also given the power to draft preliminary legislation related to the agreements.

The Chapúltepec Accords were signed on January 16, 1992, in Mexico City. The accords resolved the remaining and most contentious issues of the negotiations, those concerning the armed forces, and reaffirmed agreements reached during the past two years. Chapter I upheld the agreements stipulated in the Mexico Agreement, which effectively restructured the armed forces. Among the principles addressed in the Chapúltepec Accords were adherence to democratic values, respect for human rights, subordination of the armed forces to constitutional authorities, and national defense. The language in the accords required the armed forces to be "obedient, professional, apolitical, and non-deliberative" in their service and "respect to the political order determined by the sovereign will of the people and all political or social changes generated by that will, in accordance with democratic procedures consistent with the Constitution."[20] The accords also defined the role of the armed forces as one of national defense, as opposed to internal security: "National defense, the responsibility of the armed forces, is intended to safeguard sovereignty and territorial integrity against outside military threat"; they further specified that "the maintenance of internal peace, tranquility, order and public security lies outside the normal functions of the armed forces." To that end, the parties agreed to changes to the education and training of the armed forces to focus on human rights, respect for democracy, and the subordination to civilian authorities, including the president's authority to appoint civilians to the post of defense minister. Although the accords themselves did not specify the extent of the reduction of the armed forces agreed to in the New York Agreement, the Chapúltepec Accords did acknowledge that a plan had been submitted to the secretary general. With regard to purification, the duties and responsibilities of the Ad Hoc Commission were detailed. Finally, the National Guard, Treasury Police, National Police, Rapid-Deployment Infantry Battalions (BIRIs), and "civil defence units"—all those organizations most responsible for gross human rights violations—were to be abolished, and the National Intelligence Department was to be replaced with a State Intelligence Organization, subordinate to civilian control.

Chapter II provided for the creation of a new civilian police force, the National Civilian Police (PNC) as a separate entity from the armed forces, placing the armed forces and police under the authority of different ministries. Under

42

the accords, the PNC became the only armed police body with national juris-diction. The accords further distinguished the role of the national police from that of the armed forces by defining public security as "a service provided by the State to its citizens, free from all political considerations of politics, ideology or social position or any other discrimination; respect for human rights; the effort to prevent crime; and the subordination of the force to the constitutional authorities."[22] Additionally, the PNC's leaders were required to be civilians. In an effort to further distinguish the police from the military, the police were no longer permitted to reside in barracks and were permitted to carry only small arms. A new national public security academy was created to train recruits, and a basic level of education was established for recruits. A limited number of former members of the National Police and the FMLN were allowed to join the PNC provided they met specified criteria. Additionally, it was the designated role of the PNC to protect the right of assembly and demonstration, adding, "citizens' exercise of their political rights may not be impaired by police activities."[23] This provision underlined police responsibility to protect the rights of the citizenry rather than the rights of the state.

Chapters III and IV addressed judicial and electoral reform, reaffirming the agreements reached in the Mexico Agreement. The Chapúltepec Accords specifically addressed the National Judiciary Council's independence from the state, the role of the Judicial Training School in improving the professional training judges and attorneys, and the responsibilities of the PDDH. Chapter IV, which addressed electoral reform, was a single paragraph reaffirming the Mexico Agreement. The accords did stipulate that COPAZ appoint a special commission to propose necessary electoral reforms. Both chapters lacked specificity and were the least developed sections of the accords; the former was a single page and the latter was a single paragraph. The lack of specificity and the extent to which the reforms were left to domestic actors became a serious issue during implementation.

Chapter V addressed the socioeconomic issues of the peace accords. During the negotiations, the FMLN had been primarily concerned with military and institutional reform. Although the FMLN had based its armed struggle on battling socioeconomic injustices, the social and economic aspects of the peace accords were left until the end of the negotiations and were very limited in scope. The neoliberal policies adopted by the ARENA government were not subject to negotiation.[24] This was the position of the Cristiani administration and the FMLN, which was far more concerned about the military and human rights issues, never contested this position. According to FMLN negotiator Rubén Zamora, "The moment the FMLN agreed that we were going to negotiate with the ARENA government, the socioeconomic model was out of the discussion. Maybe we could do something on secondary issues, but the basic thing was to get to the table. This is the basic tenet of negotiations. People go to negotiate, not to sacrifice themselves."[25] According to Teresa Whitfield, it was "remarkable that socioeconomic issues even were the subject of a substantive agreement."[26] Nicaragua's experience, however, had demonstrated the danger of failing to make provisions for ex-combatants after demobilization. As such, the accords addressed five main issues: land transfer; increase and ease of loans to the agricultural sector; small business and microenterprise; reforms to permit external aid directed to community development; and measures to alleviate the social cost of structural adjustment programs. The accords also reaffirmed the commitment to privatization as a means to spread wealth to workers.[27] The land transfer program was intended to facilitate the reintegration of members of the FMLN and their supporters into society. Thus, the economic measures agreed to in the peace accords were specifically focused on rebuilding former conflict zones and the reintegration of FMLN forces through land transfer and improved access to credit—not on addressing fundamental issues of poverty and inequality.[28]

The accords also created the Forum for Economic and Social Consultation (Foro) and the National Reconstruction Plan (PRN). The purpose of the Foro was to address those socioeconomic issues not discussed in the accords, including wages, labor standards, and privatization. The Foro was to be composed of high-level government officials, specifically those with the authority to make decisions, and business and labor representatives. The terms of the Foro as specified in the accords were vague, as were the structure and issues to be addressed by the Foro. The accords required the PRN to be designed by the government within thirty days of signing the agreement for submission to the FMLN for review and comment. The National Reconstruction Plan was to focus on the reintegration of the FMLN into Salvadoran society, development of former conflict zones, issues of job creation, increase in production of basic foodstuffs, promotion of agricultural development, guarantee of basic social services, and development or redevelopment of basic infrastructure.[29]

Chapter VI specifically addressed the reintegration of the FMLN into Salvadoran society and had two main components: the reintegration of former combatants and the legalization of the FMLN as a political party. As such, the accords provided for the freedom to conduct business attributed to political parties, such as canvassing for new members, access to the media, and the right of assembly. The accords also included a special security provision for FMLN leaders following the signing of the peace accords. Political prisoners being held by the government were freed and those in exile were allowed to return. That said, the FMLN would still be required to complete the formal process of registering as a political party with the TSE.

Chapter VII, the last section of the accords, addressed the cessation of armed conflict. Accordingly, the ceasefire was to begin February 1, 1992, and to be completed on October 21, 1992. This section detailed agreements reached on the ceasefire, separation of forces, demobilization, disarmament, and reintegration of the FMLN, as well as UN verification of these processes.[30] These provisions were to be monitored and verified by ONUSAL. Additionally, COPAZ was charged with evaluating progress made on the implementation of the agreements.

The Implementation of the Accords

The formal ceasefire began on February 1, 1992, although there had been an unofficial ceasefire since December. The United Nations Observer Mission in El Salvador (ONUSAL) was formally established by Security Council Resolution 693 in May 1991 to verify the implementation of the accords.[31] The ONUSAL mission had four responsibilities: human rights monitoring, demobilization, election monitoring, and compliance with the judicial and socioeconomic requirements of the accords (see table 2.1).

TABLE 2.1

Phases of the ONUSAL mission, 1991–95

Period	Mission purpose
July 1991–January 31, 1992	Human rights monitoring
February 1, 1992–December 15, 1992	Demobilization and disarmament of FMLN; reduction of armed forces and abolishment of security forces; establishment of PNC
December 1992–March 1994	Creation of electoral division in preparation for 1994 elections and elections monitoring
March 1994–April 15, 1995	Overview of compliance with socioeconomic issues, judicial reforms, and PNC programs

Source: Adapted from Tommie Sue Montgomery, *Peacemaking and Democratization in the Western Hemisphere* (Miami: North-South Center Press, 2000), 144.

Throughout its work, the mission repeatedly commented on issues where it believed that the parties were not living up to the agreements established in the accords. ONUSAL's documentation of communications with the parties, as well as its own reports, is extensive. A careful review of the communications reveals the difficulties faced by the mission with regard to the implementation process. While there were certainly some significant issues that related directly to the FMLN, most of the documented difficulties reveal the recalcitrance of governing elites. This was particularly notable in the areas of police and judicial reform.

Human Rights

Although the deployment of the ONUSAL human rights division was originally scheduled to occur after the ceasefire, both parties requested that the mission begin its work ahead of schedule. The secretary general's office sent a small delegation to determine if the work could be conducted in the absence of a ceasefire. The division began operations in July 1991, well before any necessary reforms related to strengthening human rights had been implemented. Although the mission expanded over time, the division's chief responsibility was to investigate and report human rights violations occurring after July 26, 1991. Violations committed before that date were entrusted to the Truth Commission. Requests for division assistance often exceeded its mandate.[32] Shortly after arriving, the division expressed some concern that "vast numbers of Salvadorians right across the political spectrum believe that the Mission will be able to prevent, or at least punish, human rights violations," although it did not have the powers to do so.[33] Reports from the division generally emphasized two challenges: the difficulty of adequately monitoring violations during conflict and failure of the judiciary to investigate or follow up on alleged violations.[34]

The deployment of the human rights division gave the UN an entrée into El Salvador while negotiations continued. It also complicated the division's work. There was a fundamental tension between ONUSAL's human rights division, which was charged with monitoring and reporting abuses committed by the parties, and the UN secretary general's office, which wanted to ensure that negotiations progressed. Should reports of violations be suppressed if they advanced the larger goal of attaining a resolution to the conflict? Would suppressing reports damage the integrity of the mission and undermine respect for human rights in the long term? On the ground, there was some sense among division staff that human rights were subservient to other aspects of the negotiations, particularly political and military concerns.[35] After the ceasefire, ONUSAL's mandate expanded to include demilitarization and demobilization, civilian policing, and elections. While this helped reduce the number of human rights violations, it also shifted emphasis to other matters. As one division official relayed to the Lawyers' Committee, "once the other divisions arrived, it was more difficult. It was clear that human rights were no longer a priority for anyone. The government had never been interested, but now not even the UN or the FMLN were interested."[36]

The National Counsel for the Defense of Human Rights (PDDH) was established in 1991. Its main function was to receive and investigate complaints of human rights abuses. While the institution had the power to make recommendations, it had no enforcement capabilities. The first national counsel, Carlos Fonseca Molina, was appointed in February 1992. Due to Fonseca's own lack of experience in human rights advocacy and the general disinterest of the Cristiani administration, the institution got off to a slow start.[37] Relations with the human rights division and human rights organizations were strained, and it was not until 1994 that the national counsel and ONUSAL began working together to strengthen the institution. The appointment of Victoria Marina Velásquez de Avilés to the PDDH in 1995 helped to transform the institution.[38] Velásquez de Avilés became an outspoken defender of human rights and denounced abuses by state institutions, particularly the PNC. Public confidence in the PDDH rose considerably during her tenure, in large part due to her leadership.[39] She was rewarded for her efforts with a 10 percent budget cut in 1997, which reduced the capabilities of the institution at a critical time.[40]

Security and Policing

The second phase of implementation was the restructuring and reduction of the armed forces, abolition of security forces, and the creation of a new civilian police force, and the demobilization of the FMLN. Within one year of the signing of the accords, the armed forces had effectively been reduced by one-half, from 63,175 to 31,000.[41] Because the reduction was completed a full year ahead of schedule, some have speculated that the original number of troops had been inflated.[42] The demobilization of the Rapid-Deployment Infantry Battalions (BIRIs) was delayed by three months, but the process was completed on March 31, 1993.[43] The change in the armed forces was not only notable for the reduction in forces but also for the general willingness with which the military accepted its new role in Salvadoran society. Not all aspects of demilitarization went so smoothly. The UN appointed three Salvadoran civilians to the Ad Hoc Commission, a mechanism agreed to in the accords to review military records and purge human rights offenders. It was the first time that any military in Latin America had allowed an external review of its forces.[44] Beginning in May 1992 the commission reviewed military-personnel files and documentation from human rights organizations, and met with members of the U.S. Defense Department and congressional and human rights groups in the United States.[45] Due to the three-month time constraint, the commission was able to interview only approximately 230 officers—a mere 10 percent of all officers in the armed forces. In September 1992, the commission delivered its confidential report to President Cristiani and UN Secretary General Boutros-Ghali, which called for the removal of 102 officers, including Defense Minister René Emilio Ponce. Protests from the military high command led to stalling tactics by Cristiani. Despite the agreement that named officers were to be removed within sixty days, only twenty-three had been formally dismissed by January 1993.[46] It required significant pressure from abroad and the release of the Truth Commission's report to force the removal of remaining officers.[47]

The dissolution of internal security forces accompanied the reduction of the armed forces. The National Guard and the Treasury Police were scheduled to be dismantled by March 1992. Instead, they were renamed and incorporated directly into the armed forces.[48] ONUSAL intervened in what it considered to be a violation of the accords. The security forces were officially dissolved by the end of June 1992, although there was little doubt that some members continued to function on their own. Additionally, the National Intelligence Directorate (DNI) was dissolved and replaced by a new civilian State Intelligence Organ (OIE) in June 1992.

The FMLN's registration as a political party was dependent on certification of its demobilization. In January 1992 the Legislative Assembly passed a law on national reconciliation that permitted the return of FMLN members from abroad, including the General Command. On February 1 the FMLN began the process of establishing itself as a political party by collecting signatures and presenting them to the Supreme Electoral Tribunal. By May the FMLN began to press for its legalization as a political party, going so far as to hold a rally to mark its beginnings as a political party later that month.[49] On July 30, 1992, the FMLN was officially recognized by the government of El Salvador as a "political party in formation." However, the government also submitted a request to the TSE that the FMLN not be formally recognized until it had fully demobilized. The TSE responded that the FMLN's final registration would not be granted until ONUSAL verified its total disarmament and demobilization.[50] The United Nations certified on December 15, 1992, that the FMLN had successfully disarmed and it was registered as a political party.

The FMLN's failure to completely disarm was exposed when an arms cache belonging to the Popular Forces of Liberation (FPL) was discovered following an explosion in Managua, Nicaragua, in June 1993. In a letter to the UN secretary general, FPL leader Salvador Sánchez Cerén stated that the FPL had retained the arms only out of profound distrust for the Armed Forces of El Salvador (FAES) and had no intention of remilitarizing the conflict.[51] The FMLN subsequently disclosed more than one hundred additional arms deposits in El Salvador and neighboring countries. In August 1993, ONUSAL was able to verify that all FMLN arms had been destroyed and that the FMLN no longer constituted a combatant force. Despite this transgression, the FMLN's status as a political party was not revoked and the ceasefire was never broken.

The deployment of the new National Civil Police (PNC) began in March 1993 under the guise of ONUSAL's police division, which was deployed in February 1992.[52] Recruits for the new force were drawn from the existing police (20 percent), the FMLN (20 percent), and new recruits (60 percent), provided they met requirements laid out in the New York Agreement. Dismantling old policing structures, however, did not proceed as quickly or as cleanly as hoped. Funding shortfalls and delays in opening the new National Academy for Public Security (ANSP) resulted in the deferred deployment of the new police force.[53] Although the agreements clearly stated that the National Police would be responsible for public security until its units could be replaced by the PNC, there was also the expectation that the National Police would be phased out as the PNC was deployed. Instead, the National Police training school continued to operate and graduate students, which contributed to the *growth* of the National Police.[54] The continued functioning of the National Police deprived the PNC of vital resources. During the transition period (1992–94), the National Police received $77 million while the PNC received only $45 million and the ANSP received $22 million.[55] Moreover, more than one thousand personnel from the National Guard and Treasury Police, and entire BIRI units were transferred into the National Police. In December 1992, the GOES and the FMLN agreed, without consulting the UN, to the transfer of low-ranking officers from the armed forces and other units. Known as Plan 600, the agreement provided FMLN guerrillas with benefits in a time of scare resources.[56] ONUSAL complained that such transfers were "incompatible with the thrust of the accords and contravene their spirit," which had clearly mandated the screening of PNC personnel in response to FMLN concerns about human rights records of National Police officers.[57] The government justified these actions based on growing crime rates (see chapter 5).[58]

Concerns about the lack of adequate training, impunity and continuing human rights abuses were common during the transition.[59] Some members of the former security apparatuses were reluctant to submit to the new institutions and they quickly came to dominate the new police force, although cases of strife between former FMLN and former security officers were relatively few.[60] In June 1993 the government appointed former military officer Oscar Peña Durán as the PNC's operations director. During his ten months in office, Peña transferred two units of the National Police into the PNC—the Special Investigations Unit (SIU) and the Anti-Narcotics Division (UEA), for the latter of which Peña was the former head—a clear violation of the peace accords. Peña not only flagrantly violated the peace accords through the appointments and his refusal to allow ONUSAL's continued training of new units, but he also evaded COPAZ consultations that were mandated by the accords. ONUSAL described the refusal of its police training as "a self-defeating move," though later evidence would suggest that the decision was, in fact, designed to preserve elite control over the new police force.[61] Despite protests from ONUSAL and increasing reports of human rights violations by the PNC, the Cristiani administration exhibited little political will in enforcing these aspects of the accords. In fact, Cristiani attempted to delay the dissolution of the PN until June 1994, presumably in hopes that a new administration would be able to shirk international verification and any responsibilities of further compliance with the accords.[62] The veil of impunity, however, was lifted in June 1994 when a dozen agents in National Police uniforms robbed a bank in broad daylight, killing six and wounding five others.

The incident, which generated public outrage and exposed the extent of the ongoing impunity, was caught on video and broadcast on television and in print media.[63] Shortly thereafter, it was announced that the National Police would be dissolved. Despite significant delays, the PNC was fully deployed in October 1994 and had a force of seventy-two hundred officers by 1995. By then, however, the damage to the PNC had been done.[64]

Socioeconomic Reforms

The final stage of the ONUSAL mission concentrated on the socioeconomic issues addressed in the Chapúltepec Accords. The three main provisions of the socioeconomic section of the accords addressed land transfer, the creation of the Foro, and a national development plan. The Land Transfer Program (PTT) was intended primarily as a process by which to reintegrate FMLN combatants and their supporters into society, not as a means to redress the serious land issue that had plagued the country for more than one hundred years.[65] The land transfer program was complicated by titling and verification problems, as well as political disputes. Determining ownership before occupation and designating proper recipients was time consuming and sometimes impossible.[66] Additionally, the process was confusing for beneficiaries. Many misunderstood the terms of the accords and were surprised to discover that they would actually have to purchase the land, albeit on favorable terms (6 percent interest and a thirty-year repayment plan). There was also significant political tension and mistrust between the FMLN and ARENA that delayed the transfers, particularly with regard to ARENA's notion that land transfers were considered "rewards" for FMLN supporters in advance of the 1994 elections.[67] At one point, the FMLN halted demobilization and the government responded by stalling on the purification of the armed forces.[68] In October 1992 the UN developed a plan designed to distribute one hundred thousand *manzanas* of land to some 25,000 civilians and 22,500 ex-combatants (15,000 soldiers and 7,500 FMLN, about three manzanas (about two hectares) each.[69] The agreement did not resolve the many problems associated with the program. Some beneficiaries did not want to move, some could not be located, some died, while still others complained about the quality of the land. Landowners were not willing to sell or resented the bureaucracy of the Land Bank. Land costs, which had been depressed by the war, increased significantly after the conclusion of the conflict. Despite numerous delays and much political wrangling, the land transfer process was near completion in 1997. By the time the Land Bank was dissolved in January 1998, 36,089 beneficiaries had received some 103,300 hectares, or 10 percent of agricultural land.[70]

The Foro, which was intended as a forum for government, business, and labor to address issues such as labor rights, wages, privatization and other issues, died shortly after its creation, in September 1992. The business sector initially refused to participate because of land invasions by peasants in connection with the land transfer program. During its brief tenure, the Foro reached agreement on the ratification of the ILO conventions, twelve of which were ratified by the Legislative Assembly by 1995.[71] The business sector halted participation in late 1993 due to the upcoming March 1994 elections. The Foro was reestablished as the Consejo Superior del Trabajo, although it never met. One UN report laid the blame squarely on the shoulders of the business community: "the Forum did not fulfill its original mandate."[72]

The failure of the Foro was demonstrative of the unwillingness of the Cristiani government to allow open discussion of its economic policies. Neither the Cristiani administration nor the private sector favored labor's participation in the policymaking process and made no effort to promote or sustain the Foro. According to Miguel Sáenz, "The private sector understood that it was the instrument that could start the debate, which would lead to agreements for the economic and social transformation [of the country], so it killed it."[73] Rubén Zamora called the Foro "a disaster" and suggested that the FMLN might have been naive to believe that the Foro would be able to address significant socioeconomic issues, given Cristiani's opposition to it.[74] Thus, not only was the neoliberal model off the table at the peace accords, but the one mechanism created by the peace accords to address socioeconomic issues was quickly abolished. As such, there was little if any opportunity for labor to participate in policymaking. This failure to incorporate labor into the policymaking process relegated labor to the same position that it was in before the peace accords—outside the system, gaining attention for its demands through strike activity.

The government launched the National Reconstruction Plan (PRN) in 1992 after the inclusion of recommendations from the FMLN and the United Nations Development Program (UNDP). The FMLN and the UNDP were critical of the PRN to the extent that project development lay largely in the hands of the government and marginalized other participants; infrastructure was given priority over other needs of the former conflict zones; and the target area of the PRN was geographically too small.[75] The government responded to these criticisms by easing potential participation for NGOs, increasing the number of targeted municipalities from 84 to 115 (of a total 262), and redefining some programs to give a greater emphasis to the development of human capital over infrastructure.[76] While the government changes to the PRN marked some improvement, the problem of NGO participation was never fully resolved. NGOs were required to apply to the National Reconstruction Secretariat for funding, and those associated with the Left were often excluded.[77]

The PRN had three main areas: investment projects (infrastructure, ex-combatant programs), technical assistance (small UNDP projects), and democratic institutions (National Civilian Police, Human Rights Ombudsman).[78] Of those, investment projects received the most donor funding, giving the PRN a focus on the reconstruction of the infrastructure of the former conflict zones. The government established the Secretariat for National Reconstruction (SRN) to oversee the reconstruction process, which was designated as the distributor of funds to those projects. Additionally, the UNDP was instrumental in the reconstruction process. The UNDP, which was specifically included in the accords as a third party at the insistence of the FMLN, was responsible for the development of reinsertion and reconstruction programs.[79] The government hoped to raise $800 million for the reconstruction effort, and by 1994 it had succeeded in raising more than $900 million.[80]

The Ministry of Planning (MIPLAN), the government agency in charge of the PRN, estimated that the war cost $1.5 billion in infrastructure alone, with a replacement cost of $1.63 billion. In addition, the 1986 earthquake caused $1.2 billion in damages.[81] During the peace process, El Salvador received assurances from many countries, including the United States, that funding for reconstruction would be forthcoming. Indeed, many believed that the bulk of the funding responsibility would fall on the United States. Of the $698.9 million in external assistance from individual country donors, $535.9 million was from the United States. The Inter-American Development Bank was the single largest multilateral donor, providing $558.8 million of the $929.4 million donated by those groups.[82] Despite the significant amount of aid available to the reconstruction process, some areas were prone to significant shortfalls, especially "high-priority" programs. High-priority programs—such as the demobilization of the National Police, the creation of the PNC, and democratic and judicial reform—experienced significant shortfalls, as donors considered them too problematic. While the United States allotted more than 75 percent of its funding to these programs, other donors contributed 78 percent of their funding to lower-priority programs.[83] Non-U.S. donors contributed a mere $21 million to the PNC, land transfer, and democratic and judicial institutional programs, while contributing $261 million to physical infrastructure programs.[84] This resulted in an anticipated shortfall of $311 million.[85]

As a result of such donor funding discrepancies, many programs that were the cornerstones of the peace accords suffered serious funding shortfalls. The impact of these shortfalls was significant and was particularly evident in the case of the PNC, where funding shortfalls resulted in woefully inadequate resources for the deployment of the new police force. According to Tommie Sue Montgomery, in one department 230 police officers shared seven vehicles and two motorcycles to serve an area the size of metropolitan Atlanta, Georgia. Other police precincts had no phones, radios, or vehicles.[86] Similarly, funding shortfalls impeded the work of the public ministry's office (including the attorney general) and delayed the land transfer program and judicial reform. Thus, funding shortfalls of high-priority programs jeopardized the peace process by neglecting the very programs that were mandated by the accords.

Truth, Justice, and Reconciliation in El Salvador's Captured Peace

The importance of transitional justice to the peacebuilding process has been increasingly recognized by the international and scholarly communities. The purpose of transitional justice, which may include judicial and nonjudicial mechanisms, is to provide recognition to the victims of human rights abuses committed during war. The most common transitional justice mechanisms are truth commissions, prosecutions, reparations, institutional reforms, and memorialization.[87] Transitional justice also necessarily entails confronting and reconciling the past. While some of the institutional reforms created by the peace accords may ultimately contribute to transitional justice, the process in El Salvador has been quite limited. To date, the most significant state-sanctioned element of transitional justice was the truth commission and its report. As demonstrated below, even that was undermined by the Salvadoran government.

The Truth Commission

The Commission on Truth for El Salvador, agreed to in the Mexico Agreement, was overseen by the United Nations. The commission, chaired by former Colombian president Belisario Betancur, began its work in July 1992 and published its report in March 1993, two months later than the original mandate. During the course of its investigation, the commission received more than seven thousand complaints from victims and witnesses and collected additional evidence from human rights organizations. The commission also conducted forensic investigations, including an exhumation at the site of the 1981 El Mozote massacre. In all, more than twenty-two thousand complaints were documented. The overwhelming majority (95 percent) of those accused in the complaints were classified as "agents of the State, paramilitary groups allied to them, and the death squads."[88] Some 60 percent of complaints involved extrajudicial killings, more than 25 percent involved disappearances, and more than 20 percent included torture. More than 75 percent of the complaints received by the commission pertained to events that occurred from 1980 to 1983, with approximately 50 percent of those occurring in 1980 and 1981. The commission also noted that 95 percent of complaints involved incidents in rural areas.[89]

The report, *From Madness to Hope,* identified both patterns of violence and specific cases attributed to State agents and death squads, the most prominent of which included the assassinations of Archbishop Óscar Romero, the Jesuits, the FDR leadership, Attorney General Mario Zamora, the American churchwomen, the murder of four Dutch journalists, and numerous civilian massacres. The report also documented the FMLN's execution of mayors from 1985 to 1988 and other extrajudicial killings, including the murders of U.S. marines in the Zona Rosa in 1985. Most of the report, however, focused on the abuses and violence committed with impunity by state agencies and their affiliates. Among the report's findings in individual cases, the commission concluded that Roberto D'Aubuisson ordered the assassination of Archbishop Romero; that the murder of the American churchwomen was planned before their arrival at the airport and that high-ranking officials impeded the investigation; and that Col. René Emilio Ponce gave the order to kill Father Ignacio Ellacuría and "to leave no witnesses," which was followed by a widespread cover-up. In its investigation of civilian massacres, such as those at El Mozote, Río Sumpul, and El Calabozo, the commission determined that the armed forces had engaged in a systematic policy of targeting civilians:

> Everything points to the fact that these deaths formed part of a pattern of conduct, a deliberate strategy of eliminating or terrifying the peasant population in areas where the guerrillas were active, the purpose being to deprive the guerrilla forces of this source of supplies and information and of the possibility of hiding or concealing themselves among that population.
>
> It is impossible to blame this pattern of conduct on local commanders and to claim that senior commanders did not know anything about it. As we have described, massacres of the peasant population were reported repeatedly. There is no evidence that any effort was made to investigate them. The authorities dismissed these reports as enemy propaganda. Were it not for the childrens skeletons at El Mozote, some people would still be disputing that such massacres took place.
>
> [...]
>
> No action was taken to avoid incidents such as this. On the contrary, the deliberate, systematic and indiscriminate violence against the peasant population in areas of military operations went on for years.[90]

The Cristiani administration initially attempted to prevent the findings of the commission from being publicized but was unsuccessful in its attempts to persuade the FMLN to support that position.[91] Unlike many truth commissions, the Salvadoran report named individual actors allegedly responsible for human rights violations. Although the Cristiani government initially supported identifying those guilty of committing abuses, its position changed once it became clear that high-ranking officials would be implicated.[92] Threats of coups and retaliations, which had occurred during negotiations, soon resurfaced. Cristiani asked that the publication of the report be delayed until after the 1994 elections. The commissioners held firm in their decision, arguing that telling the "complete truth" meant naming names.[93] As a result, more than forty individuals were named. Defense Minister René Emilio Ponce, himself named in the report in connection with the Jesuit murders, and other members of the high command called the report, "unfair, incomplete, illegal, unethical, biased and insolent."[94] Other members of the military high command directed their anger toward Cristiani, who, they suggested, had been "irresponsible" in having agreed to the commission.[95]

There were numerous other criticisms of the report. First, at the behest of the FMLN, there were no Salvadorans on the commission. The organization argued that the high levels of polarization and distrust between the government and FMLN would make it difficult to find mutually acceptable, neutral Salvadoran investigators and that using Salvadorans to take testimony would reduce the number of victims and witnesses willing to provide testimony.[96] Indeed, many Salvadorans feared retribution if they were to testify about government abuses. But as Ana Guardado and others have noted, this decision not only prevented Salvadoran citizens from becoming full participants in the process but also meant that there was no government ownership of the report.[97] Not only did the Cristiani administration refuse to accept the findings of the commission, but no effort was made to distribute the report, as had become common practice in other cases.[98] Instead, Cristiani urged Salvadorans to forget the past. As described below, the refusal to acknowledge the report's findings or assign responsibility for acts of violence seriously impeded reconciliation by perpetuating two very distinct narratives of the war.

Second, the context in which the commission conducted its work constrained not only the collection of testimony but limited the prospects for meaningful reform. The truth commission was the result of the negotiations between the Salvadoran government and the FMLN, which is somewhat unusual in the establishment of truth commissions.[99] One of the chief purposes of truth commissions, as opposed to trials, is to focus on the victims rather than the perpetrators. However, as observed by Popkin, "neither the UN nor the parties to the conflict made any systematic effort to consult with Salvadoran civil society, victims and their relatives, or even Salvadoran human rights groups. Nor did the parties recognize that the right to truth and justice could not be foreclosed by their negotiations."[100] This undermined the victim-centered approach supposedly afforded by truth commissions.

Third, the commission's work was carried out in the midst of the transition rather than following the transition, as El Salvador's elections weren't scheduled until March 1994. Thus, ARENA's incumbency meant that the "old regime" and the "new regime" were one and the same.[101] For obvious reasons, truth commission investigations and the release of their reports generally occur after regime change or transitional elections, as was the case in Argentina, Chile, Guatemala, Peru, and South Africa. Those responsible for the abuses in El Salvador were still in power. As such, it should be of little surprise that the Cristiani administration did not endorse the commission's findings.

Fourth, there was general dissatisfaction with the investigation of cases related to the FMLN. The Lawyers' Committee on Human Rights referred to it as being one of the "weakest" sections of the report.[102] The vast majority of the cases in the report were those attributed to the armed forces and state security agencies, which was a reflection of both the commission's mandate and the disproportionate number of abuses committed by the state.[103] However, the commission erroneously assumed that documentation of FMLN abuses could be provided by the Salvadoran and U.S. governments and conducted little investigation in this regard.[104] For example, there was no investigation of summary executions within FMLN ranks, which many considered to be one of the chief offenses by the FMLN. As such, the report offered little new information about FMLN abuses. Additionally, those abuses that were included in the report, most of which the FMLN had already acknowledged, were attributed to a single group within the FMLN, the People's Revolutionary Army (ERP).[105] The government and its supporters used this lack of an adequate investigation into FMLN abuses to delegitimize the report.

Finally, the commissioners considered it beyond the scope of the mandate to investigate the role that the United States played in the conflict. This was particularly disconcerting since several of the cases of abuse presented in the report were committed by U.S.-trained units, such as the Atlacatl Battalion. Former U.S. ambassador to El Salvador Robert White was particularly critical of the omission: "The whole backdrop to the report that is missing is the U.S. role in not only tolerating violence in El Salvador but also encouraging it."[106]

The Commission's Recommendations

The recommendations made by the commission involved punitive measures, institutional reforms, and societal reparations to promote reconciliation. While the truth commission had no prosecutorial powers, the parties had agreed that its recommendations would be binding. Many of the commission's recommendations reaffirmed changes agreed to in the peace accords, but most were never implemented. In the absence of the judicial capacity to punish those responsible for the violations in the report, the commission made a number of punitive recommendations. First, the commission recommended the dismissal of military officers and civil servants named in report. Second, the commission recommended that all those named in the report, including members of the FMLN, be disqualified from holding public office for at least ten years and be barred permanently from serving in any capacity related to public security or national defense. Finally, the commission called for the resignation of the entire Supreme Court of Justice.[107] With respect to purging members of the armed forces, the Truth Commission succeeded where the Ad Hoc Commission had failed. Several officers were removed as a result of being named, although they were allowed to retire with full honors and benefits.[108] A new Supreme Court was elected in 1994, but the former president of the Supreme Court was appointed to the Inter-American Juridical Committee of the Organization of American States.

The commission also made recommendations regarding structural problems related to the violence. Of particular concern was the strengthening of civilian control of the military and the promotion of training in democracy and human rights among the armed forces. The commission also recommended that Article 173 of army regulations, which requires a subordinate to obey *all* orders (even illegal ones) from a superior, be repealed. Additionally, the commission urged the strengthening of the National Counsel for the Defense of Human Rights (PDDH) by increasing the number of offices and its powers of inspection at detention sites. The rights of detainees, particularly with regard to extrajudicial confessions and the criminal code, were also addressed. The commission also called for the investigation of death squads, which threatened to undermine the peace process. A series of political assassinations of ARENA and FMLN leaders in 1993 led to the establishment of the Joint Group for the Investigation of Politically Motivated Illegal Armed Groups, in December 1993. In its report, published in July 1994, the joint group identified a connection between current activity and groups active during the war and stated that "political destabilization of the peace process appears . . . to be the direct objective. The perpetrators of the attacks proceed in security, showing signs of considerable organization and planning."[109] The report also highlighted the relationship between death squads and organized crime (see chapter 5).

Also of particular importance were the recommendations for judicial reforms that addressed the excessive powers and politicization of the courts. The commission recommended that judges be appointed by the independent National Council of the Judiciary agreed to in the peace accords instead of the Supreme Court of Justice, and that judges be responsible to the new council. The commission also recognized the need to strengthen the judicial system through improved training and resources. The commission's assessment of the judiciary and of the slow pace of judicial reform was particularly pointed:

> The structure of the judiciary is still substantially the same as it was when the acts described in this report took place. The reforms of the judicial system agreed on during the peace process have been implemented to only a limited extent, so that they have yet to have a significant impact which translates into a transformation of the administration of justice. What is more, the judiciary is still run by people whose omissions were part of the situation which must now be overcome, and there is nothing to indicate that their customary practices will change in the near future.[110]

Supreme Court President Mauricio Gutiérrez Castro, a member of ARENA with connections to ARENA deputies, was a major impediment to judicial reform. His steadfast defense of the separation of powers, particularly that the judiciary was not required to implement orders given by the executive branch, slowed the pace of judicial reform. Of course, he also had less "principled" reasons for stalling reform. Gutiérrez Castro had been named in the Truth Commission's report for unprofessional behavior and his refusal to cooperate with the commission's investigations.[111] There was a clear unwillingness to accept technical assistance offered by international organizations to improve the functioning and independence of the judiciary. As noted by Popkin, "the institutional reluctance to accept foreign technical and professional assistance seemed to reflect a widespread resistance to changing the status quo."[112] The implementation of judicial reforms was greatly improved by the election of an entirely new Supreme Court of Justice in 1994. In 1996 the Legislative Assembly passed a new Criminal Procedures Code, and extrajudicial confessions were invalidated in 1997 by a constitutional amendment. It was progress, but many other pressing issues, particularly judicial incompetence and corruption, remained.

Reparations to victims of state abuses have become an important aspect of the truth and reconciliation process, one also established by international law. While reparations may include financial recompense, they also include rehabilitation, satisfaction (acknowledgment), and guarantees of nonrepetition.[113] The commission's recommendations for victim compensation were ignored by the government. Material reparations, which the commission suggested should total no less than 1 percent of international assistance, were never made to victims. The commission also recommended the creation of a national monument to the victims of the war. Although the recommendation received no support from the government, a group of Salvadoran NGOs called the Comité pro Monumento de las Víctimas Civiles de Violaciones de Derechos Humanos organized the project. In December 2003 the Monument to Memory and Truth was unveiled in Parque Cuscatlán, in San Salvador. The black granite wall, inspired by the Vietnam memorial in Washington, DC, was inscribed with the names of nearly thirty thousand victims.

The Amnesty Law

Access to justice for crimes committed during the war evaded most Salvadorans. In March 1993 the Legislative Assembly passed the General Amnesty Law for the Consolidation of Peace a mere five days after the Truth Commission released its report. The possibility of amnesty was not ruled out by the truth commission, which stated that it was a decision for the Salvadoran people.[114] While an amnesty law had been contemplated by both the GOES and the FMLN during the peace negotiations, the scope of the 1993 amnesty law was far greater than anticipated by the FMLN.[115] The National Reconciliation Law, passed in January 1992, was designed to integrate FMLN leaders into the political system and did not apply to those convicted by juries, as in the case of the UCA murders, or to those named in the Truth Commission's report.[116] The 1993 amnesty law prevented not only criminal prosecutions for abuses during the war, but the trying of civil cases and investigations regarding the status of victims as well.[117] Col. Guillermo Benavides and Lt. Yusshy Mendoza, who were convicted of participating in the UCA murders in 1991, were released under the amnesty law. Despite multiple reports by the by the Inter-American Court of Human Rights (IACHR) and findings in 1994 and 1999 that the law constituted "a violation of the international obligations it undertook when it ratified the American Convention on Human Rights," successive ARENA administrations refused to repeal the law.[118] In fact, Emily Braid and Naomi Roht-Arriaza argue that El Salvador has been the "country least compliant with IACHR decisions."[119] As such, there was no domestic legal recourse for crimes committed during the war, either in criminal or civil venues. It's also worth noting that the amnesty was also contrary to the wishes of the general population. In a poll taken shortly before the signing of the peace accords, 48 percent of respondents disagreed with any potential amnesty law, saying that it would be contrary to justice. Only 31 percent supported a potential amnesty at the time.[120]

Absent domestic remedies, some victims sought justice in foreign courts. In 2000 the families of Maura Clarke, Jean Donovan, Ita Ford, and Dorothy Kazel sued former National Guard director Carlos Eugenio Vides Casanova and ex-defense minister José Guillermo García in U.S. federal court under the 1991 U.S. Torture Victim Protection Act (TVPA).[121] The jury found the defendants not liable, apparently due to confusion over whether or not they exercised "effective command" over their troops. Although the families appealed, the judge refused to grant a new trial. Vides Casanova and García were sued again in U.S. court in 2002, this time by Salvadorans. In *Romagoza et al. v. García et al.*, four torture survivors (Juan Romagoza Arce, Neris Gonzales, Carlos Mauricio, and Jorge Montes) sued the generals under the TVPA. This time, Vides Casanova and García were found liable and the jury awarded $54.6 million in damages.[122] Although the case was overturned by the 11th Circuit Court of Appeals in February 2005, the court vacated its ruling in August 2005 and in January 2006 issued a new ruling upholding the original verdict.

In 2005, Col. Nicolas Carranza, ex-vice minister of defense and former head of the Treasury Police, was sued in federal court in Memphis. Jurors in *Chavez v. Carranza* found Carranza liable for crimes against humanity, including torture and extrajudicial killings. The jurors awarded four of the five plaintiffs $500,000 each in compensatory damages and $1 million each in punitive damages, a total of $6 million. After hearing of the verdict, Salvadoran president Tony Saca called him a hero to democracy.[123] Former U.S. ambassador Robert White testified for the plaintiffs in both the García and Carranza cases.

In *Doe v. Saravia*, Salvadoran Air Force captain Álvaro Rafael Saravia was found liable in a California federal court in 2004 for organizing the murder of Archbishop Romero under the U.S. Alien Tort Claims Act (ATCA), which allows the victims of human rights violations committed in other countries to seek relief in U.S. court. The plaintiff, an unnamed family member of the archbishop, accused Saravia of planning the murder and equipping, transporting, and paying the assassin. A default judgment for $10 million was issued against Saravia, who disappeared after receiving the complaint. He was the first individual to be held responsible for Romero's assassination in a court of law. Curiously, Saravia resurfaced in March 2010, at the thirtieth anniversary of Romero's death, in rural El Salvador. In an interview with the Salvadoran newspaper *El Faro*, Saravia recounted the story of Romero's assassination but denied being involved in its planning. Now living among the misery and poverty of El Salvador's marginalized rural population, Saravia reflected, "How would a man not become a guerrilla when he's watching his children die of hunger?"[124]

In 2008 the Center for Justice and Accountability (CJA), which had sponsored the other lawsuits, filed charges in Spain against former president Cristiani and more than a dozen members of the armed forces for their involvement in the 1989 Jesuit murders. Unlike the previous cases, this was a criminal rather than a civil case. In May 2011 the Spanish National Court issued an indictment for twenty former military officers, nine of whom subsequently turned themselves in, though the Salvadoran Supreme Court declined to arrest them without an extradition request from Spain.[125] Despite the issuance of an extradition request in November 2011, the Salvadoran Supreme Court has yet to honor that request. The extradition request for the sole defendant residing in the United States, Inocente Orlando Montano, who was sentenced to twenty-one months in U.S. prison on an immigration violation in 2013, is still pending.[126]

Unreconciled

Reconciliation is one of the most critical components of postwar peacebuilding.[127] Reconciliation is not simply about contrition and forgiveness, although those are certainly aspects of it. In peacebuilding, reconciliation refers to the redefinition of relationships between former rivals, coming to a common understanding of the past, and developing new modes of resolving conflict.[128] It is obvious to any observer that the war is still omnipresent in the Salvadoran narrative; it remains largely unaltered despite the peace process and more than two decades of peace. By eschewing the truth commission's report and passing a broad amnesty law, the Salvadoran government effectively denied Salvadorans the opportunity for reconciliation.

Beyond the denial of justice or reparations, certain Salvadoran actors continue to undermine reconciliation through their continued support of the Cold War narrative. While the calculated use of this narrative is particularly prominent during election cycles (as discussed in chapter 3), it is routinely resuscitated for political purposes. Not only has this hindered both vertical and horizontal reconciliation, it has reinforced a legacy of impunity that has facilitated the captured peace.

The peace process failed to reconcile Salvadoran society, and local actors used the politics of divisiveness for their own gain. The lack of a military victory for either side resulted in the transference of rivalries to the postwar context. Both sides remained convinced of the "rightness" of their cause. The adversarial relationship between ARENA and the FMLN came to define postwar politics. As one commentator phrased it, peace became "war by other means."[129] Additionally, the unwillingness of the Cristiani administration to accept the findings of the Truth Commission, much less implement any of its recommendations, had serious repercussions for the prospects of societal reconciliation. Neither ARENA nor the armed forces accepted responsibility for the violence. Successive ARENA administrations continued to promote the narrative that the war was a defensive one against "communist aggression," a story greatly at odds with the findings of the Truth Commission. Curiously, it was also a narrative at odds with public opinion. In a 1988 poll, fewer than 5 percent of respondents believed that communist intervention was a cause of the war.[130] As such, El Salvador remains conflicted between two views of the past. This conflict was reinforced by the 1993 amnesty law, which eliminated any access to justice for victims and their families.

There can be little doubt that the government's reaction to the truth commission's report not only denied many Salvadorans access to justice but also reinforced a legacy of impunity and limited prospects for reconciliation. One of the most cherished elements of the narrative is the continued adulation of Roberto D'Aubuisson, who ultimately capitulated to the peace process, as a national hero. Shortly after the release of the commission's report, key figures in ARENA, including Vice President Francisco Merino and San Salvador mayor Armando Calderón Sol defended D'Aubuisson, underscoring the Right's refusal to accept its role in the violence. ARENA politicians routinely visited (and kissed) his grave at El Cementerio General de los Ilustres and his photograph adorned the walls of many ARENA offices.[131] His image is ever present at party conventions. As recently as April 2014 party leaders stood in front of a massive backdrop of D'Aubuisson, fists raised and singing the party's Cold War anthem. An obelisk, built using government funds, was erected in his honor in Antiguo Cuscatlán, in the middle of a traffic circle. It is emblazoned with nationalistic slogans often attributed to the party icon. A resolution was introduced into the Legislative Assembly in February 2007 to declare D'Aubuisson, along with former president Duarte, the "son of highest merit."[132] The resolution was withdrawn days later after considerable protest from the opposition and civil society. In November 2014, San Salvador mayor and ARENA's 2014 presidential candidate Norman Quijano announced plans to rename a major street (Calle San Antonio Abad) in the capital after D'Aubuisson.[133] That plan dissipated following ARENA's loss of San Salvador in the March 2015 elections. During the celebrations surrounding the May 2015 beatification of slain Archbishop Oscar Romero, the party claimed to honor Romero and his message of reconciliation while simultaneously distancing itself from his death and defending the party's founder. ARENA party president Jorge Velado reminded all that D'Aubuisson, who is widely known to be the intellectual author or Romero's assassination, had never been convicted of a crime related to Romero's death and that the assassination had taken place prior to the founding of the party.[134]

The Elections of the Century

ONUSAL's mission expanded in May 1993 via SC Resolution 832 to include election observation.[135] While the Chapúltepec Accords created the TSE to replace the existing electoral commission (the CCE), recommendations regarding electoral reform were to be determined by a special commission appointed by COPAZ. (Electoral reform is discussed in greater detail in chapter 3.)

During peace negotiations, El Salvador held its regularly scheduled legislative and municipal elections in 1991.[136] Those elections laid the groundwork for the 1994 elections in two respects: they opened electoral competition to parties of the center-left; and the composition of the TSE, which would coordinate future elections, would be determined by those parties in power. Although the 1991 municipal and legislative elections were held in the midst of negotiations, the campaign was hardly peaceful. There were numerous reports of violence and fraudulent activity during the campaign and on election day.[137] Additionally, elections were not held in twenty-one municipalities located in conflict zones controlled by the FMLN. While seven parties participated in the elections, including the center-left Democratic Convergence (CD), the FMLN did not participate. As a consequence, the FMLN had no representation within the TSE in coordinating the 1994 elections. ARENA won 39 of the 84 seats in the Legislative Assembly, followed by the PDC with 26, the PCN with 9, and the CD with 8 seats.[138] The CD's Rubén Zamora was elected vice president of the assembly with the support of ARENA. According to Zamora, "The most important political message to emerge was to show the army that the political left could behave responsibly and to show the guerrillas that it was possible to win and move forward on political, economic, and social grounds without continuing the war."[139] While the FMLN did not recognize the elections as legitimate, they did set the precedent for the participation of the Left.

In September 1993, ONUSAL's mandate was expanded to the observation of the 1994 elections. ONUSAL's electoral division was charged with observing the TSE to ensure impartiality; monitoring registration and electoral rolls; observing the general conditions surrounding the campaign and elections (including freedom of expression, organization, and assembly); observing voter education efforts; receiving and assessing complaints and taking them to the TSE if necessary; and placing election observers at all polling sites on election day.[140] The division had thirty-six staff working in ONUSAL offices throughout the country. During its six months of operation the division met regularly with the TSE and political parties, as well as dozens of NGOs, media outlets, analysts, and other electoral observation teams. Division teams averaged nine visits to each of the country's 262 municipalities, a near herculean task for such a small staff.[141]

Voter registration was one of the greatest challenges facing the TSE and ONUSAL. Fewer than 2 million Salvadorans had voter registration cards and some 750,000 eligible voters would need to be registered before the elections. The electoral register contained duplicate entries and the names of deceased, problems that were unlikely to be resolved before the elections. There were also serious problems with the voter registration process, described by some analysts as "cumbersome" and "byzantine." The procedure for obtaining a *carnet*, the voter identification card, was needlessly complicated and time consuming.[142] Additionally, potential voters were required to obtain a birth certificate and a *cédula* (a national identity card) at their own expense. Neither of these documents was common, particularly in rural areas or former conflict zones, where public buildings were frequent targets of the war. As many as seventy-four thousand voter registration applications were denied because the applicants failed to provide birth certificates. Not surprisingly, the number of invalidated applications in former conflict zones was three times higher than the national average.[143] There was also clear evidence of politicization of the registration process by local mayors and the TSE, both of which were dominated by ARENA.[144] Some mayors delayed the return of documents necessary for timely registration or charged outrageous document fees, while the TSE was generally unresponsive to complaints by the FMLN. The result was what Stahler-Sholk refers to as the "*de facto* disenfranchisement of the poor."[145] Pressure and resources from ONUSAL and USAID helped improve the process but could not overcome months of indifference by the TSE. When voter registration closed, in January 1994, approximately 2.7 million voters, 85 percent of the voting age population, had been registered. It was anticipated that three hundred fifty thousand of those voters would not have their carnet before the elections.

Public campaign funding, like the distribution of seats on the TSE, was based on the vote share in the 1991 elections. As with representation on the TSE, this meant that the FMLN received no public financing. The disparities in campaign expenditures were palpable. It is estimated that ARENA spent some $12 million on the campaign, compared to the FMLN's $270,000.[146] These resources allowed ARENA to dominate the airwaves and print media, made easier by the fact that many media outlets were ARENA supporters. ARENA also benefited from ads sponsored by the government and independent supporters, both a violation of the electoral code. ONUSAL's electoral division observed that the ads run by independent or anonymous supporters of ARENA were "strongly hostile to the FMLN" and "contrary to the spirit of peace and reconciliation."[147] Indeed, many of the ads, which contained images of the war and implied threats of the resumption of conflict, were clearly intended to frighten and intimidate voters. This, in addition to the assassination of party leaders and activists during 1993, created an environment of fear. Although the UN described the level of campaign violence as "limited," Stahler-Sholk observed that voters were reticent in their support for parties, particularly the FMLN, and that the "climate was adversely affected by continued killings by death squads and the constant reminder of past violence."[148] A report one week before the elections described the conditions as "generally adequate" for holding free and fair elections.[149]

Elections for president, Legislative Assembly, mayors, and the Central American Parliament (PARLACEN), were held on March 20, 1994. ONUSAL's "massive" presence on election day included nine hundred observers who were dispatched throughout the country. There were as many as two thousand additional election observers from national and international delegations. A team of forty ONUSAL observers was charged with monitoring the official vote count by the TSE. Despite some problems at the polls, the report of the secretary general found "no serious incidents affecting law and order on election day, and no ballot-rigging."[150] The report, however, did call attention to the serious concerns about problems with the electoral roll and noted that some voters with cards were unable to vote, affecting an estimated 2 percent of the electorate. Others were unable to vote because their names had been used by others. The report also highlighted a number of other concerns, including polling stations that opened late, insufficient public transport to polls, and crowded polling centers that made it difficult for voters to find their individual voting stations.[151] Approximately 1.4 million voters, about 52 percent of registered voters, participated in the election. Given the momentousness of the elections, the abstention rate was much higher than anticipated.[152]

The 1994 elections offered a greater choice of political representation than ever before. Seven parties, including the FMLN-CD coalition, offered presidential candidates. ARENA nominated San Salvador mayor Armando Calderón Sol, while the FMLN-CD nominated Rubén Zamora. Nine parties participated in the legislative and local elections, including several smaller parties across the political spectrum. ARENA's Calderon Sol won 49 percent of the vote, just shy of the simple majority needed to avoid a second round of voting. FMLN-CD candidate Zamora won 24.9 percent, followed by the PDC's Fidel Chávez Mena, with 16.4 percent. Calderón Sol easily defeated Zamora in the second round of voting, in May, 68 percent to 32 percent. While ARENA won 39 seats in the assembly, the FMLN won a respectable 21 seats, followed by the PDC with 18, the PCN with 4, and the CD with 1 seat. Its alliance with the PCN ensured that ARENA would have a majority, albeit slim, in the assembly. ARENA also dominated the municipal elections, winning 206 of the 262 mayoralties. The PDC won 29 mayoralties, the FMLN won 13 plus an additional 2 in coalition races—far fewer than expected—and the PCN won 10 mayoralties. While the FMLN's electoral fortunes in municipal races were clearly affected by registration problems experienced in ex-conflict zones, ARENA also benefited considerably from the generalized fear of violence and uncertainty surrounding the peace process.[153] It was clear from the campaign that old rivalries, and society in general, had yet to be reconciled. While the elections had been touted by the UN as the culmination of the Salvadoran peace process, it was clear that much work remained to be done.

The Achievements and Limitations of the Peace Accords

The Chapúltepec Peace Accords brought tremendous change to El Salvador. The military was placed under civilian control for the first time in the country's history, and state-sponsored terrorism ceased to be the modus operandi of the police and the armed forces. The FMLN transformed from a guerrilla movement to a political party, and other opposition parties and their affiliated organizations, including labor, were legalized and functioned without fear of recrimination. Important advances were made with regard to the protection of human rights. While implementation of the accords was not without its problems, the ceasefire was never broken, the military was successfully restructured, and paramilitary and security forces were dismantled. The importance of these achievements should not be underestimated.

While the Salvadoran peace process and the Chapúltepec Accords have widely been considered one of the most successful UN peacebuilding efforts, there were also serious deficiencies that contributed to a captured peace. Perhaps most important, the peace process failed to account for the power of the country's entrenched elites or the advantages of incumbency wielded by ARENA, which became particularly evident during the implementation phase and were reaffirmed in the 1994 elections. Though the accords were broad in scope, they did not effectively deal with many of structural realities of power—both formal and informal—that were the result of a deeply patrimonial political culture and desire to maintain the status quo. While political, military, and policing reforms set forth in the accords were significant, the accords failed to take into account what many Salvadorans perceived to be the root causes of the conflict—social and structural injustices.[154] The peace accords did not redress the socioeconomic inequalities that had long defined the country; nor did they confront the neoliberal economic model being implemented by the Cristiani administration. The FMLN, despite its opposition to the neoliberal model, accepted this outcome as a price of the negotiated peace.[155] In sum, elites were able to make peace with the FMLN by sacrificing the military, whose support modernizing elements deemed unnecessary, given their economic objectives, while preserving their economic program. Likewise, the elites accepted competitive elections, but ARENA's incumbency ensured that they had control of all key institutions. The combination of the two enabled elites to effectively capture the peace.

The complete and effective implementation of the accords rested on the shoulders of the both parties to the agreement, though the ultimate responsibility lay with the Cristiani administration. The lack of political will evidenced by the Cristiani administration in carrying out key reforms undermined the peace process. Delays in purging the armed forces, the presence of National Police structures and officers in the new PNC, and the lack of support for judicial, electoral, and human rights reforms, land transfers, and the Foro, all serve as reminders that the implementation phase is often where peace is truly won or lost, diluted, or strengthened. Additionally, the unwillingness of the Cristiani administration to support the findings of the Truth Commission and the passage of the amnesty law prohibited reconciliation and reinforced a legacy of impunity that continues today. As seen in the following chapters, these factors had a profound impact on the quality of El Salvador's peace.

Chapter 3

Electoral Politics in the Postwar Era

Parties, Polarization, and Participation

> Democracy in El Salvador is a hostage of the
> political class.
>
> —Salvador Sanabria, 2006[1]

ENSURING EL SALVADOR'S successful transition to democratic governance
was a key component of the peace process. The United Nations and the
parties to the peace accords viewed democratization as a means to achieve
peace. The most significant aspects of the Chapúltepec Accords, including
military and police reforms, electoral and judicial reforms, and guarantees
for human rights, were intended to facilitate this process. As discussed in
chapter 2, these reforms were essential to ending political violence, creating
political space for opposition political parties, and guaranteeing both the
human and civil rights of El Salvador's citizens. The successful transformation and reintegration of the FMLN was also an important step toward
creating representative government. In the more than twenty years since
the peace accords were signed, the country has routinely held free and fair
elections. The FMLN's 2009 presidential victory marked the first successful
democratic transfer of power to an opposition party in the country's history.[2]

Beneath the surface, however, there were troubling signs that all was not well with Salvadoran democracy. As demonstrated in the previous chapter, ARENA's incumbency and its control of institutions enabled it to capture the peace. This had significant consequences for the quality of democracy that followed. Capture resulted in the politicization of many of the country's institutions, which reduced possibilities for representation, undermined democratic norms and practices, and failed to respect the spirit and letter of the peace accords. The growing electoral challenge to this entrenchment by the FMLN resulted in a highly polarized political environment, which analyst Álvaro Artiga describes as "the institutionalization of conflict."[3] This chapter explores the extent to which ARENA was able to manipulate the rules of the newly established democratic game through its control of the TSE and the electoral process, the dominance of political parties in the country's new democracy, the growing polarization of parties, and the extent to which these factors impacted political participation and Salvadorans' confidence in the country's democracy and institutions.

The Electoral System in El Salvador

Knowing the rules of the political game is critical to understanding political outcomes. In a democracy, the rules define the parameters of electoral competition and, in turn, shape the policy outcomes. As noted by Gary Wynia, "Games come in many different forms. In some players are closely matched and each is given a reasonable chance of winning. Most parlor games are like that. Few political contests are so competitive, however. More common is a type of competition in which the prospects for winning are unevenly distributed, in some cases because the rules discriminate against certain players, and in others because the resources needed to win are distributed unequally."[4] The negotiations occurred under the auspices of the 1983 constitution, meaning that many of the rules of the game were established before peace negotiations (see chapter 2).

El Salvador uses both simple-majority and proportional-representation (PR) systems in its elections. In presidential contests, 50 percent plus one is required to win in the first round. In the event that the first place candidate does not receive the required share of the vote, the top two contenders will move on to a second round of voting. A second round of voting has occurred twice, in 1994 and 2014, since El Salvador's transition to democracy. El Salvador's presidents serve a five-year term, and may run for one nonconsecutive term. Unlike many other countries in the region, there has been no attempt to change the constitution to allow for additional terms. The country is divided into fourteen departments, which are represented by eighty-four deputies in the Legislative Assembly. Deputies are elected to three-year terms. The Salvadoran constitution stipulates that elections for the Legislative Assembly are to be conducted using proportional representation. The Hare system of quotas and surpluses used in El Salvador has benefited small parties in small districts, particularly the PCN.[5] Prior to 2006, elections for the Legislative Assembly were conducted via a mixed electoral system. Sixty-four seats were filled by proportional representation, while an additional twenty were filled using a national list through proportional representation. La plancha, as the national list was known, was ruled unconstitutional in 2002 (and again in 2003) because the deputies assigned to each department were not based on population.[6] In 2005, Article 13 of the electoral code was changed; la plancha was eliminated and a new code implemented.[7] As of 2006, all the assembly's eighty-four seats were directly elected in multimember districts. The TSE uses the same ballot for the election of representatives to the Central American Parliament (PARLACEN). Elections for the country's 262 municipalities are conducted using a simple plurality vote. Mayors are elected for three-year terms. Until 2015, the winner of the mayor's race, who only needed a plurality, determined the makeup of the entire city council.

Electoral Reforms and the TSE

The general climate of distrust that characterized the peace negotiations had significant consequences for institutional reform. In his elaboration of the game analogy, Wynia stated, "Games are not played in a vacuum. Three things will always influence their design and operation: culture, economic structures, and state structures."[8] In El Salvador's case, the rules were defined by an elite political culture dedicated to preserving the status quo. The Supreme Electoral Tribunal (TSE) is one of the clearest examples of this problem. It is the chief electoral authority in the country, yet it is widely regarded as weak, politicized, and corrupt. A 2008 IUDOP poll found that 78.2 percent of respondents had little or no trust in the TSE, and 69 percent of respondents had little or no confidence in the electoral process.[9] By

2014 the number of people expressing little or no trust had improved to 48.5 percent, and those expressing little or no confidence in the electoral process had improved to 51.1 percent.[10] Although there are no data that explain the improvements, one might speculate that changes to the electoral code in 2013 and the improved administration of the TSE under the FMLN helped in this regard. The discussion of the TSE below highlights the extent to which the institution has been subject to manipulation by political parties, especially ARENA, which has undermined the electoral process.

Salvadoran elections are governed by the TSE, the electoral body created by the peace accords. The new electoral tribunal replaced the CCE, which had been created in 1981 by the junta in order to convene elections for the 1982 Constituent Assembly. Article 208 of the constitution states that the function of the TSE is to run and monitor elections, including counting votes. The TSE is also responsible for the electoral roll, now known as the National Registry of Natural Persons (RNPN). Although the accords stipulated that the TSE would be composed of members without any party affiliation, that has not been the practice. In fact, the composition of the TSE runs counter to any intention set forth by the accords. The TSE is composed of five members, three from the top three parties in the last election and two appointed by the Supreme Court of Justice (CSJ). The TSE's president is appointed from the party that won the greatest number of votes in the last presidential election, and until recently has been dominated by ARENA and its allies. Procedural changes in 2006 reduced the number of magistrates required to approve changes from four of five to only three of five magistrates, further concentrating power in the hands of the dominant party.[11] While proponents on the Right argued that this change would make the TSE more efficient, it also enabled ARENA and its allies to bypass the FMLN's magistrates. Over the years, TSE membership has been subject to political machinations. Following the 2004 elections, the PCN was allowed to retain its seat on the TSE even though it failed to win enough of the vote share to legally remain a political party. The FMLN protested the move to the Supreme Court, stating that the seat should have been shared by the CDU and the PDC. In 2007 the Supreme Court reaffirmed the PCN's place on the TSE. By law, the TSE was obligated to dissolve all three minor parties for failing to win the required 3 percent of the vote. Both the PDC and the PCN submitted appeals to the Supreme Court, which were granted. In 2011 the Supreme Court struck down its own 2007 ruling and dissolved the parties, which reformed under different names to participate in the 2012 elections.

Not surprisingly, the TSE has been dominated by partisan power plays that have impeded important electoral reforms and, at times, violated the constitution. Ricardo Córdova and Carlos Ramos note evidence of a marked deterioration of electoral institutions in the 2004 and 2006 elections, wherein the TSE failed to sanction parties for violating electoral rules, failed to respond to complaints, and was generally partisan in its decisions.[12] During the 2004 elections the FMLN submitted more than fifty complaints concerning various violations, none of which were upheld by the ARENA-dominated body. During that same election the TSE delayed the disbursement of campaign funds to the FMLN, limiting its ability to respond to ARENA attack ads that were thought to be particularly influential with voters.[13] A 2009 report by the EU's Election Observation Mission found that members of the TSE "seem to first consider themselves as representatives of their political party and only secondarily as representatives of the institution."[14] The TSE routinely failed to respond to complaints about violations of campaign and election laws, which demonstrated both a lack of political will and institutional capacity. Common violations included campaigning before the official start of the electoral campaign, violations of propaganda laws, use of public resources for the conduct of a campaign, distribution of material goods during the conduct of a campaign, and failure to collect outstanding debts from political parties. One area of significant weakness for the TSE was campaign financing.[15] Political parties in El Salvador receive public funds based on the number of votes won in the last election. While the TSE reimbursed parties for eligible campaign expenses, there were no limits on private donations, and parties were not required to report their finances.[16] According to former TSE magistrate Félix Ulloa, "The biggest fraud isn't at the polls; it's in the money and financing of the campaigns."[17] The failure of campaign finance reform primarily benefited ARENA, which routinely outspent the FMLN (its closest competitor) and other parties in elections. The party spent three times as much as the FMLN on political advertisements in the 1994, 2004, and 2006 elections, and more than double the FMLN in 2009.[18] In 2009 it was estimated that ARENA spent almost $11 million on advertisement, compared to the FMLN's $5.2 million. Much of the money fueling these campaigns was "dark money," which benefited both ARENA and the FMLN.

Beyond the selective application of the law, the politicization of the TSE and a lack of political will to create a more inclusive notion of democracy also stymied electoral reform as mandated by the peace accords. The Electoral Review Board (JVE), composed of one member from each registered political party, was created by COPAZ to monitor electoral reform. It was the responsibility of the JVE to monitor the TSE and all electoral activities, including the issuance of the voting documentation. The JVE was also charged with making recommendations for electoral reforms to the TSE, although it was generally ignored.[19] While some key reforms were implemented over time, many were met with great resistance. President Calderón Sol appointed a special commission charged with developing proposed electoral reforms. The proposed reforms included the creation of a national voter registry, residential voting, and the establishment of proportional representation in municipal elections.[20] Although the RNPN was established in December 1995, none of the other proposed reforms were implemented at that time. Instead, the 1996 electoral law passed by the Legislative Assembly sought to restrict representation by requiring political parties to win 3 percent of the valid vote to maintain their legal status as parties, increasing the number of signatures required to form a political party to 2 percent of the valid vote and providing public campaign money to parties *after* the election.[21]

One of the most significant electoral reforms was the introduction of the universal identification card (DUI), which served as a national identity card, driver's license, and voter registration card. Before 2003, Salvadorans had to obtain a statement from their municipal official before proceeding to the registration office to actually register, a tiring process that often required several trips. Critics often cited the difficulties of obtaining a carnet as one of the reasons for low voter turnout.[22] Some suggested that maintaining this system, established during the 1980s to prevent fraud, was a tool to suppress voter turnout.[23] Following the introduction of the DUI, voter turnout increased significantly. Some 2.3 million voters participated in the 2004 elections, about 1 million more than in 1999. Still, there were some problems with the DUI. While those who registered during the initial registration period received their DUIs at no cost, the fee for the document after that period, or for replacements or renewals, was $10. The cost was prohibitive for some Salvadorans and created a financial barrier to voting.[24] In an effort to address this problem, the government announced in 2010 that it would provide DUIs free of charge in the thirty-two poorest municipalities in the country. It was estimated that more than ninety-eight thousand residents would benefit from this program.

Despite the introduction of the DUI, problems remained with the voter registration lists. The problem became more apparent following El Salvador's 2007 national census, the first since the 1992 census. The 2007 national census revealed that the Salvadoran population was much smaller than previously thought. While the government had projected the population at 7.1 million, the census revealed that the Salvadoran population was 5,744,113, only slightly more than the 5,118,599 Salvadorans accounted for in the 1992 census. The census also revealed that fewer than 3.5 million Salvadorans were of voting age.[25] The electoral register contained approximately 4.2 million voters, roughly seven hundred thousand more than the number of eligible voters in the census. Some of this was explained by the number of registered Salvadorans living abroad and other technical issues. The census also revealed the changing demographics of the country, which had become more urban since 1992.[26] The census findings clearly demonstrated the need to update the electoral register and reapportion El Salvador's voting districts. Despite the recommendations of the Organization of American States, the TSE failed to update the electoral register to conform to the census in advance of the 2009 elections.[27]

For years, the ARENA-dominated TSE failed to implement numerous electoral reforms that would increase participation and improve representation, including many of those recommended by the special commission.[28] The TSE resisted calls for residential voting, as specified in Article 136 of the electoral code. The lack of residential voting had been a persistent criticism of analysts and international observer missions since the transition to democracy. Critics charged that the refusal to implement the policy was a deliberate strategy to suppress voter turnout.[29] Polling stations were delineated by last name, not by place of residence. For example, those surnames ending with Aa–Co were required to vote at a single polling station, which may or may not have been the station closest to the voter's place of residence. This system required many voters to travel considerable distances on election day.[30] While the government attempted to alleviate this inconvenience by providing buses to polling stations, those actions were not sufficient to correct the problem. Although residential voting was supposed to be effective with the implementation of the DUI for the 2004 elections (see Legislative Decrees 293 and 834), it was postponed until the 2006 legislative and municipal elections, when it was introduced in seven municipalities across the country as a "test."[31] Residential voting was then implemented throughout the Department of Cuscatlán for the 2009 elections and was considered successful. Only in 2014, when ARENA no longer controlled the TSE, was residential voting extended throughout the country—twenty years after what was called the election of the century.

Among the most salient issues to emerge in the postaccord environment was voting rights for Salvadorans living abroad. By some estimates, more than 2 million Salvadorans reside outside El Salvador, most of them in the United States. According to a report from Salvadoreños en el Mundo, as much as half of El Salvador's voting population lives abroad.[32] Unlike many other nationals living outside their country of origin, Salvadorans had no means of voting outside El Salvador. In recent years Salvadorans abroad began organizing and advocating the use of absentee ballots for Salvadorans living in the United States, especially given the role that their remittances play in sustaining the Salvadoran economy. Neither ARENA nor the FMLN were supportive of proposals for absentee balloting, albeit for different reasons. While the FMLN is predominantly concerned about the possibilities of fraud, ARENA consistently claimed that the constitutionality, expense, and lack of institutional capacity prohibit such a change.[33] In the 2009 presidential elections, the TSE established a half-hearted "trial" to determine if Salvadorans living abroad wanted to vote in elections. Proponents of the absentee ballots argued that the experiment was designed to fail.[34] The trial required Salvadorans living abroad to return to El Salvador to vote rather than establishing a system of absentee or consulate voting. The Flor Blanca stadium was designated as the voting center for Salvadorans living abroad. Approximately thirty-five thousand Salvadorans abroad were issued special DUIs in advance of the elections, and the TSE ordered forty thousand ballots for the voting center. Given the impediments to returning to El Salvador to vote, only 165 people voted at Flor Blanca. During my time with my electoral observation delegation at Flor Blanca, international observers easily outnumbered voters. Many Salvadorans who did return, including those in my delegation, voted in their place of residence rather than the stadium. Of course, most Salvadorans abroad could not afford the flight home or perhaps had questionable residential status abroad. As with residential voting, it took a change in leadership at the TSE to push through the reform. Salvadorans living abroad were granted the right to vote in elections for all offices in 2013.

The 2014 presidential election was the first in which they were eligible to vote. Of the 10,337 overseas registered voters, 1,909 voted in the first round and 2,334 voted in the second round. Just over 60 percent of their votes went to the FMLN.[35]

In addition to residential voting and voting abroad, more progress toward electoral reform was made during the Funes administration. In 2011 the Constitutional Court ruled that slate voting limited voters' right to select their own representatives and that prohibiting independent candidates was illegal. In the 2012 elections, voters were finally able to vote for a candidate rather than a party. A new electoral code, adopted in 2013, addressed both these issues. Other important changes included the sanctioning of attack ads (which the TSE attempted to enforce in several instances in the 2014 campaign), the establishment of a quota system requiring that 30 percent of candidates on party lists for the legislature be women, and that members of municipal councils would be assigned based on the proportionality of the vote rather than the old winner-take-all system.[36] The changes in the municipal elections went into effect for the 2015 elections. Additionally, in 2014 the Supreme Court struck down the provision of the electoral code that prohibited cross voting. These reforms were expected to increase voter turnout and improve political representation.

Despite this progress, the politicization of the institution remains a significant problem for the TSE. As a part of its legal wrangling surrounding the 2014 elections, ARENA filed a lawsuit with the Constitutional Chamber of the Supreme Court seeking to disqualify two TSE magistrates—TSE president Eugenio Chicas of the FMLN and Walter Araujo, formerly of ARENA—due to their membership in political parties. Notably, it was not only the first time ARENA had challenged the party affiliation of TSE magistrates, it was also the first time the presidency of the TSE had been held by the FMLN during a presidential election.

Elections and Parties in Postwar El Salvador

Since the signing of the peace accords, El Salvador has held five presidential elections (1994, 1999, 2004, 2009, 2014) and seven rounds of legislative and municipal elections (1994, 1997, 2000, 2003, 2006, 2009, 2012, 2015). While not without minor issues, each of these elections was deemed free and fair by domestic and international observer groups. This represents an important

79

step toward the democratization of Salvadoran politics, which had long been plagued by fraudulent, noncompetitive elections. El Salvador's first postwar elections were held in 1994 and have been dubbed the "elections of the century" in recognition that they were the first generally free and fair, competitive elections, including parties from across the political spectrum, in the country's history. The elections reshaped the landscape of Salvadoran politics, since the FMLN emerged from these elections as the second force in Salvadoran politics.[37]

El Salvador's political parties became the dominant expression of political life in the postwar era. An interviewee once said to me, "We don't have a democracy; we have a partiocracy, and it has corrupted everything. It has created a vicious circle of noncompliance and impunity."[38] There was truth in this observation. In essence, the basis for democracy in the country was "partyarchy." According to Michael Coppedge, characteristics of partyarchy include (1) the control that parties maintain over nominations for office, (2) electoral laws that require citizens to vote for a party rather than a candidate, (3) party discipline that requires legislators to vote with the party, (4) citizen organizations that are penetrated or co-opted by political parties, (5) a media system that is either owned or operated by parties and that limits voter information, and a (6) commitment to basic elements of polyarchy (freedom of expression, universal suffrage, formal institutions), which may be undermined by partyarchy.[39] While the second characteristic was resolved by electoral reform in 2013, the other elements persist. Though not discussed in detail in this study, the country's media are concentrated in the hands of the economic elite.[40] Coverage both during and outside of election cycles has consistently favored ARENA.[41] Additionally, studies demonstrated that the media also had a significant influence over legislation governing them.[42] Until the 2014 tax reform, newspapers had been exempt from paying taxes. The consequences of this partyarchy can be seen not only in the functions of institutions (such as the TSE, above), but also in the crisis of representation discussed later in this chapter.

In El Salvador, this partyarchy was, in part, the result of the institutionalization of the conflict between ARENA and the FMLN. It was both a reflection of wartime structures and attitudes as well as the failure of reconciliation. This conflict dominated political life in the country, often relegating important policy issues to the background. As a result, El Salvador's party system was characterized by a high level of polarization. The political climate became increasingly polarized as the FMLN's political fortunes increased, especially between 1997 and 2003.[43] The two dominant parties, ARENA and the FMLN, both trend very close to their respective extremes on the left-right ideological scale (see table 3.1). In a study on the dimensions of polarization in parliaments, Cristina Rivas Pérez found that the FMLN and ARENA differed most significantly on the issues of state intervention and values (religious conviction and attitudes on abortion, divorce, and the Catholic Church). Both parties shared favorable views of the military and trended more toward authoritarianism than democracy.[44]

TABLE 3.1

Evolution of the polarization of ARENA and the
FMLN in the Legislative Assembly, on a scale of 1 (left) to 10 (right)

	ARENA	FMLN
2000–2003	8.05	2.28
2003–2006	8.42	1.72
2006–2009	8.61	1.31

Sources: Manuel Alcántara and Cristina Rivas, "The Left-Right Dimension in Latin America Party Politics," paper presented at the Annual Meeting of the American Political Science Association, Philadelphia, PA, August 30–September 3, 2006; Instituto Interuniversitario de Iberoamérica, Universidad de Salamanca, "El Salvador (2006-2009)," *Elites Parlamentarias Latinoamericanas,* no. 34 (October 2008), http://americo.usal.es/oir/elites/Boletines_2008/boletin_34_ESal_P.pdf.

Rather than subsiding over time, party polarization increased from 2000 through 2009, with the FMLN experiencing the largest shift. One possible explanation of the increased polarization between ARENA and the FMLN is that it coincided with increased electoral competition between the two parties. As the FMLN's electoral prospects improved and ARENA's hold on incumbency was threatened, both parties moved further toward their respective poles. There was a notable increase in the level of polarization surrounding the 2004 presidential elections, in which ARENA revived its Cold War narrative against FMLN's former guerrilla commander Schafik Handal. Polarization was even more pronounced in the 2014 presidential elections. On a scale of 1 (left) to 10 (right), the FMLN's Salvador Sánchez Cerén scored a 1.54, while ARENA's Norman Quijano scored a 9.25. For comparison, GANA's Tony Saca, a former ARENA president, scored a 6.52.[45] Beyond being a mere characteristic of the party system, polarization was also a tool used by parties to galvanize support.[46] Parties, particularly ARENA, frequently discussed public policy issues in highly ideological terms and drew upon historic images and rhetoric to rally their bases.

Parties in the Postwar Era

The internal machinations of most of El Salvador's political parties, with the notable exception of the FMLN, were largely unchanged by the peace process and the transition to democracy.[47] The electoral prospects of some have risen while others have fallen, yet today's parties generally represent the same cleavages as they did in the war. Two of these parties, ARENA and the FMLN, were products of the war. While the accords placed significant emphasis on reforming a range of political institutions, they did not address political parties. Nor are there any electoral laws governing the internal structure or behavior of parties. The discussion below of internal dynamics of the major (ARENA, FMLN) and minor (CD, PCN, PDC) parties in the postwar era highlights issues of control and party discipline that have reinforced partyarchy at the expense of broader representation.

ARENA

The Right, historically divided between the agrarian elites and the agro-industrial elites, presented a generally united front throughout the war.[48] By 1989, however, this unity was showing signs of wear. The appointment of Alfredo Cristiani, a member of the agro-industrial elite, as the head of ARENA, in 1985, and the subsequent neoliberal project have been sources of significant contention within the Right. The emergence of the neoliberal elite in the mid 1980s served to modernize ARENA as a political party (see chapter 2). By the 1988 legislative elections, ARENA was downplaying the anticommunist discourse in favor of economic modernization and negotiations with the FMLN. Cristiani considered negotiations with the FMLN to be a key component in the revitalization and modernization of the Salvadoran economy. Some elites, particularly those among the traditional agrarian oligarchy, were opposed to negotiations with the FMLN and referred to Cristiani's group as the "Red Millionaires."[49] UCA vice rector Rodolfo

Cardenal summarized the opposition to the peace accords as a perceived attack on the very existence of the agrarian elite:

> The most resistant sector of this group is tied to agricultural exports and deplores the end of militarism because, historically, it was the instrument the oligarchy used to avoid economic development and social and political transformation. The peace accords did not question the capitalistic system or the democratic state but rather oligarchic capitalism and its corresponding militarized state. The accords provide a great opportunity to defeat the oligarchy and its political and economic model and put an end to the militarism that has permitted its dominance for decades and has impeded the economic and political development of El Salvador.[50]

While initial opposition to the peace accords was considerable among the agrarian elite, it was short lived. In an attempt to placate the more conservative Founders Faction within ARENA, Cristiani nominated conservative San Salvador mayor Armando Calderón Sol to head the party and thus secured his candidacy for president in the 1994 elections. Despite Calderón Sol's electoral victory, his accession to power did little to halt conflict within the party. Shortly after his inauguration, tensions within ARENA increased dramatically. Members of the ultraright within the party formed the Liberal Democratic Party (PLD) in April 1995, charging that party traditionalists were being excluded from decision making. Others defected to the rightwing PCN. The PLD's founder, Kirio Waldo Salgado, leveled corruption charges against the Calderón Sol government that resulted in the resignation of two cabinet members.[51] Salgado was a particularly outspoken critic of ARENA. Additionally, Salgado, along with Director of Privatization and Modernization Alfredo Mena Lagos, publicly accused Cristiani of fraud in connection with bank privatization.[52] While these matters appeared to have been common knowledge within the party, this was the first time the accusations had been aired publicly, a demonstration of the seriousness of the division within ARENA.

ARENA's significant losses in the 1997 legislative and municipal elections resulted in the complete overhaul of ARENA leadership, including the resignation of Gloria Salguero Gross, president of the National Executive Council (COENA) and member of the Founder's Faction.[53] Cristiani, to the dismay of many among the Founder's Faction, assumed the presidency of

COENA in an attempt to revamp the party's image and economic policies in preparation for the 1999 presidential elections. Cristiani and Calderón Sol supported different candidates for the presidential race; Calderón Sol's choice triumphed in the end. Francisco Flores, former ARENA deputy and minister of the presidency, handily defeated the FMLN's candidate. Following the presidential contest, ARENA's attentions turned to the San Salvador mayor's race. The party chose Luis Cardenal, a well-respected businessman and political analyst. Cardenal's attack campaign, ordered by party leadership, backfired.[54] The fallout from Cardenal's loss in the 2000 San Salvador mayor's race was significant, particularly for COENA, because it drew harsh criticism from the Founder's Faction, which blamed Cristiani for the results. As with previous electoral failures, ARENA attempted to revamp itself. Within months, Cristiani resigned from his post as the head of COENA and was replaced by Walter Araujo. During Araujo's tenure as ARENA president, the Founder's Faction established the ARENA League to the Rescue (LAR), a group dedicated to returning ARENA to its founding principles. The LAR was opposed to Araujo and by August 2001 Araujo had resigned and was replaced by business magnate Roberto Murray Meza. The LAR, which was not represented in the new COENA, criticized the makeup of the committee, which was dominated by *técnicos* and business elites. By March 2002, Murray Meza resigned and was replaced by Archie Baldocchi, president of the Banco Agrícola, further demonstrating the disarray and division among the Right.[55]

By 2003 the pattern was becoming clear: election losses equaled a shake-up in COENA. Disappointing results in the 2003 legislative and municipal elections resulted in the replacement of twelve of COENA's thirteen members. The new COENA president, coffee magnate José Antonio Salaverría Borja, immediately began preparations for the 2004 presidential elections. It was under his leadership that the primary system for candidate selection was used for the first time. ARENA selected Elías Antonio Saca González as its presidential candidate for the 2004 race. Tony Saca, a former sportscaster and president of the National Association of Private Enterprise (ANEP), was viewed as a departure from Flores and past presidents. Former ARENA presidential candidate Rodrigo Ávila noted, "Tony was not the president's candidate, nor was he COENA's candidate. He was elected because the base was allowed to speak up. That is a very historic change in the way ARENA elected its candidate."[56] While Saca was popular with the base, he was not as popular with some members of the party's rank and file leadership. He was as polarizing in the party as he was in his dealings with the FMLN. Various high-ranking ARENA officials described him as either "uneducated," a "smart guy," "an entertainer," "pragmatic," or "hopelessly corrupt."[57]

In March 2008, ARENA again held internal primaries to select the 2009 presidential candidate. Rodrigo Ávila, the former head of the PNC, was elected by a wide margin—1,770 of 2,800 votes. His strongest competition in the primary had been Vice President Ana Vilma de Escobar, who, despite having the highest preelection poll numbers of any of the candidates, won a mere 36 votes. There was immediate suspicion of the results as de Escobar and others accused Saca of manipulating the vote. Ávila's loss in the presidential elections resulted in a major overhaul of COENA, including the return of Cristiani as its head in June 2009. The growing split between the Saca faction and the party's traditional power base resulted in the defection of twelve ARENA deputies, who signaled their displeasure by voting with the FMLN in the legislative assembly. An internal investigation determined that Saca had used his position as head of COENA to direct members to vote for Ávila rather than de Escobar.[58] There was also strong reason to believe that he was behind the defections in the legislature. After refusing to resign, Saca was expelled from ARENA in December 2009.[59] The breakaway deputies from ARENA officially formed the Grand Alliance for National Unity (GANA) in April 2010 after presenting the TSE with the required fifty thousand signatures to form a political party. GANA's national coordinator, Rafael Morán, claimed the party's goal was to create a more socially conscious, less extreme right.[60] GANA would soon prove itself to be a formidable competitor for ARENA.

The FMLN

The history of division within the FMLN[61] is well documented.[62] Far from being an isolated, internal matter, the divisions within the FMLN have been the subject of numerous discussions both during and after the war. Each of the FMLN's five organizations, which subscribed to their own ideology and formula for revolution, developed their own networks and functioned more or less independently of one another throughout much of the war.[63] The five organizations shared a unity of purpose in overthrowing the existing regime, which sustained them throughout the war. Ultimately, while each of the five groups militarily shared the same short-term military goal, they varied significantly on the desired long-term political and socioeconomic outcome. Thus, once the armed struggle ended, historic differences reemerged. Like other guerrilla organizations, the FMLN faced the challenge of transitioning from guerrilla movement to political party.[64] The verticalism and discipline inherent in most guerrilla organizations was not compatible with democratic practices often associated with political parties. With the exception of the PCS, none of the guerrilla organizations had any prior experience in the day-to-day operations of a political party. While the peace accords created political space for the FMLN's reinsertion into Salvadoran society, the peace process did little to turn the FMLN into a modern, viable political party.

> Essentially, the basic problem, after the signing of the Peace Accords, was that the incorporation into civilian life of the FMLN members did not bring with it an internal discussion concerning the change, which a such new reality presupposed. On the contrary, it appears as if the challenge for the creation of a new political party was taken up as a mere strategy, which simply replaced the armed struggle as a means of taking state power.[65]

Thus, the FMLN's transition from war to peace was more complicated than merely laying down weapons and participating in the electoral process.

Divisions within the FMLN emerged shortly after the signing of the peace accords. The fissuring of the FMLN became more pronounced in advance of the 1994 elections, especially with concern to selecting a candidate. As it turned out, this would again be an issue for the party in the 1999 presidential elections. Joaquín Villalobos of the People's Revolutionary Army (ERP) favored an alliance with the center in an effort to "steal" some of the vote from ARENA and initially supported the Christian Democrats' Abraham Rodríguez in his bid for the presidency.[66] Others disagreed; the party ultimately joined a coalition with the Democratic Convergence (CD) and the National Revolutionary Movement (MNR) to support the candidacy of CD leader, and former FDR leader, Rubén Zamora. Following the "elections of the century" the FMLN found itself in a quagmire that it had managed to avoid for more than a decade. On May 1, 1994, during the first session of the General Assembly, seven FMLN deputies from the ERP and National Resistance (RN) broke rank and voted for ARENA deputy Gloria Salguero Gross for assembly president. In exchange for their votes, former ERP commander Ana Guadalupe Martínez was elected to one of the assembly's vice presidential positions and

Eduardo Sancho of the National Resistance (RN) was elected to a secretarial position.[67] Days later, FMLN general coordinator Schafik Handal issued a statement that the FMLN would not recognize the deputies and accused ERP commander Villalobos of entering into a pact with the ARENA government. On May 10 the seven deputies and Villalobos were suspended from the FMLN. The ERP and the RN formally broke with the FMLN in December 1994 and established the Democratic Party (PD) in March 1995. The defection of two high-profile FMLN commanders, Villalobos and Martínez, and six other deputies foretold of the growing tensions within the Left. The PD openly criticized the FMLN for its lack of vision in creating a peacetime identity for the party and for its Cold War mindset. In turn, the FMLN accused the PD of being "neoliberal." This language, accusations of being "neoliberal" or "Stalinist," would come to frame the debate within the FMLN.

The very public rupture between the ERP and the FMLN revealed the difficulties the various organizations had faced in maintaining unity during the war. The subsequent tension between the Renovador (Reformist) and the Ortodoxo (Orthodox) factions for control of the FMLN has led to public exposure of their internal squabbling.[68] The FMLN's internal divisions occupied print space almost daily in *El Diario de Hoy* and *La Prensa Gráfica*, the two largest daily newspapers in El Salvador that happened to be owned by ARENA allies. Not surprisingly, the tensions within ARENA discussed above rarely received any press. The conflicting desires to remain true to the character of the revolutionary movement (Ortodoxos) and the desire to evolve into a more viable political party (Renovadores) were the core tensions within the FMLN. For the Ortodoxos, democracy was merely a path to socialism, while the Renovadores embraced participatory democracy as an end. These divisions reflected the ideological underpinnings of the guerrilla organizations established in the 1970s. The Popular Forces of Liberation (FPL), generally represented by the Ortodoxo faction, historically favored a socialist society while the other groups and some FPL, now part of the Renovadores, desired a democratic society. In addition, many of the guerrilla leaders from the war became leaders of the FMLN party, which further exacerbated old divisions and rivalries.

Additionally, the transition from guerrilla movement to political party made the FMLN an electoral party rather than a mass party, detracting from its ability to mobilize its traditional base as it did in the 1970s and 1980s. Among the FMLN's traditional base, there was a feeling of abandonment by the party, which seemed interested only in courting the base during elections.[69] The FMLN's infighting prevented it from cultivating its relationships with its base in nonelection years. This was, in part, an enduring traditional characteristic of the party system in El Salvador wherein parties revolve solely around elections. And while the Left's traditional base continued to support the FMLN during elections, its capacity to organize daily in support of the FMLN was dramatically reduced. FMLN deputy Gerson Martínez described the base as "exhausted" following the war.[70]

Following the 1997 municipal and legislative elections, the FMLN looked forward to the 1999 presidential race. The party's improved showing in the 1997 elections, made more impressive by the defections of well-known members, provided only temporary unity. The process of selecting a presidential ticket became a public debacle that highlighted the FMLN's inability to contain, much less overcome, their differences. As evidence of further fracturing, the FMLN held three conventions before they agreed on a presidential ticket. The first convention, on August 15, 1998, was a tug of war between the Ortodoxo nominee, Victoria Marina Velásquez de Avilés (the former national counsel for the defense of human rights), and the Renovador candidate, San Salvador mayor Héctor Silva.[71] Neither nominee received the votes necessary to win the nomination, and since neither faction was willing to concede, a second convention was scheduled for two weeks later.[72] Weary of factionalism and unwilling to sacrifice the reputation he had built as mayor in such a public showdown, Silva withdrew his nomination at the second convention. The Ortodoxo ticket of de Avilés and Salvador Arias again failed to win a majority of the votes necessary. A third convention was held in September 1998 in which Renovador Facundo Guardado and ex-commander Nidia Díaz won the FMLN's presidential and vice presidential nomination. The details of the nominating conventions were played out in public view in El Salvador's daily papers. The FMLN made a public spectacle of its internal dynamics, giving credence to the perception that the FMLN was too embroiled in a power struggle to present a viable option, let alone govern the country.[73]

Not surprisingly, the FMLN's Guardado-Díaz ticket lost the presidential election in the first round of voting to ARENA's Francisco Flores, 52 percent to 29 percent.[74] Following the election, Guardado resigned his position as the party's general coordinator and blamed the Ortodoxo faction for the electoral loss, claiming that they had offered halfhearted support for the ticket and failed to mobilize the FMLN's base. Ortodoxo leader Schafik Handal blamed Guardado's abandonment of the socialist platform for the loss.[75] However, the vast majority of people I interviewed blamed the FMLN's loss on the political infighting during the nomination process and Guardado's candidacy, irrespective of platform or support, stating that he simply did not embody the professionalism, intellect, or charisma necessary to hold the office. By April the two factions were formally recognized by the party.[76] In July 1999, Fabio Castillo, an Ortodoxo, was elected the FMLN's general coordinator. Castillo's broad popularity provided temporary unity following the electoral debacle, as he vowed the FMLN would unite to win the 2000 elections.

A series of controversial moves by Renovadores early in 2001 was the cause of outrage among some Ortodoxo leaders. On October 1, 2001, former FMLN presidential candidate and Renovadores faction leader Facundo Guardado, was expelled from the FMLN for "sins" against the party following a three-month trial by the party's Tribunal de Honor. His offenses included his support of dollarization, failure to attend the FMLN's May convention, traveling to Spain with a government delegation following the 2001 Salvadoran earthquakes, and his display of disrespect for the party in the media by encouraging a boycott of the FMLN's national convention.[77] In an interview with *La Prensa Gráfica,* Guardado stated he would not leave the FMLN and that no authority other than God could force him to do so.[78] The fallout from Guardado's expulsion was significant. On October 4, 2001, seven FMLN representatives voted with ARENA in favor of ratification of a free-trade agreement with Chile despite threat of punishment by Handal, while hundreds marched to the FMLN headquarters in protest of the expulsion.[79] Most significantly, San Salvador mayor Héctor Silva threatened to leave the FMLN in protest. The formal expulsion of five Renovador deputies from the FMLN, in March 2002, was merely another setback for the unity of the party.[80] The definitive split came, however, in April 2002 when the Renovadores announced that they were forming their own political party, the Reformist Movement Party (PMR).[81] The PMR released an analysis of the internal problems of the FMLN entitled "The FMLN Is Dead."[82] The PMR, which claimed to be a social democratic party, expressed interest in building alliances with other parties, including the CDU, PDC, and PSD, but not ARENA or the PCN.[83] Though the party was soon defunct, its president, Facundo Guardado, once exclaimed,

"We are going to be the most important force in El Salvador. The force of the new century."[84]

With the Renovadores out of the party, the Reformistas emerged as the new opponents to the Ortodoxos. The fundamental tensions within the party remained the same: party governance and modernization. The Reformistas, like the Renovadores, also favored building alliances with other center-left parties at the national level, as it had done at the local level. Party infighting continued to plague the FMLN in its selection for the 2004 presidential candidate. Internal party primaries pitted polarizing party boss Schafik Handal against the popular reformist mayor of Santa Tecla, Óscar Ortiz. Handal narrowly defeated Ortiz, with only one-third of registered party members voting in the primary. Handal's subsequent defeat in the 2004 presidential elections led to increased division within the party. Many anticipated that Handal's defeat would result in a party revolt, allowing the Reformistas, also known as La Fuerza por el Cambio, to take control of the party apparatus. Shortly after Handal's defeat, the Reformistas began holding meetings and campaigning for the party's internal elections.[85] In November 2004 party members went to the polls to choose between the Reformistas and the Ortodoxos. Only half the party's registered voters turned out, and Handal ally Medardo González beat Fuerza candidate Óscar Ortiz for the general coordinator position amid allegations of fraud and irregularities. The elections further solidified Ortodoxo dominance of the party, with fifty of fifty-five seats on the FMLN's National Council.[86] The fissure continued the following year. In June and July 2005, three FMLN deputies, two mayors, and several hundred local leaders and members left the party. Most significantly, the FMLN's strength in the Legislative Assembly was reduced to twenty-seven from thirty-one seats due to the defections and expulsions. The defectors then formed a new center-left party, the Democratic Revolutionary Front (FDR). As with the two prior spin-off parties, the FDR failed to win any seats and was disbanded.

Given the Ortodoxo dominance within the party, the selection of Mauricio Funes as the 2009 presidential candidate was a surprise. It was, in some respects, a measure of conciliation between the two factions. It was also an exceedingly pragmatic choice, one that enabled the FMLN to capitalize on the fact that Funes, a popular journalist, was not even a member of the FMLN. He often found himself at odds with FMLN leadership during his administration, which were often as much about his leadership style as they were about ideology.[87] The selection of Salvador Sánchez Cerén, Funes's vice president, rather than Óscar Ortiz as the 2014 presidential candidate represented a shift back toward the Ortodoxo faction and reinforced the idea that the party could better control an external reformist (Funes) than an internal one (Ortiz).

Smaller Parties across the Spectrum

Other political parties began the process of transition and realignment to postwar politics as well. Smaller parties, particularly those at the center of the political spectrum, found it difficult to survive. The three parties that had modest success—the PCN, the PDC, and the CD—discovered it was necessary to align themselves with one of the two larger parties. But they often lost their identity in the process.[88] That is not to say that they have not wielded influence in Salvadoran politics. On the contrary, the failure of either the FMLN or ARENA to capture a majority in the Legislative Assembly forced them to build alliances with the smaller parties. For its part, the PCN has been seen by many as an extension of ARENA, as has the PDC for the most part.[89] With its strength in rural areas of the country, the PCN was the primary beneficiary of the declining vote share of ARENA and the PDC.[90] Between 1994 and 1997 the PCN nearly tripled its number of deputies in the assembly, and it increased its municipalities fivefold between 1994 and 2000.[91] Its presence as the third force in Salvadoran politics enabled the party to bargain alliances for increasing power. Although the presidency traditionally goes to the party with the most seats, ARENA, the PCN, and the PDC voted together to prevent the FMLN from holding the presidency. In exchange for its support, the PCN's Ciro Cruz Zepeda has been elected president of the Legislative Assembly three times (May 2002–April 2003, May 2003–April 2006, May 2009–April 2012), even though the party held a small fraction of the seats in the assembly. After being disbanded in 2011, the party's name changed to National Coalition (CN), but returned to using the PCN acronym in 2012 after adding "Party" to its name. But ARENA's legislative dominance was derailed by the emergence of Tony Saca's Grand Alliance for National Unity (GANA). In the assembly, GANA often voted with the FMLN during the Funes administration. Following GANA's split with ARENA, the party voted with the

FMLN to elect Sigfrido Reyes as the assembly's first FMLN president, in 2011. It won eleven seats in the 2012 legislative elections, making it the third-largest party in the assembly.

The two other minor parties did not fare as well. The PDC continued its precipitous decline since the end of the war, losing more than 50 percent of its mayors and nearly 75 percent of its deputies from 1994 to 2000. It lost its legal standing as a political party twice, once following the 2004 elections and again in 2011. It participated in the 2012 elections as the Party of Hope (Partido de la Esperanza) before changing its name back later in 2012. The CD, which emerged as an opposition party in advance of the 1989 presidential elections, has been the only small, center-left party to enjoy any political success. Former party president Rubén Zamora wanted to establish a viable political center that was independent of the two poles.[92] It was a formidable challenge in a country where the political center was a virtual no man's land. The CD aligned itself with the FMLN in the assembly, although its vote share was often too small to have a significant impact. It did, however, help the FMLN in coalition races at the local level, most notably with San Salvador mayor Héctor Silva Argüello. Although the CD aligned with the FMLN in the 1994 and 1997 elections, the party chose not to do so in the 2000 elections. Instead, the CD joined with the PD to form the United Democratic Center (CDU). In the 2004 elections, the CDU aligned with the PDC to run former mayor Silva as its presidential candidate. Despite being the most popular politician in the country, Silva fared poorly in the race. The party reconfigured itself again by forming Democratic Convergence (CD) in 2005, a party composed of the CDU and former members of the FMLN and the PDC. The CDU chose not to run a presidential candidate in 2009 and instead endorsed the FMLN ticket. Several members of the CDU were appointed to the Funes administration, including Héctor Dada as minister of the economy.

Electoral Politics after the Elections of the Century

In her assessment of the 2004–2009 elections, Sonja Wolf describes El Salvador's democracy as "electoral authoritarianism," a regime with all the trappings of a democracy (elections, space for dissent, opposition parties, etc.) but where the dominant power maintains control over electoral outcomes in order to defend its interests.[93] Her characterization underscores the extent to which ARENA combined the trappings of liberal democracy with illiberal practices. ARENA's desire to hold on to power is demonstrated by the politicization of public institutions and its manipulation of the electorate and political space.

Much of Calderón Sol's tenure was dedicated to the implementation of the remaining reforms mandated by the peace accords, including the dissolution of security agencies and the deployment of the PNC, the land transfer program, and electoral reforms. He also devoted significant energies to the privatization of state-owned industry (see chapter 4). The FMLN remained adamantly opposed to these programs, but others, including former members of the FMLN, were willing to work with ARENA in passing the reforms. The Pacto de San Andrés, signed by President Calderón Sol and former FMLN commander Joaquín Villalobos in 1995, committed the PD to support neoliberal reforms. In exchange for the PD's agreement to back privatization and tariff reduction measures, the Calderón Sol government agreed to fight corruption and promote human development.[94] In fact, the PD was the only party to vote with ARENA on increasing the value-added tax (IVA) from 10 percent to 13 percent, an increase that was opposed by both the Left and some in the business sector. The alliance ended when ARENA failed to uphold its end of the bargain and the PD, and particularly Villalobos, was discredited.[95]

The 1997 elections were the first legislative and municipal elections to occur after the transitional elections. The elections were notable in two key respects. First, a range of political parties from across the political spectrum fielded candidates. While only seven parties participated in the 1991 municipal elections, nine participated in 1994 and thirteen in 1997. Second, the FMLN significantly increased its vote share in both legislative and municipal elections. The UNDP observed that the electoral gain by the FMLN in the Legislative Assembly between 1994 and 1997 resulted in "an equilibrium between the ARENA and FMLN parties creat[ing] political space more favorable to the consensus-building efforts."[96] The FMLN won twenty-seven legislative seats (up from twenty-one) and forty-eight mayoralties (up from thirteen), including San Salvador.[97] While the FMLN was clearly gaining ground on the electoral playing field, other parties lost voters' support that was not recaptured by the FMLN. In fact, between the 1994 and 1997 elections ARENA lost 209,474 votes, a decrease of 35 percent, while the FMLN only gained 81,898.[98] Additionally, the PDC, which did respectably in the 1994 elections, experienced a significant decline in the 1997 elections, losing more than one-half of its deputies and mayors.

TABLE 3.2

Selected results for legislative elections by number of deputies, 1994–2015

Party/year	1994	1997	2000	2003	2006	2009	2012	2015
ARENA	39	28	29	27	34	32	33	35[e]
FMLN	21	27	31	31[a]	32	35	31	31
PDC	18	10	5	5	6	5	1[b]	1
PCN	4	11	14	16	10	11	6[c]+1[d]	6[f]
CDU	1	2	3	5				
CD					2	1	1	
GANA							11	11
Other	1	6	2					

Source: Tribunal Supremo Electoral.
[a] Two deputies defected in 2005, so it held only 29 seats going into the 2006 elections.
[b] In 2012 the PDC ran under the name Party of Hope (PES).
[c] The National Conciliation Party (PCN) became the National Coalition Party (*also* PCN) in 2011.
[d] Coalition with PES.
[e] Three of those in coalition with the PCN.
[f] Two of those in coalition with the PDC.

TABLE 3.3

Selected results for municipal elections by number of municipalities, 1994–2015

Party /year	1994	1997	2000	2003	2006	2009	2012	2015
ARENA	207	162	127	113	147	122	116	129
FMLN	13	48	67	61	54	75	85	85
FMLN coalition	2	3	10	12	5	21	9[b]	
PDC	29	15	16	15	14	9	4+1[c]	7
PCN	10	18	33	50	39	33		20
CDU	0	0	4	5+6				
CD					2	1+1[a]	3	1
GANA							17	19
CN							24+3[d]	
PSD								1

Source: Tribunal Supremo Electoral.
[a] CD coalition with FDR.
[b] Includes 8 municipalities in coalition with CD and 1 municipality in coalition with PES.
[c] PES coalition with GANA.
[d] CN coalition with PES.

The FMLN was buoyed by its successes in the 1997 elections and began looking forward to the 1999 presidential elections. Following a prolonged and heated nominating convention, the FMLN selected former guerrilla and Renovador Facundo Guardado as its candidate for president in the 1999 elections. The media coverage surrounding the nominating conventions was intense and disparaging. That said, Flores's uncontroversial (if not banal) candidacy, and a low level of interest in the election, resulted in a resounding defeat for the FMLN.[99] ARENA's Flores trounced Guardado, 52 to 29 percent. Although Flores initially vowed to appoint a cabinet representing broad sectors of society, one of his earliest appointments was telling of things to come. Flores appointed Mauricio Sandoval, who had been implicated in the 1989 murder of the Jesuits, as the director of the PNC.

The Flores Years: Sowing the Seeds of Division

The deepening of the neoliberal model under Flores resulted in increased tensions in Salvadoran society (see chapter 4). In fact, El Salvador's most significant popular protests in the postaccord era were in response to the proposed privatization of health care services during his tenure.[100] According to Jack Spence, there were fifty-four strikes between Francisco Flores's inauguration, in June 1999, and the March 2000 election, most in response to privatization initiatives.[101] In October 1999 the health workers' union of the Salvadoran Institute of Social Security (STISSS) and the doctors' union (SIMETRISSS) launched a five-month strike prompted by the failure of the ISSS to make good on agreements reached in 1997 and 1998 regarding wages, working conditions, and the promise of participation in any discussions of the restructuring of the public health system. Additionally, the Flores administration planned to privatize two hospitals and had already begun to contract out certain services (laundry, food, etc.) to private vendors. President Flores blamed the FMLN, which openly sided with the workers, for politicizing the strike and using the strike for its own purposes. The strike climaxed on March 6 when demonstrators near Hospital Médico Quirúrgico and Hospital Rosales in San Salvador were showered with tear gas, which also entered the ventilation systems of the hospitals causing further injury to patients. The excessive use of force confirmed to many that Flores's appointment of Sandoval was imprudent. Several former presidents of the Colegio Médico successfully intervened to mediate the strike that ended on March 10, 2000, two days before the municipal and legislative elections.

The FMLN became the largest political party in the country and secured its presence in some of the largest municipalities, including those in
the coffee-growing regions of the west, in the 2000 municipal and legislative
elections. The FMLN did particularly well at the local level (see table 3.2).
While the FMLN gained four seats in the Legislative Assembly, it increased
its number of mayoralties from fifty-one in 1997 to seventy-seven in 2000. As
in 1997, ARENA posted significant losses in the municipal elections, down to
127 from 162 in 1997 and 207 in 1994. In many respects, the election was a referendum on the first year of the Flores administrations. In a poll taken shortly
after the 2000 elections, 49 percent of those polled believed that the Flores
administration was doing a "bad" job of governing the country, while only
37 percent thought he was doing a good job.[102] A majority, nearly 57 percent,
said that the economy was worse under Flores, and 53 percent responded that
crime had increased during the first year of that administration.[103] Additionally, Flores seriously miscalculated the public reaction to his handling of the
Social Security workers' strike, in which he appeared arrogant and refused to
mediate the four-month strike until days before the election.

Flores's leadership style, which was widely regarded as autocratic, and
his unwillingness to work with the opposition was particularly evident in
his handling of the 2001 earthquakes. On January 13 and February 13, 2001,
powerful earthquakes registering 7.6 and 6.6 on the Richter scale struck El
Salvador. Approximately thirteen hundred Salvadorans died in the quakes;
eight thousand were seriously injured. More than three hundred thousand
homes were destroyed or damaged, as were numerous schools, hospitals,
and businesses.[104] The quakes caused nearly $3 billion in damage. Years
of deforestation, overdevelopment, and lax building codes contributed to
the devastation.[105] Landslides, such as the one that struck the Las Colinas
neighborhood of Santa Tecla and the El Carmen coffee plantation near
the Chichontepec volcano, buried hundreds. Thousands of aftershocks
forced many Salvadorans to sleep in the streets, fearful of being trapped in
their homes by another quake. In Santa Tecla, FMLN mayor Óscar Ortiz
established a tent city to house the newly homeless. By April, more than
twenty-one hundred people were living in the tent city in Santa Tecla.
The coordination between the Flores administration, which had resisted
calls for decentralization, and municipalities following the January quake
was nonexistent. Initial relief efforts were highly centralized, which complicated the distribution of aid. The establishment of the Committee for

National Solidarity (CONASOL), composed of businessmen with ties to ARENA, to distribute aid was met with skepticism by various sectors of society. Monsignor Gregorio Rosa Chávez referred to the committee as a "branch of the official party."[106] Flores's exclusion of the opposition and civil society from the development of the reconstruction plan revealed the extent of partisan nature of his administration.[107] Even the most innocuous overtures by the FMLN to assist in planning were rebuffed by the administration.[108] As one relief worker stated, "A group of people who are very powerful and who control key positions in ARENA think they are still in the 80's in many ways, people who do not see as reasonable the idea that you can rebuild the country with the rebels. For some people here the war is not over."[109] Only at the last minute did Flores finally concede to include Óscar Ortiz, in his capacity as the head of the mayor's association (COMURES), and Monsignor Gregorio Rosa Chávez in a visit to Madrid, Spain, to request foreign aid.

The privatization of health care resurfaced in 2002 when the National Encounter for Private Enterprise (ENADE), a conference for the business community, introduced several proposals to privatize part of the health care system. In complete disregard for the agreement reached in 2000, Flores endorsed the proposals and promised to create working groups to develop the plan.[110] STISSS and SIMETRESSS launched a seven-month strike, from September 2002 until June 2003. A total of six "white marches," so named because all the participants dressed in white, were held between October 2002 and June 2003, some of them attracting as many as two hundred thousand participants. The FMLN openly participated in the marches and supported antiprivatization legislation.[111] The FMLN introduced its legislation in November, which passed with the aid of the PCN. The legislation was overturned one month later, as the PCN returned to ARENA's fold. San Salvador mayor Héctor Silva offered to mediate a settlement in the strike, but Flores insisted that he first renounce his intention to seek reelection. The offer alienated Silva from the FMLN and ended his chances of being named as their presidential candidate in the 2004 elections.[112] An agreement was finally reached in June 2003 whereby the Flores government agreed to continue consultations per the 2000 agreement and to rehire the striking workers.[113]

As in 2000, the 2003 legislative and municipal elections were held during a significant strike of public-sector workers. An IUDOP poll revealed that 55 percent of respondents disagreed with Flores's handling of the strike.[114] Despite this disapproval, there was little change in the distribution of the seats in the assembly. The FMLN maintained its thirty-one seats while ARENA lost two. Both ARENA and the FMLN lost municipalities, to the benefit of the PCN. The PCN won fifty mayoralities, more than they won in 2000. Following more lackluster results for ARENA in the 2003 legislative and municipal elections, Flores announced his antigang plan, known as Mano Dura. The plan, modeled on one created by Honduran president Ricardo Maduro, authorized soldiers to work with the police in an effort to crackdown on crime. The plan also included harsh penalties for merely being a member of a gang (or even appearing to be a gang member), which was grounds for arrest and punishable with a prison sentence of two to five years, and proposed to treat children as young as twelve as adults. As many as three thousand alleged gang members were arrested in the first three months of the plan, although most were released after the elections. The PDDH, FMLN, and human rights organizations were critical of the plan, which did little to address the root causes of the crime wave and violated human rights. The FMLN argued that municipal governments would be more effective at managing the problem, to which Flores responded that the FMLN and others concerned about human rights violations were soft on crime and even complicit in their crimes.[115] Numerous judges also opposed the plan, claiming it was unconstitutional to arrest someone for *being* a gang member, not committing an actual crime. Despite these concerns, Mano Dura was approved for a six-month period.

2004: Things Get Ugly

Concerns about public security dominated the 2004 presidential campaign. ARENA selected former ANEP president, sportscaster, and political unknown Tony Saca as its candidate. ARENA's campaign focused on two main issues, both transnational in nature: gangs and remittances. Saca used both issues to heighten the sense of insecurity in the country, first by suggesting that an FMLN victory would result in the loss of the much-needed remittances that Salvadorans (and indeed the entire Salvadoran economy) were dependent on and then by couching the violence in terms of "terrorism." An internal ARENA memorandum referred to the war on gangs as "an immediate chance for the party to tie in to a winning issue" in advance of the 2004 presidential elections.[116] It was a move carefully calculated to distract voters from ARENA's failures to deliver on the economic front, and it had the added benefit of unifying disparate members of ARENA's traditional sector who had been increasingly isolated since the end of the war.[117] It also reflected a false dichotomy that was increasingly accepted within Salvadoran society, that security and human rights were mutually exclusive. Alleged criminals, it seemed, had too many rights. Only authoritarian-style policies could control crime. This tension contributed to growing political polarization, particularly with regard to support for certain policies and perceptions of violence.

ARENA's campaign assault was made easier by the FMLN's selection of Schafik Handal as its presidential candidate. Many had presumed that the party might select former San Salvador mayor Héctor Silva, but his involvement in the resolution of the 2002–3 STISSS strike ended his relationship with the FMLN. The United States had hoped to influence the outcome of the FMLN's presidential primary, which was a battle between Handal and the more moderate mayor of Santa Tecla, Óscar Ortiz. It did not work. In June 2003, U.S. ambassador Rose M. Likins granted an interview to the Salvadoran daily *La Prensa Gráfica* in which she stated that future U.S.-Salvadoran relations would hinge on the next president and that "some of the signs, actions and discourse of the Frente are cause for worry." Two weeks later, Daniel Fisk, U.S. deputy assistant secretary of state for hemispheric affairs, publicly questioned the FMLN's commitment to democracy and suggested that the FMLN's program could have been written in Havana. Handal, the former head of the PCS, had demonstrated himself to be a reasonable and apt negotiator during peace negotiations and was widely acknowledged to be one of the most capable legislators in the Legislative Assembly. He was also one of the party's most recognizable and controversial leaders, who became a lightning rod for personal attacks even before the campaign season officially began.[118] ARENA's Rodrigo Ávila acknowledged, "the FMLN has given us a big gift."[119] Handal's campaign vowed to withdraw Salvadoran troops from Iraq, reinstitute the colón, and ensure that El Salvador would not ratify the Central America Free Trade Agreement (CAFTA)—all of which drew the ire of the United States, which openly campaigned against him.

Likins's interview, along with Fisk's comments, later became the basis for ARENA's television and radio ads that stated an FMLN victory would severely alter relations with the United States, particularly with regard to remittances from Salvadorans living in the United States. One of ARENA's print ads declared, "Only Tony Saca can guarantee the security of your remittances" ("solo Tony Saca te garantiza la seguridad de tus remesas"). In another ad, a woman sits at her dining table reading a letter from her son who lives in the United States. The letter states that this could very well be the last money that he is able to send her. She is in tears, her husband consoling her. The son's letter closes imploring the mother not to vote for Handal. It is hard to overstate the importance of remittances to El Salvador; the nation's economy depended on them (see chapter 4). Remittances, money sent back to El Salvador from Salvadorans living and working overseas, exceeded $2 billion annually at the time. The urban working class and rural poor comprised the majority of the recipients of remittances. These sectors form the traditional base of the FMLN. In a preelection poll, approximately one-quarter of respondents said they received remittances.[120]

On March 17, 2004, just five days before the election, U.S. Representatives Dana Rohrabacher (R-California), Dan Burton (R-Indiana), and Tom Tancredo (R-Colorado) each threatened that a victory by the "communist/ FMLN presidential candidate" would be a national security concern. In their remarks Burton labeled the FMLN a "pro-terrorist party,"[121] while Rohrabacher claimed that the FMLN "waged war for years to establish a communist dictatorship in El Salvador."[122] Additionally, each noted the $2 billion in remittances sent home by Salvadorans living and working in the United States and stated that an FMLN victory should lead to a review of the temporary protected status of nearly three hundred thousand Salvadorans. Suddenly, TPS was a matter of "national security." Burton called for the termination of TPS and stated that it would be "urgent to apply special controls to the flow of remittances" if the FMLN won the election. Rohrabacher and Tancredo also suggested reconsideration of TPS and remittances policies.[123] While El Salvador's electoral laws prohibit political campaigning for a period of fifteen days before election day, these statements were printed as *news* stories in the Salvadoran daily newspapers. The message, again, was simple: if Handal won, Salvadorans would be returned to El Salvador and remittances would dry up.

The numerous characterizations of Handal as a terrorist, including those by the aforementioned congressmen, were present throughout the campaign. An ad emerged during the Salvadoran elections wherein Schafik's image blended with that of Osama bin Laden and the World Trade Center attacks. One group, Mujeres por la Libertad, repeatedly placed ads in Salvadoran papers that referenced his supposed ties to terrorists. The images invoked scenes of destruction and children with assault rifles, and the ads offered voters Handal's "résumé" from the war. The United States was very clear in its message that the future of U.S.-Salvadoran relations could be dramatically altered if the Left won the 2004 presidential elections. It should be of no surprise that when asked which party would be able to maintain better relations with the United States, 77 percent of respondents said ARENA, while only 12 percent said the FMLN.[124] Remittances aside, Salvadorans have a keen interest in staying on the good side of the United States. More than seventy-five thousand people lost their lives during El Salvador's civil war, and the overwhelming majority of those casualties were caused by the country's U.S.-sponsored military. The words and deeds of the United States weigh heavy in this tiny country. The election results echoed this. Saca easily defeated Handal in the first round of voting, 57 to 36 percent. Silva, once considered a favorite to win the 2004 race, won only 3.9 percent of the vote. The elections were the most polarizing since the peace accords were signed.[125] But worse was yet to come.

The intense polarization surrounding the 2004 elections defined Saca's term in office. Saca focused his attention squarely on the gang issue. Saca's approach to the gang problem was three pronged: antigang legislation, increasing the role of the military in police patrols, and blaming the FMLN. Shortly after assuming office, Saca proposed a heightened version of Mano Dura, known as Super Mano Dura. That legislation criminalized gang membership and reformed penal codes to extend prison sentences (see chapter 5). Saca also authorized increased military patrols. The addition of two more social and gang prevention programs, Mano Amiga (Friendly Hand) and Mano Extendida (Extended Hand), was a response to critics of his authoritarian approach to the crime wave. Neither ever received any real support.

As noted by Wolf, the 2006 campaign bore a striking resemblance to the 2004 campaign in its tenor.[126] Repeated warnings of the consequences of an FMLN victory were contrasted with the "successes" of President Saca. In fact, Saca had an unusually heavy, and illegal, presence in the campaign.[127] In January 2006, just six weeks before the legislative and municipal elections, Saca accused the FMLN of being "partners in disorder and destabilization" with the gangs. He appealed to the public to vote for ARENA candidates to help him pass important anticrime legislation that the FMLN had been opposing. Politically motivated rulings against popular FMLN and FDR mayoral candidates by the TSE were clearly intended to eliminate competition for the Right, while complaints of voter intimidation went unchecked.[128] In January 2006, Schafik Handal died upon returning from the inaugural celebration for Evo Morales in Bolivia, leaving many to wonder about the impact his death would have on party factionalism.[129] Handal was succeeded by Salvador Sánchez Cerén, the last of the FMLN's original leaders. Some speculated that Handal's death would give a boost to the FMLN in the 2006 legislative and municipal elections, although the party's poll numbers were already improving in the weeks before Handal's death. The 2006 election results were, in fact, mixed for the FMLN. In the Legislative Assembly the party won thirty-two seats (one more than in 2003, in addition to seats recuperated from defectors). At the local level, the results were more sobering. In addition to losing fourteen municipalities, there were a number of near losses for the FMLN. The FMLN almost lost the mayoralty of San Salvador, a post it had held since 1997. Violeta Menjívar narrowly defeated ARENA candidate Rodrigo Samayoa by forty-four votes. The TSE's delay in announcing the final election results led to a clash between FMLN supporters and police, as many suspected fraud. Thanks to Saca's popularity and divisions within the FMLN, ARENA fared well in the 2006 elections, increased it seats in the assembly, and increased its mayoralties from 113 to 147. ARENA's allies, however, did not fare as well; the PCN won thirty-nine municipalities, down from fifty-two, and the PDC won fourteen municipalities.

Following the elections, Saca introduced legislation designed to limit a range of political activity. Saca claimed that growing unrest, in the form of protests and crime, necessitated stricter laws to maintain stability. The October 2006 Special Anti-Terrorism Law (Ley Especial contra Actos de Terrorismo) criminalized common means of protest, including demonstrations and marches (see chapter 5). Labeling protest as an act of "terrorism" necessarily restricted political space for peaceful activities and served to limit criticism of government policies. In addition to underscoring the authoritarian tendencies of the administration, the law also reinforced the dominance of El Salvador's political parties as the only legitimate form of political participation.

2009: A Way Forward?

Due to El Salvador's election cycle, 2009 was the first time since 1994 that elections for all offices would be held concurrently. For reasons that were entirely political, the ARENA-dominated TSE decided hold legislative and municipal elections two months earlier than the presidential elections. The hope was to prevent the popularity of FMLN candidate Mauricio Funes from spilling over into local races.[130] The FMLN won 35 seats in the Legislative Assembly, followed by ARENA with 32 and the PCN with 11. The FMLN also substantially increased its share of mayoralties from 58 to 96 (75 on its own and 21 in coalitions) after a poor performance in 2006 while ARENA dropped from 148 to 122 municipalities. But the FMLN lost the big prize. San Salvador, which had been held by the FMLN since 1997, went to ARENA. Shortly after the January elections, the PDC and the PCN withdrew their presidential candidates, leaving only ARENA and the FMLN to participate in the March elections.[131]

Twenty years of ARENA policies failed to deliver economic growth or economic opportunity for a majority of Salvadorans, many of whom were leaving the country in record numbers to seek employment in the United States (see chapter 4). The "iron fist" policies of two administrations failed to address the country's crime wave and actually exacerbated violence (see chapter 5). ARENA also fielded a less than spectacular candidate, one that had weak backing from traditional powers within the party. Rodrigo Ávila was the then (and former) director of the PNC and had been a legislator for ARENA. Public-opinion polls had shown serious dissatisfaction with various ARENA administrations and their policies for more than a decade. Ávila's running mate, former minister of the economy Arturo Zablah, had been the intended nominee of the fledging FDR party. His name had also been floated as a potential candidate for the FMLN in the past. A vocal critic of ARENA's economic policies, Zablah was added to the ticket in order to appeal to more moderate voters.

In 2006, the FMLN leadership announced that it would discontinue the use of primaries to select candidates. Many analysts, myself included, were disappointed and believed that this was an indication that the party was perhaps de-democratizing. This decision to halt primaries and place the candidate selection process solely within the hands of the party's leadership actually turned out to be a shrewd move on the part of the FMLN. The last two primaries delivered former combatants favored by militants within the party, neither of whom were truly viable candidates. So the FMLN leadership delivered a pragmatic surprise—Mauricio Funes. Funes, who had been a popular political-news analyst, was not a member of the FMLN. It was a carefully calculated move that signaled that the FMLN was no longer content to be the party in opposition. His running mate, former FPL leader Salvador Sánchez Cerén, was a nod to the party's base, although former ERP commander Joaquín Villalobos claimed that the choice meant that Funes would take a back seat to the Ortodoxo faction of the party.[132] Funes enjoyed significant support from a group of businessmen known as the Friends of Mauricio, which included Carlos and Francisco Cáceres, Luis Lagos, and Gen. David Munguía Payés.

ARENA's 2009 campaign was reminiscent of campaigns in 2004 and 2006, associating the FMLN with the region's most prominent leftists. Billboards appeared with images of Funes surrounded by Hugo Chávez, Fidel Castro, and Daniel Ortega; another invited vice presidential candidate Sánchez Cerén to leave the country, adding in English "in the name of El Salvador." Many of the negative television and radio ads that appeared were not sponsored by ARENA but by a group called Fuerza Solidaria. The organization was founded by Venezuelan Alejandro Peña Esclusa, a vocal opponent of Hugo Chávez. While a number of members of the U.S. Congress pledged neutrality, Congressman Dana Rohrabacher again claimed the FMLN was a "pro-terrorist party," "an ally of Al-Qaeda and Iran," and claimed that the FMLN trafficked arms to Colombia's FARC rebels. He again called for the termination of temporary protected status for Salvadorans in the United States.[133] To its credit, the Obama administration issued a statement of neutrality in the days before the election.

Still, it was far more difficult to cast Funes as a radical or a communist than previous FMLN candidates. Funes was well known to the public, having hosted a popular news program on television for several years. In an IUDOP poll before the presidential election, 65 percent of respondents said that they did not believe that an FMLN victory would result in increased influence by Cuba and Venezuela. Fifty-five percent of respondents said that ARENA had waged a dirty campaign.[134] Funes's campaign focused on twenty years of failed ARENA policies. His campaign slogan, *Esta vez es diferente,* promised to deliver the change that Salvadorans wanted. The comparisons to U.S. President Barack Obama and Luiz Inácio Lula da Silva of Brazil were almost unavoidable, if not overt. Funes promised to promote reconciliation, address corruption and impunity, and fight crime. He criticized the country's reliance on remittances and ARENA's failure to create a productive economy. He was, however, careful to distance himself from prior

FMLN platforms that called for the reversal of dollarization and withdrawal from CAFTA. Finally, he pledged to maintain good relations with the United States without being subservient.

More than five thousand domestic and international election observers attended the presidential election. On occasion, observers vastly outnumbered the voters.[135] Voting was calm on election day; only a few minor infractions were reported. As Ávila had once presciently said about Tony Saca, "We need to go back to our roots, to do social programs, to go really deeply into the poverty issue, and we need to really strengthen other efforts in the free market. We need to do a lot of things. This could be our last go. I'm totally sure that if we don't do these things, Tony Saca will be our last president."[136] The party's failure to accomplish these goals cost them the election. In March 2009, Mauricio Funes won the presidential election with just over 51 percent of the vote, and on June 1, 2009, Saca transferred power to Funes. The transfer marked the first peaceful, democratic alternation of power between political parties in El Salvador's history.

Twenty Years Later

Mauricio Funes assumed the presidency during the most difficult period since the end of the war. The global recession had a devastating impact on El Salvador's economy; crime and violence (which were already high) increased; and confidence in democracy and government institutions was at its lowest in over a decade. Despite this, Funes maintained a high level of popular support (generally 70 percent or higher) throughout his tenure. His approval ratings were the highest of any president since the signing of the peace accords. Funes's popularity dipped in 2011 amid the first of two constitutional crises. The first crisis was provoked in June 2011 by the approval of Decree 743, which required unanimity among the five Constitutional Court magistrates. Funes, who signed the decree into law, argued that the measure would promote democracy by forcing consensus among judges, while critics charged that it would have effectively made the judiciary toothless.[137] The decree, opposed by only the FMLN during the legislative vote, was declared unconstitutional by the Constitutional Court and was ultimately repealed amid protests by civil society and even ARENA allies, such as ANEP.[138] Apparently, the decree had been introduced at Cristiani's behest amid rumors that the 1993 amnesty law (and perhaps CAFTA) was going to be repealed by the Supreme Court.[139] In stating that ARENA would work to repeal Decree 743, Cristiani said he was certain that the amnesty law (which he described as the "cornerstone of El Salvador's democracy") would not be repealed.[140] Inasmuch as the incident revealed the lengths that ARENA would go to in order to defend its interests and its apparent connections with the judiciary, the episode also raised serious questions about Funes's motivations for signing the law.

By all accounts, Funes had a difficult working relationship with the FMLN, which occasionally sought to distance themselves from his policies. Funes's response to the country's crime wave (see chapter 5) included increasing the presence of the military in the police and creating an unpopular gang truce. But Funes's commitment to human rights (discussed in chapter 2) and social programs (chapter 4) were popular. Additionally, his handling of the second constitutional crisis, which involved the politicized nature of the election of Supreme Court magistrates, appeared to help him regain ground lost during the first crisis.[141] If the 2012 legislative and municipal elections were, as ARENA argued, a referendum on Funes, things did not bode well for the FMLN in 2014. ARENA won thirty-three seats in the assembly, followed by the FMLN with thirty-one. GANA won eleven seats and became the third-largest party in the legislature, a distinction long held by the CN (formerly PCN), which won only six seats. ARENA won 119 mayoralties, including San Salvador and other former FMLN strongholds. The FMLN won eighty-five mayoralties, plus an additional nine in coalition races, followed by the CN with twenty-four and GANA with seventeen. While ARENA held the most seats in the legislature, GANA and the smaller parties often joined the FMLN in a voting bloc.

Shortly after assuming office, Funes announced a $587 million Anti-Crisis Plan (see chapter 4). The most popular element of that program targeted access to education by providing free school uniforms and shoes, school supplies, and school lunches for students from kindergarten through ninth grade.[142] Not surprisingly, the minister of education, Vice President Sánchez Cerén, who had been a teacher himself, was consistently the highest-rated member of Funes's cabinet.[143] Although there was support for the selection of popular Santa Tecla mayor Óscar Ortiz as the 2014 presidential candidate, the FMLN selected Sánchez Cerén with Ortiz as his running mate. The selection of the former FPL commander, one of the last historic leaders in the party, provided ample opportunity for ARENA to revive the war narrative.

While the attacks focused primarily on Sánchez Cerén's past (referring to him as a "terrorist" and "mass murderer"), it's worth noting that Ortiz had been an FPL guerrilla as well.

As its presidential candidate, ARENA selected San Salvador mayor Norman Quijano, who had won 63 percent of the vote in the 2012 mayoral election. Quijano's platform represented a return to ARENA's formula of neoliberalism (including privatization) and militarized solutions to public security. Tony Saca became the first president in postwar El Salvador to run for reelection. Saca's party, GANA, joined with the PCN and the PDC to create Unidad which sought to stake out the middle ground between the two parties. Saca pledged to maintain and expand some of the FMLN's more popular social programs, while promoting policies popular with the Right—reactivation of the agricultural sector, as well as police expansion and job creation to deal with gangs.

Public-opinion polls in advance of the 2014 elections revealed a dramatic shift in the perception of the FMLN. Approximately 50 percent of those polled said that the FMLN was prepared to govern, an improvement from 2004, when 57.3 percent said the FMLN was *not* prepared to govern.[144] When asked which party had the most capacity to reduce poverty, 41.3 percent said the FMLN, while only 23.1 percent said ARENA. Perhaps surprisingly, respondents also believed that the FMLN had more capacity to create jobs than ARENA (37.3 percent to 28.7 percent) and to control the cost of basic services (44 percent to 24.7 percent). Perceptions about the capacity to control crime were roughly even (33.5 percent for ARENA and 33.3 percent for the FMLN), while over 20 percent said "none."[145]

While changing perceptions of the FMLN and the favorable evaluation of the Funes administration no doubt helped Sánchez Cerén's candidacy, it was the "December surprise" that appeared to have swayed many voters. In December 2013 the attorney general opened an investigation into corruption allegations against former president Francisco Flores. Flores, who was the campaign director for Quijano's campaign, was accused of embezzling $15 million in donations from Taiwan, though there were indications that the amount could be significantly more.[146] His case, described in great detail in the next chapter, dominated headlines and embarrassed the Quijano campaign.

Sánchez Cerén won the first round of voting with 48.93 percent of the vote, just shy of the vote share needed to avoid a runoff. Quijano came in second with 38.96 percent, followed by Saca with 11.44 percent. Although polls after the second round gave Sánchez Cerén a significant lead (some as much as 16 percent), it soon became clear that Quijano wasn't giving up without a fight. Quijano launched an impressive (and polarizing) ground campaign to get out the vote. His campaign exploited the turmoil in Venezuela, claiming that would be El Salvador's future under a Sánchez Cerén administration. There were also claims that the FMLN was allied with gangs and they would be voting for the leftists, a claim helped along by ARENA's conservative allies in the United States.[147] An IUDOP poll conducted before the second round underscored the vitriol of ARENA's campaign. Whereas 74 percent of respondents said the FMLN's campaign was very good or good, only 41.5 said the same of ARENA. Additionally, 41.4 percent said that the FMLN's image had improved over the past few months (19.5 said it had declined) compared to 15.8 percent of respondents saying that ARENA's image had improved, while 38.2 percent said it had worsened.[148] Moreover, the Flores scandal continued to plague Quijano's campaign. In an IUDOP poll before the second round, 37 percent of respondents said they weren't voting for Quijano because of the accusations against Flores.

Before the votes had even been counted, both Sánchez Cerén and Quijano declared themselves the victors—much to the chagrin of the TSE, which had asked candidates to refrain from doing so. Quijano's election night rally, however, took an ugly turn when the candidate proclaimed that the TSE was trying to commit a "Chavista-style fraud" to deny him victory and that the military was watching and would "make democracy." His remarks, which were widely criticized, created an unprecedented tension and underscored the extent to which some elements in the Right had failed to change. Days later Defense Minister David Munguía Payés appeared on television to reaffirm that the military's role was one of obedience. The preliminary results showed that Sánchez Cerén had narrowly defeated Quijano, by about six thousand votes. While the TSE called for calm, ARENA mounted an assault on the electoral system, claiming various forms of fraud, urging its supporters into the streets, and petitioning for the annulment of the elections, although international and domestic observer groups said the election was transparent and clean. ARENA also demanded a vote-by-vote recount, a remedy not provided by Salvadoran election law, which only stipulates a recount of the *actas* (tallies).[149] The recount of the actas confirmed that Sánchez Cerén had won the election with 50.11 percent of the vote to Quijano's 49.89, a margin of approximately sixty-three hundred votes. The election set several precedents: (1) it was the closest margin of victory in any of El Salvador's presidential elections; (2) voter turnout *increased* by some quarter million (about 5 percent) between the first and second rounds of voting, with ARENA alone gaining more than four hundred thousand in the second round; and (3) a record number of Salvadorans (3,004,845) voted in the second round. While turnout for the second round was only 60.64 percent (down from 62.92 in 2009 and 66.16 in 2004), Sánchez Cerén was elected with the greatest number of votes (1,496,815) in Salvadoran history. He was also El Salvador's first guerrilla president, joining several others in the hemisphere.

Electoral politics continued to be polarized in the March 1, 2015 legislative and municipal elections. Notably, it was the first time that voters were able to select candidates for the legislative assembly from different parties.[150] The failure of the TSE's computer system resulted in a one-month delay as officials proceeded with a manual recount. Although the TSE announced results by the end of the month, the Constitutional Chamber of the Supreme Court ordered a recount due to irregularities and prohibited deputies from taking their seats. The recount, which did not alter the TSE's original seat count, was completed two and a half months after the election. Although international observers found no evidence of fraud, the election results, unsurprisingly, revealed a divided country. While ARENA won 35 seats to the FMLN's 31, their alliances with smaller parties meant that the power in the assembly was split in half (see table 3.2). ARENA won the most municipalities, including Roberto D'Aubuisson Jr.'s victory in Santa Tecla, a post formerly held by vice president Oscar Ortiz, but it lost San Salvador. The FMLN's Nayib Bukele, considered a rising star in Salvadoran politics, defeated ARENA's Edwin Zamora to win San Salvador.

Political Participation

Political participation is important to peacebuilding for the same reasons that it is important to democracy. While political participation is a way for citizens to express demands, it also plays an important role in creating responsibility, trust, tolerance, and social capital among the citizenry. Deficits in these areas are often associated with lower support for democratic norms and the emergence of autocratic regimes.[151] The nature of Salvadoran politics since the signing of the peace accords served to undermine political participation.

Political space was dominated by political parties, which developed few, if any, channels to facilitate dialogue between themselves and the citizenry. Beyond elections, few mechanisms existed to encourage broader participation or channel demands into the policymaking process. The lack of information or public consultation about major policy issues, such as privatization of public services, dollarization, or CAFTA (see chapter 4), reinforced the exclusionary nature of El Salvador's postwar democracy.

One of the most obvious expressions of this discontent was the high rate of abstention in postwar elections. Some of this could be attributed to the country's history of repression and fraudulent elections, but that would not explain why Salvadorans participated at lower rates than their Nicaraguan neighbors, who shared similar experiences. Indeed, only 55 percent of registered Salvadorans voted in the 1994 "elections of the century," compared to 78 percent voter turnout in Nicaragua's 1990 elections. William Barnes's comparison of the "founding elections" in postwar El Salvador and Nicaragua revealed that Nicaragua's significantly higher voter turnout was a result of two decades of emphasis on popular mobilization, the accessibility of both registration and voting centers, and high levels of trust in the electoral process.[152] In other words, Nicaraguans were encouraged to participate and their participation was facilitated by a competent, trusted electoral commission. Abstention rates increased following the 1994 elections. Abstention rates for presidential elections increased to nearly 57 percent in 1999 before decreasing significantly to about 32 percent in the 2004 election. At least some of this decline in the abstention rate may be due to the "DUI effect"— ID cards improved the voter registration process. Given the level of interest in the 2009 presidential campaign, it was somewhat surprising that abstention increased to more than 38 percent in those elections. Curiously, while voter abstention in the first round of 2014 presidential voting was more than 45 percent, abstention rates *decreased* approximately 5 points in the second round of voting. Abstention rates for legislative and municipal elections have generally been higher than presidential elections, reaching almost 60 percent in 2006.

There was, of course, no single explanation for the rate of abstention. Explanations for low voter turnout in El Salvador included both structural impediments and political culture. A 2006 study by Ricardo Córdova Macías and José Miguel Cruz found that Salvadorans were reluctant to admit that they did not intend to vote. Salvadorans frequently cited personal reasons to explain why *they* do not vote but explained *other's* abstention as a result of apathy, lack of trust, not having a DUI, or not liking the candidates.[153] Despite some advances in recent years, structural impediments to voting remained. While the introduction of the DUI and improvements to the national registry removed some of the barriers to registration, the process of registering remained unnecessarily complicated. Important reforms that would facilitate voting, such as residential voting, weren't implemented until two decades after the peace agreements were signed.

Perhaps the most compelling explanation for abstention had to do with the common perception of political parties as self-serving and irrelevant to people's daily lives. Slightly more than one-third of Salvadorans expressed trust in political parties or felt that political parties listened to the average person.[154] According to political analyst Córdova, "The parties have a monopoly on representation and there is no link of representation [between people and the parties]. For me, the high levels of absenteeism are no longer due to technical problems. The people are disconnected from the system. They are not interested and do not feel represented. Period."[155]

Simply put, Salvadorans did not feel represented by their elected officials. When asked who political parties served, most respondents said that the parties worked for themselves.[156] Perhaps some of this was due to the nature of the Salvadoran electoral system. Until changes made in 2012, Salvadoran voters voted for political parties, not candidates. Only party banners appeared on ballots. Under this closed-list system, political parties selected their representatives with little or no input from voters. While not an uncommon practice in proportional-representation systems, it contributed to the disconnect between voters and their representatives. According to one USAID official, "the fact that *diputados* represent the party and not the people is the biggest barrier to citizen participation."[157] Even when this process was reformed, only about half of respondents knew the names of candidates for deputies in their departments.[158] As such, elected officials were responsible to the party rather than the electorate. As further evidence of this disconnect, recent surveys found increasing apathy and lack of interest in politics.[159]

Additionally, many Salvadorans did not feel represented by the parties that they had to choose from. Approximately one-third of the Salvadoran electorate had no party identification.[160] In a 2012 IUDOP poll, nearly half of respondents gave their preferred party as "none," with only 23.1 percent choosing the FMLN and 21 percent selecting ARENA.[161] Despite the level of polarization among Salvadoran political parties, Salvadorans' ideological orientation spread fairly evenly across the political spectrum, with peaks at the center and poles.[162] That said, Salvadorans' ideological self-placement has not been static. Dinorah Azpuru detected shifts in the ideological orientation of voters in the postwar period. Voters moved to the right from 1991 to 2004, with a significant increase from the 1999 to the 2004 elections (6.07 to 6.89), followed by a dramatic shift to the left in 2009 (6.89 to 4.96).[163] This popular shift to the left coincides with the FMLN's shift to the left discussed earlier. While the ideological orientation of voters at extremes (what we might refer to as the "hard vote") was important to parties, only those who were able to capture the centrist voters were able to win presidential election. Centrist voters appeared to weigh their evaluation of presidential performance with policy proposals in determining their vote.[164] This was certainly true in 2014, when most voters indicated that they were voting based on the quality of proposals (23.8 percent of ARENA voters and 31.5 percent of UNIDAD voters) and for change (26.7 percent of FMLN voters) rather than ideology.[165]

Voting, of course, is only one form of political participation.[166] Salvadorans also exhibited low levels of political participation in other areas, including community activism. Few participate in political party events, although the number did increase from 9 percent in 2004 to 14 percent in 2012.[167] Only 22 percent indicated that they had contacted a local official, and a mere 7 percent had contacted a legislative deputy.[168] Salvadorans also had the lowest level of protest participation in Central America. Only 4 percent of respondents claimed to have participated in a protest during the last year.[169] Community activism, which had never been particularly high, also declined in 2012.[170] Some of this decline may have been due to rising fear associated with the country's crime wave, as Salvadorans reported spending more time in their homes and less time in their communities.

Despite Salvadorans' level of political participation, they generally expressed strong support for democratic governance. That, however, changed as a result of the failure to address serious social and economic problems, as well as crime. While support for electoral democracy remained high in 2012, at 82 percent ("democracy is preferable to any other form of government"), it represented a 12.5 percent decline from 2004.[171] Compared to regional means, support for a military coup under certain circumstances was relatively high, at 43 percent.[172] Support for democratic norms, including tolerance for some forms of political participation, also declined during that period. There was an increase in tolerance for certain political activities (running for office, freedom of speech, voting, and protest) from 1995 to 1999, but it decreased between 1999 and 2004.[173] After a brief increase in tolerance levels between 2004 and 2006, tolerance declined more than 10 points from 2006 to 2012.[174] As with support for democracy, the declining levels of tolerance coincided with increasing levels of polarization between the major parties, crime, and economic instability.

The number of Salvadorans who thought the country was very democratic decreased throughout the Saca administration, from 21 percent in 2004 to 10.5 percent in 2008. That number improved slightly under Funes, to 13.6 percent in 2012. The total percentage of the population who believed that there was little or no democracy increased 7 percentage points during Saca's tenure, to 50.1 in 2008, but declined to 40.3 percent in 2012, under Funes.[175] This is not surprising given the authoritarian nature of some of the policies implemented by the Saca administration. More than half the respondents (57.2 percent) reported feeling very dissatisfied with the level of democracy in the country in 2008; those numbers improved in 2012 under Funes, to 44.2.[176] These data reinforced John Booth and Mitchell Seligson's finding of a gap between supply and demand of democracy, the level of discontent with the level of democracy in El Salvador. In a 2004 survey of eight countries throughout Latin America, El Salvador had the highest discrepancy between democratic supply and demand.[177] These perceptions were accompanied by a decline in trust in institutions. The 2008 LAPOP survey revealed a decline in trust in *all* institutions between 2004 and 2008. There were marked decreases (more than 15 percent) of confidence in elections, the TSE, the police, and national government.[178] Confidence in all state institutions improved during the Funes administration, although there was a decline in confidence in many institutions between 2010 and 2012.[179]

Captured Democracy

El Salvador's postwar politics signified, in many respects, a continuation of the war. Elites' capture of the state through their political party, ARENA, enabled them to forestall electoral reforms that could potentially threaten their electoral prospects. Their control of the legislature assured them near dominance of political appointments and public policy during critical years of peacebuilding. As the FMLN threatened its electoral dominance, ARENA intensified its struggle to hold onto power using polarizing tactics. The political tug-of-war that dominated political life in El Salvador framed major policy issues (such as privatization and crime) as an electoral strategy rather than public policy. Political parties, consumed by their conflicts with one another and their own internal strife, remained distant from the citizens they claimed to represent. As the parties failed to address the country's most serious problems, Salvadorans increasingly expressed dissatisfaction with their elected officials and the institutional trappings of their new democracy. The alternation in power following the FMLN's victory in the 2009 presidential elections offered some prospects for hope. There were notable improvements in the administration of the TSE, as well as public confidence in institutions and appraisals of democracy. But was it too little, too late? As the next two chapters reveal, two decades of ARENA's political dominance had reaffirmed a culture of economic and social exclusion that threatened the quality of El Salvador's peace.

Chapter 4

El Salvador in the Neoliberal Era

> They used to say that the Salvadoran oligarchy
> consisted of fourteen families. Now, I say, there are
> five: Banco Cuscatlán, Banco Agrícola Comercial,
> Banco Salvadoreño, Banco Hipotecario, and Banco
> Desarrollo. The bankers are the new oligarchs.
>
> —José Alfredo Dutríz[1]

THE POSTWAR ECONOMY in El Salvador has been largely defined by the so-called neoliberal economic policies of four successive ARENA administrations. Many questioned the wisdom of introducing neoliberal reforms while building peace—and for good reason.[2] Postwar societies, unlike other societies in transition, have special considerations: infrastructure has been destroyed, bloated defense budgets have reduced expenditures on health and education, economies have contracted and illegal economies formed, capital and humans have fled, and the environment has been degraded. Wars also create new forms of poverty and inequality in addition to those that preceded the conflict. Additionally, with peace also comes the cost of reconstruction, the reintegration of ex-combatants and resettlement of displaced persons, as well as the return of government services. Postwar societies must essentially rebuild their economies, as well as state and social institutions.

For many, the retraction of the state from the public sphere at the point when it is needed most is antithetical to peacebuilding.[3]

The Cristiani administration began the process of liberalizing the economy in accordance with structural adjustment agreements with international financial institutions before peace negotiations, of one of chief benefits of its incumbency. Because Cristiani refused to negotiate on the neoliberal reforms his administration was implementing, and the FMLN accepted this to get to the negotiating table, there was little substantive discussion on whether or how to redress socioeconomic exclusion during peace negotiations. The socioeconomic section of the peace accords was primarily aimed at addressing reintegration and land transfer programs for ex-combatants (see chapter 2). The Forum for Economic and Social Consultation (Foro), which was supposed to create an opportunity for dialogue between the government, business, and labor, collapsed due to a lack of political will on the part of both the Cristiani administration and the business community. The failure to address substantive socioeconomic issues during the peace negotiations is perhaps one of the greatest shortcomings of the peace process. This chapter analyzes not only the application and impact of neoliberal economic policies during the administrations of Alfredo Cristiani, Armando Calderón Sol, Francisco Flores, and Antonio Saca, but also explores the extent to which elites have benefited from these policies—often at the expense of the country's development. ARENA was able to pursue these policies, despite the growing political power of the FMLN and disenchantment within its own ranks because (1) alliances made with smaller parties of the Right, such as the PCN, enabled it to control various institutions and (2) traditional elites (or hardliners) within the party would not risk an FMLN administration. As shifting alliances began to change, during the Funes administration, opportunities to augment economic policy increased—although the constraints on Funes, largely the result of twenty years of ARENA policy, limited the scope of that change.

El Salvador's War Economy and the Rise of Neoliberalism

The imposition of agrarian reform and the nationalization of key industries—notably Decree 75, which nationalized the coffee export process and created the National Coffee Institute (INCAFE) to manage these exports and the banks in 1980—were designed to undercut support for the FMLN guerrillas. The United States initially encouraged these policies and, once in power, the

Duarte government implemented additional policies aimed at gaining support from the working class, including increases for public-sector employees, a minimum wage for urban workers, and increased access to credit and price controls.[4] These programs, however, did little to bolster the economy. In fact, the number of those living in poverty increased throughout the 1980s.[5] By 1984 the United States was encouraging liberal economic reforms, which were resisted by Duarte for fear that they would increase support for the guerrillas. Through the creation of the Salvadoran Foundation for Economic and Social Development (FUSADES), a think tank composed mostly of a new generation of industrialists, the United States developed a local entity to support its economic vision for El Salvador. Wood's analysis of the transformation of elites' willingness to negotiate a democratic transition provides key insights as to the profound impact the war economy had on elite preferences and behavior. The reforms implemented during the junta and the Duarte years undermined traditional agricultural elite interests. This added to the uncertainty created by the war, which resulted in the divergence of investment away from coffee and into new enterprises. Finally, the influx of remittances that Salvadorans sent home created new opportunities in the financial and commercial sectors that had not previously existed.[6] These three factors contributed to the shift by many elites away from agro-export and into emerging sectors.[7] In 1985, FUSADES released its proposal for economic reforms, "La necesidad de un nuevo modelo económico para El Salvador," which articulated its vision for economic reform. The proposal argued that sustainable growth and increased employment were incompatible with the import substitution model in place, and it recommended a new model based on the diversification of exports and a free-market economy.[8] These new elites soon came to dominate ARENA, which heavily influenced the party's economic policies. The presidential victory of Alfredo Cristiani, himself a member of the board of directors of FUSADES, in 1989 paved the way for economic reform consistent with the neoliberal principles advocated by the United States, international financial institutions, and, of course, FUSADES.

El Salvador in the Neoliberal Era

ARENA's application of the neoliberal model has been a detriment to sustainable peace in El Salvador for three main reasons. First, ARENA's economic policy failed to address the structural causes of poverty and inequality in El Salvador. The belief that sustained economic growth alone would be sufficient to alleviate poverty and inequality was one of the guiding principles of the current economic model; it was also highly reminiscent of elite economic thought one hundred years earlier. Not only did economic policies fail to deliver sustained growth, but any measures undertaken to alleviate poverty were superficial, insufficient, and strictly within the confines of ARENA's vision of neoliberalism. Second, the economic policies of the past four administrations exacerbated historic patterns of socioeconomic exclusion. While overall poverty declined following the end of the war, the persistence of poverty and inequality represented a serious challenge to building sustainable peace. Despite official claims about the "successes" of economic policy in contributing to improvements in these areas, it was remittances—not economic reforms or policy initiatives—that reduced poverty and inequality. Third, economic policy in El Salvador was designed to benefit those in power. The greatest beneficiaries of the privatization process have been members of government and their supporters. Not only did the privatization process further concentrate wealth in the hands of a select few, but complementary (and some would argue necessary) policies were only selectively applied so as not to harm special interests. The close relationship between big business and ARENA provided a small segment of society with disproportionate levels of access to policymakers and influence over economic policy. Corruption has been endemic, though rarely punished. This has led observers from across the political spectrum to question whether the model is indeed neoliberal, or just old-school patrimony repackaged as something new.

Cristiani and the Spoils of Privatization (1989-94)

The influence of FUSADES on the Alfredo Cristiani administration is difficult to overstate. Not only was most of Cristiani's cabinet composed of FUSADES technocrats but he adopted the FUSADES 1989 proposal as his own economic platform.[9] Cristiani's economic plan had four main goals: reduce the state's participation in the economy, generate sustained growth, make efficient use of the country's resources, and create conditions to eradicate poverty.[10] These goals would be accomplished through the promotion of exports and the liberalization of the market, both of which were considered key to generating economic growth.[11] Shortly after taking office, in

June 1989, the Cristiani administration negotiated the terms of a $75 million structural-adjustment loan package with the IMF. The negotiation of this and other loan packages had a significant influence on the socioeconomic elements of the peace accords, including the National Reconstruction Plan (PRN) (see chapter 3).[12] Cristiani's policies, as implemented, consisted of the reduction of tariffs from 290 to 0 percent to 20 to 5 percent over a two-year period, elimination of price controls, elimination of export duties, liberalization of interest rates, and the introduction of the value-added tax (IVA). Additionally, Cristiani moved to privatize key industries such as coffee (INCAFE), the sugar industry (INAZUCAR), and the banks.

Both business and agrarian elites initially supported the neoliberal model introduced by Cristiani.[13] Economist Alexander Segovia offers three reasons for this: the crisis in agriculture forced agrarian elites to explore new opportunities; vast amounts of Salvadoran capital had left the country during the war; and a generational change occurred within the most important economic groups.[14] In short, elites couldn't continue with their old model and the new model promised increased access to the global economy. For the business sector, the neoliberal model would promote growth through foreign investment, export promotion, and market liberalization. For the agrarian sector, the neoliberal model would result in the privatization of two key industries: coffee and sugar.

The Cristiani administration wasted no time in embarking upon the privatization process, and the banks were among the first state-owned enterprises to be privatized. Under the 1991 Law of the Banks, which governed the privatization of the banks, individual bidders were permitted ownership of no more than 5 percent per shareholder. According to several sources, *prestanombres,* or false names, were used to purchase shares in excess of the legal limit.[15] Another source indicated that, while he was unsure of the use of false names, there were other ways to get around the law, such as using the names of housekeepers, chauffeurs, spouses, and even deceased relatives to purchase shares.[16] Because the privatization of the banks occurred before the peace accords, while there was still little political opposition or oversight, such illegal practices were generally unknown to the public. As described by one source, "the [Cristiani] administration used government resources to clean up the banks to sell them, and then purchased them themselves. They literally became bankholders for free."[17] President Cristiani himself gained a controlling interest in El Salvador's largest bank, Banco Cuscatlán.

Irregularities in the bank privatization process resulted in monopolistic practices in the financial sector, particularly in controlling interest rates.[18] The "financial piñata," as Alfredo Mena Lagos, minister of modernization under Calderón Sol, referred to it, "created private monopolies from state monopolies."[19] By the end of the decade, three banks owned 60 percent of the capital in the country.[20] In 2007, Citibank bought Banco Cuscatlán for a reported $1.5 billion.

The privatization of the banks also underscored an important shift among economic elites. Whereas directors of banks before nationalization, in 1980, had typically been members of the coffee elite (including the Guirola, Escalante-Sol Millet, Regalado Dueñas families), many of the new shareholders (Simán, Dutriz, Baldochi Dueñas, Zablah, and Cristiani, to name a few) were members of the agro-industrial business elite.[21] This, combined with the decline of the agricultural sector and the overt influence of FUSADES and the business sector over economic policy, was evidence of the waning power of agrarian elites in the postwar environment.

While elites split over the nature and outcome of bank privatization, a concern that would emerge in future criticisms of the model, other aspects of the model were well received. In fact, its implementation during Cristiani's tenure generated considerable growth, an average of 5 percent during his tenure. This growth was bolstered by initial privatizations and new foreign investment following the signing of the peace accords. Additionally, inflation declined from 20 percent in 1992 to 10 percent by 1994.[22] Nontraditional exports increased significantly, from $244.7 million in 1989 to $448.3 million in 1993. The new *maquiladora* sector also played a key role in attracting investment and created thousands of new jobs, more than doubling employment in that sector between 1989 and 1993.[23]

Other aspects of the economy were less encouraging. Cristiani's poverty eradication program was largely premised on the belief that sustained economic growth would benefit all Salvadorans, or trickle-down economics.[24] The two main social programs created to offset the costs of adjustment, the Social Rescue Plan (SRP) and the Social Investment Fund (SIF), had little impact. According to Orr, the SRP basically amounted to a repackaging of existing programs consisting of subsidies and job creation programs, while the SIF was a four-year plan funded largely by the Inter-American Development Bank (IDB) aimed at the delivery of health, education, and sanitation services throughout the country.[25] Neither program adequately addressed the structural causes of El Salvador's poverty and inequality—in part, because the government viewed poverty as a result of the war.[26] This thinking reflected a long tradition of radical liberal (see chapter 1), wherein elites viewed themselves as the modernizers of the economy and inequality as a natural by-product of development. While total poverty numbers dropped from 55.2 percent in 1988–89 to 50.4 percent in 1992–93 and extreme poverty declined from 23.6 to 20.8 percent, the numbers of those living in extreme poverty in urban areas increased from 23.3 percent to 29.6 percent for the same period.[27] The rise in inequality and urban extreme poverty added to the perception that Cristiani's policies were incompatible with the peace accords and did not address socioeconomic inequalities or poverty. The assessment by Ricardo Perdomo, minister of the economy under Duarte, was that El Salvador had "achieved macroeconomic stability at the price of poverty and unemployment."[28]

Remittances—money sent home by Salvadorans living abroad—played a key role in sustaining both the national and many household economies. While remittances totaled only 3.5 percent of GDP in 1989, they represented 8.1 percent of GDP by 1992.[29] Remittances alleviated the social costs of structural-adjustment policies immediately after the war by keeping inflation under control, promoting economic growth, and supplementing the incomes of the poor.[30] Citing a wartime study by Segundo Montes, Segovia notes that remittances constituted 47 percent of family income where at least one relative lived in the United States. A study conducted immediately following the end of the war found that remittances increased the incomes of the urban and rural poor by one-third.[31] The impact of neoliberal reforms on the Salvadoran economy and population would have been significantly worse had it not been for the dramatic increase in remittances that coincided with the end of the war.

Other critics of Cristiani's economic policies also began to question the extent to which they were truly neoliberal.[32] Some within the business community were particularly concerned by the lack of monetary flexibility and high interest rates, which limited access to credit and appeared antithetical to the administration's adherence to free-market policies.[33] The selective manner in which neoliberal reforms were applied and the bank privatization scandal led some to assert that the model was not actually neoliberal, but rather something more patrimonial and reminiscent of the nineteenth-century oligarchy. According to Rubén Zamora:

The tension in ARENA really has nothing to do with being neoliberal. If you talk to the so-called moderates, they are neoliberal in thinking when it comes to their business, but they are not neoliberal. They are exactly the same thing as the bankers. The bankers think they are neoliberal but they want what comes through the protection of the banks. They are not neoliberals. They are very protectionist. That is why I think that at the center of this whole thing the question is not between neoliberals versus non-neoliberals. The question is a neoliberal idea being shared by the private sector but with a party that is patrimonialist—that is really against neoliberals. The result is very paternalistic. They [ARENA] use neoliberalism to justify a lot of patrimony.[34]

Calderón Sol (1994–99): The Deepening of the Neoliberal Conflict

During his presidency, Armando Calderón Sol deepened the neoliberal reforms of the Cristiani administration. Unlike Cristiani, Calderón Sol filled his cabinet with businessmen, not administrators or technical experts.[35] Robert Rivera Campos credits a 1993 report by Central Bank adviser Manuel Enrique Hinds with influencing the administration's policies, particularly his recommendations for economic integration with the North American market and the privatization of the telecommunications and energy sectors.[36] The goal was to turn El Salvador into a large free-trade zone.[37] Calderón Sol lowered tariffs dramatically, increased the IVA from 10 percent to 13 percent, and eliminated nearly twelve thousand public-sector jobs during his first two years in office (see table 4.1). His convertibility plan, which pegged the Salvadoran colón to the U.S. dollar at a rate of 8.75 to 1, was a step toward dollarization. Each of these policies provoked reaction from the business community, many of whom questioned whether the economy could withstand the dramatic reduction in tariffs and the convertibility plan.[38]

The growth that the Salvadoran economy enjoyed under Cristiani began to slow under Calderón Sol, despite the privatization of key industries in 1998.[39] The most dramatic economic contraction occurred in 1996, when GDP growth registered a mere 1.7 percent (see table 4.2). The economic decline in 1996 resulted in a sharp increase in poverty and inequality. In 1996, the national poverty level increased sharply, from 52.9 percent in 1995 to 58.1 percent, and rural poverty increased from 29 to 37 percent.[40]

TABLE 4.1

Key reforms implemented by the Cristiani and Calderón Sol administrations

	Cristiani	Calderón Sol
Trade policy	Reduction of tariff range from 290–0 to 20–5%; elimination of export duties	Reduction of the tariff floor to 0% for capital goods
Fiscal policy	Institution of IVA of 10%	Increase IVA from 10% to 13%
Monetary policy	Liberalization of interest rates; creation of Banco Multisectorial de Inversiones to promote private sector investments	Convertibility plan pegging colón to U.S. dollar at 8.75 to 1
Financial sector	Bank privatization	
Privatization	Instituto Nacional del Café (INCAFE), Instituto Nacional de Azúcar (INAZUCAR), Banco Nacional de Fomento Industrial (BANAFI), Corporación Salvadoreña de Inversiones (CORSAIN)	Administración Nacional de Telecomunicaciones (ANTEL), Superintendencia General de Electricidad y Telecomunicaciones (SIGET), pensions
Modernization of the state		Elimination of 11,500 public-sector jobs by 1997[a]

Source: Adapted from Oscar Melhado, *Retos económicos de fin de siglo* (San Salvador: UCA Editores, 1997), 93, 122.

[a] This was approximately 10 percent of the public sector. In 1997 the central government employed 100,696 citizens.

TABLE 4.2

Growth of gross domestic product, 1989–98 (percent)

1989	1990	1991	1992	1993	1994	1995	1996	1997	1998
1.0	4.8	3.6	7.5	7.4	6.0	6.4	1.7	4.2	3.5

Source: Banco Central de Reserva de El Salvador (BCR), *Indicadores económicos anuales, 1994–2001.*

The increase in rural poverty coincided with a significant decline in the agricultural sector. Business and agrarian elites began to argue that the administration's policies were promoting the financial sector at the cost of the agricultural sector, which remained flat between 1994 and 2000 while the financial sector enjoyed an average growth rate of 12 percent during the same period (see table 4.3). The impact of liberalization policies had a negative effect on the agricultural sector, which suffered from a lack of comparative advantage and poor access to credit. This resulted in a growing increase in the agricultural trade deficit after 2000.[41] The growth of the financial sector in comparison to the agricultural sector created further divisions within the Right and bolstered the argument that Cristiani and his brethren had sacrificed the rest of the economy for their own personal gain. Agriculture continued to suffer after other sectors recovered the following year. Hurricane Mitch, which pummeled Central America in late October 1998, also had a significant impact on the agricultural sector. While El Salvador was spared the more devastating effects of the hurricane, there was significant damage in the country's eastern regions due to flooding. The decline in agricultural production resulted in shortages of key goods and increases in food prices (nearly 7 percent in 1998).[42]

TABLE 4.3

Economic growth by sector, 1994–2000 (percent)

	1994	1995	1996	1997	1998	1999	2000
Agriculture	-2.4	4.5	1.3	.4	-.7	.9	-.8
Industry	7.4	6.9	1.7	8.0	6.6	3.7	4.5
Construction	11.5	6.1	2.7	6.2	7.1	2.2	-2.3
Financial services	20.2	16.4	2.7	12.6	8.9	15.4	5.1

Source: Banco Central de Reserva de El Salvador (BCR), *Indicadores económicos anuales, 1994–2001.*

The FMLN, which had been opposed to the neoliberal model since its imposition, had some measure of success in tempering the neoliberal program under Calderón Sol. Following the 1997 elections, ARENA held only a single-seat advantage over the FMLN in the Legislative Assembly. This allowed the FMLN significantly more influence over the policy process than it enjoyed in previous years. Its first attempt at exercising its newfound strength was during the controversy surrounding the proposed privatization of El Salvador's National Telecommunications Company (ANTEL), in June 1997. The FMLN, together with every other party except ARENA, voted to repeal Legislative Decree 900, the law privatizing the telecommunications industry.[43] The Legislative Assembly then established a commission to review the law and establish new procedures in the privatization process. When ANTEL was finally privatized, in 1998, 51 percent of shares were up for bids, 15 percent was sold to ANTEL employees, 25 percent of the shares remained in the hands of the state, and 9 percent was offered on the stock market. It was only a partial success for the FMLN, which was opposed to the privatization of the industry. It was, however, a stark contrast to the bank privatization, wherein the state retained no ownership. The opposition also halted the privatization process for the duration of Calderón Sol's term.

The trade deficit worsened during Calderón Sol's tenure (see table 4.4). Rather than promoting exports, as was originally intended, Salvadorans were consuming well in excess of what they were producing, due in part to remittances. Imports increased from $3.7 billion in 1997 to $4.9 billion in 2000, while exports only rose from $2.4 billion to $3.0 billion during the same period, resulting in a growing trade imbalance.[44] For the business community, this was evidence that the government had failed to develop the export sector as stipulated by the model. It also reaffirmed the economy's dependence on remittances. For the agrarian elite, it was further evidence that the economy was being managed in ways inimical to their interests.

TABLE 4.4

Trade deficit, 1995-2000 (in billions of U.S. dollars)

1995	1996	1997	1998	1999	2000
1.677	1.433	1.320	1.513	1.583	1.998

Source: Banco Central de Reserva de El Salvador (BCR), *Indicadores económicos anuales 1994-2001.*

Francisco Flores (1999-2004): Stagnation, Privatization, and Dollarization

In 1999, Francisco Flores inherited the legacy of the Cristiani and Calderón Sol administrations. The economic decline that began in the Calderón Sol administration worsened during his administration, bringing growth to a standstill. In addition to the lack of growth, inequality was on the rise. In 1996 the ratio between the richest quintile and the poorest quintile was 15:1; this ratio increased to 18.0 in 1999 and to 19.6 in 2002.[45] These problems were exacerbated by Flores's policies, particularly the extension of the IVA to include medicine and items in the basic food basket, during his first month in office, and dollarization, in 2001.[46] The public had become increasingly pessimistic about the economy. Although he soundly defeated FMLN candidate Facundo Guardado in the first round of voting, public opinion was decidedly opposed to the economic policies of the previous administration. An IUDOP poll revealed that 84.1 percent of respondents believed Flores should change the economic policies of the Calderón Sol administration.[47] While 30.3 percent believed that he should follow the "New Alliance" platform that he had run on, which promised to fight inequality, reactivate agriculture, create jobs, fight crime and provide for the overall health and well-being of all Salvadorans, an equal number believed he should adopt other plans, including the CND's *Plan de nación* (19.4) and the FUSADES *Crecimiento con participación* (11.9) (see below).

The neoliberal model was criticized by both the Left and the Right for its failure to address El Salvador's most pressing problems: jobs and poverty. While the FMLN was the most vocal critic of these policies, the business community and elements within the Right were also critical of the model. Their critique addressed four main concerns: (1) lack of development of the export sector, (2) concentration of wealth in the financial sector, (3) dependence on remittances and failure to use them in a manner that would produce long-term benefits, and (4) the failure of the model to address poverty.[48] When Flores arrived in office, there were three major proposals being circulated that attempted to address these problems: ANEP's *Manifesto*, FUSADES's *Crecimiento con participación*, and the CND's *Plan de nación*.

ANEP'S MANIFESTO

Business leaders complained about the lack of openness and transparency in the privatization process, as well as the effects of that process on the financial industry. Juan Héctor Vidal, the former executive director of the National Association of Private Enterprise (ANEP), believed that the lack of transparency and competition was slowly strangling the potential for the productive sectors in society by limiting access to credit and charging unusually high interest rates.[49]

I think we didn't take advantage of privatization to promote competition and to take advantage of this privatization process to open the opportunities for more people who could invest in the shares as a product of the privatization. [Ineffective policies] have been the cause of the emergence of some kind of monopolies or illegal holdings that at this moment are affecting the possibility of the country to create wider space for openness, to accelerate the economic process to the extent that some groups control the financial system.[50]

The Association of Medium and Small Salvadoran Businesses (AMPES) also claimed that restricted access to credit had been harmful to small-business owners. In 1996, ANEP unveiled its *Manifesto,* criticizing the policies of the Calderón Sol administration and offering a plan for long-term development. The plan focused on increased domestic savings, reduced dependence on remittances, increased educational spending, reduction or partial elimination of the value-added tax (IVA), regional integration to increase competitiveness, and sustainable development. Ironically, the ANEP plan also expressed a desire to create an alliance between business and labor. This, after the business community, with the aid of Cristiani, essentially eliminated the Foro, which was created by the peace accords for that express purpose. The plan also focused on environmental protection and sustainable development as key components of any economic program.

ANEP offered a second proposal in advance of the 2000 elections, focusing on the modernization of the state. The plan also supported the reactivation of various sectors of the Salvadoran economy, including agriculture, construction, tourism, and small business.[51] In fact, the ANEP proposal shared numerous similarities with the FMLN's 1997 program, including alleviation of poverty, environmental protection, strengthened democracy, increased national savings, and the promotion of agriculture and industry.[52] In the days preceding the 2000 elections, ANEP's president stated that while they were not with the FMLN, they agree and support their criticisms of the current model. According to former ANEP president Vidal, "Sometimes I retain better relations with the opposition than with ARENA."[53]

FUSADES: CRECIMIENTO CON PARTICIPACIÓN

When Cristiani became president, in 1989, he adopted the policy recommendations of FUSADES as his own. When he left office, the organization could no longer assume that its recommendations would be accepted with no reservations. While neither Calderón Sol nor Flores had Cristiani's links to FUSADES, the organization still had significant influence within ARENA. Cristiani remained as the chair of ARENA's national executive committee, COENA, until being forced to step down following the 2000 elections. In 1999 FUSADES published its economic proposal, *Crecimiento con participación: Una estrategia de desarrollo para el siglo XXI,* and offered it to the newly installed Flores government. The proposal, directed by Chilean economist Sebastian Edwards, focused on increases in rural education and health spending, decreased government spending, increased savings, elimination of subsidies on diesel and other fuels, and improvements in tax collection. The proposal also called on the Flores government to accelerate the privatization process, which had been halted in 1998. According to one FUSADES economist, tension between FUSADES and successive ARENA administrations was driven by the government's failure to modernize the state apparatus in concert with its economic policies.[54]

THE CND'S PLAN DE NACIÓN

Unlike the ANEP and FUSADES proposals, the National Development Commission (CND) was a broad-based organization composed of representatives from government, business, NGOs and other community organizations, and citizens. The CND was initiated by President Armando Calderón Sol in 1997 at the behest of the IDB, which insisted on an economic proposal that included citizen participation.[55] The announcement of the creation of the CND also followed very closely on the heels of losses for ARENA in the 1997 legislative and municipal elections. Thirty-nine institutions, including NGOs from the Right and Left, business organizations, and regional institutions, provided resources to support the project. In 1998 and 1999 the CND conducted meetings in each of El Salvador's fourteen departments to determine the greatest areas of concern and potential solutions for the individual departments. In total, there were fifty-two workshops and fourteen departmental assemblies.[56] The CND presented its findings in 1999 in the *Plan de nación,* emphasizing regional development, decentralization, reactivation of the productive sectors, and Central American integration.[57]

One of the most crucial aspects that differentiated the *Plan de nación* from the other proposals was its emphasis on citizen participation. The series of meetings in each department provided the opportunity for citizens to express their thoughts on development priorities within the departments. As such, the plan was El Salvador's most comprehensive and inclusive development proposal. Nine of the fourteen departments claimed unemployment as the top priority of any development plan (see table 4.5). Crime, public insecurity, and poverty were also major concerns. Some departments, particularly FMLN strongholds during the war such as Morazán and Chalatenango, complained of marginalization and lack of investment.

TABLE 4.5
Prioritization of problems by department

Department	First	Second	Third
Ahuachapán	Unemployment	Reduced citizen participation	
Cabañas	Unemployment	Poverty	Loss of natural resources
Chalatenango	Unemployment	Deforestation	Departmental marginalization
Cuscatlán	Precarious economic and social situation	Failure to support agriculture	Crime
La Libertad	Lack and deterioration of roadways	Public insecurity	Unemployment
La Paz	Unemployment	Poverty	Public insecurity
La Unión	Departmental marginalization	Poor roads and means of communication	No economic or social investment
Morazán	Unemployment	Extreme poverty	Departmental marginalization
San Miguel	Reduction in farming, industry, and other economic activities	Public insecurity and crime	
San Salvador	Unemployment	Inadequate education system	Concentration of power and resources
San Vicente	Unemployment		
Santa Ana	Crime	Poor access and quality of education	
Sonsonate	Unemployment		
Usulután	Unemployment	Poverty	

Source: El Salvador, Comisión Nacional de Desarrollo, *Bases para el plan de nación* (San Salvador: CND, 1999).

The proposals for departmental development are outlined in table 4.6. Nearly half of all departments (six of fourteen) listed the development or reactivation of agriculture as key to departmental development. This is particularly noteworthy because it has been a key component in the FMLN, ANEP, and FUSADES plans. Additionally, eight departments believed that the development of tourism would benefit departmental development. Six departments listed construction and improvements of highways as key components of their development. Some, including Cuscatlán, Santa Ana, and San Salvador, specifically cited citizen participation as the cornerstone to any development plan. La Unión, which complained of departmental marginalization and a lack of social and economic investment, emphasized decentralization and the role of local government in the development process. Interestingly, only one of the forty-two proposals mentioned free trade zones.

By tapping into citizen participation, one of the most underused resources in the country, the CND was able to offer one of the most sweeping development proposals to date. What was perhaps most striking about the CND plan was the broad definition applied to development when compared to the FUSADES and ANEP plans. However, when the CND plan was presented to the government, in October 1999, it received a tepid response from the Flores administration, which claimed to have its own plan for economic development.[58] Days later, and after much criticism, Flores said he supported the plan but called on individuals to implement it on their own. For many, it was further evidence of the chasm between government policies and citizen needs. Many questioned the message that was sent by the government encouragement of citizen participation followed by the dismissal of the results. "What do you suppose happens when you invite someone to participate [in the planning] but don't listen to them?" asked Roberto Cañas. "Do you think they will participate again?"[59]

THE FMLN'S 2000–2003 LEGISLATIVE PROGRAM

The FMLN's 2000–2003 legislative program, while short on technical merit, shared some attributes with the aforementioned ANEP, FUSADES, and CND plans. All promoted increases in spending on education and health care, citizen participation, and reduction of the fiscal deficit. Like the ANEP plan, the FMLN supported the reduction of the IVA to 10 percent, favored protection of some productive sectors, and opposed the convertibility policy

TABLE 4.6

Top three development proposals by department

Department	First	Second	Third
Ahuachapán	Development and diversification of agriculture	Construction of highways	Tourism
Cabañas	Construction of highways	Development of tourism	Development of agriculture
Chalatenango	Economic and social compensation for Lempa River region	Development and diversification of agriculture	
Cuscatlán	Diversification of agriculture	Organization of citizens to develop and negotiate a plan of development	Tourism
La Libertad	Reactivation of the harbor; agriculture	Development of tourism	Construction and improvement of roadways
La Paz	Development of tourism	Reactivation of agriculture	Education; practice of values
La Unión	Improvement and construction of highways	Strengthening of local government	Involution
Morazán	Construction of highways	Development of industry	Development of agriculture
San Miguel	Attention to youth	Enhanced sectoral organization	Decentralization of the state
San Salvador	Government support for the productive sector	National policy of employment	Prioritization of national proposal for education
San Vicente	Development and growth of agriculture, artisans, and tourism	Municipal alliances enhancement of	Development and communications
Santa Ana	Organization; citizen participation	Education; family communication	
Sonsonate	Reactivation of agriculture	Development of tourism	Establishment of free-trade zones
Usulután	Reactivation of farming	Development of tourism	Construction of highways

Source: El Salvador, Comisión Nacional de Desarrollo, *Bases para el plan de nación* (San Salvador: CND, 1999).

on the grounds that it contributed to the overvaluation of the colón. Like the CND plan, the FMLN plan supported decentralization. However, the FMLN plan varied dramatically from the others in the role that it prescribed to the state to manage the economy. The FMLN's plan advocated the suspension of privatization along with the creation of mechanisms to guarantee the functioning of the market. The program also proposed that the Central Bank set a ceiling for interest rates at 15 percent and that the state be required to purchase 30 percent of its goods and services from micro, small, and medium-size businesses. It also called on the state to regulate utilities, subsidize water consumption for lower-income families, and increase spending on health care. The FMLN supported decentralization through an allocation of 10 percent of the national budget to municipal governments, an increase from the 6 percent allocated in 1997. Critics claimed the FMLN's program failed to offer much in the way of funding these proposals and, while the program supported access to credit for small and medium businesses, there was little in the proposal that would generate much-needed growth. Further, the platform reinforced the Right's contention that the FMLN was antimarket, and was labeled "populist" in one critique of the platform.[60]

PRIVATIZATION AND DOLLARIZATION

The Salvadoran economy stalled under the Flores administration, and the tension over the neoliberal model peaked during his tenure. The defining feature of the Flores administration was the continuing retraction of the state from the public sphere. In addition to the elimination of exemptions from the IVA, Flores also eliminated utility subsidies and increased taxes on microenterprise and small business. Economic growth slowed considerably during his administration (see table 4.7), and his major economic initiatives were met with widespread public resistance. Of these, the proposed privatization of the health care system (discussed in chapter 3) and dollarization were the most contentious.

TABLE 4.7

Growth of gross domestic product, 1999–2007 (percent)

1999	2000	2002	2003	2004	2005	2006	2007
3.4	2.0	2.3	2.3	1.8	2.8	4.2	4.7

Source: Banco Central de Reserva de El Salvador (BCR), *Indicadores económicos, Indicadores económicos 2002–2006*, and *Memoria de labores 2007*.

While plans to dollarize the economy had been in the works since the Calderón Sol administration, it was Flores who succeeded in dollarization. El Salvador's colón had been pegged to the U.S. dollar since 1994 at a rate of 8.75 to 1. Flores announced his intent to dollarize the economy in November 2000. The Law of Monetary Integration passed only a week later, despite FMLN protests. The law went into effect on January 1, 2001. There was very little pubic debate on the policy, and little information was provided to the public as dollars went into circulation.[61] According to Manuel Hinds, the chief architect of the policy, part of the goal was to prevent future administrations from devaluing the currency—particularly in response to demands from coffee growers that wages were too high. Dollarization would force antiquated sectors to modernize and break the influence of the oligarchy.[62] While one of the primary positive effects of dollarization was supposed to be the reduction of interest rates, critics argued that the country was not experiencing high interest rates at the time of dollarization.[63] Former minister of the economy Arturo Zablah described it as "a cure for a disease we didn't have." One of the side effects of dollarization was the phenomenon of "rounding up" prices by vendors, which created inflation for the poorer consumers.[64] The two powerful earthquakes that struck El Salvador in January and February 2001, which caused an estimated $3 billion in damage and left tens of thousands homeless, exacerbated the immediate effects of dollarization among the affected poor.

REMITTANCES: THE NEW FOUNDATION OF THE SALVADORAN ECONOMY

Remittances continued to play a very important role in sustaining the Salvadoran economy during the Flores years. The dramatic increase in remittances throughout the 1990s helped sustain the economy during a period of stagnation. By 2000, remittances totaled $1.75 billion, nearly 50 percent of exports and 13 percent of GDP.

TABLE 4.8

Annual remittances, 1991–2000 (millions of U.S. dollars)

1991	1992	1993	1994	1995	1996	1997	1998	1999	2000
790	858	864	963	1,061	1,086	1,200	1,285	1,350	1,751

Source: Central Reserve Bank of El Salvador.

Note: The Central Bank's account of remittances includes only remittances tracked by official channels. By some estimates, actual remittance figures may be as much as 15 percent more than official estimates.

Some argued that remittances may have reduced opposition to the neo-liberal reforms.[65] This sentiment was echoed by FUNDE economist Roberto Rubio:

> I think there are symptoms of social conflict manifested by the social security crisis. This government [Flores's] has beaten the world record for strikes. I think they had nine conflicts. If we continue with the same economic situation, the social condition will not be the same. Because this [crisis] means a deterioration, we will be having more problems. There will be more social pressures, but because the movement is weak, the money coming in plays the role of a buffer. Maybe that's why there hasn't been a social explosion, like in Brazil, where they robbed supermarkets, or in Guatemala, where people run to the streets when the price of transport goes up. Here there is some social response, but it is very weak.[66]

Thus, cuts in social spending, unemployment, and inflation were partially ameliorated by the influx of remittances. One analyst likened the situation to "a pressure cooker with a leak that stops it from bursting."[67]

In addition to offsetting the costs of adjustment and a stagnant economy, remittances stimulated the growth of businesses in the formal and informal sectors. Salvadoran banks opened branches in U.S. cities with large Salvadoran populations such as Los Angeles and Washington, D.C., which both eased the transfer of remittances and generated fees for the banks—banks owned by the same individuals who created the economy that made mass migration a necessary evil for many Salvadorans. Former president Cristiani's bank, Banco Cuscatlán, reportedly processed as much as one-third of the remittance market, while Banco Agrícola handled about 12 percent of the market.[68] Telecommunications companies and regional airlines, like TACA, also expanded their services.[69] Salvadorans contracted *viajeros*, or couriers, to transport goods and money between the United States and El Salvador. Viajeros represented only one form of what Patricia Landolt, Lilian Autler, and Sonia Baires refer to as entrepreneurs of the new migrant economy.[70] New shopping malls, such as La Gran Vía owned by the Siman family, provided opportunities for Salvadorans to spend their remittances. Thus, remittances were fueling development in the absence of any coordinated development policy.

Antonio Elias Saca (2004–9): Neoliberal Populism

The Saca administration's economic policy continued ARENA's policies, although his policies could best be described as reinforcing rather than deepening the model. Saca, a former president of ANEP, inherited a stagnant economy, growing public debt, and popular dissatisfaction with the economy. El Salvador's public debt increased substantially under Francisco Flores; most startling was the increase in external debt, which had grown from $2,789 million to $4,780 during his tenure.[71] By 2004 the external debt exceeded 38 percent of GNP, the maximum level acceptable by International Monetary Fund standards.[72] The rhetoric behind Saca's economic program focused on programs designed to alleviate these problems. Saca's economic program was not as clearly defined as those of the previous three administrations, and it suggested a curious blend of neoliberalism and populism. While he openly embraced the ratification of CAFTA, he also appealed to the party's poor, rural base with antipoverty programs and promises of tax reform. Saca's philosophical differences with his predecessors were reflective of the differences between FUSADES and ANEP; the former being more transnational in its orientation and the latter being more focused on domestic business interests.[73] His slogan, Growth with a Human Touch, was a play on similar repackaging of neoliberal reforms by international financial institutions at that time.

Saca, whose election campaign focused on his abilities to maintain good relations with the United States and guarantee the continued flow of remittances, reiterated Flores's commitment to the Central America Free Trade Agreement (CAFTA). On December 18, 2004, El Salvador became the first Central American country to ratify CAFTA; the measure passed with forty-nine of eighty-four votes. The agreement went into effect March 1, 2006. As with dollarization, there was little public discourse or consultation on the issue. The chaotic nature of the vote on CAFTA, as detailed by Rose Spalding, highlights the extent to which the legislation was rushed to a vote for political expediency.[74] Critics of the trade agreement, known in El Salvador by the acronym TLC (Tratado de Libre Comercio), argued that there were insufficient provisions to protect labor and the environment and that the country's dwindling agricultural sector would not be able to compete with the United States.[75] Corresponding legislation, such as laws pertaining to intellectual property rights, often resulted in violent protests, particularly among vendors in the informal sectors.

Saca's antipoverty plan consisted of five programs: a Common Health Fund (FOSALUD), Red Solidaria, Jóvenes, Conéctate, and Microcrédito. Of these, the two most ambitious were FOSALUD and Red Solidaria. In an effort to meet the United Nations' Millennium Development Goals, Red Solidaria targeted the one hundred poorest municipalities in the country, with the intention of increasing access to education, health, and nutrition. Additionally, the program sought to improve women's autonomy by directing payments to the female head of households. FOSALUD was approved eighty-four to seventy-eight by the Legislative Assembly in December 2004. Although the program and its funding were not as comprehensive as the FMLN and other center-left parties hoped for, many believed it was a step in the right direction. The program was funded, in part, through a "sin tax" on cigarettes, alcohol, and firearms. The program proposed to create fifty new twenty-four-hour health clinics throughout the country. Saca also signed a compact with the Millennium Challenge Corporation (MCC, referred to as FOMILENIO in El Salvador) in 2007. The five-year agreement delivered $461 million in investment and poverty reduction. Half the funding was devoted to roadways, while the other half went to the agricultural sector, community development, and other projects.[76] Despite Saca's emphasis on eradicating poverty and generating growth, Salvadorans had a decidedly bleak perception of his tenure. In a 2008 IUDOP survey 80 percent of respondents believed the economy had grown worse under Saca, and a sizable majority (62.4 percent) said that Saca's social programs had done little to combat poverty.[77] In fact, nearly 70 percent said poverty was worse in 2007 than the previous year. In a poll the previous year, more than half of respondents said that the *Red Solidaria* campaign was merely propaganda.[78] The continuing and dramatic increase of remittances had little bearing on Salvadorans' perceptions of the economy, as they became increasingly concerned that the economic downturn in the United States would have an impact on remittances.[79]

One of the greatest problems faced by Saca was how to fund these programs. The lack of economic growth, growing public debt, and limited tax revenues complicated any proposed increase in public spending. El Salvador's highly regressive tax structure placed a significant burden on the poor and middle classes while sparing the country's wealthy. The IVA (value-added tax) was the single largest source of tax revenue for the Salvadoran government (see table 4.9). Although previous governments withstood pressure from international financial institutions to increase tax revenues, it became increasingly clear that some type of reform would be necessary to offset the mounting public deficit.[80] Saca's modest reform proposal was met with protest by ANEP and the business community, which insisted that any increase in taxes would limit investment.[81] In the end, Saca's tax reform consisted only of measures targeting and punishing tax evasion. The FMLN refused to vote on the bill after its own proposal, which proposed shifting the tax burden away from the IVA and to those in higher income brackets, was quickly dismissed. Although income tax revenues increased during the 2006 fiscal year, the IVA continued to represent approximately 50 percent of El Salvador's total tax revenues. Additionally, it was anticipated that CAFTA would reduce the revenues derived from customs duties in the future. The availability, or lack thereof, of tax revenues had a significant impact on public expenditures. El Salvador had one of the lowest rates of government expenditure on education and health care expenditure in the region, increasing from 1.8 percent in 1991 to a mere 2.8 percent of GDP in 2005. Health care expenditures in 2005 were 3.4 percent of GDP.[82] Expenditures on health and education as a percentage of GDP were greater during the height of the war than during the peace.[83]

TABLE 4.9

Selected tax source revenues, 1995–2011 (millions of U.S. dollars)

Year	Taxes (total)	Income tax	Custom duties	Value-added tax
1995	1,079	301	199	470
1996	1,096	305	163	541
1997	1,149	323	146	593
1998	1,228	351	146	650
1999	1,275	393	148	669
2000	1,344	429	141	714
2001	1,449	431	146	809
2002	1,746	457	155	837
2003	1,916	503	178	911
2004	2,048	534	177	952
2005	2,259	668	181	1,104
2006	2,647	788	200	1,308
2007	2,724	933	204	1,389
2008	2,886	1,004	179	1,460
2009	2,609	949	138	1,521
2010	2,883	996	150	1,432
2011	3,193	1,127	167	1,547

Source: Central Reserve Bank of El Salvador.

In 2006 remittances exceeded $3.3 billion, almost 20 percent of GDP. According to the UNDP, 80 percent of remittances were used for consumables (primarily food) while another 11 percent were used for education and medical expenses.[84] The study found, however, that remittances had little to no impact on issues affecting long-term development, such as levels of education.[85] Additionally, only a small portion of remittances went to savings or investment, presumably because recipients directed those resources toward meeting basic needs. As a result, remittances drove up consumption rates. In a 2010 report, the UNDP revealed that El Salvador had one of the world's highest consumption rates.

TABLE 4.10

Annual remittances, 2000–2009 (billions of U.S. dollars)

2000	2001	2002	2003	2004	2005	2006	2007	2008	2009
1.751	1.911	1.935	2.105	2.548	2.830	3.316	3.695	3.831	3.465

Source: Central Reserve Bank of El Salvador.

In addition to offsetting the costs of structural adjustment, remittances have played a key role in alleviating both poverty and inequality among recipients.[86] In 2008 migrant remittances totaled $3.8 billion, approximately 17 percent of GDP. Approximately one-quarter of Salvadoran households relied on remittances.[87] The municipalities with the greatest number of households receiving remittances were located in the north and east of the country, primarily in Cabañas, La Unión, Morazán, and San Miguel—among them some of the departments most affected by the war. Salvadorans increasingly viewed migration as an employment opportunity. In a 2005 IUDOP survey, 53.6 percent said they had an immediate relative living in the United States. Nearly 48 percent of respondents indicated that they wanted to leave El Salvador, primarily to improve their economic situation or find work.[88] Remittances played a significant role in alleviating poverty. The UNDP study estimated that remittances reduced the national poverty level by 7 percent. The poverty rate among nonrecipients was 11 percent higher than recipients, while the number of nonrecipients living in extreme poverty was more than twice that of recipients. Recipients lived in better conditions; they were more likely to have homes made from modern building materials and to have electricity and running water in the home.[89] There was conflicting evidence as to whether remittances had a positive impact on school enrollments. A UNDP study found that remittances had a positive effect on school enrollments for younger children, while a 2010 study by Pablo Acosta found that there was virtually no significant impact on schooling.[90] That same study found that girls benefited from remittances more than boys and that they were almost eleven times more likely to stay in school than girls whose families did not receive remittances.[91] Curiously, one observation was that students who completed their education were also more likely to migrate in search of better opportunities.[92] Remittances also reduced inequality among recipients. The Gini coefficient for those who received remittances was 0.44, as opposed to 0.52 for nonrecipients.[93]

Despite their continued increase, it was clear that remittances had difficulty keeping pace with El Salvador's rising cost of living. Beginning in 2004 there was a steady increase in consumer prices, particularly for food, health costs, and transportation, which resulted in increased poverty rates in 2006 and 2007.[94] Despite minimum-wage increases for industrial workers in 1998, 2003, and 2006, and for agricultural workers in 1998 and 2006, real wages were still lower than their 1995 levels—and before the war. This was compounded by an almost 20 percent increase in bus fares and 14 percent increase in electricity

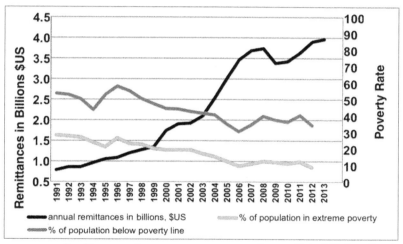

FIGURE 4.1. Remittances and poverty rates, 1991–2013. *Sources:* United Nations Development Program (UNDP); Dirección General de Estadística y Censos (DIGESTYC); Encuesta de Hogares de Propósitos Múltiples (EHPM); Banco Central de Reserva de El Salvador (BCR), all various years.

rates.[95] In 2006, Saca announced minimum-wage increases of 10 percent for those in the industrial and commercial sectors and 4 percent for maquila workers, but it was insufficient to keep up with the rising cost of living. Additionally, the increase had no impact for the 50 percent of the population employed in the informal sector. In a 2008 IUDOP poll, 82.2 percent said the cost of living had increased significantly during the past year. Half of all respondents (50.3 percent) attributed the increases to dollarization, while 17.8 percent cited unemployment. Only 13.3 percent cited the price of petroleum.[96] Growing public discontent and the inability of ARENA's programs to generate growth translated into votes against ARENA in 2009.

Mauricio Funes (2009-14): An Economy in Crisis

Mauricio Funes, the first non-ARENA president, assumed office during the worst economy since the end of the war. The global recession of 2008-9 had a significant, negative impact on the Salvadoran economy. The economy contracted 3.1 percent in 2009 as a result of the crisis, and its recovery remained stalled by low growth even after other economies in the region began to improve. El Salvador's postrecession economy has had the lowest rates of growth in Central America. In 2013, Nicaragua experienced 4.6 percent growth and Guatemala grew 3.7 percent. Even struggling Honduras mustered more than 3 percent growth. Additionally, remittances declined 11 percent in 2009 and did not return to precrisis levels until 2012. By 2013 remittances reached $3.969 billion, almost 16 percent of GDP.

TABLE 4.11

Growth of gross domestic product, 2008-13 (percent)

2008	2009	2010	2011	2012	2013
1.3	-3.1	1.4	2.2	1.9	1.7

Source: Central Reserve Bank of El Salvador.

Funes's Anti-Crisis Plan included several social programs designed to target the country's most vulnerable populations. Among the most popular were those aimed at improving access to education through free school uniforms, lunches, and school supplies, as well as the creation of low-income housing and pensions for seniors. There was also Plan de Agricultura Familiar, which targeted noncommercial, family farms. One controversial aspect of the program was the distribution of seed packages by the Ministry of Agriculture, which FUSADES, ARENA, and the U.S. embassy argued violated CAFTA rules on competition for the provision of goods and services.[97] The opposition was not surprising given the transnational interests of El Salvador's elites. In 2008 Monsanto purchased Semillas Cristiani Burkard, a leading Central American seed company, for an undisclosed sum.[98]

It was of little surprise that Funes frequently sought to placate the business sector, whose influence often exceeded that of elected officials. As one FMLN deputy once admitted, "No party can govern in this country without the private sector."[99] Funes attempted to maintain open communications with ANEP in a bid to reassure them that there would be no significant changes to the structure of the economy. Funes established the National Council for Growth as a forum for dialogue between the administration and the business sector, but even the most modest proposals were met with bitter resistance by ANEP, which often accused Funes of trying to turn El Salvador into another Venezuela.[100] In fact, despite the FMLN's long-held support for redistribution policies, de-dollarization, and its opposition to CAFTA, Funes's broader economic policy varied relatively little from those of his predecessors. While some of this may have been philosophical, much of Funes's economic policy was restrained by twenty years of ARENA policy, the country's dependence on the United States, and the realties of the global market. Remittances continued to grow throughout Funes's term, exceeding $4 billion for the first time in 2014.

TABLE 4.12

Annual remittances, 2010–14 (billions of U.S. dollars)

2010	2011	2012	2013	2014
3.539	3.648	3.91	3.969	4.217

Source: Central Reserve Bank of El Salvador.

In 2011, El Salvador became one of only four countries in the world to sign an agreement with the United States called the Partnership for Growth (PFG). The goal of the program is to help countries identify barriers to growth and address a plan to address those barriers.[101] It was determined that the country's two chief barriers were crime and insecurity and low productivity in tradables. In 2010, El Salvador had the lowest level of foreign investment in

Central America; it had plummeted during the recession after an increase from 2006–8. For every dollar that entered the country, almost four went abroad.[102] The program underscored U.S. and private-sector influence on Salvadoran policy. The United States required El Salvador to pass a law on public-private partnerships, cowritten by the United States, the IMF, and the Funes administration before agreeing to a second distribution of MCC funds.[103] In 2013 the administration introduced a Public-Private Partnership Law. One of the more controversial aspects of the original bill would have permitted the Salvadoran government to privatize public services and natural resources.[104] The FMLN succeeded in excluding many public services from privatization from the final bill. The law passed in 2013 with almost unanimous support in the legislature.

One key area where Funes differed from his predecessors was on tax reform. In 2008, 10 percent of the poorest households paid 30 percent of their income to taxes while the richest 10 percent paid only 11 percent of their earnings. The regressive nature of the tax system had long been a problem, but the business sector had always succeeded in defeating even modest reforms. Additionally, income tax burden was among the lowest in the Americas. Evasion among some of El Salvador's largest companies was egregious. One prominent example is mobile phone company Tigo, which paid only $500 in taxes in 2008 despite reported earnings of more than $450 million.[105] In 2011, Funes proposed a progressive income tax system, which the administration hoped would create $150 million in new revenue. The legislation enjoyed broad support in the assembly; only ARENA deputies voted against it. Those earning less than $503 per month would pay no taxes, while those making more than $6,200 would pay 30 percent.[106] The new tax law created more tensions between Funes and ANEP, which threatened both capital flight and shifting increased costs to consumers and workers. While income tax revenues did increase, the IVA remained the largest source of tax revenue. The reforms represented significant progress, but there was still much work to be done.

Corruption

Corruption is a problem for any state, but it poses particular challenges for peacebuilding as states in transition are particularly vulnerable to capture. It undermines rule of law, government effectiveness, economic growth, and it reinforces impunity. Additionally, corruption may reduce public trust in institutions and actors, thereby limiting state legitimacy at a critical juncture.[107]

There are few indicators that offer more compelling evidence of capture than corruption.[108] Yet, because of the hidden nature of corruption, it is often difficult to uncover—let alone measure. We do know from some widely exposed cases and anecdotal evidence that corruption has been a serious problem across administrations in postwar El Salvador, though its legacy far precedes the war. Until recently, few instances of corruption were investigated—even fewer were prosecuted. For twenty years, ARENA and its allies dominated some of the most important institutions for detecting and prosecuting corruption. The Court of Accounts, which oversees the use of public funds, was dominated by the PCN for much of the postwar period—a reward for supporting ARENA in the legislature. Supreme Court justices and the attorney general's office were also full of political appointees, again a result of ARENA's fruitful alliances with smaller, center-right parties. It's worth noting, however, that Funes's Amigos also had significant influence over his administration's policies and appointments. Corruption and impunity have undermined political and economic development. The lack of transparency in the formulation of economic policy, as best exemplified by the irregularities in bank privatization, has been common across administrations in postwar El Salvador.

El Salvador's Corruption Perceptions Index score has ranged between 3.4 and 4.2 from 1998 through 2011.[109] World Governance Indicators for Control of Corruption reflected some modest improvement between 2012 and 2013. Perceptions of corruption worsened during the Flores administration, the later years of the Saca administration, and the early years of the Funes administration (see fig. 4.2).

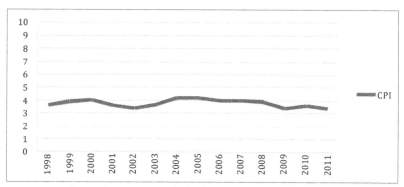

FIGURE 4.2. Corruption perception index (CPI) scores, 1998–2011. *Source:* Transparency International, Corruption Perception Index, various years.

A 2004 poll of Salvadoran businessmen from various sectors of the economy revealed what many Salvadorans had long believed: that corruption was rampant. Institutions were regarded as inefficient (the judiciary) and politicized (Court of Accounts), with indications that the law was only selectively applied. Respondents also complained of favoritism toward certain sectors of the economy, particularly construction, and in the awarding of contracts. One of the most interesting findings was in regard to policymaking. When asked who decided economic policy, half the respondents said "big business," as opposed to the 33.7 percent that believed it was the power of the president and his cabinet and the 5.2 percent that answered "deputies."[110] This study reinforced what I learned in numerous interviews with businessmen, that the lack of transparency by the government undermined the existence of a truly competitive market and that the state is essentially an extension of a very powerful business sector.[111] While there are too many instances of corruption to discuss here, several high-profile cases reveal the extent to which elites, including presidents, used public resources for their own enrichment.

In July 1997 it was discovered that the director of two financial-services companies—Inversiones, Seguras y Productivas (INSEPRO) and Financiera de Inversiones, Seguras y Productivas (FINSEPRO)—had embezzled more than $115 million (though some reports suggested it was more than twice that amount) from unsuspecting, and mostly elderly, clients.[112] The funds were diverted into businesses owned by Roberto Mathies Hill, the owner of INSEPRO and FINSEPRO. Mathies Hill, a member of one of El Salvador's wealthy coffee families, was the chair of ARENA's business sector at the time.[113] The names of those arrested read like a who's who of the country's business elites.[114] The scandal underscored the incestuous nature of the country's business elites, the financial sector, and government. The president of El Salvador's Central Reserve Bank, Roberto Orellana Milla, was the director of several businesses owned by Mathies Hill. He also happened to be one of the chief architects of Cristiani's economic policy. The FMLN, using its newfound power in the assembly, succeeded not only at having him appear before the Financial Affairs Committee to answer questions but also in compelling a vote to recommend his resignation. After a four-year investigation, Mathies Hill's trial and the rendering of the verdict took only two days. He was acquitted, as were most of the more than twenty others implicated in the scandal.[115] It was just one of several corruption scandals in the 1990s in which it is also believed that the courts protected economic elites.[116]

Corruption was also rife in state utilities. In 2002, Carlos Perla, former president of National Administration of Aqueducts and Sewers (ANDA), was accused of various acts of corruption in his capacity as the state utility's chief administrator. Perla, who was appointed by Calderón Sol in 1994, was accused of using ANDA funds to build a luxury home. He fled to France, insisting that he was being politically persecuted, but was extradited in 2003. In 2007 he was sentenced to fifteen years in prison for embezzlement.[117] In 2013 twenty-one former members of the Flores administration were accused of embezzlement in connection with a 2001 joint venture between CEL (Executive Hydroelectric Commission of the Lempa River) and Italian energy company Enel (now LaGeo). The attorney general's office alleged that the contract between CEL and Enel which resulted in Enel becoming the majority shareholder, was tantamount to "backdoor privatization" of the country's geothermal sector and had deprived the state of millions of dollars. Among the accused were Flores's minister of the economy Miguel Lacayo Argüello; Guillermo Sol Bang, former president of CEL and former party treasurer for ARENA; Jorge José Simán Zablah, former LaGeo president and a founding member of FUSADES; José Antonio Rodríguez Rivas, the former director of LaGeo and brother-in-law of President Flores; and Tom Hawk, former director of ARENA's business sector and a member of the party's political commission.[118] Amid a crumbling case and accusations of a political bias, the prosecutor withdrew charges in July 2015.[119] Also in 2013, fifteen people, including several Saca appointees, were arrested on corruption charges related to the construction of Diego de Holguín Boulevard. Renamed Monseñor Romero Boulevard in 2012, the cost exceeded the original budget by more than $100 million and took more than five years to complete.[120]

Recent allegations of corruption against past presidents have also surfaced. Allegations of corruption dogged the Saca administration. Saca was expelled from ARENA following the 2009 elections on charges that he had rigged the primary elections for the 2009 presidential nominee, misspent $219 million in government funds, used his political power to promote laws or selectively enforce laws that would benefit his business interests, used government monies to bribe deputies in the legislative assembly, and threatened local officials to support his candidates.[121] His accumulation of wealth while he was in office was substantial. According to *El Faro*, Saca's net worth grew from $197,000 between 1998 and

2003 to $3 million in 2007 and $10.5 million in 2009.[122] In the days before his departure from office, allegations of cronyism and corruption surfaced against President Funes, who had been an outspoken critic of ARENA's corruption.[123] But it was the case against former president Francisco Flores that drew the most attention. In October 2013 it was announced that Flores was being investigated for embezzling a $15 million donation from the Taiwanese government that had been intended for earthquake relief. In an appearance before a congressional panel in January 2014, Flores denied that the funds were for his personal use. Flores apparently tried to leave the country during the hearings, only to flee later to Panama.[124] In May 2014 the government issued a warrant for his arrest on charges of embezzlement, illegal enrichment, and disobedience. To date he is the only Salvadoran head of state to be officially charged with any crimes. In September 2014, Flores surrendered to Salvadoran authorities. He was initially placed under house arrest, which resulted in protests. Days later the criminal court overturned house arrest and sent him to a high-security prison, where he stayed for two months until he was returned to house arrest due to health reasons. At the time of this writing, a determination on his trial is pending.

Capture and the Economics of Exclusion

To some extent, there was nothing new about El Salvador's neoliberal era. Policies that protected, and in fact promoted, elite interest had been evident in the country since the late nineteenth century. Many Salvadorans hoped that would change after the war, but instead discovered that postwar economic policy was merely old wine in new wineskins. The application of the neoliberal model by four successive ARENA administrations was a source of contentious debate between those that argued that free-market reforms would generate growth and those that believed that a vital role still remained for the state in redressing socioeconomic problems. While the FMLN eventually succeeded in slowing the process of privatization, it was unable to halt the application of other policies. Additionally, traditional, agricultural elites who did not benefit from the privatization process, as well as some within the private sector, challenged ARENA's application of the neoliberal model as being anticapitalist and patrimonial. The lack of transparency in the application of the neoliberal model under the Cristiani and Calderón Sol administrations enriched the few and drew the ire of both the agrarian elites and the business sector. The contentious politics of the Flores administration resulted in the period of the country's greatest social unrest, as evidenced by the mass demonstrations against the privatization of the health sector (see chapter 3). Economic stagnation and dollarization disproportionately affected the poor, as did the extension of the IVA to cover food and medicine. Attempts by the Saca administration to address poverty were generally regarded as superficial, albeit an improvement. The rising cost of living and the decline in real wages that characterized his last two years in office were expressions of the model's failure to generate sustainable, equitable growth. Yet, despite mounting evidence that there were serious problems in the economic model, ARENA and its supporters were unwilling to discuss any modifications to the model. Rampant corruption further reinforced that the government designed policy to benefit a select few. The special relationship enjoyed by FUSADES during the Cristiani and ANEP during the Flores and Saca administrations (and perhaps the Friends of Mauricio during the Funes administration) added to the perception that policy was designed to reward leaders and their cronies and punish detractors.

ARENA's policies exacerbated existing socioeconomic tensions and failed to invigorate the economy. The economic growth that initially accompanied the application of the model from 1990 to 1995 declined significantly in 1996 and was stagnant by 2000. The economy is still struggling to recover from the 2008 recession, lagging behind its neighbors. While overall poverty decreased following the end of the war, income concentrations were higher than before the war. While poverty decreased, so did the country's middle class, while the ranks of the "vulnerables" (those living between the middle class and poverty) increased.[125] Absent economic growth or any clear policy to reduce poverty and inequality, it was clear that the sustained influx of remittances, El Salvador's single largest source of foreign exchange, played a significant role in alleviating poverty and inequality, particularly among the rural and urban poor. With coffee on the decline and maquiladoras shifting operations to China and other lower-wage countries, Salvadorans became the country's most valuable export. Their exodus exposed the vulnerability of ARENA's economic policies, which had done little to create a productive economy. Clearly the economic policies imposed since the end of the war had done little to create opportunity or security for the majority of Salvadorans. Economic exclusion, which had been a root cause of the war, persisted during the peace. That exclusion, as we will see in the next chapter, has had profound consequences on Salvadoran society.

Chapter 5

The Politics of Exclusion

Migration, Crime, and Society in the Postwar Era

> Elsewhere people talk about trust, human capital, and
> knowledge but here we talk about feeding our people to
> turn them into little machines—like the witch in Hansel
> and Gretel who feeds the kids so she can eat them.
>
> —Orlando de Sola, 1999[1]

SOCIAL EXCLUSION AND MARGINALIZATION in El Salvador have political
and economic roots that preceded the peace accords. While the peace
accords delivered an end to the civil war, many Salvadorans felt that the
problem of marginalization remained unaltered by the peace process. Many
cited poverty and inequality as evidence of continued exclusion, symptoms
of the captured peace. While some of this was the result of deficiencies in the
peace accords, much of it was also a reflection of the country's deep legacy
of exclusion coupled with a lack of political will to address these problems
in the postaccord environment. Unresolved political rivalries and the
application of neoliberal economic policies contributed to marginalization
of various sectors across Salvadoran society. This growing marginalization
was evidenced by three interrelated phenomena in postwar society: mass
migration, crime and violence, and the ongoing conflict over political space

between civil society and the state. These phenomena were the byproducts of state policy, which had been designed to serve elite interests.

Migration

The phenomenon of migration is not new to El Salvador. The country's land patterns, growing population, and economic development resulted in migration as early as the turn of the twentieth century. While early migration predominately focused on Honduras, some migrants went to the United States in search of work.[2] Industrialization and the decline of the agricultural sector led to an increase in migration to the United States during the 1960s. Still it was not until the onset of the war that Salvadorans began migrating to the United States in large numbers. More than one million Salvadorans left the country in search of refuge during the 1980s, including more than half a million who came to the United States. Salvadorans who migrated to the United States during the war represented a broad cross-section of society, and tended to be more urban and more educated than the general population of El Salvador.[3] Those who could not afford to migrate to the United States went to Mexico and other parts of Central America.[4] The dispersal and dislocation of Salvadorans had a profound impact on the country for years to come.

Unlike Cubans and Nicaraguans who came to the United States during the same time period, Salvadorans were considered by the U.S. government to be principally economic migrants rather than refugees and thus not eligible for asylum.[5] Obviously, admitting that Salvadorans were fleeing a repressive regime would have complicated the continuation of U.S. military aid. Salvadoran refugees established organizations, such as El Rescate and the Central American Resource Center, to assist migrants in securing legal status. The sanctuary movement, a campaign composed of numerous religious denominations, emerged during the 1980s as a powerful advocate for the fair treatment of Salvadorans and other Central Americans seeking asylum in the United States.[6] By 1986 more than four hundred congregations had joined the movement. In addition to providing material aid to refugees, and sometimes smuggling them across the border, the movement also provided legal assistance. However, in 1991 the U.S. district court in San Francisco approved a settlement in one class action suit, *American Baptist Churches v. Thornburgh,* that required the INS to offer asylum hearings to those

Salvadorans and Guatemalans whose prior applications had been denied. It also specified that decisions on individual cases would be made independent of U.S. foreign policy.[7] Salvadorans were able to apply for asylum under the American Baptist Churches (ABC) agreement until January 1, 1996. In the years before the expiration of the agreement, asylum applications increased dramatically. While there were 6,781 applications in 1992 and 14,616 in 1993, the number of applications rose to 75,860 in 1995 and 65,588 in 1996. Still, only a small portion of those (234 in 1995 and 198 in 1996) were granted asylum. It was not until the 1997 Nicaraguan Adjustment and Central American Relief Act that those Salvadorans covered by the ABC agreement were allowed to apply for permanent residence. One notable advance in the interim was the Immigration Act of 1990, which established temporary protected status (TPS). TPS applied to those individuals fleeing countries experiencing ongoing conflict, natural disaster, and "extraordinary and temporary conditions." Under the original timetable, Salvadorans residing in the United States since September 19, 1990, were eligible for TPS, which provided work authorization and prevented them from being deported.

Salvadorans were redesignated for TPS after the 2001 earthquakes. Since that time there have been numerous extensions. The extensions have resulted in massive public-relations campaigns by the Salvadoran government. During the 2002 reregistration push, Francisco Flores recorded television ads and phone messages for Salvadorans living in the United States, reminding them to register, and community organizations and consulates held registration drives.[8] By November 2004 over 290,000 Salvadorans had TPS. During the 2005 TPS reregistration period, Tony Saca traveled to the United States to personally encourage eligible Salvadorans to reregister. The Salvadoran government planned a vigorous registration campaign to ensure immigrants made the deadline. In addition to television ads and recorded messages, the government sent more than 350,000 registration booklets through the mail.[9] The most recent extension allowed eligible Salvadorans to remain in the United States until September 2016. There is no way to predict whether another extension will be granted, but it has become increasingly difficult to explain the extensions under the specifications of TPS. Additionally, while TPS has ensured that hundreds of thousands of Salvadorans can legally live and work in the United States, it has also created a precarious status for Salvadorans living in the United States Not only are the extensions not guaranteed, but those with TPS status are unable to return to El Salvador.[10] The result is a "refugee-like, quasi-documented, non-citizen status" that makes it difficult for those Salvadorans to "belong" to either state.[11]

Migration to the United States increased significantly after the end of the war, prompted by growing crime and a lack of economic opportunities.[12] By some estimates, 20 percent of the Salvadoran-born population lived in the United States.[13] Because most of them were undocumented, precise estimates of the number of Salvadorans currently living in the United States are unavailable. According to the 2000 census, there were 817,336 native-born Salvadorans living in the United States. In 2010 the U.S. Census Bureau estimated that there were almost 1.7 million, an increase of 151.7 percent from 2000. In 2011, Salvadorans became the third-largest group of Latino origin.[14] Most NGOs working with the Salvadoran community estimated the number to be between 2 and 2.5 million. According to the Salvadoran Ministry of Foreign Relations, in 2005 there were more than 3.2 million Salvadorans living outside the country, including more than 2.8 million in the United States. According to their data, the five largest populations were in Los Angeles (800,000), Washington, DC (550,000), New York (340,000), San Francisco (327,000), and Houston (206,500). The only city with more Salvadorans than these cities is San Salvador (1.5 million). For this reason, the United States was widely referred by Salvadorans to as Department 15, a reference to the country's fourteen departments.

While the Salvadoran government had a very distant relationship with the Salvadoran population in the United States during the war, the growing influence of remittances in the economy and increased migration led to efforts to improve ties with the community.[15] In 2002 the Flores administration created the General Directorate for Attention to the Communities Abroad (DGACE) to assist migrants and build ties with the home country. In 2004 the government established the Vice Ministry of Foreign Affairs for Salvadorans Living Abroad. The government also developed a social investment fund, United for Solidarity (Unidos), that provided grants for development projects to municipalities in what Sarah Gammage describes as "state-led engagement with the diaspora."[16] This engagement was facilitated through the development of hometown associations and transnational networks, which played an increasing, albeit limited, role in local development.[17] Unidos, which ended in 2005, was managed by the Social Investment Fund for Local Development (FISDL) and was closely associated with ARENA, which alienated some hometown associations. In fact, ARENA municipalities received significantly more funds than municipalities governed by other parties, which deepened mistrust of the short-lived program.[18]

This mass migration was an important source of support for migrants' families and the Salvadoran economy. Remittances helped offset the costs of structural adjustment and have alleviated both poverty and inequality among recipients (see chapter 4).[19] In 2014 migrant remittances totaled $4.2 billion. Continued migration flows and remittances cemented El Salvador's status as a transnational society and heightened its dependence on the United States. For many, the decision to make the perilous journey to the United States was a necessary one. Rising living costs and depressed wages made it increasingly difficult to survive (see chapter 4). To make the journey, many relied on the use of *coyotes,* essentially smugglers of humans. Coyotes typically charged between $5,000 and $10,000 for their services, which included passage through Guatemala, Mexico, and across the U.S. border. Few Salvadorans could afford such costs and often leveraged possessions, including their homes, to pay for the journey. Those caught returned home with nothing, which necessitated another attempt at the journey to pay their new debts. Some coyotes developed reputations as thieves and thugs, sometimes abandoning migrants or holding them for ransom. Others, however, became local heroes. In March 2006, Narciso "Chicho" Ramírez, a former coyote, was elected mayor of San Francisco Menéndez. Ramírez was well known among his constituents, having smuggled many of their family members abroad.[20]

There were concerns, however, that not all the effects of migration and remittances were positive. First, there was some indication that remittances contributed to a growing divide within Salvadoran society between those who received remittances and those who did not. As evidenced by the UNDP's 2005 study, there were significant disparities in the distribution of remittances across departments and within municipalities. Such disparities added to the sense of exclusion among nonrecipients. Second, there were growing concerns that migration was tearing the social fabric of El Salvador. Studies suggested that migration contributed to the disintegration of the family, which some argued led to an increase in crime and gang membership among youth. Those households receiving remittances were more likely to be single-parent nuclear families or extended families (e.g., grandparents) raising children.[21] Some 40 percent of the children of migrants lived in households without one or both parents, and the uncertainty about when or if they would see their parents again caused many to suffer from depression.[22] As U.S. immigration policies tightened and anti-immigrant rhetoric increased, migrants chose to remain in the United States rather than risk returning to visit or collect loved ones. Some opted to use coyotes to have their children sent to them, a dangerous and worrisome trend.[23] The crisis of unaccompanied minors came to a head in June 2014, when it was revealed that almost fifty thousand children from Central America, including 9,850 Salvadoran youths, had been apprehended by the U.S. Border Patrol within eight months.[24] Finally, others raised concerns that those receiving remittances had become "lazy" and were choosing not to work. Levels of unemployment among heads of households who receive remittances were nearly double the rate for nonrecipients.[25] In a stroke of irony, unwanted jobs in the rural sector were increasingly filled by migrant workers from Nicaragua and Honduras, for whom the wages were significantly higher than at home. By some estimates, as many as two hundred thousand migrants from those countries were working in El Salvador.[26]

Crime and Violence

Empirical evidence clearly demonstrates that social and economic violence are likely to increase in postconflict societies. Explanations for this, while varying and complex, tend to focus on the vacuum left by the period between the demobilization of old police and military forces and the deployment of new forces, as well as the availability of arms.[27] The weakness of other institutions charged with the implementation of the rule of law, particularly the judiciary, also helps create an environment for lawlessness. Additionally, postwar economies are often economies in distress, both from the toll of war and the price of peace. Another less frequently discussed but also important dynamic is the reverse diaspora, which necessitates the reabsorption of returning populations. While existing literature largely addresses the problem from the perspective of the reintegration of refugee populations as a means of preventing future conflict, these populations may also compete for scarce economic resources in vulnerable economies.[28]

The crime wave that began in the 1990s has been characterized by elevated levels of violent crime, particularly homicides. Some of this violence has its roots in historic socioeconomic patterns of inequality and repression that predate the peace accords. Other aspects of the violence can clearly be traced to institutional weaknesses, elite political culture invested in the maintenance of the status quo, and the lack of political will to implement key reforms. In this sense, violence persists due to enduring patterns of political, social, and economic exclusion unremedied by the peace process. As early as January 1993, ONUSAL expressed concerns about the impact of rising crime on democracy: "The widespread perception of insecurity and magnitude of the crime wave may inhibit the feeling of safety that peace was expected to bring, thereby hindering the process—necessary to the consolidation of democracy—of overcoming the culture of fear and intimidation."[29] El Salvador's violence was further exacerbated by the state's policies aimed at controlling violence. The application of repressive and arbitrary anticrime policies resulted in an *increase* in violent crime and undermined popular support of democratic norms essential to the peacebuilding process.

Explaining the Causes of Persistent Violence

Just as there was no single root cause to the war, there is no single explanation for the postwar crime wave that continues to undermine peace, security, and democracy in El Salvador.[30] The main contributors to the ongoing violence, however, were weak institutions, socioeconomic marginalization, a history of using violence to resolve conflicts, and migration patterns.

WEAK INSTITUTIONS AND IMPUNITY

The rapid dissolution of the armed forces and the lack of a transitional security plan resulted in a security gap in postwar El Salvador. The transition from the National Police (PN) to the new National Civilian Police (PNC) force was not without its problems. The government continued to funnel resources into the PN, systematically depriving the new PNC of funds. Additionally, shifting unqualified personnel and entire units of old security agencies into the PNC served to undermine the spirit and letter of the peace accords. Many of those transferred became high-ranking officials within the PNC, and almost half of them would later be investigated for corruption and ties to illicit organizations, including drug trafficking and death squads.[31] Among the transfers was Ricardo Menesses, a former army officer who worked in intelligence, the narcotics division, and was later named director of the PNC, had known ties to José Natividad Pereira "Chepe" Luna, one of the country's most wanted traffickers, who evaded police capture for years based on insider information.[32] Aptly referred to as the PNC's "original sin" by Héctor Silva Ávalos, these transfers not only corrupted the culture and effectiveness of the new police force, but it soon made the state vulnerable to the influence of organized crime.

Few high-ranking officers were ever investigated for their alleged ties to organized crime or other criminal activity. There were the occasional purges, such as those that followed the 1994 bank robbery discussed in chapter 2. Evidence that PNC members were involved in various forms of organized crime, including extortion, kidnapping, and drug trafficking, led the National Public Security Council to establish the PNC's cleansing commission. In 2000 and 2001 more than fifteen hundred members of the PNC were fired in response to the commission's report, but most of them were low-ranking officers.[33] Police purges under the Saca and Funes administrations also tended to focus on purging low-ranking officers. Though there have been some convictions for criminal activity, investigations of high-ranking officers or attempts to address structural issues within the police have been virtually nonexistent—if not outright discouraged. When the inspector general of Funes's PNC Zaira Navas began investigating several police commissioners for their alleged links to drug trafficking and organized crime, she encountered significant opposition. In opposition to her efforts, José Antonio Almendáriz, a PCN deputy, proposed a special commission to investigate *her*. Navas resigned in 2012 after the new PNC director, Francisco Salinas, appointed an intelligence officer who was being investigated for his links to organized crime.[34]

Police corruption also had a significant impact on popular perceptions about the police and its ability to fight crime. Salvadorans were reluctant to report crimes to the police, both for fear or retribution and for fear of police shakedowns. In 2007 the National Counsel for the Defense of Human Rights (PDDH) received almost twenty-eight hundred complaints, 67 percent of them involving the PNC.[35] According to one UNDP study, 44 percent of respondents believed that police officers were involved in criminal activity.[36] High levels of crime and corruption within the PNC had a significant impact on the organization's reputation.[37] While public confidence in the armed forces was higher than other public institutions, there were troubling revelations that military officers were involved in arms trafficking. As the gangs' access to sophisticated levels of weaponry increased, rumors swirled that they were getting some of their weapons from the armed forces. In November

2014 a former army lieutenant was sentenced to seven years in prison for arms trafficking.[38] Reports of police abuses and extrajudicial killings, including a particularly damning report by *El Faro* on a 2015 police massacre of suspected gang members, raised concerns about police professionalism amid growing crime.

Judicial reform was one of the most difficult areas of reform, in part due to the extent of the corruption of the judiciary, a shortage of well-educated lawyers and judges, and the historic politicization of the judicial process. Unlike the reforms to the security sector, the peace accords made little specific provision for judicial reform. This led to disarticulation and public disputes between the two institutions charged with rule of law. As with certain segments of the old security sector, members of the Supreme Court initially resisted many of the reforms. Political will, not resources, held up judicial reform. The new penal code, designed to professionalize and modernize the criminal justice system, was finally passed in April 1998.[39] These changes, however, did not compensate for the insufficient resources available to prosecutors and the lack of coordination between the police and attorney general. The prosecutor's office was woefully underfunded and lacked qualified personnel. According to Charles Call, only one-third of the prosecutors in 1997 were attorneys.[40] Moreover, the PNC's inadequate training in investigative techniques hindered the job of prosecutors. In fact, as many as 60 percent of arrests never made it to trial.[41] In 2005 only 14 percent of murders were brought to trial, and a mere 4 percent resulted in convictions.[42] A 2014 study by the IUDOP revealed that between 2009 and 2013, only 6.5 percent of cases initiated resulted in a judgment.[43] When cases did make it to trial, witnesses discovered that there were no provisions for their protection. This low capacity within the criminal justice system not only failed to protect citizens but also reinforced public perceptions that institutions were weak and ineffective.

MARGINALIZATION

Numerous studies cite marginalization and income inequality as key variables in elevated levels of social violence.[44] Marginalization in postwar societies may be heightened due to the economic costs of war, such as periods of lost growth, capital flight, the destruction of infrastructure, loss of employment, and lack of access to education. Marginalization and inequality have long been dominant features of Salvadoran society and were the root causes of the war. Despite the government's contention that the poverty and inequality were the result of the war, the end of the war did not resolve these problems. In fact, neoliberal policies made the concentration of wealth more extreme. Low growth rates during the late 1990s resulted in a nearly 6 percent increase in the national poverty rate, and inequality increased between 1996 and 2002. Although government data showed a steady decline in poverty between 1996 and 2005, some doubted the accuracy of the state's methodology. At least some of this reduction was due to the influx of remittances.

In the past, the highest levels of extreme poverty were found in rural areas. While marginalization in rural areas remains a serious problem, rising levels of urban poverty have been associated with crime. Extreme poverty in urban areas rose significantly in the immediate postwar period (see chapter 4).[45] Some of this was due to the dramatic increase in postwar urban migration exposed by the 2007 national census, as those living in the countryside migrated in search of work. In 2005 as much as 60 percent of the Salvadoran workforce was employed in the informal sector, including one-half of those living in urban areas. Most workers, including those employed in the formal sector, did not have pensions.[46] In 2008, 58 percent of the poor lived in urban areas.[47] A recent UNDP study on urban poverty and exclusion revealed that approximately 2 million Salvadorans, one-half the urban population, lived in precarious urban settlements (*asentamientos urbanos precarios,* AUPs), essentially urban slums. Almost 60 percent of households in these settlements lacked basic sanitation. Seventy-five percent of young adults ages eighteen to twenty-four lacked the basic education necessary to pursue higher education and, as a result, had reduced opportunities for employment. Studies have shown that high levels of exclusion among urban youth, especially males, were a strong predictor for elevated crime rates.[48] They were also the most common victims of crime.

THE HISTORY OF VIOLENCE AS A MEANS OF RESOLVING CONFLICT

While Salvadoran elites (as well as nonelites), have tried to draw distinctions between war violence and postwar violence, numerous studies suggest a relationship between violence during war and the continuation of violence during postwar years.[49] This "continuum of violence" was seen as an extension of the conflict, which becomes part of a society's cultural norms.[50] More than seventy-five thousand Salvadorans died in the civil war. The tortured bodies of the regime's victims were often left along the roadside or in public places to heighten the sense of fear and insecurity among the population.

However, violence as a means of resolving conflict in El Salvador was not merely a result of norms established during the war. The use of violence to resolve social conflicts was deeply rooted in Salvadoran history (see chapter 1). The government and elites routinely used repression as a means of societal control throughout the late nineteenth and much of the twentieth centuries. The use of violence as a means of settling conflict was not limited to the state and elites. Interpersonal violence has also been quite high. Ricardo Córdova, José Cruz, and Mitchell Seligson found that El Salvador had higher rate of homicide than the rest of the region before the war and that the current violence is "neither a result of the civil war nor sudden social conflict."[51] According to Cruz and Luis González, El Salvador had the highest homicide rate in the hemisphere during the 1970s at about thirty per one hundred thousand.[52] This, along with historic patterns of state violence, suggests a deeply embedded level of cultural violence that has persisted beyond the end of the civil war. As one gang member said in a NACLA interview, "We saw and we learned—even if we didn't want to—violence was in us."[53] The absence of transitional justice or attempts at societal reconciliation as well as the continued use of the war narrative, have reinforced enduring patterns of cultural violence.[54]

MIGRATION FLOWS

As outward migration flows have increased, so has the number of deportees who have been returned from the United States. Since 1999 more than 165,000 Salvadorans have been deported from the United States. Many of these deportations were carried out under the 1996 Illegal Immigration Reform and Immigrant Responsibility Act. More than one-third of the total deportees between 1999 and 2012 were classified as criminals (see table 5.1). It's important to note, however, that most of the criminal offenses were nonviolent. Among them were Salvadorans who had come to the United States during the war and grown up there, often recalling nothing of El Salvador—or even speaking Spanish. The isolation they experienced upon deportation led many to join gangs. The Salvadoran government blamed these deportations for the country's crime wave, as criminal deportees were routinely released into Salvadoran society without notifying local authorities. This led to calls by the Salvadoran government for increased coordination with the United States in returning deportees. The true extent to which deportees are a source of crime remains to be seen, although the rise in criminal deportations does coincide with increasing crime rates. A report by the UNODC, however, questions whether the deportees are responsible for the types of violent crimes that plague the country. Fifty-six percent of the criminal deportations in 2005 were for criminal immigration and drug offenses (half of those for possession).[55] While other violations included assault (10.3 percent), burglary and robbery (6.8 percent), and sexual assault (2.9), murder was not one of the top ten offenses listed by the U.S. Department of Homeland Security.[56] Given that so few of the criminal deportees had a history of violent crimes, it was unclear the extent to which these deportations had a significant impact on violent crime rates.[57]

In a 2006 interview with then director of the national police Rodrigo Ávila, he added that internal migration was a problem for public security. The January and February 2001 earthquakes had resulted in displacement as people moved rapidly into urban areas. He noted an overlap in places where migrants settled and those that had seen an increase in crime, such as Apopa, Soyapango, San Marcos, Armenia, which he attributed to poor planning, insufficient services, and poor security.[58]

TABLE 5.1

Deportations of Salvadorans from the United States, 1999–2013

	Total deportations	Criminal deportations
1999	4,160	2,115
2000	4,736	2,145
2001	3,928	1,895
2002	4,066	2,295
2003	5,561	3,474
2004	7,269	2,805
2005	8,305	2,827
2006	11,050	3,850
2007	20,045	4,949
2008	20,050	5,558
2009	20,844	6,344
2010	20,347	8,368
2011	17,381	8,507
2012	18,993	8,647
2013	20,862	9,440
Total	187,597	73,219

Source: Department of Homeland Security, *Yearbook of Immigration Statistics* (Washington, DC: Office of Immigration Statistics, Immigration Enforcement Actions), various years.

Statistics on Violence

Social violence is not a new phenomenon in El Salvador. The elevated homicide rates in the 1960s and 1970s translated into higher rates after the war. There was a significant increase in homicides during the latter half of the 1980s, with a dramatic increase between 1990 and 1994. From 1994 to 1995 there were 150 to 160 homicides per hundred thousand inhabitants, presumably as a result of the security gap and demobilization process. While those numbers have declined considerably, El Salvador still suffers from the highest homicide rate in the hemisphere and one of the highest in the world. Between 1990 and 2013 more than seventy-three thousand people were murdered.[59] The available data on violence in El Salvador tells a story of continuing marginalization, weak institutions, and impunity.

While there is overwhelming consensus that El Salvador suffers from elevated levels of violence, the lack of accurate statistics complicates a more nuanced assessment of the problem. Before 2005, the three most cited government sources—the National Civilian Police (PNC), the Public Prosecutor's Office (FGR), and the Institute of Forensic Medicine (IML)—all had different methodologies for calculating homicide rates.[60] For example, the FGR included all violent deaths (including car accidents) in its homicide figures, resulting in inflated statistics.[61] As such, data on homicides varied significantly across organizations within a given year. For example, in 2001 the PNC reported 2,210 homicides, while the IML reported 2,374 and the FGR reported 3,509. However, as noted by Wim Savenije and Chris van der Borgh, observable patterns in homicide rates across the three sources revealed a significant increase in homicides during the immediate postwar years, a sharp decline beginning in 1996 and significant increases between 2004 and 2005.[62]

In 2007, 17 percent of the total deaths in El Salvador were the result of homicide and another 13 percent were classified as violent deaths (suicide and auto accidents).[63] In fact, El Salvador had the highest mortality rate for automobile accidents in Latin America at 23.9 per hundred thousand.[64] Although 90 percent of the homicides in 2007 and 2008 were men, with the highest risk being between the ages of fifteen and thirty-nine, there was also a dramatic increase in homicides among women. Homicides of women increased 50 percent between 1999 and 2006.[65] Still, it was young men who were most vulnerable, as the homicide rate for fifteen-to-twenty-four-year-olds in 2007

TABLE 5.2

Homicides, 1994–2014

	Number	Rate per 100,000
1994	9,135	164.5
1995	8,485	149.7
1996	8,047	139.0
1997	8,573	145.0
1998	4,970	82.4
1999	2,270	36.2
2000	2,341	37.3
2001	2,210	35.2
2002	2,024	32.0
2003	2,172	33.0
2004	2,768	41.0
2005	3,778	55.5
2006	3,928	68.3
2007	3,497	60.7
2008	3,179	55.8
2009	4,382	71.2
2010	4,004	64.8
2011	4,360	70.1
2012	2,576	41.2
2013	2,499	39.7
2014	3,942	68.6

Sources: Data for 1994–98 obtained from the Public Prosecutor's Office (FGR); data for 1999–2006 from National Civilian Police (PNC); data for 2005–8 from Mesa Técnica de Homicidios; data for 2009–14 from Institute of Forensic Medicine (IML).

was 92.3 per hundred thousand, well above the national average.[66] According to the PNC, firearms were used in almost 80 percent of the homicides in El Salvador. In 2007, there were an estimated 429,719 firearms in the country, 280,000 of which were illegal.[67] Geographically, elevated homicide rates were concentrated in certain departments. In 2003, the departments with the highest homicide rates were Sonsonate, Santa Ana, La Paz, and La Libertad, all with rates higher than 40 per 100,000. By 2006, homicide rates in the five departments with the highest homicide rates exceeded 60 per 100,000, the highest being La Libertad, at over 80 per 100,000.[68] Sixty percent of homicides occurred in the twenty municipalities where nearly half the Salvadoran population lived.[69] By 2009, Sonsonate, La Libertad, Santa Ana, and San Salvador registered more than 80 homicides per 100,000, and by 2011 eight of El Salvador's fourteen departments were registering homicide rates of over 50 per 100,000.[70] These departments were located along popular transshipment routes for drugs and other illicit goods. Interestingly, there appeared to be relatively little connection between war and postwar violence. Departments that saw high levels of violence during the war, including Chalatenango and Morazán, had homicide rates well below the national average.[71]

Most homicides in El Salvador, 81 percent in 2007 and 2008, occurred in public spaces. In addition to homicides, El Salvador experienced elevated levels of more generalized public violence, including assault and robbery. This resulted in heightened perceptions of insecurity in public places, particularly public transportation, markets and commercial venues, automobiles, and even the workplace.[72] In El Salvador's case, perceptions of the level of insecurity mirror reality. The country had the highest reported victimization rate in the region, at 19 percent.[73] Despite this, only a fraction of the crimes committed were actually reported to police or other officials. Only 27 percent of victims reported crimes, 42 percent said nothing would come of it, and another 24 percent said they feared reprisals.[74]

Manifestations of Violence

The high rates of violence in El Salvador could not be attributed to a single source or perpetrator. Crime clearly emanated from a wide range of actors. In addition to more generalized violence perpetrated by individuals, evidence suggested that a significant portion of El Salvador's crime wave was caused by organized violence, including youth gangs, organized-crime rings, and vigilante groups. Distinctions between groups became increasingly blurred as street gangs became involved in transnational organized crime.[75] While these types of violence dominate the public discourse, violence in the private sphere, which primarily targets women, rarely generates media attention despite evidence that it was widespread and contributed to the normalization of violence.

GANGS

Much of the emphasis on El Salvador's crime wave focused on youth gangs, often referred to as *maras* or *pandillas*.[76] Tens of thousands of Salvadorans fled the country during the civil war. Many of them emigrated to the United States, often settling in urban areas such as Los Angeles, California. Out of place and threatened by preexisting (many of them Chicano) gangs, Salvadorans either joined gangs or formed new gangs of their own. By the 1980s, U.S. gangs were making the transition from turf wars to market wars due to the introduction of cocaine. In the early 1990s changes in U.S. immigration policy led to the repatriation of Salvadoran inmates to their homeland. The United States began deporting gang members in the early 1990s, including at least one thousand Salvadorans who were deported following the Los Angeles riots.[77] The U.S. Immigration and Naturalization Service established the Violent Gang Task Force in 1992, the same year in which the transnational gang Mara Salvatrucha (MS-13) established itself in El Salvador, mixing with existing youth gangs in the country. Some gangs were even organizing with demobilized combatants from the war, which enabled them to form alliances and acquire weapons and territory quickly.[78] While there were numerous gangs operating in El Salvador, the most notorious are MS-13 and the 18th Street Gang.[79] It is difficult to estimate the exact number of gang members in the country, and numbers often vary widely. A 2007 UNODC report estimates 10,500 gang members in El Salvador, lower than either Guatemala (14,000) or Honduras (36,000).[80] In a 2012 report, the UNODC claimed there were 20,000 gang members in El Salvador (12,000 belonging to MS-13; 8,000 to 10,000 belonging to M-18), compared with 22,000 in Guatemala and 12,000 in Honduras.[81] The report based its estimates on interviews with law enforcement officials. Still others claim that the number for El Salvador is as high as 60,000.

Numerous studies have been conducted on the nature of these gangs, often focusing on the reasons for joining and the activities conducted by gang members. The literature on why youths join gangs in Central America mirrors findings on youth gangs throughout the world (including the United States) in suggesting that the most common reasons young people join gangs are lack of educational opportunities and employment, abuse and neglect at home, disintegration of the family, and societal marginalization.[82] As noted by Orlando Pérez, gangs tended to be most prevalent in the country's most marginalized urban areas, where there was an absence of employment and educational opportunities and their emergence coincided with declining social expenditures.[83] Gang members were known to engage in numerous criminal activities, including extortion, kidnapping, drug trafficking, prostitution, murder, and possibly human trafficking.[84] In recent years, gangs underwent the noticeable shift from defending their turf to taking over turf and preying on communities. The collection of rents, known collectively as *la renta*, was a common practice in gang areas. These extortion rackets preyed on local businesses, medical clinics, schools, and even neighborhoods. Of particular concern was the targeting of public transportation. Bus drivers in affected communities were forced to pay la renta in order to drive their routes. When they refused to pay, they were killed. In 2006 alone, at least seventy bus drivers were murdered.[85] As gangs became more sophisticated (see below), they were increasingly linked to organized crime and drug trafficking. There was some conflicting evidence as to the extent of the relationship between maras and organized-crime networks, although there clearly appeared to be some "horizontal" or ad hoc relationship between the two.[86] According to the 2007 UNODC study, the relationship between gangs and "the backbone of the flow seems to be in the hands of more sophisticated organized crime operations."[87] A follow-up report, in 2012, argued that gangs weren't desirable for traffickers because they control relatively small swaths of territory, lack basic skills, and have a tendency to become involved in feuds that don't generate profit.[88] Héctor Silva Ávalos' research suggests that MS-13 controls local drug markets but that the group doesn't generally move cocaine or launder money. His research also suggests that there are some powerful *cliquas* who have formed relationships with drug traffickers, but that appears to have more to do with specific leaders and geography (e.g., the cities of Sonsonate and Nuevo Concepción).[89]

The maras were the intense focus of media and political attention, much of it sensationalized. Images of heavily tattooed (often shirtless to expose their tattoos), fearsome young men dominated electronic and print media for more than a decade. They were frequently represented as something other than human and certainly not deserving of the rights afforded to citizens. This was routinely reaffirmed by public officials, as when PNC director Ricardo Menesses referred to intergang violence by stating, "those who are dying are not normal citizens but rather delinquents; the citizenry has been the least affected."[90] The maras were routinely portrayed as the primary source of violence in El Salvador. The government's media campaign on the maras clearly affected public perceptions of them. According to a 2004 IUDOP poll, more than 90 percent of respondents said gangs were a major problem for the country, but only 21 percent considered them a serious problem in their own communities.[91] Although more than 90 percent of respondents said gangs were a problem, only 10 percent claimed to have had a direct problem with gangs.[92] Whether they accurately reflected reality, these perceptions were very important in determining the level of insecurity in society. As noted by Andrew Morrison, Mayra Buvinic, and Michael Shifter, "the degree of insecurity that results from any given level of violence depends upon how this violence is perceived by the populace. Perceptions, in turn, are heavily influenced by the way the media covers violence."[93] Despite the significant focus on gangs as a source of the crime wave, there was little evidence to suggest that the gangs were responsible for the portion of the violence commonly attributed to them. While the government routinely claimed that gangs were responsible for 60 percent of the homicides, the IML attributed only 8 percent of homicides to the maras in the early 2000s.[94] By 2012 almost 31 percent of homicides were attributed to gangs.[95] Moreover, only 12 percent of the murder trials in 2006 involved known gang members.[96] This discrepancy was noted by the UNODC report, which found that "while youth gangs do represent a source of criminality, they do not appear to be responsible for a particularly disproportionate share of the murders in the countries where they predominate."[97] There were worrying indications that successive governments were overstating the nature and sophistication of gangs in order to gain funds for antigang policies, as well as to obscure the failure to tackle organized crime.[98] As homicides spiraled out of control following the truce (discussed below), the government claimed that 60 percent of homicide victims were gang members while the police countered that gang members represented only 30 percent of homicide victims.[99] Whether this discrepancy was the result of methodological differences or a lack of understanding about the nature of violence in El Salvador, it posed a serious problem for tackling the violence.

ORGANIZED CRIME AND TRAFFICKING

The proliferation of organized criminal networks is another common form of violent crime in postconflict societies, and El Salvador was no exception to that norm. Weak policing and judicial institutions, a legacy of impunity carried over from the war, and a lack of meaningful economic opportunities created an ideal environment for organized crime to flourish. ONUSAL raised concerns about the growth of organized crime and its connections to state institutions as early as 1994, noting that some among the demobilized might find it difficult to adapt to the postwar setting and would be vulnerable to organized crime.[100] One month later, the bank assault carried out by those in old National Police uniforms occurred. Because the PNC and other state officials are known to be involved with organized crime, many syndicates operate with impunity. Moreover, the emphasis on gang violence, while serious, has masked the levels of violence associated with organized crime.

The most common and sophisticated forms of organized crime included money laundering, local and international drug trafficking, auto theft rings, arms trafficking, immigrant trafficking, sex trafficking, and the trafficking of human organs.[101] Credit card skimming and cyber crimes were also becoming increasingly common. As suggested above, the collection of la renta was not limited to the maras, and at least some suggested that the maras were merely low-ranking collectors for more sophisticated organizations.[102] Organized-crime rings frequently engaged in extortion, which was often underreported for fear of retribution. For example, in 2003 only 296 cases, about 1 percent of total complaints, of extortion were reported to the PNC.[103] It was difficult to estimate the amount of organized crime due to the relative sophistication of the organizations, low reporting on related crimes, and the impunity with which they operated. Between 1997 and 2000, 11,639 complaints of organized crime were registered with the PNC. Most complaints were received in municipalities with elevated homicide rates, including San Salvador, La Libertad, Santa Ana, Sonsonate, and La Paz.[104] This suggested that there is some relationship between organized crime and the homicide epidemic. One common indicator of the potential for organized crime is the size of the informal economy. El Salvador's informal economy was approximately 48 percent of GDP, an indicator of corruption and criminal activity.[105]

By the mid- to late 2000s, drug trafficking had become a serious problem for Central America's Northern Triangle. Geographically disadvantaged in its position between Colombia and the United States, Central America had become a major transshipment location for international drug trafficking. Drug trafficking in the Northern Triangle (El Salvador, Guatemala, Honduras) rose due to increasing pressure placed on cartels by the Mexican government and the Mérida Initiative. As a result, Mexican cartels, such as the Sinaloa cartel, increased their presence in the region. In 2005 and 2006, El Salvador captured the least amount of cocaine in the region, significantly less than Guatemala or Honduras.[106] This remained unchanged in 2012, even as other countries in the region experienced increases. This imbalance suggested that either that El Salvador was not the transshipment hub that Guatemala, Honduras, and coastal Nicaragua had become or that drug trafficking was occurring with impunity.[107]

Among the more nefarious organized-crime groups in the country, were two groups of *transportistas:* the Texis Cartel and Los Perrones. The organizations move illicit goods, including drugs, for anyone willing to pay them—including Mexican drug cartels like Los Zetas. In addition to trafficking, the groups engage in theft, money laundering, and bribery. As drug trafficking increased throughout the isthmus, these groups became more sophisticated and more transnational. Los Perrones, which conducted operations in San Miguel, Usulután, La Unión, and Santa Ana Departments, was connected with Mexican drug lord "El Chapo" Guzmán from the Sinaloa Cartel and the Gulf Cartel.[108] Allegedly founded by a group of prominent businessmen, mayors, and at least one legislative deputy, the Texis Cartel reveals the depth of the penetration of organized crime in El Salvador.[109] Businesses were used as fronts for money laundering, bribes were paid to local officials, party leaders, and informants within the PNC. There was even evidence that this penetration went all the way to the presidency.[110] The Texis Cartel typically moved cocaine along the northwestern part of the country, facilitating passage between Honduras to Guatemala. Additionally, these networks began enlisting gangs to assist them in their smuggling. Gangs were paid in cocaine, which they began to sell in local markets. This increased not only their incomes but intergang rivalries as well.[111]

DEATH SQUADS

There was growing concern that the increased homicide rate was the result of the reemergence of death squads engaged in social cleansing and extrajudicial executions. Social cleansing groups and death squads first reemerged in 1993, during the security gap. Groups such as Sombra Negra (Black Shadow) in San Miguel carried out extrajudicial killings of suspected criminals from late 1994 to March 1995. Although several PNC officers and San Miguel mayor Will Salgado were charged, none were ever convicted. According to Héctor Silva Ávalos, gangs were an obstacle to organized crime syndicates, due to their ability to control territory. As such, they developed relationships with local police and used them to carry out killings.[112] In the late 1990s, organizations such as Grupo de Exterminio (Extermination Group), and La Voz del Pueblo (Voice of the People) also targeted gang members. Gangs, however, were not the only targets of social cleansing. Gays and prostitutes were also victims.[113] The dramatic increase in unexplained homicides since 2003 was attributed to death squads engaged in social cleansing.[114] In 2004, 2005, and 2006, 8.0 percent, 9.9 percent, and 13.4 percent of homicides were attributed to maras, while those attributed to "unknown" agents accounted for 28.9 percent, 48.4 percent, and 59.0 percent, respectively.[115] Perhaps most troubling were the revelations that death squads were in fact operating within the PNC.[116] Although dismissed as isolated incidents by the government, the methods used in the killings suggested otherwise. Evidence of torture was reminiscent of death squads that operated during the war.[117] Moreover, the *mano dura* policies discussed below provided ideological and rhetorical support for social-cleansing groups.[118] There appeared to be an increase in death squad activity from 2013 to 2014, again with some allegations of police involvement.[119]

VIOLENCE AGAINST WOMEN

Women were increasingly the victims of homicides in El Salvador. The homicide rate among women doubled between 1999 and 2006. A more recent report by the Salvadoran Institute for the Advancement of Women (ISDEMU), showed that murders of women increased more than 80 percent between 2008 and 2009.[120] That rate decreased dramatically by 2013, falling from 19.1 percent in 2011 to 6.5 percent of total homicides in 2013.[121] During the first half of the decade, El Salvador had the highest rate of femicides in Central America, more than double the number in Honduras and more than five times those occurring in Nicaragua.[122] A spate of particularly gruesome murders of young women from 2002 through 2004 terrified Salvadoran women and captured international attention. The tortured, mutilated bodies of women, most of whom had also been raped, were found in public spaces throughout the country. Their deaths and the condition of their bodies were reminiscent of death squad activity during the war.[123] The UN's Special Rapporteur on Violence against Women commented that the deaths reflected a "culture of hatred towards women."[124] The lack of responsiveness by state authorities to investigate and prosecute the cases underscored both the incompetence and the impunity of those organizations. Because state authorities routinely failed to investigate these cases, there was little understanding of the femicides or how they might be prevented.[125] There was increasing concern, however, that the femicides were the result of intrafamilial violence.[126]

Because much of the public discourse focused on maras and public violence, very little attention was paid to intrafamilial violence and other forms of gender-based violence.[127] Most victims of intrafamilial violence, child abuse, and sexual assault in El Salvador were women. Reports of domestic violence have increased in recent years, in part due to improvements in reporting. Complaints of domestic violence to ISDEMU increased from 4,329 in 2004 to 6,051 in 2008. According to a 2008 study by the National Family Health Survey (FESAL), nearly half of women reported being verbally abused by spouses or partners and nearly one-quarter of women reported that they had been physically abused.[128] There was also troubling evidence that interfamilial violence had become normalized in Salvadoran society. One study found that more than 56 percent of Salvadorans believed it was "normal" for a man to assault a woman.[129] In nearly 87 percent of reported cases, the abuser was the spouse or partner.[130] Despite low reporting, it was believed that rape and crimes against women and girls were widespread. More then three-quarters of rapes were perpetrated by individuals known to the women, as were more than 85 percent of sexual abuse cases.[131]

Women's economic status and limited economic opportunities often exposed them to violence. Due to a lack of employment opportunities in the formal sector, many young women sought employment as domestic laborers. According to Human Rights Watch, "95 percent of the estimated 21,500 domestics aged 14 to 19 are girls and women."[132] In a 2002 survey by the International Labor Organization's International Programme on the Elimination of Child Labor, more than 60 percent of girls reported physical or psychological abuse by their employers.[133] Sexual harassment in the formal workplace was also common. A 2008 PDDH survey revealed that approximately 42 percent of women working in government institutions had been sexually harassed in the workplace, including 68 percent of those in the PNC.[134] In 2010 the Legislative Assembly passed the Comprehensive Law for a Life Free from Violence for Women. During its first two years in force (2012–14), only sixteen of sixty-three femicides were classified as such under the law.[135] In 2011 the assembly passed the Law of Equality, Equity, and Eradication of Discrimination against Salvadoran Women. In 2012 the Funes administration also established a program known as Ciudad Mujer, led by first lady and secretary of social inclusion Vanda Pignato. The city centers provided job training, child care, health care, including psychological counseling, as well as legal and financial-planning services. While it's too early to assess the impact of this program, it was the first national government initiative designed to address gender inequality and gender-based violence.

Anti-Gang Policies and Their Effects

The postwar crime wave represented a genuine challenge for the fledgling democracy. Placing violence under the auspices of rule of law was an entirely new concept for El Salvador, and its new security institutions were undermined by both their relative newness and the failure to change the culture and personnel of those who had long been in charge of the repressive apparatus. The militarization of the police was a practice that began under the Cristiani administration in an effort to bridge the initial security gap. Joint patrols between police and military routinely patrolled the Comalapa Highway, between San Salvador and the airport. This policy was later extended to protect economic activities, such as the coffee harvest, to break up social protests, and to provide security during the 1994 presidential elections. The extraordinary levels of violence in the mid-1990s clearly overwhelmed the fledgling PNC. In February 1995, Calderón Sol approved the use of some seven thousand military personnel to support the PNC on patrol.[136] While the policy may have seemed necessary under the circumstances, it also set a dangerous precedent and undermined the spirit of the peace accords.

Crime and appropriate policy responses to it had been a matter of debate throughout the 1990s. At various times, members of both ARENA and the FMLN favored policies that were tough on crime policies. In fact, reforms to the 1998 penal code were denounced by the security and business sectors as being "too soft."[137] Although homicides declined dramatically in the late 1990s, ARENA decided to focus on crime and insecurity for purely political reasons. ARENA needed a winning issue in light of the FMLN's growing political threat (see chapter 3). Additionally, the tougher stance on crime was designed to mollify disgruntled members of the traditional Right, who were particularly affected by the rural crime wave in the late 1990s.[138] Though he had initially eschewed such calls for a tougher approach to crime, Francisco Flores capitulated to pressure from COENA and announced his antigang plan, known as Mano Dura (Iron Fist), in July 2003. The plan authorized soldiers to work with the police in joint-operation groups called Grupos de Tarea Antipandilla (GTAs) in an effort to crack down on crime. The Ley Antimaras was approved by the Legislative Assembly in October 2003 for a six-month period. The plan also included harsh penalties for merely being (or even appearing to be) a member of a gang, including arrest and two to five years in prison, and proposed to treat children as young as twelve as adults. As many as three thousand alleged gang members were arrested in the first three months of the plan, although most were released. In March 2004 the law was declared unconstitutional on numerous counts, including differentiation for crimes committed by gangs when these crimes were already in the penal code, penalizing people for their appearance or presumed gang membership, not carrying identification in public, and failing to differentiate between children and adults.[139] Saca, who had been elected on the campaign slogan *Un país más seguro*, unveiled his plan, known as Super Mano Dura, shortly after taking office. The plan continued the reliance on the use of GTAs in operations to round up suspected gang members. Images of officers in ski masks detaining *mareros* (always shirtless to expose their tattoos) were splashed across the front pages of daily newspapers, offering assurance that the plan was working. Additionally, reforms to the penal code made membership in an illicit association an aggravating circumstance in a crime, which added six to nine years to sentencing.[140] Unlike Flores, Saca also created programs aimed to prevent crime among at-risk youth and to assist those wishing to leave gang life. Mano Amiga (Friendly Hand) and Mano Extendida (Extended Hand) were initially greeted with great enthusiasm, but it soon became clear that the programs were not a priority. Underfunded and ineffective, they never received the level of support afforded Mano Dura.[141]

Muaricio Funes continued the militarized policing policies of his predecessors by ordering an additional twenty-five hundred troops to join police patrols in new antigang units for a six-month period beginning in November 2009. The following year the joint patrols were extended for another year and their presence expanded from nineteen to twenty-nine high-crime communities. Soldiers were also sent to prisons to maintain order and provide additional security. Following a particularly stunning attack on two buses that killed twenty people, in June 2010, Funes introduced new antigang legislation making membership punishable by ten years in prison. He also appointed former general David Munguía Payés as minister of justice and public security and recently retired general Francisco Ramón Salinas Rivera as the director of the PNC, a breach of the peace accords.

In March 2012, *El Faro* revealed that talks between the military's chaplain, Monsignor Fabio Colindres, and former FMLN commander Raúl Mijango and El Salvador's gangs had resulted in a truce.[142] El Salvador's gangs agreed to stop killing rival gang members and cease forced recruitment in exchange for improved prison conditions, less onerous visitor inspections, and opportunities for employment and reintegration. Gangs living in "peace zones," municipalities where they promised to cease violent activities, were eligible for reinsertion and education programs. The Funes administration repeatedly denied that it had been involved in the truce, though it was apparent that the truce could not have been negotiated without his knowledge or that of Minister of Public Security David Munguía Payés.[143] It was later revealed that the truce had been a part of the overall strategy of Munguía Payés, who had previously served as Funes' minister of defense, to reduce homicides.[144] The reaction to the truce was mixed. Some raised concerns that government negotiations with gangs had essentially turned them into political actors with political power.[145] Others claimed that the truce revealed the extent of alliance between the state and traffickers.[146] Business leaders complained that the truce didn't include extortions. The truce was also unpopular with opposition politicians, who used it for fodder in the 2014 elections, and with the public. An IUDOP public-opinion poll revealed that nearly 90 percent of respondents had little or no confidence in the truce.[147]

In 2013 the Constitutional Chamber of the Supreme Court ruled that the appointments of Munguía Payés as minister of public security and former general Francisco Salinas as director of the National Civilian Police were violations of the peace accords. Though he disagreed with the decision, Funes accepted the ruling and replaced Munguía Payés with Ricardo Perdomo and reinstated Munguía as defense minister. Salinas was reassigned to the State Intelligence Organization (OIE), replacing Perdomo, and Rigoberto Pleités became the new director of the PNC. Shortly after the dismissal of Munguía Payés, the truce began to break down. Perdomo, his replacement, opposed the truce and chose to terminate dialogue with the gangs.[148] Without support from Perdomo, the gangs had no incentive to maintain the truce. As Cruz points out, the success of the truce was completely dependent on the will of the gangs, as the government had no way to enforce it.[149]

Policy Outcomes

As evidenced by increasing homicide rates and levels of violence, the mano dura policies were ineffective. Homicide rates were actually lower in the years before the implementation of mano dura. There were 23,721 recorded homicides in El Salvador between 2003 and 2009 (the mano dura period), as compared to 8,845 homicides from 1999 to 2002, a clear indication that the policies did nothing to alleviate, and may have possibly exacerbated, the homicide epidemic. The application of mano dura policies led to the immediate increase in arrests of suspected mareros, which merely created the illusion that the government was reducing crime. There were more than nineteen thousand arrests between July 2003 and August 2004, but only 5 percent of them led to formal investigations.[150] The mass arrests led to a dramatic increase in El Salvador's prison population, which increased from 7,800 to 14,682 (87.7 percent) between 2000 and 2006.[151] By 2008 there were 19,814 prisoners in facilities designed to hold 8,227. Even with this increase in arrests, known gang members represented only about 30 percent of the prison population.[152] Prison overcrowding led to deteriorating conditions for inmates, as many as half of whom were awaiting trial.[153] The volume of arrests and poor quality of criminal investigations resulted in extended detentions for many prisoners.

In addition to being ineffective, there was strong evidence that the policies were actually counterproductive to reducing gang violence. Following a series of violent prison clashes between rival gang members, the government established the policy of separating the prison population by gang membership. As a result, gang power within prisons, intergang tensions, and violence increased.[154] Additionally, younger, less-identified gang members were housed alongside older, more advanced gang leadership, creating what some referred to as a "finishing school" for gangs.[155] This practice enabled the consolidation and strengthening of gang infrastructure.[156] There was also some indication that the mano dura policies resulted in the evolution of gangs.[157] Gang members were encouraged to eschew tattoos, the *rapado* (close shaved) hairstyle, and certain types of dress commonly associated with the maras.[158] Essentially driven underground, the gangs also became more organized, sophisticated, and expanded their territory.[159] Gangs were increasingly associated with extortion and the collection of rents from businesses, particularly the transportation sector.[160]

There has been increasing consideration given to the impact of public insecurity on the prospects for peace and democracy in postconflict, or even posttransition, societies. Crime and violence exposed weaknesses in democratic institutions and resulted in a lack of public confidence in government structures and institutions or even democratic governance.[161] The sense of insecurity created by the violence may lead the population to clamor for authoritarian responses to lawlessness. Governments may respond by "giving the people what they want" rather than exploring meaningful solutions to the problem. Responding to violence in postconflict societies has resulted in increased militarization of the police, restrictions of civil rights, and violations of human rights. In El Salvador, both the violence and the policy responses had a corrosive effect on building sustainable peace, consolidating democracy, and engendering respect for human rights. The militarization of the PNC resulted in arbitrary and repressive measures, which have undermined respect for human rights and the rule of law. High levels of corruption and impunity within the PNC and judiciary further contributed to low levels of public trust in the institutions charged with protecting the population. In a 2009 IUDOP poll, 72.5 percent of respondents said that Super Mano Dura had done little or nothing to reduce crime related to the maras.[162] When asked why homicides had increased, 26.4 percent attributed the rise to corruption in the police, 18.4 percent to soft laws, and 27.5 percent to insufficient or ill-prepared police.[163] Thus, not only did the policies represent continued authoritarian tendencies within ARENA, but they also reflected a preference among the population for punitive policies. As crime increased, so did the popularity of repressive policies that undermined democratic norms.[164] As demonstrated by Pérez, high crime rates were the most likely reason to support a coup, and crime victims were more likely to support the idea of a coup.[165] When posed with the statement that democracy was preferable to other forms of rule, 56 percent of respondents said yes in 1996, as opposed to only 38 percent in 2007.[166]

While unpopular, the truce appeared to be effective at reducing homicides. In 2012 the homicide rate dropped to 41.2 per hundred thousand, a reduction of more than 40 percent from 2011. According to the PNC, the daily homicide rate was reduced from 12 per day in 2011 to 6.8 per day in 2013. Femicides declined as well. Some argued that the reductions, while significant, did not account for the rising number of disappearances that accompanied the truce.[167] Again, the data is confusing. PNC data shows a dramatic increase in disappearances between 2010 and 2012, while IML data indicates a decrease between 2011 and 2012.[168] Following Munguía Payés' removal, homicide rates began to increase. At the beginning of the truce, the average daily homicide rate was 5.57. The daily average from January to May

2014 was 9.48, creeping closer to pretruce numbers.[169] The security situation continued to deteriorate rapidly into 2015, as the government reportedly refused to negotiate a new truce with the gangs. In July, gang threats against bus drivers resulted in a transport stoppage that paralyzed San Salvador. Violence escalated between gangs and security forces, resulting in the deadliest month on record since 1992. The Institute of Legal Medicine reported 911 homicides in August (about 30 per day) alone. In addition to increasing military patrols, the government sought to extend the country's antiterror law (discussed below) to prosecute gang members. Not only did the Constitutional Chamber rule that the antiterror law could be applied to gang members, but it also effectively ruled that the 2012 truce was illegal.Gangs could now be tried as terrorists.

Finally, the emphasis on gangs in anticrime policy masked the presence and nature of other forms of violence. Increasing evidence suggested that gangs were responsible for only a portion of the violence in El Salvador. Little was known about organized crime or social cleansing, and authorities and the media often treated these forms of violence as the exception rather than the rule. Often coming from marginalized communities and divorced from power structures, mareros were easy scapegoats in the crime wave. Moreover, the mano dura policies privileged public violence, while private violence remained marginalized from public discourse and was often legitimized.

Civil Society

The end of the war created new opportunities and immense challenges for civil society. Decades of repression had weakened El Salvador's civil society, which had been a common target of state violence. Many actors faced the complexities of evolving along with the changing political environment. As might be expected, there was a significant increase in nongovernmental organizations after the end of the war, many of which were involved in reconstruction, development, and human rights issues. Dominant discourse within postwar civil society focused primarily on issues not resolved by peace accords, namely exclusion and the neoliberal model. Despite the generally freer environment, political space for civil society became increasingly limited as it threatened the government's agenda. Moreover, the government often failed to protect the rights of citizens to organize or insure that violations of activists' civil and human rights be prosecuted.

Actors in a New Era

The Catholic Church, which had once been a major source of social activism, became decidedly more conservative in the postwar era. Following the death of Archbishop Arturo Rivera y Damas in November 1994, new leadership distanced itself from the "activist" traditions of the 1970s and 1980s.[170] The appointment of Fernando Sáenz Lacalle, the local founder of Opus Dei, as archbishop of San Salvador, in April 1995, led to a dramatic decline in social activism.[171] Sáenz Lacalle, who eschewed liberation theology as a Marxist doctrine that promoted violence, sought to distance the church from social conflicts. The dismissal of a popular priest, Jesús Orlando Erazo, in El Paisnal, forty kilometers northwest of San Salvador, in 1999 served as an example of the growing distance of the popular church from the church hierarchy.[172] Like many communities in El Salvador, crime in Aguilares has skyrocketed since the end of the war.[173] Padre Orlando, the nephew of the slain Father Rutilio Grande, organized protests against growing crime and unemployment.[174] The priest planned a march from Aguilares to Romero's tomb, in the National Cathedral, to gain attention for the problems in the community. After inviting Archbishop Sáenz Lacalle to join the march, the priest was removed for "political organizing."[175]

Popular organizations, which had been very active before and during the war, suffered from a number of weaknesses. Many organizations were unprepared for the transition from war to peace. First, many of them had no experience in development and reconstruction work and lacked technical capacity for projects introduced by international agencies.[176] Second, many of the organizations functioning during the 1970s and 1980s were created in opposition to military rule and political repression and provided relief for the economically oppressed. In essence, many groups lost their raison d'être following the peace accords and had difficulty finding new identities. Some popular organizations reemerged as nongovernmental organizations, while others continued their activities as grassroots or peasant organizations.[177] Finally, popular organizations had developed strong ties with political organizations, particularly the FMLN. This politicization had a serious impact on these organizations following the end of the war.

The Cristiani and Calderón Sol administrations were dubious about the role of popular organizations, which they perceived as instruments of the FMLN, in postwar civil society. This bias was particularly evident during the reconstruction process, when NGOs and other organizations associated with the FMLN were overlooked by the Secretariat for National Recon-struction in the reconstruction process, despite their levels of expertise in the ex-conflict zones.[178] Opposition NGOs received a mere 0.62 percent of funds distributed from February 1992 to November 1993 under the National Reconstruction Plan.[179] A majority of the funds, some 52.49 percent, were allocated to Salesian NGOs with strong ties to elites, which had maintained a close relationship with the Salvadoran government during the 1980s.[180] Additionally, a controversial NGO law, which required NGOs to be regis-tered with the state in order to receive funding, had a significant impact on these organizations.[181] When the law was first introduced, in 1995, it was so restrictive that it virtually eliminated the boundary between the state and civil society.[182] In response to remonstrations from the NGO community, ARENA subsequently rewrote and passed a revised version of the law in November 1996. Still, the law generated fear and mistrust among the NGO community.[183] The registry was maintained by the Ministry of the Interior, which exercised a great deal of control over the approval of organizations for formal status as well as the distribution of funds. This arrangement gave the government significant control over the NGO community.[184] The ap-proval process was highly politicized, as leftist NGOs or those affiliated with the FMLN faced a more difficult, lengthy approval process. For example, the Minister of the Interior threatened to "review" the status of the Cole-gio Médico for its part in the five-month strike during 1999 to 2000 at the Workers' Union of the Salvadoran Social Security Institute (STISSS).[185] Ad-ditionally, several well-respected organizations had difficulty in the gaining of approval for the registry, including the Latin American School of Social Sciences (FLACSO).[186]

High levels of politicization affected popular organizations in another way. Because many of these organizations were intertwined with various guer-rilla organizations, the internal divisions of the FMLN became a significant source of tension among and within organizations. According to Elisabeth Wood, the impact of the 1994–95 split between the FMLN and the ERP on peasant groups in Usulután was significant, causing many groups to question the nature of their alignments as well as their future efforts.[187] Michael Foley also found that the ERP-FMLN split was detrimental to some organizations, causing infighting and financial collapse in at least one prominent case.[188] Thus, while their relationships with the FMLN during the war had fostered their existence, those same relationships worked against them in the postwar era. Those organizations that developed autonomously were more likely to weather the transition. The success of Las Dignas, a prominent women's organization that focuses on women's reproductive and productive rights, was attributed to its ability to define itself as an autonomous organization before the peace accords.[189] By effectively breaking with National Resistance, which the organization did because the RN's (male) leadership wanted to control it and its finances, Las Dignas developed an identity, structure, and funding sources independent of the FMLN.

Mobilization among the popular sectors was most successful when the issues and actors were broad. Using the case of the Democratic Peasant Alliance (ADC), Flint demonstrated that a broad-based movement, capable of engaging key political actors, could play a vital role in mitigating social problems.[190] The ADC, one of El Salvador's largest peasant organizations, along with numerous other organizations from across the political spectrum, launched a campaign for agrarian-debt cancellation in 1995. The movement galvanized ex-combatants and other beneficiaries of the land transfer program agreed to in the peace accords, landowners, and various peasant organizations and NGOs. The ADC's success in sustained organizing and lobbying for debt cancellation resulted in an agreement in 1998 to cancel 85 percent of the agrarian debt.[191] The ADC's campaign played a significant role in demonstrating the potential success of broad-based mobilization; few other issues have cut across sectors the way the agrarian issue did.

The labor movement in El Salvador was also confronted with several challenges following the war. The Foro, created by the peace accords, offered the greatest opportunity for labor to become actively involved in economic policy and labor issues. After the Foro collapsed, in 1994, labor's role in developing economic proposals was effectively eliminated. The collapse of the Foro, along with privatization and politicization, has contributed to an increasingly disjointed labor movement. Like popular organizations, labor unions associated with the FMLN had a particularly difficult transition to the postwar era. A study of Salvadoran labor unions by Fitzsimmons and Anner revealed that those unions affiliated with the center-right, had traditionally focused on traditional labor issues, and were depoliticized, were more likely to survive the transition. This finding is echoed by former FENASTRAS general secretary Héctor Bérnabe Recinos: "Following 1994, we came to the conclusion that the largest and strongest organizations were those that separated their union affairs from the parties."[192] The failure to focus on the typical bread-and-butter issues was a serious impediment to organization. According to one labor leader, "we were made tough for battle but now we are not educated, not experienced enough. There is a need for pragmatic workers, with more training, who are aware of their needs."[193] Additionally, as the FMLN became more focused on transitioning to a political party, labor issues were not a priority. Because many unions had depended on the FMLN for guidance, if not outright direction, they felt "orphaned from politics, from projects, from its [labor's] duty, and betrayed by the parties, specifically the Left."[194]

Civil Society and Political Space

By the mid to late 1990s, civil society was becoming more organized and more vocal in its demands. The social security strikes of 1999 to 2000 and 2002 to 2003 (see chapter 3), were the most prominent examples of successful campaigns to influence public policy. Most protests during the late 1990s and early 2000s, like the social-security strikes, focused on opposition to the neoliberal model and its various policies. Protests, however, were not limited to the Left. Groups from across the political spectrum emerged during the mid to late 1990s to express dissatisfaction with government policy and continuing exclusion. One such group was former civilian patrol agents. Following the peace accords, that group claimed they were due compensation for their "services" provided during the war. The accords did not provide for payment or restitution to this group. The most prominent of these organizations was the Association of Salvadoran Agricultural Producers (APROAS), which claimed to represent as many as forty-five thousand former militia members. In August 1999 police killed two protesters, wounded several, and arrested nearly fifty others during a protest. It was one of many violent clashes between APROAS and police during the late 1990s and early 2000s. Calderón Sol initially refused to award compensation to the group but offered a settlement after protests became more violent. The group rejected the $34-per-person settlement, demanding $2,000 per person and a pension. It was later revealed that the administration had diverted 10 million colones from funds designated for Hurricane Mitch victims to the ex-patrols.[195] The funds were dispersed days before the 1999 presidential election, although the government denied allegations of vote buying. Protests continued under the Flores administration, including the days leading up to the 2000 elections.[196] While there is clearly a story here about corruption and the misappropriation of funds, it is also a story about exclusion. The protestors were from predominately poor rural communities, had received no compensation from the accords, and their demands had been ignored. As noted by an article in *Proceso,* "It is ironic that those who were formerly appreciated as a key element—even a heroic element—in the Salvadoran state are now looked down upon as rebels without a cause; but it is understandable because the benefits of peace were shared out among the politicians of the big parties and the generals, forgetting the weakest sectors in the machinery of war that they had used."[197]

By 1999 the government was becoming less tolerant of social protest—and perhaps civil society in general. As noted by Cathy McIlwaine, the government adopted a rather paternalistic attitude toward civil society (and NGOs in particular) during the peace process and early postwar period.[198] The inability to control these growing movements, let alone allow them to influence public policy, was a source of frustration for ARENA administrations. Flores, having been besieged by the first social-security strike, referred to the strikes as antidemocratic. Days before the 2000 elections, he urged voters to reject "violence and disorder" at the polls: "Today, there still are people who want to thwart our decision to choose a better future and threaten us with violent acts, strikes, and disorder."[199] The attempt, of course, was to link the strikes to the war and to paint dissent as instability. While strike activity and popular protests declined following the social security "white marches" of 2002-3, there were numerous, albeit less prominent, protests surrounding CAFTA.[200] The Popular Social Bloc (BPS), the Popular Resistance Movement of October 12 (MPR-12), and other organizations engaged in protests and shut down highways. As many as two hundred members of the MPR-12 occupied the Legislative Assembly before the CAFTA vote in protest of the agreement and government's failure to consult the population.

The period of relative tolerance for protests and demonstrations contracted further following the 2004 elections. The change coincided with Saca's rhetoric regarding the FMLN's engagement in destabilizing activities, linking protests to the crime wave. The government increasingly relied on repression to disperse demonstrations. In October 2006 the Salvadoran government approved the Special Antiterrorism Law (Ley Especial contra Actos de Terrorismo) by a narrow margin. The legislation was a response to increasingly contentious social protests against government policies. One particular protest, in July 2006 in front of the University of El Salvador (UES) over increasing bus fares and electricity rates, resulted in the shooting deaths of two police officers. The government blamed the FMLN, while the FMLN blamed police repression. The law criminalized common means of protest, such as demonstrations, marches, occupying buildings and street blockades, as acts of terrorism. Following its passage, the law was used against street vendors and striking health care workers. One of the most common targets of the law were the street vendors who filled the streets of central San Salvador, many of whom had been displaced following the December 1998 fire in San Salvador's Central Market, which displaced more than ten thousand vendors. The displacement and the growth of the informal economy swelled their ranks. Frequent raids and controversial policies have led to increasingly violent protests and clashes with police.[201]

It became increasingly clear that the intention of the antiterrorism law was to limit political space for the opposition of government policies. In July 2007 a group of protestors arrived in the town of Suchitoto to protest President Saca's visit to announce a water decentralization program, which some considered to be the beginning stage of the privatization of water. Violent clashes erupted between police and protestors, which culminated in the arrest of fourteen people, including several members of the Association for the Development of El Salvador (CRIPDES). The Suchitoto 13, as they came to be known, were arrested under the Special Antiterrorism Law and charged with terrorism. The arrests were widely condemned by the Human Rights Ombudsman (PDDH), Tutela Legal (the human rights office of the Catholic archbishop in San Salvador), the Human Rights Institute at the University of Central America (IDHUCA), and other national and international human rights organizations. Reports from Tutela Legal and the PDDH cited arbitrary arrests, the use of disproportionate force by the police, the use of physical violence against those arrested, and the presence of the armed forces and elite assault units, which violated the constitution.[202] Their findings indicated that the protestors arrested were not engaged in violence and had even asked police to facilitate peaceful protest. According to Tutela Legal, the purpose of the operation was not to restore public order but rather to terrorize the community and the social movement more generally. In August 2007 deputies from ARENA and the PCN voted to change Article 348 of the penal code to increase the prison term for public disorders from four to eight years.[203] The concern, of course, was that the law would be applied to those engaged in peaceful protest, such as the Suchitoto 13. Under significant pressure, the charges were eventually reduced to public-disorder charges and ultimately dismissed in February 2008. Critics charged that the application of the law to peaceful protest against privatization demonstrated ARENA's willingness to subvert democratic norms in favor of the neoliberal model. While the law did not appear to be widely applied to protestors during the Funes administration, it remained in effect at the time of this writing.

Even when the government did not actively repress protests, its failure to support a more open political climate was notable. While the controversy over the Pacific Rim Mining Corporation (now OceanaGold) highlighted the potential for civil society to influence public policy, government failure to properly investigate or prosecute the murders of several prominent antimining activists generated fear within civil society and reinforced perceptions of impunity. Pacific Rim, based in Vancouver, began operations in El Salvador in 2002. It was one of many mining companies to return to El Salvador after the end of the civil war. During the past decade, residents in mining communities had noticed skin rashes, dead livestock, and withering crops, all of which they later associated with pollution from the mining industry. Communities began to organize antimining groups and coordinated their activity with environmental and human rights organizations. In 2005, Pacific Rim announced its plan to expand activities at the El Dorado gold mine in San Isidro, Cabañas, El Salvador's second poorest department. Activists were concerned about the environmental impact of mining, particularly the use of cyanide. Using cyanide to dissolve gold eliminates the need to mine in open pits, which keeps costs low and profits high.[204] Cyanide in mining not only pollutes water sources but is known to cause grave long-term environmental impacts as well.[205] By the company's own estimate, two tons of cyanide daily (nearly seven hundred tons per year) would be used in the El Dorado mine.[206] Residents also feared that the mining would also put a strain on precious natural resources, especially water. According to *Envío*, "the company declared it would use 10.4 liters of water per second, almost 900 million liters daily, in the El Dorado mine alone—the same amount an average family uses in twenty years. In Sensuntepeque, the capital of Cabañas, drinking water arrives only once a week as it is."[207] Given the lack of water (potable or not) in rural areas, such a practice would deprive local residents of a vital natural resource.

The antimining campaign was led by a broad cross section of civil society, including environmental and human rights organizations, community residents, and the Catholic Church.[208] The Conference of Bishops of the Roman Catholic Church in El Salvador issued numerous statements opposing the mining activities. The new archbishop of El Salvador, Monsignor José Luis Escobar Alas, even incorporated it into his homilies, insisting that the mining activities would bring harm to both residents and the environment.[209] La Mesa Nacional Frente a la Minería Metálica (La Mesa) in El Salvador, which won the Letelier-Moffitt International Human Rights Award in 2009, served as the umbrella organization for the various groups. The organizations relied on protests and road blocks to prevent companies from conducting mining activity.

In 2007 the IUDOP conducted a survey about mining in twenty-four municipalities with mining exploration licenses. Nearly 70 percent of respondents opposed mining in their communities. A 2015 follow-up poll registered growing opposition, with some 76 percent saying that they were opposed to mining projects.[210] Respondents were primarily fearful of water contamination. The survey also revealed that most respondents were neither informed nor consulted by local governments about mining in their municipalities. Skeptical of claims by Pacific Rim that mining would create jobs, 67.6 percent said that the mines would contribute little to the community. Respondents also identified a wide variety of social ills that they associated with the mining industry, including alcoholism, crime, the spread of HIV/AIDS, and violence against women and children.[211] The company engaged in a public-relations campaign to influence public opinion. Their television and radio ads extolled the benefits of what they called green mining. One strange series of television ads featured images of Fidel Castro and George Bush together, to suggest that people of all ideologies should favor the mining.[212] The company's campaigning in communities included the distribution of school supplies, fertilizer, and livestock vaccine.[213]

Like so many other key protests in recent years, the Pacific Rim controversy played a role in the 2009 presidential elections. In February 2009, one month before the presidential elections, the Saca administration bowed to public sentiment and pressure from the antimining campaign and rejected the company's request for a mining permit. Saca, ever the rhetorical populist, said he'd rather pay the company than issue the permit, and referred to the concept of green mining as "superficial."[214] Shortly thereafter, Pacific Rim announced that it would sue El Salvador through its U.S. subsidiary under provisions in the Central America Free Trade Agreement (CAFTA). The company sought $300 million in lost investments and future earnings. In June 2012 the World Bank's International Center for the Settlement of Investment Disputes ruled that Pacific Rim could not sue El Salvador under CAFTA-DR, which was expanded to include the Dominican Republic in 2004, due to lack of proper standing, but that the company could sue under El Salvador's 1999 investment law.[215]

Moving the issue to arbitration did little to resolve the social conflict already brewing in local communities. From June to December 2009, three antimining activists in Cabañas were murdered. The tortured body of Marcelo Rivera, a member of the Association of Friends of San Isidro Cabañas (ASIC), was found on June 30. Rivera, a respected environmental activist, was also a member of the FMLN's local board of directors and was very active in local politics. In fact, he complained of fraud in the 2009 mayor's race. Not surprisingly, authorities claimed that his death was related to generalized crime and was not a politically motivated killing, a claim that FESPAD and others promptly rejected.[216] Four gang members were arrested for the crime, and three were sentenced to forty years in prison. The fourth suspect, who had been released from prison because he was a minor, was later killed, as was another young man who testified at the trial.[217] The police and the attorney general's office claimed the gangs were hired as hit men to settle a feud, though who exactly ordered the hit was never investigated.[218] In December 2009, Ramiro Rivera, a member of the Cabañas Environmental Committee (CAC), and his wife were killed in Trinidad, Sensuntepeque, despite being accompanied by a PNC security detail.[219] He had been shot several times on one occasion, in August 2009, but survived. Days later Dora Alicia Sorto Recinos, also a member of the Cabañas Environmental Committee, was murdered in front of her young son. She was eight months pregnant. Police arrested Óscar Menjívar, reportedly a paid promoter of Pacific Rim, for Ramiro Rivera's August attack after being identified by Rivera. Menjívar, who had also been accused of assaulting several other antimining activists, was acquitted in March 2010. There have been no charges in the murder of Ramiro Rivera, nor that of Dora Alicia Sorto.

Threats against antimining activists and their supporters were common and clearly aimed at intimidating activists. Radio Victoria in Cabañas, which covered antimining activity, was repeatedly attached and its journalists targeted with death threats. The threats and intimidation began in

2006 but increased significantly following their coverage of the death of Marcelo Rivera. The PDDH's Óscar Luna ordered an investigation into the death threats.[220] A fact-finding mission to Cabañas by the organization Voices on the Border in February 2010 described "a climate of intimidation and insecurity that reflects a culture of chronic impunity. . . . The delegation found that this climate of impunity and violence has resulted in obstruction of justice, inadequate investigations by government authorities, and a chilling affect on civic participation"[221] Additionally, the mayor of San Isidro, the same one whom Marcelo Rivera accused of fraud in the 2009 elections, admitted to the delegation that he had accepted financial payments from Pacific Rim. The failure to properly investigate or prosecute these crimes underscored the authorities' lack of commitment to protecting political space for civil society.

Exclusion and the Paucity of Peace

The story of postwar society in El Salvador is one that belies some of our most fundamental notions of peacebuilding. Economic policies designed to benefit a few failed to create a productive economy or reduce social conflict. As a result, more Salvadorans leave the country now than during the war, many of them in search of jobs and security. The lack of employment opportunities and disintegration of the family that resulted from migrations helped further marginalize the country's youth, some of whom sought refuge in gang life. Social violence replaced political violence, making El Salvador one of the most violent countries in the world. Successive administrations have been incapable of reducing the violence, and the government's authoritarian solutions to the problem (as well as some appointments) have been in direct contradiction to the peace accords. The transfer of security agents, some with ties to organized crime, into the new PNC undermined security and allowed criminality to flourish within its ranks and throughout society. Finally, the conflict over the neoliberal model continued to be a source of conflict between social sectors and the government, which increasingly used authoritarian measures to capture political space. Both the crime wave and the political violence surrounding social protests underscored high levels of impunity among state agencies. As evidenced in earlier chapters, popular support for democratic norms eroded over time and Salvadorans became increasingly skeptical about promises of peace.

Chapter 6

Reclaiming the Captured Peace

THE AIM OF THIS BOOK has been to highlight the role that elite interests can play in undermining peacebuilding, even in cases generally considered successful by outsiders. While local elites may placate peacebuilders with the apparent agreement to liberal reforms, they may also adopt or continue long-standing practices and attitudes that undermine those same reforms. Their ability to do so may be heightened through their status as incumbents, which offers them strategic advantages throughout the peacebuilding process. While the difficulty of overcoming these advantages is merely one of a number of challenges confronted by peacebuilders in postconflict environments, outcomes suggest that confronting the norms and structures of entrenched elites should be an important component of peacebuilding. This, of course, is easier said than done.

El Salvador is a cautionary tale of the prospects for peacebuilding, even under the most favorable of circumstances.[1] In comparison to other cases (such as Afghanistan, Bosnia, Cambodia, Rwanda), El Salvador was certainly less complex: two parties facing a military stalemate agreed to settle an essentially political dispute at the negotiating table in the context of a favorable regional and international environment. There can be little doubt that the UN, and ONUSAL in particular, played a constructive role in El Salvador's peace process.[2] Yet as UN documents reported on countless occasions, the will of entrenched elites posed a number of serious problems for implementation and institutional reform.

Salvadoran elites, through their governing political party, ARENA, were not only able to limit the scope of the negotiations largely to institutional reform that they would oversee, they were also able to minimize their losses by manipulating various aspects of implementation. The Cristiani and Calderón Sol administrations implemented most of the key elements of the accords, though not always with transparency or on time. This was particularly evident in police reform, which has had profound consequences for the quality of peace in El Salvador. The transfer of members and units of old security organizations not only enabled elites to maintain control over the new police but also opened the institution to corruption and organized crime. ARENA's insistence that electoral and judicial reforms be approved through the Legislative Assembly under the auspices of the 1983 constitution as well as its control of the TSE, gave ARENA significant control over the content and implementation of the reforms. Because the FMLN did not participate in the 1991 elections, the party had no representation in the assembly other than their allies in the CD during that time. The only mechanism for recommending or monitoring reforms before 1994, COPAZ, was often marginalized in the policy process. ARENA's domination of the legislature, either alone or in concert with its allies, enabled it to control the policy agenda. Its control over the legislature also endowed it with the opportunity to dominate other institutions that were elected by the body, such as the courts, the electoral tribunal, the prosecutor's office, and the Court of Accounts.

Manifestations of the Captured Peace

Democratization has been a basic tenet of every post–Cold War, UN-brokered peace settlement.[3] The belief that democracy is a means by which to achieve lasting peace should prompt us to ask serious questions about the *quality* of democracy that sustains peace. The dual processes of democratization and peacebuilding have rarely delivered both peace *and* liberal democracy.[4] Low-intensity democracies, such as El Salvador, are not uncommon in postwar settings. These democracies emphasize electoral politics at the expense of broader participation and representation.[5] The emphasis on elections as democracy is evident in the case of El Salvador. One of the most prominent characteristics of postwar politics in El Salvador is the extent to which the conflict between the two parties has been institutionalized. El Salvador's democracy has largely been defined as a competition between two rival political parties—ARENA and the FMLN. This dominance of political life by parties, referred to as partyarchy, has politicized institutions and undermined the consolidation of democracy. Through its role in the TSE, ARENA and its allies chose not to implement reforms that would increase representation and participation, fearing that it would come at an electoral cost to them. The TSE also routinely failed to enforce election laws, particularly as they pertained to violations committed by ARENA and its allies. Through the implementation of policies such as the NGO law or the antiterrorism law, the party has also been able to restrict political space for civil society. As such, ARENA has controlled the political environment, deliberately limiting space, representation, and opportunities for dialogue. Citizens do not feel represented by political parties and have little trust in them or the institutions that govern the electoral process (see chapter 3). This has translated into voter abstention, low levels of other forms of participation, general dissatisfaction with the quality of democracy, and increased support for nondemocratic practices. Rampant corruption and the government's inability to address the country's serious social and economic problems have also had a significant impact on Salvadorans' appraisal of democracy, as well as the peace. In a 2012 IUDOP poll taken twenty years after the signing of the peace accords, almost 50 percent of respondents said little or none of the peace accords had been fulfilled. Only 35 percent said things were better since the signing of the peace accords, *down* from more than 54 percent in 2001. Fifty-seven percent expressed little to no satisfaction with the functioning of democracy.[6]

The absence of any meaningful transitional justice process has also had profound consequences for El Salvador's peace. The findings of the Truth Commission placed much of the blame for abuses committed during the war on the state. Cristiani's dismissal of the commission's findings, the failure to distribute the report, and the sweeping amnesty law denied Salvadorans access to an accurate historical account of the war and created an enduring legacy of impunity. The Salvadoran government did not print and distribute the commission's report until 2014, under FMLN president Sánchez Cerén. Neither the state, nor ARENA, nor the armed forces accepted any responsibility for the violence that killed seventy-five thousand Salvadorans and displaced one million more. But ARENA's irresponsibility in this matter goes well beyond the denial of justice. In the more than two decades since the end of the war, the party has continued to use its war narrative in the course of everyday politics. It has been used during election cycles to create fear and uncertainty among voters; it has been used in everyday rhetoric to slander ideas, policies, or individuals that threaten its interests; it has been used to justify repressive policies to combat crime and control social protest. Beyond serving as a simple narrative, it is a key component of the party's ideology. Victims of the war are not only denied compensation and access to justice, they are revictimized by the continued denial of the abuses, such as the proposal to name a major artery after Roberto D'Aubuisson.

The situation grew worse under the Flores and Saca administrations as electoral politics became highly polarized. Threatened by the FMLN's growing success in elections, ARENA invoked inflammatory rhetoric to defame its opponent. As an electoral strategy during the campaigns in 2004, 2006, 2009, 2012, and 2014, ARENA stoked public fear about crime, violence, and instability. When asked in a recent interview whether party polarization was the principle obstacle to dealing seriously with violence, former security minister Francisco Bertrand Galindo responded, "It has always been that way."[7] This politicization of violence had a significant impact on public opinion, which increasingly demonstrated support for authoritarian solutions. Public confidence in institutions, particularly those charged with the administration of justice and security, has declined in recent years, as have levels of tolerance and support for democratic norms. While support for democracy as a regime remained high, these trends indicated a deterioration of democratic values among Salvadorans.

The literature on peacebuilding has become increasingly critical of the inability of the liberal peace to address the root causes of conflicts and deliver sustainable peace. Such reforms reduce the state's capacity to respond to the needs of the population. As demonstrated by the case of El Salvador, the application of economic policies that benefited elites perpetuated a political, economic, and social order inconsistent with the principles that guide peacebuilding. The privatization process of several sectors was marred by corruption that resulted in the creation of monopolies, leading some to question whether the model was really neoliberal at all. Many interviewees, on the right and the left, believed that wealth was more concentrated after the war than before it, even though indicators of inequality improved. The socioeconomic exclusion that resulted from neoliberal policies led to mass migration, contributed to rising violence, and created a fundamental tension between civil society and the state.

The postwar political and economic context has had a profound impact on El Salvador's societal development. Economic policies failed to reduce inequality, promote development, or generate sufficient employment opportunities. As a result, Salvadorans began looking outward to support their families. The 2007 national census revealed that the population had not grown since 1992, a reflection of the scale of Salvadoran migration. This mass migration has become a safety net for both Salvadorans and the government, but not without profound cost. The disintegration of the family structure, the dangers of the journey northward, and the precarious status of the millions of undocumented Salvadorans living in the United States are only a few of the negative consequences associated with migration. Moreover, the reliance on remittances as a development strategy reveals the weaknesses of more than two decades of economic policy. Approximately 80 percent of remittances are used for consumption, an indication that recipients are using them simply to sustain themselves. Without remittances, countless Salvadorans would be plunged deeper into poverty.

Social exclusion has also contributed to rising crime. El Salvador has one of the highest homicide rates in the world, and many Salvadorans perceive the current violence to be worse than during the war.[8] The sustained crime wave that emerged after the war has dominated discourse within and about the country for the past several years, and many worry that it constitutes the greatest threat to peace. Much of the attention has focused on gangs, although evidence clearly suggests that the maras are responsible for only a portion of the violence. Scapegoating gangs has diverted attention from other nefarious perpetrators of violence, including organized crime and death squads. That both continue to operate with impunity is cause for grave concern. For some, gangs became one of the most symbolic expressions of El Salvador's continuing social exclusion. For others, they were delinquents to be "dealt with." Rather than address the root causes of violence (lack of opportunity, employment, education, etc.), the Flores and Saca governments implemented mano dura policies. These policies exacerbated the problem and homicides *increased*. Lines between policing and the military were blurred, as successive administrations showed disregard for the peace accords. The policies also demonstrated the extent to which ARENA had yet to break with its authoritarian tendencies. There were also troubling suggestions that sustained levels of violence were becoming normalized in postwar society. This was also true of domestic violence, which had become almost commonplace in Salvadoran society.[9]

As the government politicized violence and sought to link crime with instability, it also framed other forms of "disorder" as threats to the state. Civil society, suggested by many theorists to be the linchpin of developed democracies, was often viewed as a threat to the status quo. There was little voice for civil society in the formal political arena, and those groups that were connected to parties were prone to manipulation. After a period of disorientation in the immediate postwar era, popular organizations quickly learned to make use of the new political space. The social security strikes of 1999–2000 and 2002–2003 were the largest and most effective protests in the postwar era. While the protests were helpful in advancing the FMLN's agenda, popular organizations were often treated with disdain by ARENA. As politics became increasingly polarized, the Flores and Saca administrations increased their attacks on civil society. The use of force in the case of the Suchitoto 13, as well as the attempt to label peaceful protestors as terrorists, demonstrated the limitations of political space in El Salvador's democracy.

Reclaiming the Captured Peace?

The ascension of Mauricio Funes to the presidency, in June 2009, was a significant step toward the consolidation of democracy in El Salvador. The transfer of power between ARENA and the FMLN was the first peaceful, democratic transfer of power in the country's history. Funes entered office amid high hopes for change. In a December 2009 Mitofsky poll, he had the highest approval rating of any president in the hemisphere, at 88 percent, and most Salvadorans (almost 72 percent) believed that he represented a positive change.[10] An IUDOP survey on Funes' first year in office outlined the serious challenges that lay ahead for the administration. Economic issues, including job creation, reducing the cost of food, and reducing poverty, remained the most pressing concerns for Salvadorans, according to 41.1 percent of respondents.[11] His principle challenge was to revitalize a nonproductive economy whose most successful export is its own people. This is no small task, especially during a global financial crisis. Funes was also faced with the need to bridge the historic and expansive gap between rich and poor. According to 37.2 percent of respondents, crime was the most serious issue to be addressed.[12] Homicides soared during his first year in office, adding to the country's growing sense of insecurity. The gang truce, while producing some apparent, albeit temporary, reduction in homicides, was unpopular and fell apart as a result of the lack of political will.

Can peace be reclaimed after elite capture? The experience of the Funes administration suggests this is a very difficult task. Nonincumbent administrations inherit the structures, policies, and challenges created by previous administrations. It is important to note that some important reforms were implemented during the Funes administration, which required alliances with smaller parties. Electoral reforms that had lingered for as long as two decades were implemented. The FMLN and its allies passed a progressive tax reform and laws on gender equality and violence against women. The Funes administration initiated a number of vital (and popular) social programs that targeted underserved populations. Finally, Funes' discourse about the war and his efforts at promoting reconciliation have diverged most significantly from prior administration. In November 2009, Funes awarded the National Order of José Matias Delgado to the six UCA Jesuit martyrs in a public act of atonement for mistakes by past governments. He also pledged that El Salvador would investigate the 1980 assassination of Archbishop Óscar Romero, determine culpability, and make reparations, though that did not happen. At a ceremony celebrating the eighteenth anniversary of the peace accords, in January 2010, Funes offered the first formal apology for the war by a Salvadoran president. In his apology he acknowledged the human rights abuses that occurred during the war and asked the Salvadoran people for forgiveness. On the twentieth anniversary of the peace accords, Funes delivered his address in El Mozote, site of the 1981 massacre that left only a single survivor. He asked for forgiveness and named those officers implicated in the massacre, though the Right and the military continued to celebrate these officials implicated in human rights abuses. These acts represented the first attempt by the government to reconcile Salvadoran society. His recognition of the need to heal war wounds represented an important acknowledgment of the role that reconciliation plays in building peace and democracy in El Salvador. As meaningful as these acts were, it was also clear that there would be limits to his efforts. In December 2012 the Inter-American Court of Human Rights found the Salvadoran government guilty in a case brought by family members of victims of the El Mozote massacre. The court ordered the state to reopen the investigation of the massacre, as amnesty laws do not protect the state from war crimes. In September 2013, El Salvador's attorney general announced he would reopen the investigation. Later that month

Archbishop José Luis Escobar decided to close Tutela Legal, the Catholic Church's human rights office established in 1982 by Salvadoran archbishop Arturo Rivera y Damas. For more than thirty years the office had collected reports on human rights abuses, and it was rumored that the closure was linked to the fear that the evidence collected by the office could be used to prosecute war crimes. At the time of this writing, the status of Tutela Legal's collection was uncertain. It was, however, certain that prosecuting wartime crimes would be very difficult without them.

That said, there were a number of difficulties in advancing any larger political or economic agenda. First, the Funes administration was successful in advancing legislation only to the extent that it was able to build voting alliances with smaller right-wing parties, a strategy perfected by ARENA. The long overdue tax reform is a good example of this. While the administration was able to introduce several social policies designed to alleviate poverty and inequality, the administration was helpless to make any more significant structural changes to the economy. The reasons for this inability, of course, are not entirely to do with domestic politics. Globalization, foreign dependence, and market forces would make any substantive change nearly impossible for such a small economy of scale. The Partnership for Growth and the P3 legislation, required by the United States, are good reminders of the realities of power inequities between El Salvador and the United States. Funes regularly faced strong resistance from business elites, especially ANEP, on even the most modest of reforms. In protest of his policies, elites "boycotted" the economy, investing capital in other countries in the region (particularly Nicaragua) despite the desperate need for investment at home.

Second, the legacies of past policies created a form of path dependence that limited policy options available to the Funes administration. The criminality and corruption within the PNC limited the abilities of the institution to effectively manage the country's crime epidemic. In this context, Funes had few options but to continue with the militarized-policing policies of his predecessors. The truce and its few accompanying social programs might have played an important role in reducing incentives for gang violence had the administration been willing to own it as a matter of official policy. But even if the truce had endured, it would have addressed only a portion of the criminal violence plaguing the country. Growing corruption and the infiltration of state institutions by organized crime, which began within the PNC, now threatened the state at every level.

The experiences of Funes suggests that his successor, Salvador Sánchez Cerén, will face significant difficulties in advancing any agenda that threatens elite interests or significantly alters the advantages of incumbency that ARENA has developed over time. The FMLN's continued position of strength in the legislature will depend on maintaining alliances with other parties. Legislative elections in May 2015 left Sánchez Cerén with a divided legislature for most of his tenure. Like Funes, Sánchez Cerén met with the business community shortly after confirmation of his election in an attempt to allay their fears about his agenda. He also made trips to the United States and to neighboring countries in Central America. Several of his appointments reaffirmed his commitment to Funes's policies and underscored the continued influence of business elites. While Sánchez Cerén published the Truth Commission's report in August 2014, it appeared unlikely there would be any attempt to address wartime violations or comply with IACHR findings to repeal the amnesty law. Path dependence in policy appeared to be the strongest in terms of security. Faced with rising homicides in 2014–15, Sánchez Cerén continued the practice of militarized policing and created three new military batallions to fight rising crime. Moreover, Sánchez Cerén applauded the Supreme Court's ruling that allowed gangs to be tried as terrorists, though the FMLN opposed the antiterror law when it was introduced in 2006. Attempts by the administration to raise funds for security initiatives via tax proposals were, not surprisingly, met with strong resistance by ARENA and the business sector.

Lessons of the Captured Peace

What can peacebuilders and others learn from El Salvador's captured peace? More important, what can be done to prevent captured peace in future peacebuilding efforts? I have attempted to illustrate the power that entrenched elites, particularly incumbents, have over peace processes and the implications for the subsequent postwar period. This power does not suggest, however, that peacebuilders do not or cannot play a constructive role in mitigating the advantages of such incumbency.

All Politics Is Local

As the literature on peacebuilding increasingly demonstrates, the failure to take into account local norms and practices (as well as the exclusion of civil society) has been one of the chief deficiencies of peacebuilding.

Peacebuilding's focus on democratizing elections and institutional reform is not sufficient to overcome deeply rooted norms and structures, which may be difficult to identify and even more difficult to dismantle. Yet without an understanding of how elite entrenchment works in different contexts, there is little hope of preventing elite capture in postwar peacebuilding. Moreover, the focus on statebuilding, while vital, often fails to address the state-society relationship. This is especially challenging in a state like El Salvador, where patronage relationships between voters and parties date back more than a century. While interviewing candidates in 2000, 2004, and 2006, I routinely encountered people who were looking for work or goods from candidates in exchange for their votes. None of them viewed this as anything inappropriate; it was simply accepted practice. Failure to recognize and address clientelistic practices and patronage networks, which are often deeply engrained in institutions *and* society, can compromise institutional reform.

Power Sharing

Power-sharing agreements have become increasingly common in postwar peacebuilding. Evidence suggests that when parties enter power-sharing arrangements, they are more likely to fully commit to the peace process.[13] While much of the research on this topic focuses on how such agreements can build confidence and insure the durability of agreements, I would also suggest that these agreements could help overcome some of the more nefarious advantages of incumbency. Because the Salvadoran parties agreed to use the 1983 constitution as the basis for reforms and because all parties decided to proceed with the regular schedule of elections, the FMLN was essentially excluded from policymaking until after the March 1994 elections—more than two years after the agreements were signed. In other words, the FMLN had no formal political representation in government institutions throughout the implementation phase.[14] While the FMLN did have representation on COPAZ, it was essentially a mechanism to monitor implementation, not a policymaking body. COPAZ was often marginalized by other institutions and was generally considered ineffective.

Capacity Building

Among the many advantages that incumbents enjoy is the knowledge of governance and capacity to function as a political party. ARENA benefited from significant support from the United States, and from the assistance provided to groups such as FUSADES. While guerrilla movements, like the FMLN, may have demonstrated excellent organizational capacity during the war, most have little or no experience with democratic governance or party organization. This was certainly true of the FMLN, which received very little assistance in its transition from rebel movement to political party.[15] Experience from other cases suggests that strengthening the capacity of these groups could offset some of the advantages of incumbency. The most notable example is the case of RENAMO, in Mozambique, which was the beneficiary of a $17 million UN trust fund established to aid its transition.[16] Had the FMLN benefited from such a fund, it might have been in a stronger position to demand judicial reforms or might not have made concessions to the Cristiani administration to transfer army officers and units into the PNC.

Strengthening Institutions and Addressing Impunity and Corruption

ONUSAL recognized that several of El Salvador's institutions were weak, and encouraged reforms and offered training in these areas. Because the relative weaknesses of these institutions could be manipulated by ARENA for its own gain, reforms were sometimes delayed and training offers denied. This, combined with the absence of any accountability for crimes committed during the war, encouraged impunity in institutions charged with ensuring the country's postwar transition. In the future, peacebuilders might consider an institution-strengthening body such as the International Commission against Impunity in Guatemala (CICIG) to work in concert *with* the transition. The body was instituted in Guatemala well after the signing of the peace accords to address ongoing corruption and impunity, and has recently been a point of discussion in El Salvador and Honduras. Because the state was unwilling or incapable of addressing impunity on its own, the technical assistance offered through such a mechanism has the potential to strengthen institutions while exposing criminality within them.

ELITE CAPTURE can be difficult to overcome and, as demonstrated here, the failure to do so can have dire consequences for the quality (and sometimes sustainability) of peace. El Salvador represents one of the cases of elite capture in postwar peacebuilding, but it appears equally (if not more) enduring in cases such as Cambodia and Guatemala. If peacebuilding efforts are to succeed, they not only must build new institutions and invigorate citizen participation, but must break patterns of patronage and clientelism that make capture possible. It is hoped that the lessons provided herein can contribute to a greater understanding of the role of local actors, specifically incumbent elites, in peacebuilding. The role of elite actors in peacebuilding remains woefully understudied, and there is no doubt that this study merely offers a glimpse of the work that remains to be done.

Notes

Abbreviations

CIDAI   Centro de Información, Documentación y Apoyo a la Investigación
ISDEMU   Instituto Salvadoreño de Desarrollo de la Mujer
IUDOP   Instituto Universitario de Opinión Pública, Universidad Centroamericana José Simeón Cañas
UNDP   United Nations Development Programme
UNODC   United Nations Office on Drugs and Crime

Introduction: Elites, Peacebuilding, and the Problem of Capture

1. Salvador Sánchez Cerén, interview by author, San Salvador, October 2006.

2. United Nations, "The Situation in Central America: Procedures of the Establishment of a Firm and Lasting Peace and Progress in Fashioning a Region of Peace, Freedom, Democracy and Development Assessment of the Peace Process in El Salvador: Report of the Secretary General" (New York: United Nations Department of Public Information, 1997).

3. United Nations, "The Situation in Central America: Progress in Fashioning a Region of Peace, Freedom, Democracy and Development," Report of the Secretary General. August 11, 2005, A/60/218 (New York: United Nations Department of Public Information, 2005).

4. Instituto Universitario de Opinión Pública (IUDOP), "Los salvadoreños y salvadoreñas evalúan el cumplimiento de los Acuerdos de Paz," *Boletín de Prensa* 24, no. 1 (2012).

5. Charles Call, "The Mugging of a Success Story: Justice and Security Reform in El Salvador," in *Constructing Justice and Security after War*, ed. Call (Washington, DC: U.S. Institute of Peace, 2007), 29–67.

6. Boutros Boutros-Ghali, *An Agenda for Peace: Preventive Diplomacy, Peacemaking and Peacekeeping* (New York: United Nations, 1992), 32.

7. See Johan Galtung, "An Editorial," *Journal of Peace Research* 1, no. 1 (1964): 1–4; Galtung, "Violence, Peace, and Peace Research." *Journal of Peace Research* 6, no. 3 (1969): 167–91; Galtung, *Peace by Peaceful Means: Peace and*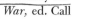

Conflict, Development and Civilization (Oslo: International Peace Research Institute, 1996).

8. Michael Barnett, Hunjoon Kim, Madalene O'Donnell, and Laura Sitea, "Peacebuilding: What Is in a Name?," *Global Governance* 13, no. 1 (2007): 35–58.

9. See, for example, Immanuel Kant, *To Perpetual Peace: A Philosophical Sketch,* trans. Ted Humphrey (Indianapolis: Hackett Publishing, 2003); David A. Lake, "Powerful Pacifists: Democratic States and War," *American Political Science Review* 87, no. 1 (1992): 624–38; Christopher Layne, "Kant or Cant: The Myth of the Democratic Peace," *International Security* 19, no. 2 (Fall 1994): 5–49; E. Michael Brown, Sean M. Lynn-Jones, and Steven E. Miller, eds. *Debating the Democratic Peace* (Cambridge, MA: MIT Press, 1996); James Lee Ray, "Does Democracy Cause Peace?," *Annual Review of Political Science* 1, no.1 (1998): 27–46.

10. Attempts at measuring success in peacebuilding commonly lead to the dilemma of "infinite regress," referring to the difficulty of measuring something with no identifiable end. See Fen Osler Hampson, *Nurturing Peace: Why Peace Settlements Succeed or Fail* (Washington, DC: U.S. Institute of Peace, 1996), 9. For a discussion of peacebuilding as statebuilding, see Carrie Manning, "Local Level Challenges to Post-conflict Peacebuilding," *International Peacekeeping* 10, no. 3 (2003): 25–43.

11. Charles T. Call, "Ending Wars, Building States," in *Building States to Build Peace,* ed. Call and Vanessa Wyeth (Boulder: Lynne Rienner, 2008), 1.

12. Christoph Zürcher, "The Liberal Peace: A Tough Sell?," in *A Liberal Peace: The Problems and Practices of Peacebuilding,* ed. Susanna Campbell, David Chandler, and Meera Sabaratnam (London: Zed Books, 2011), 69–88. Though El Salvador is absent from Zürcher's analysis, it would not be considered a liberal democracy based on his methodology.

13. Barnett, Kim, et al., "Peacebuilding," 52.

14. Virginia Page Fortna, "Peacekeeping and Democratization," in *From War to Democracy: Dilemmas of Peacebuilding,* ed. Anna K. Jarstad and Timothy D. Sisk (New York: Cambridge University Press, 2008), 39–79.

15. Thomas Carothers, "The End of the Transition Paradigm," *Journal of Democracy* 13, no. 1 (2002): 9.

16. See Mark Duffield, *Global Governance and the New Wars: The Merging of Development and Security* (London: Zed Books, 2001); Roland Paris, *At War's End: Building Peace after Civil Conflict* (New York: Cambridge University Press, 2004); Michael Pugh, "The Political Economy of Peacebuilding: A Critical Theory Perspective," *International Journal of Peace Studies* 10, no. 2 (2005): 23–42; Roger Mac Ginty and Oliver P. Richmond, eds., *The Liberal Peace and Post-war Reconstruction: Myth or Reality?* (New York: Routledge, 2009);

Richmond, ed., *Palgrave Advances in Peacebuilding: Critical Developments and Approaches* (New York: Palgrave Macmillan, 2010).

17. Paris, *At War's End*, 6–7.

18. See Charles T. Call, *Why Peace Fails: The Causes and Prevention of Civil War Recurrence* (Washington, DC: Georgetown University Press, 2012).

19. Ole Jacob Sending, "The Effects of Peacebuilding: Sovereignty, Patronage and Power," in *A Liberal Peace? The Problems and Practices of Peacebuilding*, ed. Susanna Campbell, David Chandler, and Meera Sabaratnam (London: Zed Books, 2011), 55–68.

20. Miles Kahler, "Statebuilding after Afghanistan and Iraq," in *The Dilemmas of Statebuilding: Confronting the Contradictions of Postwar Peace Operations*, ed. Roland Paris and Timothy D. Sisk (New York: Routledge, 2009), 292.

21. Roman Krznaric, "Civil and Uncivil Actors in the Guatemalan Peace Process," *Bulletin of Latin American Research* 18, no. 1 (1999): 1–16. See also Susanne Jonas, *Of Centaurs and Doves: Guatemala's Peace Process* (Boulder: Westview Press, 2000).

22. In this work I use Michael Burton, Richard Gunther, and John Higley's definition of elites, meaning "persons who are able, by virtue of their strategic positions in powerful organizations, to affect national political outcomes regularly and substantially." As such, I focus my analysis almost exclusively on right-wing elites, the military, and ARENA and its associates until 2009. Prior that time, the FMLN's ability to influence outcomes was fairly limited. "Introduction: Elite Transformations and Democratic Regimes," in *Elites and Democratic Consolidation in Latin America and Southern Europe*, ed. John Higley and Richard Gunther (New York: Cambridge University Press, 1992), 7.

23. David Roberts, "Statebuilding in Cambodia," in *The Dilemmas of Statebuilding: Confronting the Contradictions of Postwar Peace Operations*, ed. Roland Paris and Timothy D. Sisk (New York: Routledge, 2009), 151–53.

24. See Jack Snyder, *From Voting to Violence: Democratization and Nationalist Conflict* (New York: Norton, 2000).

25. David Roberts, *Liberal Peacebuilding and Global Governance: Beyond the Metropolis* (New York: Routledge, 2012), 28–31; Michael Barnett, Songying Fang, and Christoph Zürcher, "Compromised Peacebuilding," *International Studies Quarterly* 58, no. 3 (2014): 613–14.

26. Michael Barnett and Christoph Zürcher, "The Peacebuilder's Contract: How External Statebuilding Reinforces Weak Statehood," in *The Dilemmas of Statebuilding: Confronting the Contradictions of Postwar Peace Operations*, ed. Roland Paris and Timothy D. Sisk (New York: Routledge, 2009), 24.

27. Ibid., 25.

28. Ibid., 35.

29. Barnett, Fang, and Zürcher, "Compromised Peacebuilding."

30. Anna K. Jarstad and Roberto Belloni, "Introducing Hybrid Peace Governance: Impact and Prospects of Liberal Peacebuilding," *Global Governance* 18, no. 1 (2012): 1.

31. Roger Mac Ginty, *International Peacebuilding and Local Resistance: Hybrid Forms of Peace* (Basingstoke: Palgrave Macmillan, 2011); Mac Ginty, "Hybrid Peace: The Interaction between Top-Down and Bottom-Up peace," *Security Dialogue* 41, no. 4 (2010): 391–412.

32. Oliver P. Richmond, *A Post-liberal Peace: The Infrapolitics of Peacebuilding* (Abingdon, UK: Routledge, 2011).

33. Jarstad and Belloni, "Hybrid Peace Governance," 1–2.

34. For works on regulatory capture, see George J. Stigler, "The Theory of Economic Regulation," *Bell Journal of Economics and Management Science* 2, no. 1 (1971): 3–21; Jean-Jacques Laffont and Jean Tirole, "The Politics of Government Decision-Making: A Theory of Regulatory Capture," *Quarterly Journal of Economics* 104, no. 4 (1991): 1089–127. On interest group influence over public policy, see Theodore Lowi, *The End of Liberalism: The Second Republic of the United States,* 2nd ed. (New York: Norton, 1979).

35. Cited in Joel Hellman and Daniel Kaufmann, "Confronting the Challenge of State Capture in Transition Economies," *Finance and Development* 38, no. 3 (2001): 31–35.

36. Sanjay Pradhan, *Anticorruption in Transition: A Contribution to the Policy Debate* (Washington, DC: World Bank, 2000), 9.

37. Ibid., 26.

38. See Jean-Philippe Platteau, "Monitoring Elite Capture in Community-Driven Development," *Development and Change* 35, no. 2 (2004): 223–46; Melissa T. Labonte, "From Patronage to Peacebuilding? Elite Capture and Governance from Below in Sierra Leone," *African Affairs* 111, no. 442 (2011): 90–115; Pranab K. Bardhan and Dilip Mookherjee, "Capture and Governance at Local and National Levels," *American Economic Review* 90, no. 2 (2000): 135–39; Aniruddha Dasgupta and Victoria A. Beard, "Community Driven Development, Collective Action and Elite Capture in Indonesia," *Development and Change* 38, no. 2 (2007): 229–49.

39. See Christine Cheng and Dominik Zaum, eds., *Corruption and Post-conflict Peacebuilding: Selling the Peace?* (Abingdon, UK: Routledge: 2012); Madalene O'Donnell, "Post-conflict Corruption: A Rule of Law Agenda?," in *Civil War and the Rule of Law,* ed. Agnès Hurwitz and Reyko Huang (Boulder: Lynne Rienner, 2008), 225–60.

40. Ibid., 225.

41. Labonte, "Patronage to Peacebuilding," 94.

42. Daron Acemoglu and James A. Robinson, "Persistence of Power, Elites and Institutions," *American Economic Review* 98, no. 1 (2008): 267–93.

43. James Mahoney, *The Legacies of Liberalism: Path Dependence and Political Regimes in Central America* (Baltimore: Johns Hopkins University Press, 2001), 4–9.

44. Roberts, *Liberal Peacebuilding*, 30.

45. Ho-Won Jeong, *Peacebuilding in Postconflict Societies: Strategy and Process* (Boulder: Lynne Rienner, 2005), 112–13.

46. Kahler, "Statebuilding after Afghanistan," 292–93.

47. I thank Bill Stanley for suggesting this language, which so perfectly captured the essence of my work.

48. Elisabeth Jean Wood, *Forging Democracy from Below: Insurgent Transitions in South Africa and El Salvador* (New York: Cambridge University Press, 2000), 52–75.

49. Kevin Murray, Ellen Coletti, Jack Spence, et al., *Rescuing Reconstruction: The Debate on Post-war Economic Recovery in El Salvador* (Cambridge, MA: Hemisphere Initiatives, 1994), 6. The economic program being implemented by the Cristiani administration was "simply not on the table" during the peace negotiations. This was at the insistence of the Salvadoran government and with tacit acknowledgment by the FMLN. Roberto Cañas and Rubén Zamora, interview by author, San Salvador, 1999.

50. This was aided, in part, by the fact that a number of important reforms lacked specificity. Several analysts have noted the consequences of the lack of specificity of reforms in peace accords, which inevitably reduced enforcement and increased disputes over those reforms. See, for example, David Holiday and William Stanley, "Building the Peace: Preliminary Lessons from El Salvador," *Journal of International Affairs* 46, no. 2 (1993): 415–38; Tommie Sue Montgomery, "Getting to Peace in El Salvador: The Roles of the United Nations Secretariat and ONUSAL," *Journal of Interamerican Studies and World Affairs* 37, no. 4 (1995): 139–72.

51. Holiday and Stanley, "Building the Peace," 425–27.

52. Lawrence Michael Ladutke, *Freedom of Expression in El Salvador: The Struggle for Human Rights and Democracy* (Jefferson, NC: McFarland, 2004), 9.

53. See Antonio Cañas and Héctor Dada, "Political Transition and Institutionalization in El Salvador," in *Comparative Peace Processes in Latin America*, ed. Cynthia J. Arnson (Washington, DC: Woodrow Wilson Center Press, 1999), 69–95.

54. See Holiday and Stanley, "Building the Peace," 415–38.

55. Cañas and Dada, "Political Transition," 71.

Chapter 1: Elites and the Salvadoran State

1. Héctor Lindo-Fuentes, *Weak Foundations: The Economy of El Salvador in the Nineteenth Century* (Berkeley: University of California Press, 1990), 189–90.

2. The actual number was somewhat larger and likely closer to sixty families. See Víctor Bulmer-Thomas, *The Political Economy of Central America since 1920* (New York: Cambridge University Press, 1987).

3. Elisabeth Jean Wood, *Forging Democracy from Below: Insurgent Transitions in South Africa and El Salvador* (New York: Cambridge University Press, 2000), 25.

4. James Mahoney identifies six criteria that define radical liberalism in el Salvador and Guatemala: (1) massive expansion of commercial agriculture; (2) incorporation into international markets; (3) emergence of an agrarian bourgeoisie with significant political power; (4) emergence of a centralized state apparatus; (5) emergence of a polarized rural class structure; and (6) emergence of a powerful military-coercive apparatus. Among the five Central American countries, the last two criteria are unique to El Salvador and Guatemala. Mahoney, *The Legacies of Liberalism: Path Dependence and Political Regimes in Central America* (Baltimore: Johns Hopkins University Press, 2001), 35–39.

5. For an extensive history of El Salvador's colonial economy, see Murdo J. MacLeod, *Spanish Central America: A Socioeconomic History, 1520–1720* (Berkeley: University of California Press, 1973).

6. Lindo-Fuentes, *Weak Foundations*, 88.

7. This pressure was effective due to the relatively decentralized nature of the Salvadoran state at that time. For a discussion of this strategy, see Robert G. Williams, *States and Social Evolution: Coffee and the Rise of National Governments in Central America* (Chapel Hill: University of North Carolina Press, 1994), 69–75.

8. Lindo-Fuentes, *Weak Foundations*, 117.

9. Ibid., 127.

10. Jeffrey M. Paige, *Coffee and Power: Revolution and the Rise of Democracy in Central America* (Cambridge, MA: Harvard University Press, 1997), 105–6.

11. Aldo A. Lauria-Santiago, *An Agrarian Republic: Commercial Agriculture and the Politics of Peasant Communities in El Salvador, 1823–1914* (Pittsburgh: University of Pittsburgh Press, 1999), 164–65.

12. Lindo-Fuentes, *Weak Foundations*, 151.

13. Ibid., 150.

14. Tommie Sue Montgomery, *Revolution in El Salvador: From Civil Strife to Civil Peace*, 2nd ed. (Boulder: Westview, 1995), 30.

15. Erik Ching, *Authoritarian El Salvador: Politics and the Origins of the Military Regimes, 1880–1940* (Notre Dame, IN: University of Notre Dame Press, 2014), 53–71.

16. Ibid., 57.

17. Williams, *States and Social Evolution,* 211, 223.

18. Lindo-Fuentes, *Weak Foundations,* 152.

19. Williams, *States and Social Evolution,* 75–79.

20. Philip J. Williams and Knut Walter, *Militarization and Demilitarization in El Salvador's Transition to Democracy* (Pittsburgh: University of Pittsburgh Press, 1997), 15.

21. Ibid., 16.

22. Ibid., 17.

23. Enrique Baloyra, *El Salvador in Transition* (Chapel Hill: University of North Carolina Press, 1982), 28–29. Baloyra refers to the relationship between control of production, export, finance, and land tenure as the "magic square."

24. The Association of Coffee Processors and Exporters (ABECAFE) was created in 1961. The Cafetelera and ABECAFE represent the competing interests of the coffee elite.

25. Baloyra, *El Salvador in Transition,* 7.

26. Montgomery, *Revolution in El Salvador,* 32.

27. Carlos Acevedo, "The Historical Background to the Conflict," in *Economic Policy for Building Peace: The Lessons of El Salvador,"* ed. James K. Boyce (Boulder: Lynne Rienner, 1996), 20.

28. James Dunkerley, *The Long War: Dictatorship and Revolution in El Salvador* (London: Verso, 1983), 22.

29. Ibid.

30. Acevedo, "Historical Background," 20.

31. Paige, *Coffee and Power,* 107.

32. Dunkerley, *Long War,* 22.

33. Montgomery, *Revolution in El Salvador,* 36.

34. Ibid.; Dunkerley, *Long War;* Elisabeth J. Wood, "Peace Accords and Postwar Reconstruction," in Boyce, *Economic Policy,* 73–106; William Stanley, *The Protection Racket State: Elite Politics, Military Extortion, and Civil War in El Salvador* (Philadelphia: Temple University Press, 1996); Thomas Anderson, *Matanza: El Salvador's Communist Revolt of 1932* (Lincoln: University of Nebraska Press, 1971). Estimates of the death toll vary. The most common estimate appears to be thirty thousand (Montgomery, Dunkerley), but some (Wood, Stanley) put the number closer to fifteen thousand. See also Anderson for an extensive discussion of the matanza, its causes, and effects.

35. Stanley, *Protection Racket State.* Stanley aptly refers to this phenomenon as a "protection racket."

36. Montgomery, *Revolution in El Salvador,* 39.

37. Ching, *Authoritarian El Salvador,* 262–66.

38. Paige, *Coffee and Power*, 122–24.

39. Héctor Lindo-Fuentes, Erik Ching, and Rafael A. Lara-Martínez, *Remembering a Massacre in El Salvador: The Insurrection of 1932, Roque Dalton, and the Politics of Historical Memory* (Albuquerque: University of New Mexico Press, 2007), 217–49.

40. Stanley, *Protection Racket State*, 59–60.

41. Ibid.

42. The 1886 constitution prohibits self-succession. Castañeda was able to serve a second term because he argued that his first term was merely the completion of Araujo's term.

43. Montgomery, *Revolution in El Salvador*, 42–43.

44. Williams and Walter, *Militarization and Demilitarization*, 39. Reelection was prohibited by the constitution.

45. Ibid., 38.

46. Stanley, *Protection Racket State*, 71.

47. Ibid.

48. Montgomery, *Revolution in El Salvador*, 44.

49. Many of the junior officers who had trained abroad were impacted by the modernization of the region in comparison to El Salvador. See Williams and Walter, *Militarization and Demilitarization*, 38.

50. Williams and Walter, *Militarization and Demilitarization*, 40.

51. Stanley, *Protection Racket State*, 68.

52. Montgomery, *Revolution in El Salvador*, 37–39. Also see Montgomery for a more detailed analysis of the political cycle of regime change.

53. Williams and Walter, *Militarization and Demilitarization*, 21.

54. Those parties include Pro-Patria (1931–44); the National Union Party (PUN) (1944–50; the PRUD (1950–61); and the PCN (1961–79).

55. Baloyra, *El Salvador in Transition*, 36.

56. Williams and Walter, *Militarization and Demilitarization*, 47.

57. Montgomery, *Revolution in El Salvador*, 38.

58. Baloyra, *El Salvador in Transition*, 37.

59. Montgomery, *Revolution in El Salvador*, 52.

60. Baloyra, *El Salvador in Transition*, 44. Acción Comunitaria later became a department of the municipal administration.

61. Montgomery, *Revolution in El Salvador*, 61.

62. Baloyra, *El Salvador in Transition*, 189.

63. Stanley, *Protection Racket State*, 86–87.

64. Ibid., 87.

65. See Hugh Byrne, *El Salvador's Civil War: A Study of Revolution* (Boulder: Lynne Rienner, 1996), 25; Montgomery, *Revolution in El Salvador*, 64–65.

66. Baloyra, *El Salvador in Transition*, 64. Baloyra estimates that as many as fifty to one hundred thousand armed peasants participated in these "anticommunist" networks.

67. Ibid. Baloyra refers to this group as "the disloyal Right."

68. Montgomery, *Revolution in El Salvador*, 72.

69. Baloyra, *El Salvador in Transition*, 86–88.

70. Ibid., 73–74.

71. Paige, *Coffee and Power*, 195.

72. Lindo-Fuentes, Ching, and Lara-Martínez, *Massacre in El Salvador*, 240–41; Stanley, *Protection Racket State*, 107–32.

73. Note the use of *disappear* as a transitive verb. "To disappear someone" and "the disappeared" are translations from the Spanish and came into use in Latin America during the military juntas of the 1970s.

74. John A. Booth and Thomas W. Walker, *Understanding Central America*, 2nd ed. (Boulder: Westview, 1993), 103.

75. Approximately fifty-five thousand Salvadorans were killed between 1980 and 1984. See Booth and Walker, *Understanding Central America*, table 10).

76. For a full discussion of the massacre, see Mark Danner, *The Massacre at El Mozote* (New York: Vintage, 1994).

77. Theresa Whitfield, *Paying the Price: Ignacio Ellacuría and the Murdered Jesuits of El Salvador* (Philadelphia: Temple University Press, 1995), 169–70.

78. Cynthia McClintock, *Revolutionary Movements in Latin America: El Salvador's FMLN and Peru's Shining Path* (Washington, DC: U.S. Institute of Peace, 1998), 267–71.

79. The five other assassinated leaders were Juan Chacón, Manuel Franco, Enrique Barrera, Dorteo Hernández, and Humberto Mendoza.

80. For a discussion of the FDR during this period, see Dunkerley, *Long War*, 166–68.

81. Montgomery, *Revolution in El Salvador*, 114.

82. The Popular Forces of Liberation (FPL), the People's Revolutionary Army (ERP), the Armed Forces of National Resistence (FARN), the Revolutionary Party of Central American Workers (PRTC), and Armed Forces of Liberation (FAL).

83. The FDR and FMLN were allied during the early 1980s, but the relationship weakened as the war continued. Over time, the FMLN acquired increasing experience, so that by the late 1980s the FDR was essentially nonoperational although many of its representatives traveled abroad and drew attention to the cause.

84. Cynthia Arnson, *Crossroads: Congress, the Reagan Administration, and Central America* (New York: Pantheon Books, 1989), 41–42.

85. Byrne, *El Salvador's Civil War*, 61.

86. The Carter administration temporarily halted aid in December 1980 following the murders of U.S. Maryknoll nuns. Following the January 1981 FMLN offensive, the administration approved the resumption of military aid at increased levels. See Martin Diskin and Kenneth Sharpe, "El Salvador," in *Confronting Revolution: Security through Diplomacy in Central America*, ed. Morris Blachman, William Leogrande, and Sharpe (New York: Pantheon Books, 1986), 59; Arnson, *Crossroads*, 50. In addition, aid to Nicaragua was halted on grounds that it had aided the FMLN in the offensive.

87. That said, some hardliners within El Salvador's extreme right, such as D'Aubuisson, believed that the Reagan administration was soft on communism.

88. See Jeane Kirkpatrick, "Dictatorships and Democracy," *Commentary* 68, no. 5 (November 1979): 34–45.

89. Arnson, *Crossroads*, 50.

90. See Byrne, *El Salvador's Civil War*, 75–76. According to a 1981 U.S. Security Assessment, there were three main goals for U.S. policy in El Salvador: to avoid a coup by the extreme right; to maintain a government that is committed to democracy and change via reforms; and to improve economic growth in an effort to thwart a coup.

91. The Reagan Doctrine reinforced the administration's focus on the East-West conflict, pledging aid to anticommunist rebels, which were viewed as democratic, throughout the globe. Support of anticommunist rebels, such as the Contras in Nicaragua, was viewed as vital to U.S. national security and was accompanied by a policy to "roll back" communism through military means.

92. Booth and Walker, *Understanding Central America*; Byrne, *El Salvador's Civil War*.

93. Booth and Walker, *Understanding Central America*, 90–91.

94. See Dunkerley, *Long War*, 200–202; Montgomery, *Revolution in El Salvador*, 156–60.

95. Craig Pyes, "ARENA's Bid for Power," in *El Salvador: Central America in the New Cold War*, ed. Marvin E. Gettlemen, Patrick Lacefield, Louis Manashe, and David Mermelstein (New York: Grove Press, 1987), 165–74.

96. Marguerite Johnson and James Willwerth, "El Salvador: Taking a Chance on Elections," *Time Magazine*, December 21, 1981.

97. Diskin and Sharpe, "El Salvador," 64–65.

98. Rubén Zamora, *El Salvador, heridas que no cierran: Los partidos políticos en la post-guerra* (San Salvador: FLACSO Programa El Salvador, 1998), 53–54.

99. Montgomery, *Revolution in El Salvador*, 182.

100. Ibid., 190.

101. Alexander Segovia, "The War Economy of the 1980s," in *Economic Policy for Building Peace: The Lessons of El Salvador*, ed. James K. Boyce (Boulder: Lynne Rienner, 1996), 37.

102. Montgomery, *Revolution in El Salvador,* 190.

103. Segovia, "War Economy," 39.

104. Ibid., 40.

105. Ibid., 39.

106. In fact, a group of moderates, including D'Aubuisson's vice presidential candidate, split with ARENA shortly after the 1984 elections to form the Liberation Party (Partido Liberación).

107. Ibid., 42.

108. Kenneth Johnson, "Between Revolution and Democracy: Business Elites and the State in El Salvador during the 1980s" (PhD diss., Tulane University, 1993). See Johnson for an in-depth analysis of the transition of ARENA during the 1980s.

109. Several scholars suggest that the failure of the Soviet state actually had greater ideological ramifications for the Right than it did for the FMLN, which always employed its own brand of Salvadoran-style socialist doctrine.

110. See Joaquín Villalobos, "A Democratic Revolution for El Salvador," *Foreign Policy,* no. 74 (Spring 1989): 103–22.

111. United Nations, *The United Nations and El Salvador, 1990–1995* (New York: United Nations Department of Public Information), 9–10.

112. CD candidate Guillermo Ungo won 3.8 percent and the MAC, a splinter group of the PDC, won 1 percent.

113. Wood, *Forging Democracy,* 52–77.

114. It's worth noting that the far right was never far from the center of power, as demonstrated by Cristiani's selection of Gen. Rafael Bustillo as defense minister. The United States opposed the appointment, and Cristiani conceded. Bustillo was later named by the Truth Commission as the intellectual author of the murder of the UCA Jesuits.

115. Margaret Doggett, *Death Foretold: The Jesuit Murders in El Salvador* (Washington, DC: Georgetown University Press, 1993), 8.

116. Montgomery, *Revolution in El Salvador,* 219.

117. Victims of the 1989 UCA murders include Ignacio Ellacuría, rector of the UCA; Ignacio Martín-Baro, founder and director of the UCA's Institute of Public Opinion (IUDOP); Segundo Montes, founder and director of the UCA's Institute on Human Rights (IDHUCA); Joaquín López y López; Anando López; Juan Ramón Moreno; and Elba and Celina Ramos, the Jesuits' housekeeper and her daughter.

118. For a full discussion of the crime, conspiracy, and judicial proceedings, see Doggett, *Death Foretold.*

119. Montgomery, *Revolution in El Salvador,* 222. That amount was one-half the planned aid package. The other half of that aid was restored following the murder of two U.S. Marines in 1991.

120. The term *negotiated revolution* was coined by Álvaro de Soto, assistant UN secretary general Javier Pérez de Cuéllar, during negotiations.

Chapter 2: Making the Captured Peace

1. Rubén Zamora, interview by author, San Salvador, October 1999.

2. United Nations, *The United Nations and El Salvador, 1990–1995* (New York: United Nations Department of Public Information, 1995), 10; Teresa Whitfield, "The Role of the United Nations in El Salvador and Guatemala: A Preliminary Comparison," in *Comparative Peace Processes in Latin America*, ed. Cynthia J. Arnson (Washington, DC: Woodrow Wilson Center Press, 1999), 261.

3. Whitfield, "Role of the United Nations," 262.

4. Álvaro de Soto and Graciana del Castillo, "Obstacles to Peacebuilding," *Foreign Policy*, no. 94 (Spring 1994): 139.

5. Whitfield, "Role of the United Nations," 268. According to Whitfield, Pérez de Cuéllar was particularly concerned that the peace process be completed by the end of his term, on January 1, 1992, as there was no guarantee that his successor would be Latin American and thus share the same level of interest in resolving the conflict.

6. Tommie Sue Montgomery, "Getting to Peace in El Salvador: The Roles of the United Nations Secretariat and ONUSAL," *Journal of Interamerican Studies and World Affairs*, 37, no. 4 (Winter 1995), 139–72; Whitfield, "Role of the United Nations"; Diana Villiers Negroponte, *Seeking Peace in El Salvador: The Struggle to Reconstruct a Nation at the End of the Cold War* (New York: Palgrave Macmillan, 2012); David Holiday and William Stanley, "Under the Best of Circumstances: ONUSAL and the Challenges of Verification and Institution Building in El Salvador," in *Peacemaking and Democratization in the Western Hemisphere*, ed. Tommie Sue Montgomery (Miami: North-South Center Press, 2000), 37–65; Terry Lynn Karl, "El Salvador's Negotiated Revolution," *Foreign Affairs* 71, no. 2 (Spring 1992): 147–64.

7. See John Paul Lederach, *Preparing for Peace: Conflict Transformation across Cultures* (New York: Syracuse University Press, 1995); Johan Galtung, "Conflict Resolution as Conflict Transformation: The First Law of Thermodynamics Revisited," in *Conflict Transformation*, ed. Kumar Rupesinghe (New York: St. Martin's Press, 1995), 51–64.

8. United Nations Security Council, "Report of the Secretary-General on the situation in Central America; contains the text of the Geneva Agreement (4 April 1990) and the Caracas Agreement (21 May 1990) signed by the Government of El Salvador and the FMLN," A/45/706-S/21931, November 8, 1990.

9. Ibid.

10. Ibid. In fact, the FMLN delegation consulted with labor, church representatives, and human rights organizations before each round of negotiations. See Susan D. Burgerman, "Building the Peace by Mandating Reform: United Nations–Mediated Human Rights Agreements in El Salvador and Guatemala," *Latin American Perspectives* 27, no. 3 (May 2000): 79.

11. Ibid.

12. The UN maintained a presence in El Salvador after the ONUSAL mission closed on April 30, 1995, through the UN Mission in El Salvador (MINUSAL), whose original six-month term that began in May 1995 was extended through April 1996.

13. Ibid.

14. United Nations, "Letter dated 8 October 1991 from El Salvador transmitting the text of the Mexico Agreement and annexes signed on 27 April 1991 by the Government of El Salvador and the FMLN," A/46/553-S231–30, October 9, 1991.

15. Ibid.

16. Ibid.

17. Margaret Popkin, *Peace without Justice: Obstacles to Building the Rule of Law in El Salvador* (University Park: Pennsylvania State University Press, 2000), 101.

18. Ibid., 97.

19. United Nations, "Letters dated 26 September 1991 and 4 October 1991 from El Salvador transmitting texts of he New York Agreement and the Compressed Negotiations, signed on 25 September 1991 by the Government of El Salvador and the FMLN," A/46502-S/23082, September 26, 1991.

20. United Nations, "Letter dated 27 January 1992 from El Salvador transmitting the entire text of the Peace Agreement between the government of El Salvador and the FMLN, signed at Chapultepec Castle in Mexico City on 16 January 1992," A/46/864-S/23501, January 30, 1992.

21. Ibid.

22. Ibid.

23. Ibid.

24. Rubén Zamora and Roberto Cañas, interviews by author, San Salvador, October and November 1999. Also see Whitfield, "Role of the United Nations," 273.

25. Rubén Zamora, interview by author, San Salvador, October 1999.

26. Whitfield, "Role of the United Nations," 273.

27. The accords also state that the privatization process "shall also avoid monolopolistic practices, while guaranteeing business freedom and consumer protection." United Nations, "Letter dated 27 January 1992 from El Salvador

transmitting the entire text of the Peace Agreement between the Government of El Salvador and the FMLN, signed at Chapúltepec Castle in Mexico City on 16 January 1992," A/46/864-S/23501, January 30, 1992.

28. Elisabeth J. Wood, "Peace Accords and Postwar Reconstruction," in Boyce,, *Economic Policy*, 82.

29. United Nations, "Peace Agreement," A/46/864-S-23501, in *The United Nations and El Salvador, 1990-1995* (New York: United Nations, 1995), 193-230.

30. Ibid.

31. For a detailed account of the ONUSAL mission, see Lawyers' Committee for Human Rights, *Improvising History: A Critical Evaluation of the United Nations Observer Mission in El Salvador* (New York: The Committee, 1995).

32. See United Nations, "Report of the ONUSAL Human Rights Division for November and December 1991," A/46/876-S/23580, February 19, 1992.

33. United Nations Security Council, "Report of the Secretary-General on ONUSAL and the first report of the ONUSAL Human Rights Division," A/45/1055-S/23037, September 16, 1991.

34. United Nations, "Report of the ONUSAL Human Rights Division for the period from 1 January to 30 April 1992," A/46/935-S24066, June 5, 1992; United Nations, "Report of the ONUSAL Human Rights Division for November and December 1991," A/46/876-S/23580, February 19, 1992; United Nations, "Report of the Secretary-General on ONUSAL and the first report of the ONUSAL Human Rights Division," A/45/1055-S/23037, September 16, 1991.

35. Lawyers' Committee for Human Rights, *Improvising History*, 18-19.

36. Ibid., 19.

37. Popkin, *Peace without Justice*, 167-68; Charles T. Call, "Assessing El Salvador's Transition from Civil War to Peace," in *Ending Civil Wars: The Implementation of Peace Agreements*, ed. Stephen John Stedman, Donald Rothchild, and Elizabeth M. Cousens (Boulder: Lynne Rienner, 2002), 406.

38. Velásquez de Avilés had previously served as the deputy national counsel for children.

39. Popkin, *Peace without Justice*, 173-74; Call, "El Salvador's Transition," 407.

40. Popkin, *Peace without Justice*, 172.

41. Ricardo Córdova Macías, "Demilitarizing and Democratizing Salvadoran Politics," in *El Salvador: Implementation of the Peace Accords*, ed. Margarita S. Studemeister (Washington, DC: U.S. Institute of Peace, 2001), 27; Phillip J. Williams and Knut Walter, *Militarization and Demilitarization in El Salvador's Transition to Democracy* (Pittsburgh: University of Pittsburgh Press, 1997), 162-63.

42. Williams and Walter suggest that the military high command may have inflated initial numbers to give the appearance of a more dramatic reduction.

They suggest that the actual number was closer to forty to forty-two thousand rather than the reported sixty-three thousand.

43. The demobilization of the BIRIs was originally scheduled for December 1992, but the FMLN used its own demobilization as a tool in the land transfer stalemate. As a result, the high command refused to demobilize until the FMLN had done so.

44. Williams and Walter, *Militarization and Demilitarization*, 163.

45. Ibid., 156.

46. Montgomery, *Revolution in El Salvador*, 241.

47. Williams and Walter, *Militarization and Demilitarization*, 157.

48. Ibid., 153–54.

49. United Nations, *The United Nations and El Salvador*, doc. 41, sec. 5, 43.

50. United Nations, *The United Nations and El Salvador*, doc. 56, sec. 7, 65–67.

51. United Nations, *The United Nations and El Salvador*, doc. 82, annex 2 (B).

52. The chief responsibility of the division was monitoring the National Police; training Auxiliary Transitory Police (PAT), which was responsible for security in ex-conflict zones until the PNC could be deployed; and overseeing the deployment of the PNC.

53. Facilities designated for use by the ANSP were frequently annexed by old security forces; some were subjected to vandalism. See Call, "El Salvador's Transition," 400.

54. In response to the discovery, the secretary general stated, "This is clearly not what was intended in the Peace Agreement and is especially disturbing when linked to the apparent reinforcement, rather than reduction, of the National Police."

55. Lawrence Michael Ladutke, *Freedom of Expression in El Salvador: The Struggle for Human Rights and Democracy* (Jefferson, NC: McFarland, 2004), 135.

56. Héctor Silva Ávalos, *Infiltrados: Crónica de la corrupción en la PNC, 1992–2013* (San Salvador: UCA Editores, 2014), 90.

57. United Nations Security Council, "Report of the Secretary-General on all aspects of ONUSAL's operations," S/25812, May 21, 1993.

58. The Cristiani administration used crime as an excuse not to reduce the National Police. See United Nations Security Council, "Report of the Secretary-General on ONUSAL's activities from 21 November 1993 to 30 April 1994," S/1994/561, May 11, 1994.

59. Jack Spence, George Vickers, and David Dye, *The Salvadoran Peace Accords and Democratization: A Three Year Progress Report and Recommendations* (Cambridge, MA: Hemisphere Initiatives, 1995), 5–8.

60. Charles Call, "The Mugging of a Success Story: Justice and Security Reform in El Salvador," in *Constructing Justice and Security after War*, ed. Call (Washington, DC: U.S. Institute of Peace, 2007), 39.

61. United Nations, *The United Nations and El Salvador,* doc. 109, sec. 3, 42(d).

62. See Ladutke, *Freedom of Expression,* 135.

63. Ladutke offers a critical assessment in the role that the "dominant" media played in aiding the Cristiani administration in obfuscating responsibilities associated with the implementation of the accords, particularly with regard to public security and the truth commission's report.

64. For a detailed account of police reform in El Salvador and the relationship between the PNC and organized crime, see Silva Ávalos, *Infiltrados.*

65. Antonio Cañas and Héctor Dada, "Political Transition and Institutionalization in El Salvador," in Arnson, *Comparative Peace Processes in Latin America,* 69–95. The land transfer program was not intended to resolve issues of inequality but was an attempt to resolve the issue of lands occupied by ex-combatants and their supporters.

66. For a detailed discussion of the land transfer program and problems of implementation, see Spence, Vickers, and Dye, "Salvadoran Peace Accords," 13–17. For a follow-up discussion of the PTT, as well as an analysis of the 1996 agrarian debt law and its impact on the PTT, see Jack Spence, David R. Dye, Mike Lanchin, and Geoff Thale, *Chapúltepec: Five Years Later: El Salvador's Political Reality and Uncertain Future* (Cambridge, MA: Hemisphere Initiatives, 1995), 36–42.

67. Ibid., 15.

68. Ariane de Bremond, "The Politics of Peace and Resettlement through El Salvador's Land Transfer Program: Caught between the State and the Market," *Third World Quarterly* 28, no. 8 (2007): 1544.

69. Paramilitaries were excluded from the agreement, which became a serious source of tension during the mid to late 1990s.

70. De Bremond, "Politics of Peace and Resettlement," 1538.

71. Tommie Sue Montgomery, "The United Nations and Peacemaking in El Salvador," *North-South Issues* 4, no. 3 (1995): 4.

72. United Nations, *The Situation in Central America: Procedures of the Establishment of a Firm and Lasting Peace and Progress in Fashioning a Region of Peace, Freedom, Democracy and Development Assessment of the Peace Process in El Salvador: Report of the Secretary General* (New York: United Nations Department of Public Information, 1997), 34.

73. Miguel Sáenz, interview by author, San Salvador, March 2000.

74. Rubén Zamora, interview by author, San Salvador, October 1999.

75. Wood, "Peace Accords," 87.

76. Ibid., 88.

77. For a complete discussion of this issue, see Kevin Murray, Ellen Coletti, Jack Spence, et al., *Rescuing Reconstruction: The Debate on Post-war*

Economic Recovery in El Salvador (Cambridge, MA: Hemisphere Initiatives, 1994): 16-19.

78. Ibid., 11.

79. Ibid., 43.

80. Ibid., 12.

81. Segovia, "The War Economy of the 1980s," in Boyce, *Economic Policy*, 31.

82. James K. Boyce, "External Resource Mobilization," in Boyce, *Economic Policy*, 131.

83. Ibid., 135.

84. Ibid., 135-40. Boyce discusses four reasons for the funding priorities of non-U.S. donors: constraints on the volume of aid; the free-rider question; political impediments; and skepticism about the success of programs.

85. Ibid.

86. Montgomery, *Revolution in El Salvador*, 240-41.

87. For a more detailed discussion on transitional justice, see Neil J. Kritz, ed., *Transitional Justice: How Emerging Democracies Reckon with Former Regimes*, 3 vols. (Washington, DC: U.S. Institute of Peace, 1995); Martha Minow, *Between Vengeance and Forgiveness: Facing History after Genocide and Mass Violence* (Boston: Beacon Press, 1999); Ruti G. Teitel, *Transitional Justice* (New York: Oxford University Press, 2000); Priscilla B. Hayner, *Unspeakable Truths: Facing the Challenge of Truth Commissions* (New York: Routledge, 2001).

88. United Nations, *From Madness to Hope: The 12-Year War in El Salvador, Report of the Truth Commission for El Salvador*, appendix to UN doc. S/25500, April 1, 1993 (San Salvador: United Nations, 1993), 43.

89. Ibid., 44.

90. Ibid., 126.

91. Montgomery, *Revolution in El Salvador*, 243.

92. As stated in the Truth Commission's report, "at the beginning of its [the truth commission's] mandate, it received hints from the highest level to the effect that institutions do not commit crimes and therefore that responsibilities must be established by naming names. At the end of its mandate, it again received hints from the highest level, this time to the opposite effect, namely, that it should not name names, perhaps in order to protect certain individuals in recognition of their genuine and commendable eagerness to help create situations which facilitated the peace agreements and national reconciliation."

93. Hayner, *Unspeakable Truths*, 18.

94. Doggett, *Death Foretold*, 264.

95. Ibid., 262.

96. Lawyers' Committee for Human Rights, *Improvising History*, 123-24; Popkin, *Peace without Justice*, 122.

97. Ana Guardado, "Outsiders in El Salvador: The Role of an International Truth Commission in a National Transition" *Berkeley La Raza Law Journal,* 22, no. 2 (2012): 433–57; Lawyers' Committee for Human Rights, *Improvising History,* 141–42.

98. Popkin, *Peace without Justice,* 122. In both Chile and Argentina the new civilian administrations publicly accepted the findings of the reports, and efforts were made to disseminate the report to the public. The Argentine report, *Nunca más,* has sold over three hundred thousand copies. Although Chile's *Rettig Report* was published in newspapers, wider plans for dissemination were forestalled by a series of political assassinations.

99. As Guardado points out with the cases of Argentina and Chile, some of the more successful truth commissions are established by presidential decrees following the transition of power. Guatemala, like El Salvador, was established during UN negotiations, and the truth-seeking process was also conducted in the absence of serious structural reforms.

100. Ibid., 111.

101. Luc Huyse, "Justice after Transition: On the Choices Successor Elites Make in Dealing with the Past" *Law and Social Inquiry* 20, no. 1 (Winter 1995): 51–78.

102. Lawyers' Committee for Human Rights, *Improvising History,* 130.

103. As stated in the commission's mandate, "The Parties recognize the need to clarify and put an end to any indication of impunity on the part of officers of the armed forces, particularly where respect for human rights is jeopardized." As a result, the commission recognized that one of its chief tasks was to focus on the armed forces.

104. Lawyers' Committee for Human Rights, *Improvising History*; Popkin, *Peace without Justice,* 117–19.

105. While certainly not the primary cause of the coming split within the FMLN, it fostered animosity within the organization.

106. Dorothy Vidulich, "U.N. Salvador report prompts U.S. criticism—El Salvador death squads investigation." *National Catholic Reporter.* March 26, 1993.

107. United Nations, *From Madness to Hope,* Report of the Truth Commission for El Salvador, 172–77.

108. Hayner, *Unspeakable Truths,* 119–20.

109. United Nations, "Report issued on 28 July 1994 by the Joint Group for the Investigation of Politically Motivated Illegal Armed Groups (extract: conclusions and recommendations)," S/1994/989, October 22, 1994.

110. United Nations, *From Madness to Hope.*

111. Emily Braid and Naomi Roht-Arriaza, "De Facto and De Jure Amnesty Laws: The Central American Case," in *Amnesty in the Age of Human Rights*

Accountability: Comparative and International Perspectives, ed. Francesca Lessa and Leigh Payne (New York: Cambridge University Press, 2012), 171.

112. Popkin, *Peace without Justice,* 253.

113. Hayner, *Unspeakable Truths,* 170–71.

114. Popkin, *Peace without Justice,* 149.

115. Ibid., 152.

116. Ibid., 151.

117. Ibid., 152–57.

118. Inter-American Commission on Human Rights, "Report on the Situation of Human Rights in El Salvador" (1994), OEA/Ser.L/II.85, doc. 28 rev., 75.

119. Emily Braid and Naomi Roht-Arriaza, "Amnesty Laws," 201.

120. IUDOP, "Los salvadoreños ante los acuerdos finales de paz," *Informe,* no. 31 (1992), http://www.uca.edu.sv/publica/iudop/informes1a100/informe31.pdf.

121. For more on the case, see Ford et al. v. García, Vides Casanova, 289 F. 3d 1283 (11th Cir. 2002).

122. The damages included $14.6 million in compensatory and $40 million punitive damages. See Joshua E. S. Phillips, "The Case against the Generals: U.S. Now Home to Hundreds of Accused War Criminals and Torturers from All Over Latin America," *Washington Post,* August 17, 2003.

123. César Castro Fagoaga, "Presidente Saca defiende a ex viceministro Carranza," *El Faro,* November 7, 2005, http://www.elfaro.net/Secciones/noticias/20051114/noticias7_20051114.asp.

124. Carlos Dada, "How We Killed Archbishop Romero," *El Faro,* March 25, 2010, http://www.elfaro.net/es/201003/noticias/1416/?st-full_text=1.

125. Braid and Roht-Arriaza, "Amnesty Laws," 204–5.

126. Center for Justice and Accountability, "The Jesuits Massacre Case," http://www.cja.org/article.php?list=type&type=84.

127. See, for example, Johan Galtung, "Peace and Conflict Research in the Age of the Cholera: Ten Pointers to the Future of Peace Studies," *Peace and Conflict Studies* 2, no. 1 (July 1995), and "After Violence: 3R, Reconstruction, Reconciliation, Resolution: Coping with Visible and Invisible Effects of War and Violence," Transcend: A Peace and Development Network, July 1998, http://www.transcend.org/TRRECBAS.HTM.

128. Hayner, *Unspeakable Truths,* 161–63.

129. Carlos Dada, "La prolongación de la guerra por otros medios," in *La polarización política en El Salvador,* ed. Álvaro Artiga González et al. (San Salvador: FUNDAUNGO and FLACSO), 23–36.

130. IUDOP, "Salvadoreños ante los acuerdos finales."

131. For an additional illustration of this, see Julie M. Mazzei, "Finding Shame in Truth: The Importance of Public Engagement in Truth Commissions," *Human Rights Quarterly* 33, no. 2 (May 2011): 431–52.

132. "Proponen reconocer a Duarte y a D'Aubuisson," *La Prensa Gráfica,* February 14, 2007, http://www.laprensagrafica.net/nacion/715783.asp.

133. Israel Serrano, "Calle San Antonio Abad será nombrada Mayor Roberto d'Aubuisson," *La Página,* November 27, 2014, http://www.lapagina .com.sv/nacionales/101531/2014/11/26/Calle-San-Antonio-Abad-sera-nombrada -Mayor-Roberto-d´Aubuisson.

134. "Pope Approves Martydom Declaration of Oscar Romero, Slain Archbishop of San Salvador," *New York Times,* February 3, 2015, at http://www .nytimes.com/aponline/2015/02/03/world/europe/ap-eu-rel-vatican-romero .html?_r=0.

135. ONUSAL's electoral division was established under UN Security Council Resolution 832 in September 1993 and was dissolved April 30, 1994.

136. The elections were governed by an electoral agreement signed by political parties in 1990. One of the most significant changes was the increase in the number of seats in the Legislative Assembly from 60 to 84.

137. Montgomery, *Revolution in El Salvador,* 222–23.

138. The Nationalist Democratic Union (UDN) and the Authentic Christian Movement (MAC) each won a single seat. ARENA won 181 municipalities, followed by the PDC with 70 and the PCN with 11.

139. Rubén Zamora, "Democratic Transition or Modernization? The Case of El Salvador since 1979," in *Democratic Transitions in Central America,* ed. Jorge I. Domínguez and Marc Lindenberg (Gainesville: University Press of Florida, 1997), 177.

140. United Nations Security Council, "Report of the Secretary-General on the United Nations Observer Mission in El Salvador," S/1994/304, March 16, 1994, 1–2.

141. Ibid., 2.

142. For a detailed description of the process, see Montgomery, *Revolution in El Salvador,* 250–51.

143. UN Security Council, "Observer Mission in El Salvador," S/1994/304, March 16, 1994, 3.

144. As stated by both Montgomery and Richard Stahler-Sholk, it was believed that restricting the size of the voter pool would benefit ARENA. Montgomery, *Revolution in El Salvador,* 250; Stahler-Sholk, "El Salvador's Negotiated Transition: From Low-Intensity Conflict to Low-Intensity Democracy," *Journal of Interamerican Studies and World Affairs* 36, no. 4 (1994): 29.

145. Stahler-Sholk, "Negotiated Transition," 24–25.

146. Ibid., 24.

147. UN Security Council, " Observer Mission in El Salvador," S/1994/304, March 16, 1994.

148. Stahler-Sholk, "Negotiated Transition," 31-33.

149. UN Security Council, "Observer Mission in El Salvador," S/1994/304, March 16, 1994.

150. UN Security Council, "Observer Mission in El Salvador," S/1994/375, March 31, 1994.

151. Ibid.

152. See William A. Barnes, "Incomplete Democracy in Central America: Polarization and Voter Turnout in Nicaragua and El Salvador," *Journal of Interamerican Studies and World Affairs* 40, 3 (Autumn 1998): 63-101. In his comparison of the "elections of the century" in Nicaragua (1990) and El Salvador (1994), Barnes found that Nicaragua's significantly higher turnout (78 percent) was attributed to a political culture that emphasized democratic participation, the strong sense of professionalism within Nicaragua's electoral commission, and high levels of voter confidence that the process would be fair.

153. Leonard Wantcheckon, "Strategic Voting in Conditions of Political Instability: The 1994 Elections in El Salvador," *Comparative Political Studies* 32, no. 7 (1999): 810-34.

154. IUDOP, "Salvadoreños ante los acuerdos finales."

155. See Murray et al., *Rescuing Reconstruction,* 6. The economic program being implemented by the Cristiani administration was "simply not on the table" during the peace negotiations. This was the insistence of the Salvadoran government and the implicit understanding of the FMLN. Cañas and Zamora interviews, San Salvador, October, November 1999.

Chapter 3: Electoral Politics in the Postwar Era

1. Salvador Sanabria, interview by author, San Salvador, October 2006.

2. I do not include the transfer of power from the PDC to ARENA in 1989 because those elections were held during a war and the opposition was excluded from participating.

3. Álvaro Artiga, interview by author, San Salvador, October 2006.

4. Gary Wynia, *The Politics of Latin American Development,* 3rd ed. (New York: Cambridge University Press, 1990), 25.

5. The PCN routinely won seats well in excess of those it received through direct election. For example, in 2006 only two PCN candidates were directly elected, but an additional eight were seated as a result of the remainder vote.

6. For the ruling, see http://www.jurisprudencia.gob.sv/Exploiis/indice.asp ?nBD=1&nDoc=29317&nItem=29486&nModo=3.

7. See *Elecciones 2015,* http://www.tse.gob.sv/e107_files/downloads/codigo _electoral.pdf.

8. Wynia, *Politics of Latin American Development*, 26.

9. IUDOP, *Boletín de Prensa* 23, no. 2 (2008).

10. IUDOP, "Los salvadorenos y salvadorenas frente a las elecciones presidenciales de 2014," *Boletín de Prensa* 27, no. 1 (2014).

11. Before this change, the votes of four of five magistrates were required to approve changes to the electoral code.

12. Ricardo Córdova Macías and Carlos Ramos, "The Peace Process and the Construction of Democracy in El Salvador: Progress, Deficiencies and Challenges," in *In the Wake of War: Democratization and Internal Armed Conflict in Latin America*, ed. Cynthia J. Arnson (Washington, DC: Woodrow Wilson Center Press, 2012), 95.

13. Rafael López-Pintor, "El Salvador," in *Political Finance in Post-conflict Societies*, ed. Jeff Fischer, Marcin Walecki, and Jeffrey Carlson (Washington, DC: Center for Transitional and Post-Conflict Governance, International Foundation for Electoral Systems, 2006), 58.

14. EU Election Observation Mission, *El Salvador: Legislative, Municipal and PARLACEN Elections—2009*, January 20, 2009, http://www.eods.eu/library/EUEOM%20PS%20EL%20SALVADOR%2020.01.2009_%20en.pdf.

15. Tommie Sue Montgomery, "Getting to Peace in El Salvador: The Roles of the United Nations Secretariat and ONUSAL." *Journal of Interamerican Studies and World Affairs* 37, no. 4 (Winter 1995): 139–72," 144–56. See Montgomery also for a discussion of the various weaknesses with respect to the 1994 elections.

16. Félix Ulloa, interview by author, San Salvador, March 2000.

17. Ibid.

18. Riitta-Ilona Koivumaeki, "El Salvador: Societal Cleavages, Strategic Elites, and the Success of the Right," in *The Resilience of the Latin American Right*, ed. Juan Pablo Luna and Cristóbal Rovira Kaltwasser (Baltimore: Johns Hopkins University Press, 2014): 278–79.

19. Rafael López-Pintor, "El Salvador," in *Political Finance in Post-conflict Societies*, ed. Jeff Fischer, Marcin Walecki, and Jeffrey Carlson (Washington, DC: Center for Transitional and Post-Conflict Governance, International Foundation for Electoral Systems (IFES), May 2006): 49–60, available at http://www.ifes.org/publication/0b087c527792ae130507f80957ad3f2b/Poltiical%20Finance%20in%20Post-Conflict%20Societies-small.pdf.

20. Jack Spence, David R. Dye, Mike Lanchin, Geoff Thale, and George Vickers, *Chapúltepec: Five Years Later: El Salvador's Political Reality and Uncertain Future* (Cambridge, MA: Hemisphere Initiatives, 1997), 12.

21. Ibid., 11.

22. A carnet is the voter registration card used in El Salvador.

NOTES TO PAGES 76-78

23. Tommie Sue Montgomery, *Revolution in El Salvador: From Civil Strife to Civil Peace*, 2nd ed. (Boulder: Westview, 1995), 265; Richard Stahler-Sholk, "El Salvador's Negotiated Transition: From Low-Intensity Conflict to Low-Intensity Democracy," *Journal of Interamerican Studies and World Affairs* 36, no. 4 (1994): 29.

24. Juan José Martel, interview by author, San Salvador, October 2006.

25. DIGESTYC, *VI censo de población y V de vivienda 2007,* http://www.censos .gob.sv/util/datos/Resultados%20VI%20Censo%20de%20Poblaci%F3n%20V %20de%20Vivienda%202007.pdf, April 2008.

26. It was unclear whether the census findings would have benefited ARENA or the FMLN in redistricting. During my 2009 research, I heard claims that the redistricting would clearly benefit the FMLN, as well as claims that ARENA had manipulated the census to reduce the population in FMLN districts to give itself an electoral advantage. The only thing that was clear was that any redistricting would like reduce the total number of seats in the assembly.

27. El Salvador Solidarity, "Congressional Brief: Electoral Violations and Anomalies," U.S.-El Salvador Sister Cities, accessed February 2009, http:// elsalvadorsolidarity.org/joomla/index.php?option=com_content&task=view&id =208&Itemid=65#_edn8.

28. See also John Carey, "Political Institutions in El Salvador: Proposals for Reform to Improve Elections, Transparency, and Accountability," draft paper prepared for FUSADES, December 2013, http://www.hks.harvard.edu/fs /rhausma/elsvdr/political.pdf.

29. Roberto Rubio-Fabiàn, Antonio Morales, Tomás Carbonell, Florentín Meléndez, and Anne Germain Lefévre, "Democratic Transition in Post-conflict El Salvador: The Role of the International Community," Netherlands Institute of International Relations "Clingendael," August 2004, 109.

30. This system was further complicated by the fact that married couples may not share the same last name and may be required to travel to different polling places, a difficulty that is only exacerbated when child care and inadequate transportation is an issue. See Jack Spence, Mike Lanchin, and Geoff Thale, *From Elections to Earthquakes: Reform and Participation in Post-war El Salvador* (Cambridge, MA: Hemisphere Initiatives, April 2001), 6.

31. The seven chosen municipalities were Turín, in the Ahuachapán Department; El Paisnal, in San Salvador; Nuevo Cuscatlán, in La Libertad; San Juan Nonualco, in La Paz; Tecapán, in San Vicente; Carolina, in San Miguel; and Meanguera del Golfo, in La Unión.

32. Salvadoreños en el Mundo, "Briefing Paper on Voting Rights for 3.3 Million Disenfranchised Salvadoran Migrants Living Overseas," April 14, 2008.

33. Ibid.

34. Salvador Sanabria, interview by author, San Salvador, March 2009.

35. Embassy of El Salvador, Washington, DC, pers. comm., March 13, 2014.

36. The mayor and deputy mayor positions would still go to the party with the largest vote share.

37. There were some politically motivated killings of FMLN activists in 1994, but that pattern did not continue.

38. Alfredo Mena Lagos, interview by author, San Salvador, October 2006.

39. Michael Coppedge, *Strong Parties and Lame Ducks: Presidential Partyarchy and Factionalism in Venezuela* (Stanford: Stanford University Press, 1994), 19-20.

40. Elaine Freedman, "Mapping the Salvadoran Media," *Envio* 366 (January 2012), http://www.envio.org.ni/articulo/4483.

41. See Nataly Guzmán, "Las elecciones presidenciales de 2004: Un studio desde la prensa escrita," *ECA Estudios Centroamericanos* 59, no. 667 (2004): 419-32; Marcos Rodríguez, Danilo Padilla, and Raúl Torres, *La propaganda electoral en El Salvador (2008-2009): Monitoreo y propuestas para transparencia* (San Salvador: Fundación Nacional para el Desarrollo, 2009).

42. Freedman, "Mapping the Salvadoran Media."

43. See Álvaro Artiga González, *Elitismo competitivo: Dos décadas de elecciones en El Salvador (1982-2003)* (San Salvador: UCA Editores, 2004), 94-110.

44. Cristina Rivas Pérez, "The Dimensions of Polarization in Parliaments," in *Politicians and Politics in Latin America,* ed. Manuel Alcántara Sáez (Boulder: Lynne Rienner, 2008), 139-60.

45. Mélany Barragán Manjón, "El Salvador: Unas elecciones presidenciales marcadas por el conflicto y la polarización ideológica," *Elites Parlamentarias Latinoamericanas,* no. 57 (January 2014).

46. Jeroen de Zeeuw, "Political Party Development in Post-war Societies: The Institutionalization of Parties and Party Systems in El Salvador and Cambodia" (PhD thesis. University of Warwick, 2009), 112; Rubén Zamora, "Polarización y democracia: Un mal necesario?" in *La polarización política en El Salvador* (San Salvador: FUNDAUNGO, 2007), 63-101.

47. For a detailed discussion of El Salvador's political parties, see Rubén Zamora, *El Salvador, heridas que no cierran: Los partidos políticos en la post-guerra* (San Salvador: FLACSO, 1998); de Zeeuw, "Political Party Development," 104-10.

48. Kenneth L. Johnson, "Between Revolution and Democracy: Business Elites and the State in El Salvador during the 1980s" (PhD diss., Tulane University, 1993); Jeffrey M. Paige, *Coffee and Power: Revolution and the Rise of Democracy in Central America* (Cambridge, MA: Harvard University Press, 1997). See both sources for an in-depth discussion of the tensions between these two groups and the general ideology of Salvadoran elites.

49. Paige, *Coffee and Power*, 190.

50. Quoted in Montgomery, *Revolution in El Salvador*, 8–9.

51. Minister of Agriculture Carlos Mejía Alférez and Minister of Finance Ricardo Montenegro resigned on November 28, 1995.

52. Jack Spence et al., *Chapúltepec: Five Years Later*, 22–23.

53. Salguero Gross left in the party in 2001, saying party no longer represented her. She formed the short-lived Partido Popular Republicano (PPR).

54. Cardenal, who had been tapped by Flores, claimed that he had been wary of the internal power struggle between Cristiani and Flores and the effect it would have on his campaign. The first month of his campaign, he had "no office, no fax, no nothing, not even a card that said I was the candidate." Luis Cardenal, interview by author, San Salvador, 2004.

55. "Murray Meza renuncia a presidencia de ARENA," *La Prensa Gráfica*, March 19, 2002.

56. Rodrigo Ávila, interview by author, Santa Tecla, March 2004.

57. ARENA officials, interviews by author, San Salvador, March 2004, October–November 2006.

58. Carlos Dada, "ARENA inicia expulsión de Saca," *El Faro*, December 12, 2009.

59. Sergio Arauz, "ARENA expulsa a Saca y Saca no se da por expulsado," *El Faro*, December 14, 2009, http://www.elfaro.net/es/200912/noticias/735/.

60. "Third Party on the Rise," *Central America Report*, no. 3716, April 3, 2010.

61. Portions of this section appear in Christine Wade, "El Salvador: The Successful Transformation of the FMLN," in *From Soldiers to Politicians: Transforming Rebel Movements after Civil War*, ed. Jeroen de Zeeuw (Boulder: Lynne Rienner, 2007), 33–54.

62. Montgomery, *Revolution in El Salvador*; Cynthia McClintock, *Revolutionary Movements in Latin America: El Salvador's FMLN and Peru's Shining Path* (Washington, DC: U.S. Institute of Peace, 1998); Hugh Byrne, *El Salvador's Civil War: A Study in Revolution* (Boulder: Lynne Rienner, 1996); Wade, "El Salvador"; Michael Allison and Alberto Martín Alvarez, "Unity and Disunity in the FMLN," *Latin American Politics and Society* 54, no. 4 (Winter 2012): 89–118.

63. See Christine Wade, "The Left and Neoliberalism: Postwar Politics in El Salvador" (PhD diss., Boston University, 2003), 48–51.

64. Wade, "El Salvador"; Allison and Martín, "Unity and Disunity"; Carrie Manning, *The Making of Democrats: Elections and Party Development in Bosnia, El Salvador, and Mozambique* (New York: Palgrave Macmillan, 2008).

65. Centro de Información, Documentación y Apoyo a la Investigación (CIDAI), "The FMLN: Searching for an Identity," *Proceso* 908, June 28, 2000, http://www.uca.edu.sv/publica/proceso/proci908.html.

66. Rodríguez lost the PDC nomination and Villalobos retreated to the FMLN.

67. Montgomery, *Revolution in El Salvador*, 268.

68. The Ortodoxo faction is led by Schafik Handal and Salvador Sánchez Cerén, the Renovadores by Facundo Guardado, and the neutral Terceristas by Gerson Martínez.

69. Ilja A. Luciak, *After the Revolution: Gender and Democracy in El Salvador, Nicaragua, and Guatemala* (Baltimore: Johns Hopkins University Press, 2001).

70. Gerson Martínez, interview by author, San Salvador, March 2001.

71. The nominations for the presidential ticket were further complicated by the fact that the FMLN decided at its December 1997 convention that the presidential ticket must consist of a male-female combination. That requirement was abolished in advance of the 2004 election.

72. The FMLN requires 518 votes to win the nomination. De Avíles received 441 votes to Silva's 431.

73. CIDAI, "The Lack of Wisdom of the FMLN Convention," *Proceso* 818, August 18, 1998, http://www.uca.edu.sv/publica/proceso/proci818.html.

74. Paradoxically, the FMLN was essentially a "war" ticket represented by two former guerrilla commanders, Guardado and Díaz. The ARENA ticket, however, signaled a break with the past, positing a candidate unassociated with the war.

75. Guardado's platform provided for a continuation of the neoliberal model but with more state regulation and redistributive capacity.

76. Party unity was created in 1995, resulting in the disbanding of factional identities.

77. "FMLN expulsa a Facundo Guardado," *La Prensa Gráfica*, October 2, 2001.

78. Ibid.

79. Those deputies were later expelled from the FMLN and are creating a new party, as yet unnamed, to participate in the upcoming elections with a coalition of leftist parties.

80. The deputies continued to participate in the Legislative Assembly under the name Movimiento Renovador.

81. To participate in the 2003 municipal and legislative elections, the party will have to collect thirty-five thousand signatures.

82. "El Salvador: New Political Party Formed from Faction Farabundo Martí para Liberación Nacional," *NotiCen*, April 18, 2002.

83. "Facundistas presentan nuevo partido," *La Prensa Gráfica*, April 8, 2002.

84. "Guardado, presidente renovador," *El Diario de Hoy*, April 8, 2002.

85. The FMLN internal elections were conducted by democratic, secret ballot. Shortly after the 2006 municipal and legislative elections, the FMLN leadership announced that it would suspend this practice.

86. In fact, the Ortodoxos won thirty-four of the thirty-five seats up for election.

87. Héctor Perla, Jr., Marco Mojica, and Jared Bibler, "From Guerrillas to Government: The Continued Relevance of the Central American Left," in *The New Latin American Left: Cracks in the Empire,* ed. Jeffrey R. Webber and Barry Carr (Lanham, MD: Rowman and Littlefield, 2012), 339.

88. Ibid.

89. The PCN has on occasion voted with the FMLN against ARENA.

90. As mentioned earlier, the PCN was also the beneficiary of El Salvador's remainder vote system, which allocated it a disproportionate number of seats to votes won.

91. Due to a coalition between ARENA, the PCN, and the PDC, the FMLN did not control the Legislative Assembly. This was a matter of great contention, particularly with concern of the directorship of the assembly. The FMLN countered that the move was undemocratic and refused to participate in the directorate. Critics also question the validity of such a move by ARENA, seen as a last-ditch effort to maintain control.

92. Rubén Zamora, interview by author, Washington, DC, September 2001.

93. Sonja Wolf, "Subverting Democracy: Elite Rule and the Limit to Political Participation in Post-war El Salvador," *Journal of Latin American Studies* 41, no. 3 (August 2009): 431-33.

94. Spence et al., "Chapúltepec," 26.

95. Ibid.

96. United Nations Development Programme (UNDP), *Informe sobre Indices de Desarrollo Humano en El Salvador* (San Salvador: UNDP, 1997), 32.

97. There are 84 seats in the Legislative Assembly and 262 municipalities in El Salvador. Counting coalitions, the FMLN took 54 mayoralties in 1997.

98. José Miguel Cruz, "¿Por qué no votan los salvadoreños?," *Estudios Centroamericanos* 53, nos. 595-96 (1998): 449-72, table 10.

99. IUDOP, "Los salvadoreños frente a las elecciones presidenciales 99," *Boletín de Prensa* 16, no. 2 (1999): 99.

100. For more background on the strike, see Paul Almeida, *Waves of Protest: Popular Struggle in El Salvador, 1925-2005* (Minneapolis: University of Minnesota Press, 2008), 194-204.

101. This number, while telling of the discontent toward Flores' program, is a significant decline from the 1980s, when such activity would have been far riskier. Byrne cites two hundred strikes in 1985 alone. Byrne, *El Salvador's Civil War,* 144. See also Lisa Kowalchuck, "Can Movement Tactics Influence Media

Coverage? Health-Care Struggle in the Salvadoran News," *Latin American Research Review* 44, no. 2 (2009): 109-35.

102. IUDOP, "Encuesta de evaluación del primer año de Francisco Flores, Asamblea Legislative, Alcaldias y post-electoral," *Informe*, no. 85 (May 2000).

103. Ibid.

104. Jack Spence, Mike Lanchin, and Geoff Thale, *From Elections to Earthquakes: Reform and Participation in Post-war El Salvador* (Cambridge, MA: Hemisphere Initiatives, 2001), 34.

105. United Nations Economic Commission for Latin America and the Caribbean (ECLAC), *The January 13, 2001, Earthquake in El Salvador: Socioeconomic and Environmental Impact*, LC/Mex/L.457, February 21, 2001, http://www.bvsde.paho.org/bvsade/i/fulltext/earthquake/earthquake.pdf.

106. CIDAI, "The Falling of the Democratic Façade," *Proceso* 936, January 24, 2001, http://www.uca.edu.sv/publica/proceso/proci936.html.

107. Ismael Moreno, "Dollarization and the Earthquake: Two Manmade Disasters," *Envio*, no. 234 (January 2001), http://www.envio.org.ni/articulo/1473.

108. Spence, Lanchin, and Thale, *From Elections to Earthquakes*, 36.

109. David Gonzalez, "Santa Tecla Journal: Shovels Are Easier Than Rifles, Ex-Guerrilla Says," *New York Times*, April 4, 2001, http://www.nytimes.com/2001/04/04/world/santa-tecla-journal-shovels-are-easier-than-rifles-ex-guerrilla-says.html.

110. Kowalchuk, "Movement Tactics," 117.

111. Paul Almeida, *Waves of Protest*, 194-202.

112. Francisco Altschul, interview by author, San Salvador, November 2006.

113. In El Salvador it is illegal for workers in the public sector to strike.

114. IUDOP, "Evaluacíon del país a finales de 2002 y perspectivas electorales para 2003," *Boletín de Prensa* 17, no. 4 (2002).

115. "A 'Hard Hand': State Violence against Youth Gangs," *Proceso* 266 (September 2003), http://www.envio.org.ni/articulo/2121.

116. Ibid.

117. Sonja Wolf, "Subverting Democracy: Elite Rule and the Limits of Political Participation in Post-war El Salvador," *Journal of Latin American Studies* 41, no. 3 (2009): 448; Alisha C. Holland, "Right on Crime? Conservative Party Politics and *Mano Dura* Policies in El Salvador," *Latin American Research Review* 48, no. 1 (2013): 44-67.

118. When asked which candidate they would never vote for, 44 percent of respondents said Handal, more than double those who said they would never vote for Saca (18.8 percent). Interestingly, only 5 percent said they would never vote for Silva. See IUDOP, "Los salvadoreños frente a las elecciones presidenciales de 2004," *Boletín de Prensa* 19, no. 1 (2004).

119. Rodrigo Ávila, interview by author, Santa Tecla, March 2004.
120. The actual number is actually higher, as there is a tendency to under-report the receipt of remittances. See IUDOP, "Encuesta sobre el proceso electoral de 2004," 103, table 6.
121. "Disturbing Statement out of El Salvador," Congressional Record, March 17, 2004, pp. E394–95.
122. "El Salvador," Congressional Record E402, March 17, 2004.
123. "Election in El Salvador," Congressional Record E389, March 17, 2004.
124. IUDOP, Informe, no. 103 (2004), table 70.
125. United Nations General Assembly, Report of the Secretary-General, "The Situation in Central America: Progress in fashioning a region of peace, freedom, democracy and development," August 11, 2005, A/60/218.
126. Wolf, "Subverting Democracy," 454.
127. Salvadoran election law prohibits the head of state from participating in party activities, something that was complicated by his role as the president of COENA.
128. Wolf, "Subverting Democracy," 454–55.
129. Handal's controversial persona and poor showing in the 2004 election notwithstanding, the popular outpouring of grief at his funeral was easily one of the largest public gatherings in Salvadoran history.
130. Holding the elections separately also gave ARENA an advantage because it had more financial resources than the FMLN.
131. The PCN's presidential candidate, Tomás Chévez, an evangelical minister, refused to withdraw from the race and claimed that his rights had been violated. The PCN retaliated by expelling him from the party.
132. Joaquín Villalobos, "¿Quién gobernaría, Funes o el FMLN?," El Diario de Hoy, accessed December 30, 2008, http://www.elsalvador.com/mwedh/nota/nota_opinion.asp?idCat=6350&idArt=3182935.
133. Rep. Dana Rohrabacher, "Extension of Remarks, El Salvador Election," March 11, 2009, http://rohrabacher.house.gov/UploadedFiles/elsalvador_extension_of_remarks.PDF.
134. IUDOP, "Los salvadoreños y las salvadoreñas frente las elecciones presidenciales 2009," Boletín de Prensa 24, no. 1 (2009).
135. This was particularly true at the Flor Blanca stadium, where I began my morning. The TSE had prepared for thousands of voters from abroad to vote there, but only a few hundred showed up.
136. Rodrigo Ávila, interview by author, Santa Tecla, March 2004.
137. UN News Centre, "New Law in El Salvador Threatens Judicial Independence, UN Rights Expert Says," July 1, 2011, http://www.un.org/apps/news/story.asp?NewsID=38917&Cr=&Cr1=#.VITlGb4q8iA.

138. Tim Muth, "El Salvador's Constitutional Crisis Roils the Nation," *Christian Science Monitor*, June 16, 2001, http://www.csmonitor.com/World/ Americas/Latin-America-Monitor/2011/0616/El-Salvador-s-constitutional-crisis -roils-the-nation; Voices on the Border, "The Debate over Decree 743 Continues," June 14, 2011, http://voiceselsalvador.wordpress.com/2011/06/14/the -debate-over-decree-743-continues/.

139. Elaine Freedman, "What's behind Decree 743?," *Envio* 360, July 2011, http://www.envio.org.ni/articulo/4376; Edgarado Ayala, "El Salvador: Rumors of Amnesty Repeal Cause Panic," *Inter Press Service*, July 11, 2011, http://www .ipsnews.net/2011/07/rights-el-salvador-rumours-of-amnesty-repeal-cause-panic /; Emily Achtenberg, "A Vote for Democracy in El Salvador," *NACLA*, August 5, 2011, https://nacla.org/blog/2011/8/5/vote-democracy-el-salvador.

140. Freedman, "What's behind Decree 743?"

141. Geoff Thale, "Tensions Rise between El Salvador's National Assembly and the Supreme Court: Understanding (and Misunderstanding) the Salvadoran Constitutional Court Crisis," Washington Office on Latin America, July 18, 2012, http://www.wola.org/commentary/tensions_rise_between_el_salvador_s _national_assembly_and_the_supreme_court_understanding.

142. Perla, Mojica, and Bibler, "From Guerrillas to Government," 339.

143. IUDOP, "Los salvadoreños y salvadoreñas evalúan el tercer año de gobierno de Mauricio Funes y opinan sobre el proceso electoral de 2012," *Boletín de Prensa* 26, no. 3 (2012); IUDOP, *Boletín de Prensa* 27, no. 1 (2013).

144. IUDOP, "Los salvadoreños frente a las elecciones presidenciales de 2004," *Boletín de Prensa* 19, no. 1 (2004); IUDOP, *Boletín de Prensa* 27, no. 2 (2013).

145. IUDOP, *Boletín de Prensa* 27, no. 2 (2013).

146. David Pérez, "Corrupción atribuida a expresidente Flores aumenta $75 millones," *Contra Punto*, February 11, 2014, http://www.contrapunto.com.sv/ politica/corrupcion-atribuida-a-expresidente-flores-aumenta-75-millones.

147. Roger Noriega, "Will Elections in El Salvador Create a Narcostate?," American Enterprise Institute, February 24, 2014, http://www.aei.org/outlook /foreign-and-defense-policy/regional/latin-america/will-elections-in-el -salvador-create-a-narcostate/; Jim Demint, "High Stakes for U.S. in El Salvador's Election," *Miami Herald*, February 13, 2014, http://www.miamiherald .com/2014/02/13/3933733/high-stakes-for-us-in-el-salvadors.html

148. IUDOP, "En frente a segunda vuelta 2014," *Boletín de Prensa* 28, no. 3 (2014).

149. Michael Allison and Christine Wade, "To Rebound after Defeat, El Salvador's ARENA Must Move beyond Fear," *World Politics Review*, April 16, 2014, http://www.worldpoliticsreview.com/articles/13706/to-rebound-after-defeat

-el-salvador-s-arena-must-move-beyond-fear; Héctor Perla, Jr., "Elections in El Salvador: ARENA's Dangerous Gambit," Council on Hemispheric Affairs, March 10, 2014, http://www.coha.org/elections-in-el-salvador-arenas-dangerous-gambit/.

150. It was also the first time that voters could directly vote for PARLACEN representatives.

151. See, for example, Sidney Verba and Norman H. Nie, *Participation in America: Political Democracy and Social Equality* (Chicago: University of Chicago Press, 1987); Robert Putnam, *Making Democracy Work: Civic Traditions in Modern Italy* (Princeton: Princeton University Press, 1993); Putnam, *Bowling Alone: The Collapse and Revival of American Community* (New York: Simon and Schuster, 2000); Ronald Inglehart and Christian Welzel, *Modernization, Cultural Change, and Democracy* (New York: Cambridge University Press, 2005); Christian Welzel and Ronald Inglehart, "The Role of Ordinary People in Democratization," *Journal of Democracy* 19, no. 1 (January 2008): 126–40.

152. William A. Barnes, "Incomplete Democracy in Central America: Polarization and Voter Turnout in Nicaragua and El Salvador," *Journal of Interamerican Studies and World Affairs* 40, no. 3 (Autumn 1998): 88–89.

153. Ricardo Córdova Macías, José Miguel Cruz, and Mitchell A. Seligson, *Cultura política de la democracia en El Salvador, 2006* (San Salvador: IUDOP, 2007), 130–31.

154. Margarita Corral, "Do Parties Listen to the People? Views from the Americas," Latin American Public Opinion Project, *AmericasBarometer Insights*, no. 12 (2009).

155. Ricardo Córdova, interview by author, San Salvador, March 2000.

156. IUDOP, "En frente las elecciones legislativas and municipios 2012," *Boletín de Prensa* 26, no. 2 (2012).

157. Ken Ellis, interview by author, San Salvador, March 2000.

158. IUDOP, "En frente las elecciones," *Boletín de Prensa* 26, no. 2 (2012).

159. See, for example, Neil Nevitte, *El Salvador 2009 Benchmark Democracy Survey: Initial Findings* (Washington, DC: National Democratic Institute, 2009); IUDOP, "Encuesta de evaluación post-electoral de enero y sobre el proceso electoral de marzo" (San Salvador: IUDOP, 2009).

160. Nevitte, *El Salvador 2009 Benchmark Democracy Survey;* IUDOP, "En frente las elecciones," *Boletín de Prensa* 26, no. 2 (2012).

161. IUDOP, "En frente las elecciones," *Boletín de Prensa* 26, no. 2 (2012).

162. Artiga González, *Elitismo competitivo;* Ricardo Córdova Macías, José Miguel Cruz, and Mitchell A. Seligson, *Cultura política de la democracia en El Salvador, 2008: El impacto de la gobernabilidad* (San Salvador: IUDOP, 2008); Nevitte, *El Salvador 2009 Benchmark Democracy Survey;* IUDOP, "Encuesta de evaluación post-electoral"; Dinorah Azpuru, "The Salience of Ideology: Fifteen

Years of Presidential Elections in El Salvador," *Latin American Politics and Society* 52, no. 2 (Summer 2010): 103–38.

163. Azpuru, "Salience of Ideology," 123–24.

164. Ibid., 120–21.

165. IUDOP, "Los salvadoreños y salvadoreñas evalúan la situación del país a finales de 2013 y opinan sobre las elecciones presidenciales de 2014," *Boletín de Prensa* 27, no. 2 (2014).

166. See Robert A. Dahl, *Polyarchy: Participation and Opposition* (New Haven: Yale University Press, 1971); Inglehart and Welzel, *Modernization, Cultural Change.*

167. John A. Booth, Christine J. Wade, and Thomas W. Walker, *Understanding Central America: Global Forces, Rebellion, and Change,* 6th ed. (Boulder: Westview, 2015), 241.

168. Ibid.

169. Ibid.

170. Ibid., 245. See also José Miguel Cruz, "Social Capital in the Americas: Community Problem-Solving Participation," Latin American Public Opinion Project, *AmericasBarometer Insights* (2008).

171. Córdova Macías, Cruz, and Seligson, *Cultura política, 2008.*

172. Booth, Wade, and Walker, *Understanding Central America,* 248.

173. Córdova Macías, Cruz, and Seligson, *Cultura política, 2006,* 63–65.

174. Córdova Macías, Cruz, and Seligson, *Cultura política, 2008,* 145.

175. Córdova Macías, Cruz, and Seligson, *Cultura política, 2006,* 32–33; Córdova Macías, Cruz, and Seligson, *Cultura política, 2008.*

176. Córdova Macías, Cruz, and Seligson, *Cultura política, 2008,* 181.

177. John A. Booth and Mitchell A. Seligson, *The Legitimacy Puzzle in Latin America: Political Support and Democracy in Eight Nations* (New York: Cambridge University Press, 2009), 215–17.

178. Córdova Macías, Cruz, and Seligson, *Cultura política, 2008.*

179. Ricardo Córdova Macías and José Miguel Cruz, *Political Culture of Democracy in El Salvador and the Americas, 2012: Towards Equality of Opportunity* (Nashville: LAPOP, 2013), 157.

Chapter 4: El Salvador in the Neoliberal Era

1. José Alfredo Dutríz, interview by author, San Salvador, November 1999.

2. See, in particular, Álvaro de Soto and Graciana del Castillo, "Obstacles to Peacebuilding," *Foreign Policy,* no. 94 (Spring 1994): 69–83; James K. Boyce, *Economic Policy for Building Peace: The Lessons of El Salvador* (Boulder: Lynne

Reinner, 1996); Roland Paris, *At War's End: Building Peace after Civil Conflict* (New York: Cambridge University Press, 2004).

3. Susan Woodward, "Economic Priorities for Successful Peace Implementation," in *Ending Civil Wars: The Implementation of Peace Agreements*, ed. Stephen John Stedman, Donald Rothchild, and Elizabeth M. Cousens (Boulder: Lynne Rienner, 2002), 183–214; David Moore, "Levelling the Playing Fields and Embedding Illusions: 'Post-conflict' Discourse and Neo-liberal 'Development' in War-Torn Africa," *Review of African Political Economy* 83, no. 1 (2000): 11–28; Nicole Ball, "The Challenge of Rebuilding War-Torn Societies," in *Turbulent Peace: The Challenge of Managing International Conflict*, ed. Chester Crocker, Fen Osler Hampson, and Pamela Aall (Washington, DC: U.S. Institute of Peace, 2001): 719–36; Mitchell Seligson, "Democracy on Ice: The Multiple Challenges of Guatemala's Peace Process," in *The Third Wave of Democratization in Latin America: Advances and Setbacks*, ed. Frances Hagopian and Scott Mainwaring (New York: Cambridge University Press, 2005), 202–31.

4. Segovia, "The War Economy of the 1980s," in Boyce, *Economic Policy*, 37.

5. Ibid., 43.

6. Elisabeth J. Wood, *Forging Democracy from Below: Insurgent Transitions in South Africa and El Salvador* (New York: Cambridge University Press, 2000), 52–53.

7. Ibid., 62–63.

8. Ricardo Córdova Macías, William Pleitez, and Carlos Ramos, "Reforma política y reforma económica: Los retos de la gobernibilidad democrática," *Documentos de trabajo, Serie análisis de la realidad nacional 98-1* (San Salvador: FUNDAUNGO, 1998).

9. The 1988 proposal was coordinated by University of Chicago economist Dr. Arnold Harberger and several other international advisers. The project was funded by USAID in anticipation of Cristiani's victory. See William I. Robinson, *Transnational Conflicts: Central America, Social Change, and Globalization* (New York: Verso, 2003), 96.

10. Robert Rivera Campos, *La economía salvadoreña al final del siglo: Desafíos para el futuro* (San Salvador: FLACSO, 2005), 15.

11. Kenneth L. Johnson, "Between Revolution and Democracy: Business Elites and the State in El Salvador During the 1980s," (PhD diss., Tulane University, 1993), 311.

12. Kevin Murray, Ellen Coletti, Jack Spence, et al., *Rescuing Reconstruction: The Debate on Post-war Economic Recovery in El Salvador* (Cambridge, MA: Hemisphere Initiatives, 1994), 6.

13. Alexander Segovia, "Macroeconomic Performance and Policies since 1989," in *Economic Policy for Building Peace: The Lessons of El Salvador*, ed. James K. Boyce (Boulder: Lynne Rienner, 1996), 55.

14. Ibid.

15. Confidential interviews by author, San Salvador, November 1999, February–March 2000.

16. Confidential interview by author, San Salvador, November 1999. See also Óscar Melhado, *El Salvador: Retos económicos de fin de siglo* (San Salvador: UCA Editores, 1997), 90–91.

17. Confidential interview by author, San Salvador, October 1999.

18. Segovia, "Macroeconomic Performance," 63.

19. Alfredo Mena Lagos, interview by author, San Salvador, November 2006.

20. Ricardo Perdomo, interview by author, San Salvador, November 1999.

21. María Dolores Albiac, "Los ricos más ricos de El Salvador," in *El Salvador: La transición y sus problemas,* ed. Rodolfo Cardenal and Luis Armando González (San Salvador: UCA Editores, 2002), 165.

22. Jack Spence, David R. Dye, Mike Lanchin, Geoff Thale, and George Vickers, "Chapúltepec: Five Years Later, El Salvador's Political Reality and Uncertain Future" (Cambridge, MA: Hemisphere Initiatives, 1997), 29.

23. See Eva Paus, "Exports and the Consolidation of Peace," in *Economic Policy for Building Peace: The Lessons of El Salvador,* ed. James K. Boyce (Boulder: Lynne Rienner, 1996), 247–78.

24. Robert Orr, "Building Peace in El Salvador: From Exception to Rule" in *Peacebuilding as Politics: Cultivating Peace in Fragile Societies,* ed. Elizabeth M. Cousens, Chetan Kumar, and Karin Wermester (Boulder: Lynne Rienner, 2001), 168.

25. Ibid.

26. See ibid., 169. Orr also notes a "mismatch" between the nature of the programs and the extent of poverty, the difficulty of reaching the target populations due to the politicization of the aid, and the dependency of the programs on international funding.

27. Segovia, "Macroeconomic Performance," 64.

28. Ricardo Perdomo, interview by author, San Salvador, November 1999.

29. Segovia, "Macroeconomic Performance," 55–56.

30. Ibid., 51.

31. Ibid., 56.

32. This criticism of the model persisted well beyond Cristiani's term and was voiced by a wide cross-section of analysts and practitioners. Most striking was the extent to which references to the "new oligarchy" dominated discourse during interviews.

33. Juan Héctor Vidal, interview by author, San Salvador, November 1999; Manuel Enrique Hinds, interview by author, San Salvador, October 2006.

34. Rubén Zamora, interview by author, San Salvador, October 1999.

35. Melhado, *El Salvador*, 94–95.

36. Rivera Campos, *Economía salvadoreña*, 35.

37. Ibid., 35–36.

38. Juan Hector Vidal and confidential interview by author, San Salvador, October, November 1999.

39. Electrical distribution was privatized in January 1998 for $586.1 million. ANTEL, the Salvadoran telecommunications industry, was also privatized in 1998. The landlines and wireless components were sold separately.

40. UNDP, *Informe sobre desarrollo humano, El Salvador 2005: Una mirada al nuevo nosotros: El impacto de las migraciones* (San Salvador: UNDP, 2005).

41. Chris Gingrich and Jason Garber. "Trade Liberalization's Impact on Agriculture in Low-Income Countries: A Comparison of El Salvador and Costa Rica," *Journal of Developing Areas* 43, no. 2 (Spring 2010): 1–17.

42. Banco Central Reserva, Annual economic indicators, 1995–2002, http://www.bcr.gob.sv.

43. Legislative Decree 900 was originally passed in November 1996.

44. Banco Central Reserva, http://www.bcr.gob.sv.

45. UNDP, Cuadro 13, 480–481.

46. Arturo Zablah Kuri, *Más allá de las promesas* (San Salvador: Friedrich Ebert Stiftung, 2005), 17.

47. IUDOP, "Elecciones presidenciales 99," *Boletín de Prensa* 14, no. 3 (1999).

48. Juan Héctor Vidal, Roberto Rivera Campos, Orlando Arevalo, and confidential sources, interviews by author, San Salvador, 1999–2000.

49. Juan Héctor Vidal, interview by author, San Salvador, November 1999.

50. Ibid.

51. "ANEP's Salvadoran Manifesto," *Proceso* 912 (July 26, 2000).

52. Jack Spence, *War and Peace in Central America: Comparing Transitions toward Democracy and Social Equality in Guatemala, El Salvador, and Nicaragua* (Cambridge, MA: Hemisphere Initiatives, 2004), 32.

53. Juan Héctor Vidal, interview by author, San Salvador, November 1999.

54. Ibid.

55. David Mena, interview by author, San Salvador, July 1999.

56. Ibid.

57. "Flores impulsará Plan de Nación." *La Prensa Gráfica*, October 22, 1999.

58. Flores' plan was called the New Alliance.

59. Roberto Cañas, interview by author, San Salvador, February 2000.

60. "Sector privado rechaza plan económico del FMLN," *La Prensa*, February 23, 2000.

61. Marcia Towers and Silvia Borzutzky, "The Socioeconomic Implications of Dollarization in El Salvador," *Latin American Politics and Society* 46, no. 3 (2004): 46–47.

62. Manuel Enrique Hinds, interview by author, San Salvador, October 2006. See also Manuel Hinds, *Playing Monopoly with the Devil: Dollarization and Domestic Currencies in Developing Countries* (New Haven: Yale University Press, 2006).

63. Inflation rates in El Salvador at that time were some of the lowest in Latin America. See discussion on the benefits and costs of dollarization in Towers and Borzutsky, "Dollarization in El Salvador," 36–42.

64. See ibid., 47–49. See also Marla Dickerson, "In El Salvador, the Dollar Is No Panacea," *Los Angeles Times,* August 4, 2007.

65. Segovia, "Macroeconomic Performance," 55.

66. Roberto Rubio, interview by author, San Salvador, November 2000.

67. Roberto Cañas, interview by author, San Salvador, November 1999.

68. Manuel Orozco, *Remittances and Markets: New Players and Practices* (Washington, DC: Inter-American Dialogue, 2000); 11; Sarah Gammage, "Exporting People and Recruiting Remittances: A Development Strategy for El Salvador?" *Latin American Perspectives* 33, no. 6 (November 2006): 75, 85.

69. UNDP, *Mirada al nuevo nostros;* Gammage, "Exporting People," 87–89.

70. Patricia Landolt, Lilian Autler, and Sonia Baires, "From Hermano Lejano to Hermano Mayor: The Dialectics of Salvadoran Transnationalism," *Ethnic and Racial Studies* 22, no. 2 (1999): 298–302.

71. Central Reserve Bank of El Salvador, Annual Economic Indicators, 1995–2002; Annual Economic Indicators, 2002–2006, http://www.bcr.gob.sv.

72. External debt increased more than 54 percent between 1995 and 2004. See "The External Debt: The eternal Economic Problem," *Proceso* 1130, http://www.uca.edu.sv/publica/proceso/proci1130.html.

73. Aaron Schneider, *State-Building and Tax Regimes in Central America* (New York: Cambridge University Press, 2012), 119.

74. Rose Spalding, *Contesting Trade in Central America: Market Reform and Resistance* (Austin: University of Texas Press, 2014), 130–35.

75. FMLN officials, interviews by author, San Salvador, October–November 2006

76. "MCC Completes Successful Five-Year Compact with El Salvador," September 21, 2012, http://www.mcc.gov/pages/press/release/press-release-09212012 -elsalvadorcloseout.

77. IUDOP, "Los salvadoreños evalúan el cuarto año de gobierno de Antonio Saca," *Boletín de Prensa* 22, no. 1 (2007).

78. IUDOP, "Los salvadoreños y salvadoreñas evalúan la situación del país a finales de 2007," *Boletín de Prensa* 22, no. 2 (2007).

79. Marcela Sanchez, "Remittance Slowdown: Wake-up Call for Latin America," *Washington Post,* March 14, 2008, http://www.washingtonpost.com /wp-dyn/content/article/2008/03/13/AR2008031302147.html.

80. For a discussion of previous tax reform efforts see Schneider, *State-Building*, 128–35.

81. Saca's finance minister, Guillermo López Suárez, who was responsible for the tax reforms, allegedly resigned under pressure from ANEP and the business community, who were angry about the tax reform. He was replaced by William J. Handal, who had been a member of the board of directors of FINESPRO when the firm was closed, in 1997, amid allegations of corruption. Handal was not charged in the case. "El Salvador Finance Minister Resigns," U.S. Embassy San Salvador, April 20, 2006, http://wikileaks.org /cable/2006/04/06SANSALVADOR1027.html; "Saca Names TACA Veteran Finance Minister," U.S. Embassy San Salvador, May 2, 2006, http://wikileaks .org/cable/2006/05/06SANSALVADOR1152.html.

82. Economic Commission for Latin America and the Caribbean, *Statistical Yearbook for Latin America and the Caribbean 2007* (Santiago: ECLAC, 2008), tables 1.3.9, 1.4.5.

83. See John Booth, Christine Wade, and Thomas Walker, *Understanding Central America*, 6th ed. (Boulder: Westview, 2015), 274.

84. UNDP, *Mirada al nuevo nosotros,* 79.

85. Ibid., 86–88.

86. Christine Wade, "El Salvador: Contradictions of Neoliberalism and Building Sustainable Peace," *International Journal of Peace Studies* 13, no. 2 (Autumn–Winter 2008): 15–32.

87. UNDP, *Mirada al nuevo nostros,* 15.

88. IUDOP, "Encuesta de evaluación del año 2005," *Informe,* no. 109 (December 2005), http://www.uca.edu.sv/publica/iudop/Web/2005/informe109.pdf.

89. UNDP, *Mirada al nuevo nostros,* 84–85.

90. A. Cox Edwards and Manuelita Ureta, "International Migration, Remittances, and Schooling: Evidence from El Salvador," *Journal of Development Economics* 72, no. 2 (2003): 429–61; Pablo Acosta, "Entrepreneurship, Labor Markets, and International Remittances: Evidence from El Salvador," in *International Migration, and Economic Development, and Policy: Studies across the Globe,* ed. Çaglar Özden and Maurice Schiff (New York: Palgrave Macmillan, 2007).

91. Pablo Acosta, "School Attendance, Child Labour, and Remittances from International Migration in El Salvador," *Journal of Development Studies* 47, no. 6 (June 2011): 911, 931–32.

92. Katharine Andrade-Eekhoff, interview by author, San Salvador, October 2006. Eekhoff, who worked for UNDP at the time, relayed a story about an entire graduating class in the campo going to the mayor's office to request papers so they could migrate.

93. UNDP, *Mirada al nuevo nostros*, 17.

94. Banco Central Reserva, *Indicadores económicos, 2002–2006*, http://www .bcr.gob.sv.

95. The hikes were followed by violent protests in front of the National University. Two policemen were killed by two protestors who happened to be members of the FMLN. The Saca administration accused the FMLN of instigating the protests and claimed that the party had violated the peace accords.

96. IUDOP, "Los salvadoreños evalúan el cuarto año de gobierno de Antonio Saca y opinan sobre la coyuntura político-electoral," *Boletín de Prensa 23*, no. 3 (2008).

97. Lourdes Quintanilla, "MCC: Aún faltan requisitos previos al FOMILENIO II," *La Prensa Gráfica*, April 25, 2014, http://www.laprensagrafica .com/2014/04/25/mcc-aun-faltan-requisitos-previos-al-fomilenio-ii.

98. "Monsanto Company Announces Agreement to Acquire Semillas Cristiani Burkhard, the Leading Central American Corn Seed Company," *Monsanto*, June 19, 2008, http://news.monsanto.com/press-release/monsanto-company-announces -agreement-acquire-semillas-cristiani-burkard-leading-centra; "Free Trade Threatens El Salvador's Seed Distribution Program," *Voices on the Border*, May 2, 2014, http://voiceselsalvador.wordpress.com/category/agriculture/.

99. Miguel Sáenz, interview by author, San Salvador, March 2000.

100. "ANEP (National Association of Private Enterprise) Taking on President Funes, Again!," *Voices on the Border*, August 29, 2012, https://voiceselsalvador .wordpress.com/2012/08/29/anep-national-association-of-private-enterprise -taking-on-presient-funes-again/#comments; Yolanda Magaña, "Asamblea desplaza a ANEP de 19 instituciones autónomas del Estado," *El Mundo*, August 18, 2012, http://elmundo.com.sv/asamblea-desplaza-a-anep-de-19-instituciones -autonomas-del-estado; "¿Porqué la ANEP tiene que ser parte del Gobierno?," *Diario CoLatino*, August 22, 2012, http://www.diariocolatino.com/es/20120822 /editorial/106815/¿Porqué-la-ANEP—tiene-que-ser-parte—del-Gobierno.htm.

101. U.S. Department of State, Bureau of Western Hemispheric Affairs, *Partnership for Growth: El Salvador 2011–2015*, November 3, 2011, http://www .state.gov/p/wha/rls/fs/2011/176636.htm. Unlike the PFG, a 2012 study by the Foundation for the Study of the Application of Law (FESPAD) concluded that investment was low because the economy was stagnant due to high levels of income inequality, limited government cash flow, and low population growth due to immigration. Arguing that the economy had to grow before it could attract

investment, the study recommended focusing on reducing income inequality, increasing the minimum wage, tax reform, redistribution of wealth, and diversification of markets (such as Brazil and Argentina).

102. Leah Matthews and Erica Stahl, "Asocio público-privado en El Salvador: Análisis de impacto y recomendaciones," *FESPAD*, October 23, 2012, http://www.fespad.org.sv/wp-content/uploads/2013/08/asocio-publico-privado-en -el-salvador.pdf.

103. Lily Moodey, "P3 Legislation in El Salvador: An Aggressive Reassertion of Neoliberal Economics?," *Council on Hemispheric Affairs*, August 7, 2013, http://www.coha.org/p3-legislation-in-el-salvador-an-aggressive-reassertion-of -neoliberal-economics/.

104. Matthews and Stahl, "Asocio público-privado."

105. Sergio Arauz, "Los más pobres en El Salvador tributan el 30% de sus ingresos, y los más ricos el 11%," *El Faro*, December 15, 2011, http://www.elfaro. net/es/201112/noticias/6898/.

106. Ibid.; Juan José Dalton, "Los ricos pagarán más en El Salvador, *El País*, December 15, 2011, http://internacional.elpais.com/internacional /2011/12/15/actualidad/1323975560_734673.html; Amadeo Cabrera, "Funes sanciona reforma fiscal votada en pleno," *La Prensa Gráfica*, December 16, 2001, http://www.laprensagrafica.com/el-salvador/politica/237559-funes-sanciona -reforma-fiscal-votada-en-pleno.html.

107. John A. Booth and Mitchell A. Seligson, *The Legitimacy Puzzle in Latin America: Political Support and Democracy in Eight Nations* (New York: Cambridge University Press, 2009), 105–43.

108. Joel S. Hellman, Geraint Jones, and Daniel Kaufmann, "Seize the State, Seize the Day: State Capture, Corruption, and Influence in Transition," World Bank Policy Research Working Paper 2444, September 2000.

109. Scores from 2012 and 2013 are not provided because Transparency International changed their methodology and the data isn't comparable to previous years.

110. IUDOP, "La transparencia en el Estado salvadoraño: La perspectiva de los empresarios," *Boletín de Prensa* 22, no. 1 (2005): 8.

111. Like the admittedly more scientific UCA study, interviewees never regarded themselves as part of the select group that influenced government policy. Most "identified out" or claimed to have fallen out of favor with a given administration. It was also clear that many feared retribution for speaking out against corrupt practices. Several agreed to be interviewed only if I agreed not to tape the interview or indicate that the meeting had even occurred.

112. Serge F. Kovaleski, "Financial Scam Hits Elderly Salvadorans Hard," *Washington Post*, May, 24, 1998.

113. Edith Beltran, "Official Says El Salvador Investment Fraud Reached $100 Million," Associated Press, July 22, 1997, http://www.apnewsarchive .com/1997/Official-says-El-Salvador-investment-fraud-reaches-$100-million /id-00f5f3a6a6654dbe28c2b97087311ea5; Robert Sandals, "El Salvador: Corruption Scandal Shakes Financial System," *NotiCen, Latin America Database*, University of New Mexico, July 24, 1997.

114. The names included not only Matheis Hill but his father, Roberto Matheis Regalado, and Francisco Rodríguez Laucel, the former superintendent of the financial system.

115. Robert Sandals, "El Salvador: Verdict in Embezzlement Trial Sours Officials in Use of the Jury System," *NotiCen*, July 5, 2001.

116. In January 1999 the Real Estate Credit Bank (CREDISA) folded due to $72 million in losses amid allegations that the bankruptcy was created in order to limit the number of banks and concentrate the wealth. Pension Funds Administrator (AFP) Profuturo, which was created in 1997, was reportedly bankrupt by 1999 and its license was withdrawn in 2000 and the AFP was eventually liquidated. In an interview with the authors, the fund's director claimed this was an effort to concentrate holdings in the larger, more powerful funds—essentially driving the smaller funds out of business.

117. Alexis Henríquez, "Perla a 15 años de prisión por delitos desde la ANDA" *El Faro*, July 16, 2007, http://archivo.elfaro.net/secciones/Noticias/20070716 /noticias10_20070716.asp.

118. Elaine Freedman, "LaGeo-Enel: Chronicle of an Energy Hijacking," *Envio*, no. 379 (March 2013), http://www.envio.org.ni/articulo/4665.

119. Valeria Guzmán and Fátima Peña, "Fiscalía desiste del caso CEL-Enel y todos los acusados quedan en libertad," *El Faro*, July 4, 2015, http://www.elfaro .net/es/201507/noticias/17154/Fiscal%C3%ADa-desiste-del-caso-CEL-Enel -y-todos-los-acusados-quedan-en-libertad.htm

120. Efren Lemus, Sergio Arauz, and Daniel Valencia, "Siete capturados por corrupción en construcción del bulevar Diego de Holguín," *El Faro*, September 12, 2013, http://www.elfaro.net/es/201309/noticias/13287/.

121. Sonia Escobar, Iván Escobar, and Beatriz Castillo, "Expulsan a ex presidente Saca de ARENA," *Diario CoLatino*, December 15, 2009, http://www .diariocolatino.com/es/20091215/nacionales/74786/Expulsan-a-ex-presidente -Saca-de-ARENA.htm; "Reorganizing ARENA: The Party's Future after Avila's Defeat," embassy San Salvador, October 6, 2009, http://wikileaks.org /cable/2009/10/09SANSALVADOR947.html; "ARENA Expels Former President Saca," U.S. Embassy San Salvador, December 15, 2009, http://wikileaks .org/cable/2009/12/09SANSALVADOR1103.html.

122. Gabriel Labrador, "Ganancias de las empresas de Saca se multiplicaron hasta por 16 cuando fue presidente," *El Faro,* November 19, 2013, http://www .elfaro.net/es/201311/noticias/13936/.

123. Efren Lemus and Carlos Dada, "El presidente Funes, una cadena de favores y un spa," *El Faro,* May 26, 2014, http://www.elfaro.net/es/201405/noticias /15437/.

124. Eric Linton, "El Salvador Seeks Return of Fugitive Ex-president Francisco Flores from Panama, *International Business Times,* May 5, 2014, http:// www.ibtimes.com/el-salvador-seeks-return-fugitive-ex-president-francisco -flores-panama-1580351.

125. UNDP, "Perfil de estratos sociales en América Latina: pobres, vulnerables y clases medias," August 26, 2014, http://www.latinamerica.undp.org/content /dam/rblac/docs/Research%20and%20Publications/Poverty%20Reduction /UNDP-RBLAC-Grupos_sociales_AL-2014.PDF.

Chapter 5: The Politics of Exclusion

1. Interview by author, San Salvador, October 1999.

2. Cecilia Menjívar, *Fragmented Ties: Salvadoran Immigrant Networks in America* (Berkeley: University of California Press, 2000), 40–41.

3. Ibid., 54–55.

4. Thousands also went to Europe, where some countries had more open asylum policies.

5. For a discussion on the issue of Salvadoran migrants, see William D. Stanley, "Economic Migrants or Refugees from Violence? A Time-Series Analysis of Salvadoran Migration to the United States," *Latin American Research Review* 22, no. 1 (1987): 132–54; Richard C. Jones, "Causes of Salvadoran Migration to the United States," *Geographical Review* 79, no. 2 (April 1989): 183–94.

6. For more on the sanctuary movement, see Susan Coutin, *The Culture of Protest: Religious Activism and the U.S. Sanctuary Movement* (Boulder: Westview, 1993); Miriam Davidson, *Convictions of the Heart: Jim Corbett and the Sanctuary Movement* (Tucson: University of Arizona Press, 1988).

7. *American Baptist Churches v. Thornburgh,* 760 F. Supp. 796 (N.D. Cal. 1991)

8. Mary Beth Sheridan, "Calling All Salvadorans," *Washington Post,* November 11, 2002, http://www.latinamericanstudies.org/elsalvador/tps.htm.

9. Mary Beth Sheridan, "Salvadoran President Hails U.S. Work Plan," *Washington Post,* January 9, 2005, http://www.washingtonpost.com/wp-dyn/articles /A59873-2005Jan8.html.

10. Alison Mountz, Richard Wright, Ines Miyares, and Adrian J. Bailey, "Lives in Limbo: Temporary Protected Status and Immigrant Identities," *Global Networks* 2, no. 4 (2002): 345–46.

11. Ibid., 352.

12. Maurice Schiff and Çaglar Özden, *International Migration, Remittances and the Brain Drain* (New York: Palgrave Macmillan, 2005). As much as one-third of skilled Salvadoran labor emigrated during this time.

13. UNDP, *Una mirada al nuevo nostros: El impacto de las migraciones* (San Salvador: UNDP, 2005), http://www.pnud.org.sv/migraciones/content /view/9/105/.

14. Anna Brown and Eileen Patten, "Hispanics of Salvadoran Origin in the United States, 2011," Pew Research Center, June 19, 2013, http://www.pewhispanic .org/2013/06/19/hispanics-of-salvadoran-origin-in-the-united-states-2011/.

15. Patricia Landolt, Lilian Autler, and Sonia Baires, "From Hermano Lejano to Hermano Mayor: The Dialectics of Salvadoran Transnationalism," *Ethnic and Racial Studies* 22, no. 2 (1999): 303–5.

16. Sarah Gammage, "Exporting People and Recruiting Remittances: A Development Strategy for El Salvador?," *Journal of Latin American Perspectives* 33, no. 6 (2006): 90–91.

17. Ibid.; Menjívar, *Fragmented Ties.*

18. Katrina Burgess, "Collective Remittances and Migrant-State Collaboration in Mexico and El Salvador," *Latin American Politics and Society* 54, no. 4 (Winter 2012): 127.

19. Christine Wade, "El Salvador: Contradictions of Neoliberalism and Building Sustainable Peace," *International Journal of Peace Studies* 13, no. 2 (Autumn–Winter 2008): 15–32.

20. N. C. Aizenman, "The Migrants' Mayor," *Washington Post,* June 2, 2006, http://www.washingtonpost.com/wp-dyn/content/article/2006/06/01 /AR2006060101775.html; "People-Smuggler Campaigns in El Salvador," Associated Press, March 6, 2006, http://www.latinamericanstudies.org/elsalvador /ramirez.htm.

21. Programa Estado de la Nación—Región, *Estado de la región en desarrollo humano sostenible* (San José: Estado de la Nación, 2008), 258, http://www .estadonacion.or.cr/estado-de-la-region/region-informes-anteriores/region -informe2008.

22. Leisy J. Abrego, "Rethinking El Salvador's Transnational Families," *NACLA Report on the Americas* (November–December 2009): 28–29.

23. Catherine Elton, "El Salvador Targets Smugglers Who Transport Children," *Christian Science Monitor,* January 7, 2003, http://www.csmonitor.com /2003/0107/p07s01-woam.html/(page)/3.

24. Frances Robles, "Wave of Minors on Their Own Rush to Cross Southwest Border," *New York Times,* June 4, 2014; Adam Isacson, "How Can This Be," http://thisisadamsblog.com/post/87847867449/how-can-this-be; Ian Gordon,

"Map: These Are the Places Central American Child Migrants Are Fleeing," *Mother Jones*, June 27, 2014, http://www.motherjones.com/mojo/2014/06/map -unaccompanied-child-migrants-central-america-honduras.

25. Programa Estado de la Nación—Región, *Estado de la región en desarrollo human sostenible*, 259.

26. See, for example, Catherine Elton, "Latin America's Faulty Lifeline," *AlterNet*, March 20, 2006, http://www.alternet.org/world/33536/?page=1; Eliza Barclay, "Too Much of a Good Thing," *Houston Chronicle*, November 12, 2006; Lourdes Garcia-Navarro, "El Salvador Migration Creates Labor Shortage," NPR, http://www.npr.org/templates/story/story.php?storyId=15218365.

27. See, in particular, Charles Call and William Stanley, "Civilian Security," in *Ending Civil Wars: The Implementation of Peace Agreements,* ed. Stephen John Stedman, Donald Rothchild, and Elizabeth M. Cousens (Boulder: Lynne Rienner, 2002), 303–26; Roy Licklider, "Obstacles to Peace Settlements," in *Turbulent Peace: The Challenges of Managing International Conflict,* ed. Chester Crocker, Fen Osler Hampson, and Pamela Aall (Washington, DC: U.S. Institute of Peace, 2003), 704–6; Roger Mac Ginty, "Post-accord Crime," in *Violence and Reconstruction,* ed. John Darby (Notre Dame, IN: University of Notre Dame Press, 2006), 101–19.

28. See Howard Adelman, "Refugee Repatriation," in *Ending Civil Wars: The Implementation of Peace Agreements,* ed. Stephen John Stedman, Donald Rothchild, and Elizabeth M. Cousens (Boulder: Lynne Rienner, 2002), 273–302.

29. United Nations, "Report of the ONUSAL Human Rights Division for the period from 1 July 1992 to 31 January 1993," A/47/912-S/25521 S, April 5, 1993.

30. For a thorough discussion on the various factors of violence at the society, household, and individual levels, as well as the costs of violence, see Mayra Buvinic, Andrew R. Morrison, and Michael Shifter, "Violence in the Americas: A Framework for Action," in *Too Close to Home: Domestic Violence in the Americas,* ed. Andrew R. Morrison and María Loreto Biehl (Washington, DC: IDB, 1999), 3–34.

31. Héctor Silva Ávalos, "Infiltrators: Corruption in El Salvador's Police," *Insight Crime,* February 21, 2014, http://www.insightcrime.org/investigations/the -infiltrators-a-chronicle-of-el-salvador-police-corruption.

32. Héctor Silva Ávalos, *Infiltrados: Crónica de la corrupción en la PNC, 1992–2013* (San Salvador: UCA Editores, 2014), 170–82.

33. Spring Miller and James Cavallaro, eds. *No Place to Hide: Gang, State, and Clandestine Violence in El Salvador,* Human Rights Program (Cambridge, MA: Harvard Law School, 2009), 36.

34. Sonja Wolf, "Policing Crime in El Salvador," *NACLA Report on the Americas,* Spring 2012, 44.

35. Raúl Gutiérrez, "El Salvador: Police Nostalgic for the Past," *Inter Press Service*, February 12, 2008, http://www.ipsnews.net/2008/02/rights-el-salvador -police-nostalgic-for-the-past/.

36. UNDP, *Informe sobre desarrollo humano para América Central, 2009– 2010: Abrir espacios a la seguridad ciudadana y el desarrollo humano* (San Salvador: UNDP, 2009), 238, http://www.pnud.org.sv/2007/component/option,com _docman/task,cat_view/gid,230/Itemid,56/?mosmsg=Est%E1+intentando +acceder+desde+un+dominio+no+autorizado.+%28www.google.com%29.

37. Orlando J. Pérez, "Democratic Legitimacy and Public Insecurity: Crime and Democracy in El Salvador and Guatemala," *Political Science Quarterly* 118, no. 4 (Winter 2003-4): 630.

38. David Gagne, "El Salvador Military Official Convicted in Arms Trafficking Case," *InSight Crime*, December 1, 2014, http://www.insightcrime.org /news-briefs/el-salvador-military-official-convicted-in-arms-trafficking-case.

39. Charles T. Call, "The Mugging of a Success Story: Justice and Security Reform in El Salvador," in *Constructing Justice and Security after War*, ed. Call (Washington, DC: U.S. Institute of Peace, 2007), 53.

40. Ibid., 54.

41. Washington Office on Latin America, *Protect and Serve? The Status of Police Reform in Central America* (Washington, DC: WOLA, July 2009), 30.

42. Raúl Gutiérrez, "El Salvador: Hard-Line Policies Vs Rule of Law," *Inter Press Service*, August 11, 2008, http://www.ipsnews.net/2008/08/el-salvador -hard-line-policies-vs-rule-of-law/.

43. IUDOP, *La situacion de la seguridad y justicia 2009-2014*, 49-58.

44. See François Bourguignon, "Crime as a Social Cost of Poverty and Inequality: A Review Focusing on Developing Countries," in *Facets of Globalization: International and Local Dimensions of Development*, World Bank Discussion Paper 415 (Washington, DC: World Bank, 2001): 171-91; Buvinic, Morrison, and Shifter, "Violence in the Americas," 3-34.

45. Luis Armando González and Lilian Vega, "El Salvador: Política, sociedad y economía en 2005," *Estudios Centroamericanos* 61, no. 690 (2005): 418.

46. Guillermo E. Perry, William F. Maloney, Omar S. Arias, Pablo Fajnzylber, Andrew D. Mason, and Jaime Saavedra-Chanduvi, *Informality: Exit and Exclusion* (Washington, DC: World Bank, 2007).

47. Facultad Latinoamericana de Ciencas Sociales, Ministerio de Economía, UNDP, *Mapa de pobreza: Urbana y exclusión social El Salvador*, vol. 1, *Conceptos y metodología* (San Salvador: Algier's Impresores, 2010), 22, http://www.flacso.org.sv /files/Mapa_de_Pobreza_Urbana_y_Exclusi%C3%B3n_Social_El_Salvador.pdf.

48. See Robert Ayres, *Crime and Violence as Development Issues in Latin America and the Caribbean* (Washington, DC: World Bank, 1998); José Miguel

Cruz, Alvaro Trigueros Argüello, and Francisco González, *The Social and Economic Factors Associated with Violent Crime in El Salvador* (San Salvador: IUDOP, 1999).

49. See Ellen Moodie's compelling ethnography of postwar violence, *El Salvador in the Aftermath of Peace: Crime, Uncertainty, and the Transition to Democracy* (Philadelphia: University of Pennsylvania Press, 2010).

50. Buvinic, Morrison, and Shifter, "Violence in the Americas," 103–4.

51. Ricardo Córdova Macías, José Miguel Cruz, and Mitchell Seligson, *Cultura política de la democracia en El Salvador, 2006* (San Salvador: Instituto Universitario de Opinión, 2007), 87.

52. José Miguel Cruz and Luis Armando González, "Magnitud de la violencia en El Salvador," *Estudios Centroamericanos* 52, no. 588 (October 1997): 953–66.

53. Uzziel Peña and Tom Gibb, "El Salvador's Gang Truce: A Historic Opportunity," *NACLA Report on the Americas* 46, no. 2 (Summer 2013): 13.

54. Johan Galtung defines cultural violence as "those aspects of culture, the symbolic sphere of our existence—exemplified by religion and ideology, language and art, empirical science and formal science (logic, mathematics)—that can be sued to justify or legitimize direct or structural violence." Galtung, "Cultural Violence," *Journal of Peace Research* 27, no. 3 (August 1990): 291–305.

55. United Nations Office on Drugs and Crime, *Crime and Development in Central America: Caught in the Crossfire* (New York: UNODC, May 2007), 43.

56. Ibid.; United States, Department of Homeland Security, Office of Immigration Statistics, Immigration Enforcement Actions: 2005, *Annual Report November 2006*, http://www.dhs.gov/xlibrary/assets/statistics/yearbook/2005/Enforcement_AR_05.pdf.

57. Sonja Wolf, "Mara Salvatrucha: The Most Dangerous Street Gang in the Americas?," *Latin American Politics and Society*, 54, no. 1 (Spring 2012): 74.

58. Interview by author, San Salvador, October 2006.

59. IUDOP, *La situación de la seguridad y justicia 2009–2014: Entre expectivas de cambio, mano dura military y treguas pandilleras* (San Salvador: IUDOP, 2014), 1.

60. A unified registry, the Mesa Técnica, was created in 2005.

61. José Miguel Cruz, Álvaro Trigueros Argüello, and Francisco González, *El crimen violento en El Salvador* (San Salvador: IUDOP, 2000), 12–15.

62. Wim Savenije and Chris van der Borgh, "Youth Gangs, Social Exclusion and the Transformation of Violence in El Salvador," in *Armed Actors: Organized Violence and State Failure in Latin America*, ed. Kees Koonings and Dirk Kruijt (Boulder: Lynne Rienner, 1996), 156–57.

63. Base de Datos de mortalidad de DIGESTYC, http://www.digestyc.gob.sv

64. UNDP, *Informe sobre desarrollo humano, 2009–2010,* 71.

65. UNDP, *Seguridad paz reto país: Recomendaciones para una política de seguiridad ciudadana en El Salvador* (San Salvador: UNDP, 2007), 26–24; Amnesty International, "El Salvador," Amnesty International Report 2008, http://www.amnesty.org/en/region/el-salvador/report-2008.

66. UNDP, *Informe sobre desarrollo humano, 2009–2010,* 123.

67. Ibid., 169.

68. UNDP, *Seguridad paz reto país,* 26. The departments with the highest homicide rates in 2006 were La Libertad (80.87 per 100,000), San Salvador (65.22), Santa Ana (64.01), Sonsonate (62.48), and Cuscatlán (61.08).

69. Ibid., 26.

70. IUDOP, *Situación de la seguridad, 2009–2014,* 14.

71. Ibid., 25. Homicide rates in Chalatenango and Morazán were 10.4 and 12.4 per 100,000, respectively.

72. IUDOP, "Victimización y percepción de inseguridad en El Salvador 2009," *Boletín de Prensa* 24, no. 5 (2009).

73. UNDP, *Informe sobre desarrollo humano, 2009–2010,* 82.

74. Ibid., 245; Córdova Macías, Cruz, and Seligson, *Cultura política,* 95. The number of crimes reported to the police is down slightly from those reported by Córdova, Cruz, and Seligson, where 37.5 percent of the victimized reported the crime; nearly half of those who didn't claimed that it wouldn't do any good, and 53 percent expressed no faith in the justice system to prosecute the crimes.

75. Douglas Farah, "Central American Gangs: Changing Nature and New Partners," *Journal of International Affairs* 66, no. 1 (Fall–Winter 2012).

76. The terms have come to be used interchangeably, although *pandillas* typically referred to local gangs and *maras* referred to those gangs with transnational roots. The terminology may also be somewhat localized, with *maras* being used more frequently in El Salvador or Honduras and *pandillas* being more common in Nicaragua.

77. Donna DeCesare, "Deporting America's Gang Culture," *Mother Jones,* July–August 1999.

78. Farah, "Central American Gangs," 56–57.

79. The Barrio 18 gang was identified as a "mega-gang" in 2000 by the LAPD.

80. UNODC, *Crime and Development,* 60.

81. UNODC, *Transnational Organized Crime in Central America and the Caribbean: A Threat Assessment* (Vienna: UNODC, September 2012), 29, http://www.unodc.org/documents/data-and-analysis/Studies/TOC_Central_America_and_the_Caribbean_english.pdf

82. See María Santacruz-Giralt, José Miguel Cruz, Alberto Concha-Eastman, et al., *Inside the Neighborhood: Salvadoran Street Gangs' Violent Solidarity*

(San Salvador: Pan American Health Organization/Universidad Centroamericana, 2002).

83. Orlando J. Pérez, "Gang Violence and Insecurity in Contemporary Central America," *Bulletin of Latin American Research* 32, no. 1 (March 2013): 217–34.

84. For more on Central American gangs, see Ana Arana, "How the Street Gangs Took Central America," *Foreign Affairs*, no. 84 (May–June 2005): 98–110; Donna DeCesare, "Deporting America's Gang Culture," *Mother Jones*, July–August 1999, 44–51.

85. Raúl Gutiérrez, "Transport–El Salvador: Your Money or Your Life," *Inter Press Service*, February 15, 2007, http://ipsnews.net/news.asp?idnews=36585.

86. Diana Villiers Negroponte, *The Merida Initiative and Central America: The Challenges of Containing Public Insecurity and Criminal Violence* (Washington, DC: Brookings Institution, 2009), 15–16.

87. UNODC, *Crime and Development*, 17.

88. UNODC, *Transnational Organized Crime*, 29.

89. Héctor Silva Ávalos, pers. comm., June 27, 2014.

90. "Murder Rate Prompts Legal Reforms," *Central America Report*, February 25, 2005.

91. IUDOP, "Encuesta de victimización y percepción de seguridad en El Salvador en 2004," 2004.

92. Santacruz-Giralt, Cruz, Concha-Eastman, et al., *Inside the Neighborhood*.

93. Andrew Morrison, Mayra Buvinic, and Michael Shifter, "The Violent Americas: Risk Factors, Consequences and Policy Implications of Social and Domestic Violence," in *Crime and Violence in Latin America*, ed. Hugo Frühling and Joseph Tulchin, with Heather A. Golding (Washington, DC: Woodrow Wilson Center Press, 2003), 94.

94. UNDP, *¿Cuánto cuesta la violencia a El Salvador?* (San Salvador: UNDP, 2005), 23; UNODC, *Crime and Development*, 61.

95. IUDOP, *Situación de la seguridad, 2009–2014*, 19.

96. Raúl Gutiérrez, "Prisons Out of Control," *Inter Press Service*, March 17, 2008, http://www.ipsnews.net/news.asp?idnews=41616.

97. UNODC, *Crime and Development*, 45.

98. Wolf, "Mara Salvatrucha."

99. Valeria Guzmán, "Policía desmiente versión del gobierno de que el 60 % de víctimas de homicidios son pandilleros," *El Faro*, July 13, 2015, http://www.elfaro.net/es/201507/noticias/17173/Polic%C3%ADa-desmiente-versión-del-gobierno-de-que-el-60--de-v%C3%ADctimas-de-homicidios-son-pandilleros.htm

100. United Nations, "Report Issued on 28 July 1994 by the Joint Group for the Investigation of Politically Motivated Armed Groups," S/1994/989, 22, October 1994, in *The United Nations and El Salvador 1990–1995*.

101. UNDP, *Informe sobre desarrollo humano, 2009-2010*, 101.

102. "San Miguel, centro de extorsiones de El Salvador." *Diario La Opinión*, November 23, 2006, http://www.radiolaprimerisima.com/noticias/6596/san-miguel-centro-de-extorsiones-de-el-salvador.

103. UNDP, *¿Cuánto cuesta la violencia?*, 26.

104. Ibid., 48.

105. UNODC, *Crime and Development*, 21.

106. Ibid., 103. In 2005 and 2006, for example, El Salvador captured only 39 kg and 107 kg of cocaine, respectively. During those same two years, Guatemala captured 5,085 and 287 kg, Honduras captured 473 and 2,714 kg, and Nicaragua captured 6,951 and 9,720 kg.

107. UNODC, *Crime and Development*, 15.

108. Julieta Palcastre, "Los Perrones Collaborate with 'El Chapo' in Central America," *Diálogo*, September 26, 2013, http://dialogo-americas.com/en_GB/articles/rmisa/features/regional_news/2013/09/26/drogas-centroamerica.

109. Sergio Arauz, Óscar Martínez, and Efren Lemus, "El Cártel de Texis," *El Faro*, May 16, 2011, http://www.elfaro.net/es/201105/noticias/4079/?st-full_text=0; "Texis Cartel,*InSight Crime*, http://www.insightcrime.org/groups-el-salvador/texis-cartel.

110. Silva, *Infiltrados*, 227-31.

111. Farah, "Central American Gangs," 59-60.

112. Personal communication with author, June 27, 2014.

113. William Branigan, "Gays' Cases Help to Expand Immigration Rights," *Washington Post*, December 17, 1996.

114. Miller and Cavallaro, *No Place to Hide*, 16-17.

115. Jeannette Aguilar, "Los resultados contraproducentes de las políticas antipandillas," *Estudios Centroamericanos* 62, no. 708 (October 2007): 878.

116. "Police Accused of Corruption," *Central America Report*, September 21, 2007; Raúl Gutiérrez, "Death Squads Still Operating" *Inter Press Service*, September 4, 2007, http://ipsnews.net/news.asp?idnews=39143.

117. Miller and Cavallaro, *No Place to Hide*, 17.

118. Ibid.

119. James Bargent, "Has Gang Violence in El Salvador Sparked a Death Squad Revival?," *InSight Crime*, May 23, 2014, http://www.insightcrime.org/news-briefs/gang-violence-el-salvador-sparked-death-squad-revival; "Grupo de exterminio se ha activado en Zacatecoluca según la PNC," *La Pagina*, January 17, 2014, http://www.lapagina.com.sv/nacionales/91711/maras-El-SAlvador-PNC-inseguridad-noticias-El-Salvador-Zacatecoluca.

120. Instituto Salvadoreño de Desarrollo de la Mujer (ISDEMU), *Informe Nacional sobre la Situación de violencia contra las mujeres en El Salvador,*

http://www.unfpa.org.sv/dmdocuments/situacion_violencia.pdf. The number of homicides among men also increased during the same period, but only by about 35 percent.

121. IUDOP, *Situación de la seguridad, 2009–2014*, 7.

122. Consejo Centroamericano de Procuradores de Derechos Humanos, *Informe regional: Situación y análysis del femicidio en la región centroamericana* (August 2006), 107–8, http://centralamericasecurity.thedialogue.org/articles /informe-regional-situacion-y-analisis-del-femicidio-en-la-region-centroamericana ?lang=es.

123. United Nations, Report of the United Nations Special Rapporteur on Violence against Women to the Sixty-First Session on the Commission on Human Rights, E/CN/4/2005.72/Add.2, para. 24.

124. United Nations, "UN Expert of Violence against Women Concludes Visit to El Salvador," Office of the High Commissioner for Human Rights, March 22, 2010, http://www.ohchr.org/en/NewsEvents/Pages/DisplayNews.aspx?NewsID =9935&LangID=E.

125. Procuraduría para la Defense de los Derechos Humanos, "Informe de la Procuradora para la Defensa de los Derechos Humanos sobre el fenómeno de los feminicidios en El Salvador," 2006.

126. See Organización de Mujeres Salvadoreñas, "Violencia intrafamiliar: Frecuente causa de feminicidios en el país," *La Boletina de ORMUSA,* June 2009. http://www.ormusa.org/boletinas/2009_06_boletina.pdf.

127. See Mo Hume, *The Politics of Violence: Gender, Conflict and Community in El Salvador* (Chichester, UK: Wiley-Blackwell, 2009); Hume, "'It's as If You Don't Know Because You Don't Do Anything about It': Gender and Violence in El Salvador," *Environment and Urbanisation* 16, no. 2 (2004): 63–72; Peter Peetz, "Discourses on Violence in Costa Rica, El Salvador and Nicaragua: Laws and the Construction of Drug- and Gender-Related Violence," GIGA Working Paper 72, German Institute of Global and Area Studies, March 2008, http://www.giga-hamburg.de/dl/download.php?d=/content/publikationen/pdf /wp72_peetz.pdf.

128. ISDEMU, *Primer informe nacional sobre la situación de violencia contra las mujeres en El Salvador* (2009), 5. http://www.unfpa.org.sv/dmdocuments /situacion_violencia.pdf.

129. Consejo Centroamericano de Procuradores de Derechos Humanos, *Informe regional: Situación y análisis del femicidio en la región centroamericana* (August 2006), 44, http://www.iidh.ed.cr/BibliotecaWeb/Varios/Documentos /BD_1896785571/Informefemicidio/I%20Informe%20Regional%20Femicidio .pdf.

130. Ibid., 46.

131. Ibid., 47.

132. Human Rights Watch, "No Rest: Abuses against Child Domestics in El Salvador," January 15, 2004, http://www.hrw.org/en/reports/2004/01/14/no-rest.

133. Ibid.

134. ISDEMU, *Primer informe nacional sobre la situación de violencia contra las mujeres en El Salvador, 3.*

135. Julia Zulver, "El Salvador Elections: Putting Women's Rights on the Agenda," *al-Jazeera,* January 31, 2014, http://m.aljazeera.com/story /20141288499915469

136. Jack Spence, George Vickers, and David Dye, *The Salvadoran Peace Accords and Democratization: A Three Year Progress Report and Recommendations* (Cambridge, MA: Hemisphere Initiatives, 2004), 9.

137. Alisha Holland, "Right on Crime? Conservative Party Politics and *Mano Dura* Policies in El Salvador," *Latin American Research Review,* 48, no. 1 (2013), 58.

138. Ibid., 53–57.

139. Miller and Cavallaro, *No Place to Hide,* 40–41.

140. Ibid., 44.

141. Ibid., 43.

142. For an excellent discussion of the evolution of public security policy that resulted in the truce, see Theresa Whitfield, 'Mediating Criminal Violence: Lessons from the Gang Truce in El Salvador" (Geneva, Switzerland: Centre for Humanitarian Dialogue, June 2013), http://www.hdcentre.org/uploads/tx_news /Mediating-Criminal-Violence_01.pdf; José Miguel Cruz, "The Political Workings of the Funes Administration's Gang Truce in El Salvador" (Washington, DC: Woodrow Wilson International Center for Scholars, 2013), http://www .wilsoncenter.org/sites/default/files/JOSE%20MIGUEL%20CRUZ.pdf.

143. Óscar Martínez, Carlos Martínez, Sergio Arauz, and Efren Lemus, "Gobierno negoció con pandillas reducción de homicidios," *El Faro,* March 14, 2012, http://www.elfaro.net/es/201203/noticias/7985/; "El Salvador's Gang Truce: In Spite of Uncertainty, an Opportunity to Strengthen Prevention Efforts," Washington Office on Latin America, July 17, 2012, http://www.wola.org /commentary/el_salvadors_gang_truce_in_spite_of_uncertainty_an_opportunity _to_strengthen_prevention_e.

144. Carlos Martínez and José Luis Sanz, "La nueva verdad sobre la tregua entre pandillas," *El Faro,* September 11, 2012, http://www.salanegra.elfaro.net /es/201209/cronicas/9612/.

145. Douglas Farah, "The Transformation of El Salvador's Gangs into Political Actors," (Washington, DC: Center for Strategic and International Studies, June 21, 2012), http://csis.org/files/publication/120621_Farah_Gangs_HemFocus.pdf.

146. Héctor Silva Ávalos, pers. comm., June 27, 2014.

147. IUDOP, "Los salvadoreños y salvadoreñas evalúan la situación del país a finales de 2012," *Boletín de Prensa* 27, no. 4 (December 2012): 3.

148. Carlos Martínez and José Luis Sanz, "How El Salvador's Security Minister Dismantled Truce, Unleashed Mayhem," *InSight Crime,* May 28, 2014, http://www.insightcrime.org/news-analysis/how-el-salvadors-security-ministry-dismantled-truce-unleashed-mayhem.

149. José Miguel Cruz, "The Political Workings of the Funes Administration's Gang Truce in El Salvador, 15.

150. Aguilar, "Resultados contraproducentes," 878.

151. UNDP, *Seguridad paz reto país, 30.*

152. Aguilar, "Resultados contraproducentes," 882.

153. UNODC, *Crime and Development, 33.*

154. Aguilar, "Resultados contraproducentes," 87; Miller and Cavallaro, *No Place to Hide,* 12–13.

155. Miller and Cavallaro, *No Place to Hide,* 26.

156. Aguilar, "Resultados contraproducentes," 883–84.

157. José Miguel Cruz, *Street Gangs in Central America* (San Salvador: UCA Editores, 2007), 60.

158. Aguilar, "Resultados contraproducentes," 885.

159. Ibid.

160. Miller and Cavallaro, *No Place to Hide,* 27–29.

161. See LatinoBarómetro, *Informe 2005: Diez años de opinión pública* (Santiago: Corporación LatinoBarómetro, 2005).

162. IUDOP, "Victimización y percepción de inseguridad," 45.

163. Ibid., 73.

164. Pérez, "Democratic Legitimacy," 638.

165. Ibid., 639. See also Córdova and Cruz.

166. UNDP, *Informe sobre desarrollo humano, 2009–2010, 173.*

167. Farah, "Central American Gangs," 63.

168. IUDOP, *Situación de la seguridad, 22–25.*

169. Martinez and Sanz, "How El Salvador's Security Minister Dismantled Truce."

170. Andrew J. Stein notes a return to doctrinal rigidity among the church hierarchy that has led to decreased support for elements of the popular church. See "Religious Actors in El Salvador since 1992," paper presented at the IX International Congress of the Latin American Studies Association in Chicago, Illinois, September 24–26, 1998.

171. Rodolfo Cardenal, interview by author, San Salvador, October 1999.

172. El Paisnal is near Aguilares, the parish of Father Rutilio Grande, who was killed in 1977.

173. "Esperan apoyo de Quezaltepeque, Guazapa y El Paisnal: Aguilares al paro por secuestros," *La Prensa Gráfica,* May 17, 1999.

174. "Caso sacerdote Aguilares sigue pendiente," *La Prensa Gráfica,* November 1, 1999, http://www.laprensagrafica.com/siguen-deportaciones-a-la-espera -de-reforma.

175. See Religious Task Force on Central America and Mexico, "El Salvador: Let Us See What Becomes of the Dream," *Central America/Mexico Report* 20, no. 2 (May 2000).

176. Óscar Ríos, interview by author, San Salvador, March 2000. This is certainly not true for all opposition NGOs, some of which developed sophisticated organizational schemes and handled significant amounts of aid during the war.

177. Adam Flint, "The Reemergence of Social Movements in an Era of Neoliberal Democracy in El Salvador," paper prepared for the Latin American Studies Association Conference, Miami, March 16–18, 2000.

178. See Kevin Murray, Ellen Coletti, Jack Spence, et al., *Rescuing Reconstruction: The Debate on Post-war Economic Recovery in El Salvador* (Cambridge, MA: Hemisphere Initiatives, 1994), 16–21.

179. Ibid., 17.

180. Ibid.

181. International aid for NGOs was at its peak after the peace accords. Many Salvadoran NGOs became dependent on international aid for their day-to-day activities. Failure to be admitted to the registry caused many to shut down.

182. NGOs across the political spectrum opposed the proposal, which included the power of the superintendent to intervene in an organization's general finances and to replace officers of the organizations. See David R. Dye, Mike Lanchin, Geoff Thale, and George Vickers, *Chapúltepec: Five Years Later: El Salvador's Political Reality and Uncertain Future* (Cambridge, MA: Hemisphere Initiatives, 1997), 14; Tommie Sue Montgomery, "International Missions, Observing Elections, and the Democratic Transition in El Salvador," in *Electoral Observation and Democratic Transitions in Latin America,* ed. Kevin J. Middlebrook (Boulder: Lynne Rienner, 1998), 64.

183. Cathy McIlwaine, "Contesting Civil Society: Reflections from El Salvador," *Third World Quarterly* 19, no. 4 (1998): 663–65.

184. Ricardo Córdova, interview with author, San Salvador, March 2000.

185. The Colegio Médico is the Salvadoran equivalent of the American Medical Association.

186. Kay Eekhoff Andrade, FLACSO, interview by author, San Salvador, March 2000.

187. Elisabeth J. Wood, *Forging Democracy from Below: Insurgent Transitions in South Africa and El Salvador* (New York: Cambridge University Press, 2000), 103–4.

188. Michael Foley, "Laying the Groundwork: The Struggle for Civil Society in El Salvador," *Journal of Interamerican Studies and World Affairs* 38, no. 2 (1996): 87.

189. Kelley Ready, "Between Local Constituencies and Transnational Funding: Situating Salvadoran Feminism," paper prepared for the Latin American Studies Association Conference, Miami, March 16–18, 2000.

190. Flint, "Reemergence of Social Movements."

191. Ibid., 5.

192. Héctor Bérnabe Recinos, interview by author, San Salvador, November 1999.

193. Jorgé Artíga, interview by author, Costa del Sol, March 2000.

194. Héctor Bérnabe Recinos, interview by author, San Salvador, November 1999.

195. Jaime García, "Es ilegal el desembolso de ¢10 millones para APROAS," *El Diario de Hoy,* October 14, 1999, http://www.elsalvador.com/noticias /EDICIONESANTERIORES/octubre14/NACIONAL/nacio7.html. Approximately five thousand ex-patrols received payments of a little more than $200 each.

196. "El Salvador: Governing Party Loses Mayoral Race in Capital and Its Advantage in Legislature," *NotiCen,* March 16, 2000, http://www.thefreelibrary. com/EL+SALVADOR%3A+GOVERNING+PARTY+LOSES+MAYORAL +RACE+IN+CAPITAL+%26+ITS . . . -a060140822.

197. CIDAI, "Social Crisis: Social Solution," *Proceso* 866, August 18, 1999, http://www.uca.edu.sv/publica/proceso/proci866.html.

198. McIlwaine, "Contesting Civil Society," 666.

199. "El Salvador: Governing Party Loses Mayoral Race," *NotiCen,* March 16, 2000.

200. For a discussion of civil society and CAFTA, see Rose J. Spalding, "Civil Society Engagement in Trade Negotiations: CAFTA Opposition Movements in El Salvador, *Latin American Politics and Society* 49, no. 4 (2007): 85–114.

201. For an interesting interview with organizers of the market vendors movement and their perspectives on the law, see Erica Thompson, "What We Want: Voices from the Salvadoran Left," *Upside Down World,* April 29, 2009, http://upsidedownworld.org/main/el-salvador-archives-74 /1839-what-we-want-voices-from-the-salvadoran-left-.

202. Tutela Legal del Arzobispado, "Ante los sucesos de violencia acaecidos en la población de Suchitoto, el pasado día 2 de Julio de 2007," http://www .pddh.gob.sv/docs/InformepreliminarSuchitoto23julio07.pdf.

203. Carmen Morán, "Aprueban reformas antidisturbios," *El Diario de Hoy,* August 16, 2007, http://www.elsalvador.com/mwedh/nota/nota_completa .asp?idCat=6342&idArt=1635364.

204. Jane Perlez and Kirk Johnson, "Behind Gold's Glitter: Torn Lands and Pointed Questions," *New York Times*, October 24, 2005, http://www.nytimes .com/2005/10/24/health/24iht-web.1024gold.complete.html?pagewanted=all.

205. Ibid.

206. Elaine Freedman, "Pacific Rim Mining Company: The Kraken of Cabañas," *Envio*, no. 342 (January 2010), http://www.envio.org.ni/articulo/4143.

207. Ibid.

208. For a detailed discussion of the antimining network in El Salvador see Rose Spalding, *Contesting Free Trade in Central America: Market Reform and Resistance* (Austin: University of Texas Press, 2014).

209. Keny López Piche, "No a la minería: Saca cierra puertas a explotación de metales," *La Prensa Gráfica*, February 26, 2009, http://www.laprensagrafica.com /index.php/economia/nacional/32-nacional/20190-no-a-la-mineriasaca-cierra -puertas-a-explotacion-de-metales.html.

210. IUDOP, "Opinions and Perceptions towards Metal Mining in El Salvador," *Boletín de Prensa* 39, no. 2 (2015), http://www.uca.edu.sv/iudop/wp-content /uploads/MINE_ENG.pdf.

211. IUDOP, "Encuesta sobre conocimientos y percepciones hacia la minería en zonas afectadas por la incursión minera," *Informe*, no. 115 (November 2007), http://www.uca.edu.sv/publica/iudop/Web/2008/Resumen-IUDOP-Mineria .pdf. IUDOP, "Opinions and Perceptions towards Metal Mining in El Salvador."

212. Freedman, "Pacific Rim Mining Company."

213. Raúl Gutiérrez, "'Life Is Worth More Than Gold,' Say Anti-Mining Activists," *Inter Press Service*, February 1, 2008, http://ipsnews.net/news.asp ?idnews=41039.

214. López Piche, "No a la minería." See also Spalding, *Contesting Trade in Central America*, 175–78.

215. Lauren Carasik, "World Bank Tribunal Threatens El Salvador's Development," *al-Jazeera*, April 22, 3014, http://america.aljazeera.com/opinions /2014/4/el-salvador-worldbankpacificrimoceangoldmining.html. See also Spalding, *Contesting Trade in Central America*, 180–83.

216. "Homicidio de Marcelo no debe de quedar impune: FESPAD," *Diario CoLatino*, July 10, 2009, http://www.diariocolatino.com/es/20090710/nacionales /69042/.

217. Voices on the Border, "Monday Action Alert!," January 31, 2011, http:// voiceselsalvador.wordpress.com/2011/01/.

218. Gabriel Labrador Aragón, "Pandilleros mataron a los ambientalistas de Cabañas, dicen Fiscalía y PCN," *El Faro*, July 6, 2011, http://www.elfaro.net /es/201107/noticias/4692/.

219. "Funes: Crimen de ambientalista no quedará impune," *La Prensa Gráfica,* December 22, 2009, http://www.laprensagrafica.com/el-salvador/judicial/81487-funes-crimen-de-ambientalista-no-quedara-impune.html.

220. Gloria Silvia Orellana and Beatriz Castillo, "Periodistas denuncian amenazas a muerte," *Diario CoLatino,* July 27, 2009, http://www.diariocolatino.com/es/20090727/portada/69668.

221. Voices on the Border, "Voices on the Border's Fact Finding Mission Returns from Cabañas," http://voiceselsalvador.wordpress.com/2010/02/15/fact_finding_delegation/.

Chapter 6: Reclaiming the Captured Peace

1. David Holiday and William Stanley, "Under the Best of Circumstances: ONUSAL and the Challenges of Verification and Institution Building in El Salvador," in *Peacemaking and Democratization in the Western Hemisphere,* ed. Tommie Sue Montgomery (Miami: North-South Center Press, 2000), 57.

2. Tommie Sue Montgomery, "Getting to Peace in El Salvador: The Roles of the United Nations Secretariat and ONUSAL," *Journal of Interamerican Studies and World Affairs* 37, no. 4 (Winter 1995): 139–72; Teresa Whitfield, "The Role of the United Nations in El Salvador and Guatemala: A Preliminary Comparison," in *Comparative Peace Processes in Latin America,* ed. Cynthia Arnson (Washington, DC: Woodrow Wilson Center Press, 1999); Diana Villiers Negroponte, *Seeking Peace in El Salvador: The Struggle to Reconstruct a Nation at the End of the Cold War* (New York: Palgrave Macmillan, 2012).

3. For a discussion of the relationship between peacebuilding and democratization, see Anna K. Jarstad and Timothy D. Sisk, eds. *From War to Democracy: Dilemmas of Peacebuilding* (New York: Cambridge University Press, 2008).

4. Ibid.

5. Barry Gills and Joel Rocamora, "Low Intensity Democracy," *Third World Quarterly* 13, no. 3 (1992): 501–23; Richard Stahler-Sholk, "El Salvador's Negotiated Transition: From Low-Intensity Conflict to Low-Intensity Democracy," *Journal of Interamerican Studies and World Affairs* 36, no. 4 (1994): 13–34.

6. IUDOP, "Los salvadoreños y salvadoreñas evalúan el cumplimiento de los Acuerdos de Paz," *Boletín de Prensa* 26, no. 1 (2012).

7. Roberto Valencia, "How Not to Repeat the Failures of El Salvador's Gang Truce," *InSight Crime,* August 14, 2014, http://www.insightcrime.org/news-analysis/repeat-el-salvador-gang-truce-failures.

8. See Ellen Moodie, *El Salvador in the Aftermath of Peace: Crime, Uncertainty, and the Transition to Democracy* (Philadelphia: University of Pennsylvania Press, 2010).

9. See Mo Hume, *The Politics of Violence: Gender, Conflict and Community in El Salvador* (Chichester, UK: Wiley-Blackwell, 2009).

10. Ibid.

11. Ibid.

12. Ibid.

13. Caroline A. Hartzell and Matthew Hoddie, *Crafting Peace: Power-Sharing Institutions and the Negotiated Settlement of Civil Wars* (University Park: Pennsylvania State University Press, 2007).

14. The center-left Democratic Convergence (CD) did participate in the 1991 elections, winning eight seats. While the CD party had a close relationship with the FMLN (including the fact that some of the FMLN's negotiators were from the CD), this cannot be rightly equated with the FMLN enjoying representation.

15. Christine Wade, "El Salvador: The Successful Transformation of the FMLN," in *From Soldiers to Politicians: Transforming Rebel Movements after Civil War*, ed. Jeroen de Zeeuw (Boulder: Lynne Rienner, 2007), 33–54.

16. Carrie Manning, *The Politics of Peace in Mozambique: Post-conflict Democratization, 1992–2000* (Westport, CT: Praeger, 2002).

Selected Bibliography

Abrego, Leisy J. "Rethinking El Salvador's Transnational Families." *NACLA Report on the Americas* (November–December 2009): 28–29.

Acemoglu, Daron, and James A. Robinson. "Persistence of Power, Elites and Institutions." *American Economic Review* 98, no. 1 (2008): 267–93.

Acevedo, Carlos. "The Historical Background to the Conflict." In Boyce, *Economic Policy*, 19–30.

Acosta, Pablo. "Entrepreneurship, Labor Markets, and International Remittances: Evidence from El Salvador." In *International Migration, Economic Development, and Policy: Studies across the Globe*, edited by Çaglar Özden and Maurice Schiff, 141–60. New York: Palgrave Macmillan, 2007.

Adelman, Howard. "Refugee Repatriation." In Stedman, Rothchild, and Cousens, *Ending Civil Wars*, 273–302.

Aguilar, Jeannette. "Los resultados contraproducentes de las políticas antipandillas." *Estudios Centroamericanos* 62, no. 708 (October 2007): 877–90.

Albiac, María Dolores. "Los ricos más ricos de El Salvador." In *El Salvador: La transición y sus problemas*, edited by Rodolfo Cardenal and Luis Armando González, 153–83. San Salvador: UCA Editores, 2002.

Allison, Michael, and Alberto Martín Alvarez. "Unity and Disunity in the FMLN." *Latin American Politics and Society* 54, no. 4 (Winter 2012): 89–118.

Almeida, Paul. *Waves of Protest: Popular Struggle in El Salvador, 1925–2005.* Minneapolis: University of Minnesota Press, 2008.

Amnesty International. "El Salvador." Amnesty International Report, 2008. http://www.amnesty.org/en/region/el-salvador/report-2008.

Anderson, Thomas. *Matanza: El Salvador's Communist Revolt of 1932.* Lincoln: University of Nebraska Press, 1971.

Anner, Mark. "¿Hacia la sindicalización de los sindicatos?" *Estudios Centroamericanas* 51, nos. 573–74 (1996): 599–614.

Arana, Ana. "How the Street Gangs Took Central America." *Foreign Affairs* 84, no. 3 (May–June 2005): 98–110.

Arnson, Cynthia J., ed. *Comparative Peace Processes in Latin America.* Washington, DC: Woodrow Wilson Center Press, 1999.

———. *Crossroads: Congress, the Reagan Administration, and Central America.* New York: Pantheon Books, 1989.

Artiga González, Álvaro. *Elitismo competitivo: Dos décadas de elecciones en El Salvador (1982–2003).* San Salvador: UCA Editores, 2004.

Ayres, Robert. *Crime and Violence as Development Issues in Latin America and the Caribbean.* Washington, DC: World Bank, 1998.

Azpuru, Dinorah. "The Salience of Ideology: Fifteen Years of Presidential Elections in El Salvador." *Latin American Politics and Society* 52, no. 2 (Summer 2010): 103–38.

Ball, Nicole. "The Challenge of Rebuilding War-Torn Societies." In Crocker, Hampson, and Aall, *Turbulent Peace,* 719–36.

Baloyra, Enrique. *El Salvador in Transition.* Chapel Hill: University of North Carolina Press, 1982.

Bardhan, Pranab K., and Dilip Mookherjee. "Capture and Governance at Local and National Levels." *American Economic Review* 90, no. 2 (2000): 135–39.

Barnes, William A. "Incomplete Democracy in Central America: Polarization and Voter Turnout in Nicaragua and El Salvador." *Journal of Interamerican Studies and World Affairs* 40, no. 3 (1998): 63–101.

Barnett, Michael, Songying Fang, and Christoph Zürcher. "Compromised Peacebuilding." *International Studies Quarterly* 58, no. 3 (2014): 608–20.

Barnett, Michael, Hunjoon Kim, Madalene O'Donnell, and Laura Sitea. "Peacebuilding: What Is in a Name?" *Global Governance* 13, no. 1 (2007): 35–58.

Barnett, Michael, and Christoph Zürcher. "The Peacebuilder's Contract: How External Statebuilding Reinforces Weak Statehood." In Paris and Sisk, *Dilemmas of Statebuilding,* 23–52.

Booth, John A., and Mitchell A. Seligson. *The Legitimacy Puzzle in Latin America: Political Support and Democracy in Eight Nations.* New York: Cambridge University Press, 2009.

Booth, John A., Christine J. Wade, and Thomas W. Walker. *Understanding Central America: Global Forces, Rebellion, and Change.* 6th ed. Boulder: Westview Press, 2015.

Booth, John A., and Thomas W. Walker. *Understanding Central America.* 2nd ed. Boulder: Westview, 1993.

Bourguignon, François. "Crime as a Social Cost of Poverty and Inequality: A Review Focusing on Developing Countries." In *Facets of Globalization: International and Local Dimensions of Development,* edited by Shahid Yusuf, Simon Evenett, and Weiping Wu. World Bank Discussion Paper 415. Washington, DC: World Bank, 2001.

Boutros-Ghali, Boutros. *An Agenda for Peace: Preventive Diplomacy, Peacemaking and Peacekeeping.* New York: United Nations, 1992.

Boyce, James K., ed. *Economic Policy for Building Peace: The Lessons of El Salvador.* Boulder: Lynne Rienner, 1996.

———. "External Resource Mobilization." In Boyce, *Economic Policy for Building Peace,* 129–54.

Braid, Emily, and Naomi Roht-Arriaza. "De Facto and De Jure Amnesty Laws: The Central American Case." In *Amnesty in the Age of Human Rights Accountability: Comparative and International Perspectives,* edited by Francesca Lessa and Leigh Payne, 182–209. New York: Cambridge University Press, 2012.

Brockett, Charles D. *Political Movements and Violence in Central America.* New York: Cambridge University Press, 2005.

Brown, E. Michael, Sean M. Lynn-Jones, and Steven E. Miller, eds. *Debating the Democratic Peace.* Cambridge, MA: MIT Press, 1996.

Bulmer-Thomas, Victor. *The Economic History of Latin America since Independence.* Cambridge: Cambridge University Press, 1994.

Burgerman, Susan D. "Building the Peace by Mandating Reform: United Nations–Mediated Human Rights Agreements in El Salvador and Guatemala." *Latin American Perspectives* 27, no. 3 (May 2000): 63–87.

Burgess, Katrina. "Collective Remittances and Migrant-State Collaboration in Mexico and El Salvador." *Latin American Politics and Society* 54, no. 4 (Winter 2012): 119–46.

Burton, Michael, Richard Gunther, and John Higley. "Introduction: Elite Transformations and Democratic Regimes." In *Elites and Democratic Consolidation in Latin America and Southern Europe,* edited by John Higley and Richard Gunter, 1–37. New York: Cambridge University Press 1992.

Busumtwi-Sam, James. "Sustainable Peace and Development in Africa." *Studies in Comparative International Development* 37, no. 3 (2002): 91–118.

Buvinic, Mayra, Andrew R. Morrison, and Michael Shifter. "Violence in the Americas: A Framework for Action." In *Too Close to Home: Domestic Violence in the Americas,* edited by Andrew R. Morrison and María Loreto Biehl, 3–34. Washington, DC: Inter-American Development Bank, 1999.

Byrne, Hugh. *El Salvador's Civil War: A Study of Revolution.* Boulder: Lynne Rienner, 1996.

Call, Charles T. "Assessing El Salvador's Transition from Civil War to Peace." In Stedman, Rothchild, and Cousens, *Ending Civil Wars,* 383–420.

———. "Ending Wars, Building States." In *Building States to Build Peace,* edited by Call and Vanessa Wyeth, 1–22. Boulder: Lynne Rienner, 2008.

———. "The Mugging of a Success Story: Justice and Security Reform in El Salvador." In *Constructing Justice and Security after War,* edited by Call, 29–67. Washington, DC: U.S. Institute of Peace, 2007.

———. "Sustainable Development in Central America: The Challenges of Violence, Injustice and Insecurity." Central America 2020, Working Paper 8 (2000). http://ca2020.fiu.edu/Themes/Charles_Call/Call.pdf.

———. *Why Peace Fails: The Causes and Prevention of Civil War Recurrence.* Washington, DC: Georgetown University Press, 2012.

Call, Charles T., and William Stanley. "Civilian Security." In Stedman, Rothchild, and Cousens, *Ending Civil Wars*, 303–26.

Campbell, Susanna, David Chandler, and Meera Sabaratnam, eds. *A Liberal Peace? The Problems and Practices of Peacebuilding.* London: Zed Books, 2011.

Cañas, Antonio, and Héctor Dada. "Political Transition and Institutionalization in El Salvador." In Arnson, *Comparative Peace Processes*, 69–95.

Carothers, Thomas. "The End of the Transition Paradigm." *Journal of Democracy* 13, no. 1 (2002): 5–21.

Carr, Barry, and Steve Ellner, eds. *The Latin American Left: From the Fall of Allende to Perestroika.* Boulder: Westview, 1993.

Castañeda, Jorge. *Utopia Unarmed: The Latin American Left after the Cold War.* New York: Vintage Books, 1993.

Cheng, Christine, and Dominik Zaum, eds. *Corruption and Post-conflict Peacebuilding: Selling the Peace?* Abingdon, UK: Routledge, 2012.

Ching, Erik. *Authoritarian El Salvador: Politics and the Origins of the Military Regimes, 1880–1940.* Notre Dame, IN: University of Notre Dame Press, 2014.

Clements, Charles. *Witness to War: An American Doctor in El Salvador.* New York: Bantam Books, 1984.

Consejo Nacional para el Desarrollo Sostenible (CNDS). *Estado de la nación en desarrollo humano 1999.* San Salvador: Algier's Impresores, 1999.

Coppedge, Michael. *Strong Parties and Lame Ducks: Presidential Partyarchy and Factionalism in Venezuela.* Stanford: Stanford University Press, 1994.

Córdova Macías, Ricardo. "Demilitarizing and Democratizing Salvadoran Politics." In *El Salvador: Implementation of the Peace Accords,* edited by Margarita S. Studemeister, 27–32. Washington, DC: U.S. Institute of Peace, 2001.

Córdova Macías, Ricardo, and José Miguel Cruz. *Political Culture of Democracy in El Salvador and the Americas, 2012: Towards Equality of Opportunity.* Nashville: LAPOP, 2013.

Córdova Macías, Ricardo, José Miguel Cruz, and Mitchell A. Seligson. *Cultura política de la democracia en El Salvador, 2006.* San Salvador: IUDOP, 2007.

———. *Cultura política de la democracia en El Salvador, 2008: El impacto de la gobernabilidad.* San Salvador: IUDOP, 2008.

Córdova Macías, Ricardo, and Carlos Ramos. "The Peace Process and the Construction of Democracy in El Salvador: Progress, Deficiencies and Challenges." In *In the Wake of War: Democratization and Internal Armed Conflict in Latin America,* edited by Cynthia J. Arnson, 79–106. Washington, DC: Woodrow Wilson Center Press, 2012.

Córdova Macías, Ricardo, William Pleitez, and Carlos Ramos. "Reforma política y reforma económica: Los retos de la gobernibilidad democrática."

Documentos de trabajo, Serie análisis de la realidad nacional 98–1. San Salvador: FUNDAUNGO, 1998.

Corral, Margarita. "Do Parties Listen to the People? Views from the Americas." AmericasBarometer Insights 2009, 12. Latin American Public Opinion Project.

———. "(Mis)Trust in Political Parties in Latin America." AmericasBarometer Insights 2008, 2. Latin American Public Opinion Project.

Cousens, Elizabeth, Chetan Kumar, and Karin Wermester, eds. *Peacebuilding as Politics: Cultivating Peace in Fragile Societies*. Boulder: Lynne Rienner, 2002.

Coutin, Susan. *The Culture of Protest: Religious Activism and the U.S. Sanctuary Movement*. Boulder: Westview, 1993.

Crocker, Chester, Fen Osler Hampson, and Pamela Aall. *Turbulent Peace: The Challenges of Managing International Conflict*. Washington, DC: United States Institute of Peace, 2001.

Cruz, José Miguel. "Criminal Violence and Democratization in Central America: The Survival of the Violent State." *Latin American Politics and Society* 53, no. 4 (Winter 2011): 1–33.

———. "The Political Workings of the Funes Administration's Gang Truce in El Salvador." Washington, DC: Woodrow Wilson International Center for Scholars, 2012.

———. "¿Por qué no votan los Salvadoreños?" *Estudios Centroamericanos* 53, nos. 595–96 (1998): 449–72.

———. *Street Gangs in Central America*. San Salvador: UCA Editores, 2007.

Cruz, José Miguel, and Luis Armando González. "Magnitud de la violencia en El Salvador." *Estudios Centroamericanos* 52, no. 588 (October 1997): 953–66.

Cruz, José Miguel, Álvaro Trigueros Argüello, and Francisco González. *El crimen violento en El Salvador*. San Salvador: IUDOP, 2000.

Cuenca, Breny. "La fisura en el FMLN: Diferencias ideológicas o pugna de poder?" *Tendencias* 31 (1994): 19–21.

Dada Hizeri, Héctor. "Las elecciones de 1997: Sus resultados y la nueva distribución política." In *Las elecciones de 1997: ¿Un paso más en la transición democrática?*, edited by Dada Hizeri, 239–70. San Salvador: FLACSO, 1998.

Dasgupta, Aniruddha, and Victoria A. Beard. "Community Driven Development, Collective Action and Elite Capture in Indonesia." *Development and Change* 38, no. 2 (2007): 229–49.

Davidson, Miriam. *Convictions of the Heart: Jim Corbett and the Sanctuary Movement*. Tucson: University of Arizona Press, 1988.

de Bremond, Ariane. "The Politics of Peace and Resettlement through El Salvador's Land Transfer Program: Caught between the State and the Market." *Third World Quarterly* 28, no. 8 (2007): 1537–56.

de Soto, Álvaro, and Graciana del Castillo. "Obstacles to Peacebuilding." *Foreign Policy,* no. 94 (Spring 1994): 69–83.

Diskin, Martin, and Kenneth Sharpe. "El Salvador." In *Confronting Revolution: Security through Diplomacy in Central America,* edited by Morris Blachman, William Leogrande, and Kenneth Sharpe, 50–87. New York: Pantheon, 1986.

Dodson, Michael, Donald W. Jackson and Laura O'Shaughnessy. "Political Will and Public Trust: El Salvador's Procurator for the Defense of Human Rights and the Dilemmas of Institution-Building." *Human Rights Review* 2, no. 3 (April–June 2001): 51–75.

Doggett, Margaret. *Death Foretold: The Jesuit Murders in El Salvador.* Washington, DC: Georgetown University Press, 1993.

Downs, George, and Stephan John Stedman. "Evaluation Issues in Peace Implementation." In Stedman, Rothchild, and Cousens, *Ending Civil Wars,* 43–69.

Doyle, Michael, Ian Johnstone, and Robert C. Orr. *Keeping the Peace: Multidimensional UN Operations in Cambodia and El Salvador.* New York: Cambridge University Press, 1997.

Duffield, Mark. *Global Governance and the New Wars: The Merging of Development and Security.* London: Zed Books, 2001.

Dunkerley, James. *The Long War: Dictatorship and Revolution in El Salvador.* London: Verso, 1983.

Edwards, A. Cox, and Manuelita Ureta. "International Migration, Remittances, and Schooling: Evidence from El Salvador." *Journal of Development Economics* 72, no. 2 (2003): 429–61.

Edwards, Sebastian. *Crecimiento con participación: Una estrategia de desarrollo para el siglo XXI.* San Salvador: FUSADES, 1999.

El Salvador. Comisión Nacional de Desarrollo. *Bases para el plan de nación.* San Salvador: CND, 1998.

European Union Election Observation Mission. *El Salvador Legislative, Municipal and PARLACEN Elections 2009: Preliminary Statement.* San Salvador, January 20, 2009.

Farah, Douglas. "Central American Gangs: Changing Nature and New Partners." *Journal of International Affairs* 66, no. 1 (Fall–Winter 2012): 53–67.

Fitzsimmons, Tracy, and Mark Anner. "Civil Society in a Postwar Period: Labor in the Salvadoran Democratic Transition." *Latin American Research Review* 34, no. 3 (1999): 103–28.

Flint, Adam. "The Reemergence of Social Movements in an Era of Neo-liberal Democracy in El Salvador." Paper prepared for the Latin American Studies Association Conference, Miami, March 16–18, 2000.

Foley, Michael. "Laying the Groundwork: The Struggle for Civil Society in El Salvador." *Journal of Interamerican Studies and World Affairs* 38, no. 2 (1996): 67–104.

Fortna, Virginia Page. "Peacekeeping and Democratization." In *From War to Democracy: Dilemmas of Peacebuilding*, edited by Anna K. Jarstad and Timothy D. Sisk, 39–79. New York: Cambridge University Press. 39–79.

Galtung, Johan. "Conflict Resolution as Conflict Transformation: The First Law of Thermodynamics Revisited." In *Conflict Transformation*, edited by Kumar Rupesinghe, 51–64. New York: St. Martin's, 1995.

———. "Cultural Violence." *Journal of Peace Research* 27, no. 3 (August 1990): 291–305.

———. "An Editorial." *Journal of Peace Research* 1, no. 1 (1964): 1–4.

———. "Peace and Conflict Research in the Age of the Cholera: Ten Pointers to the Future of Peace Studies." *Peace and Conflict Studies* 2, no. 1 (June 1995): 25–36.

———. *Peace by Peaceful Means: Peace and Conflict, Development and Civilization*. Oslo: International Peace Research Institute, 1996.

———. "Violence, Peace, and Peace Research." *Journal of Peace Research* 6, no. 3 (1969): 167–91.

Gammage, Sarah. "Exporting People and Recruiting Remittances: A Development Strategy for El Salvador?" *Latin American Perspectives* 33, no. 6 (November 2006): 75–100.

Gills, Barry, and Joel Rocamora. "Low Intensity Democracy." *Third World Quarterly* 13, no. 3 (1992): 501–23.

Gingrich, Chris, and Jason Garber. "Trade Liberalization's Impact on Agriculture in Low-Income Countries: A Comparison of El Salvador and Costa Rica." *Journal of Developing Areas* 43, no. 2 (Spring 2010): 1–17.

González, Luis Armando, and Lilian Vega. "El Salvador: Política, sociedad y economía en 2005." *Estudios Centroamericanos* 61, no. 690 (2005): 409–39.

Guardado, Ana. "Outsiders in El Salvador: The Role of an International Truth Commission in a National Transition." *Berkeley La Raza Law Journal* 22, no. 2 (2012): 433–57.

Hampson, Fen Osler. *Nurturing Peace: Why Peace Settlements Succeed or Fail*. Washington, DC: U.S. Institute of Peace, 1996.

Hartzell, Caroline A., and Matthew Hoddie. *Crafting Peace: Power-Sharing Institutions and the Negotiated Settlement of Civil Wars*. University Park: Pennsylvania State University Press, 2007.

Hayner, Priscilla B. *Unspeakable Truths: Facing the Challenge of Truth Commissions*. New York: Routledge, 2001.

Hellman, Joel, and Daniel Kaufmann. "Confronting the Challenge of State Capture in Transition Economies." *Finance and Development* 38, no. 3 (2001): 31–35.

Hinds, Manuel. *Playing Monopoly with the Devil: Dollarization and Domestic Currencies in Developing Countries*. New Haven: Yale University Press, 2006.

Holbik, Karel, and Philip Swan. *Trade and Industrialization in the Central American Common Market: The First Decade.* Austin: Bureau of Business Research, University of Texas, 1972.

Holiday, David, and William Stanley. "Building the Peace: Preliminary Lessons from El Salvador." *Journal of International Affairs* 46, no. 2 (1993): 415–38.

———. "Under the Best of Circumstances: ONUSAL and the Challenges of Verification and Institution Building in El Salvador." In *Peacemaking and Democratization in the Western Hemisphere,* edited by Tommie Sue Montgomery, 37–65. Miami: North-South Center Press, 2000.

Holland, Alisha C. "Right on Crime? Conservative Party Politics and *Mano Dura* Policies in El Salvador." *Latin American Research Review* 48, no. 1 (2013): 44–67.

Hume, Mo. "'It's As If You Don't Know Because You Don't Do Anything about It': Gender and Violence in El Salvador." *Environment and Urbanization* 16, no. 2 (2004): 63–72.

Huyse, Luc. "Justice after Transition: On the Choices Successor Elites Make in Dealing with the Past." *Law and Social Inquiry* 20, no. 1 (Winter 1995): 51–78.

IUDOP (Instituto Universitario de Opinión Pública). "Los cuidadanos opinan sobre los Acuerdos de Paz y la democracia en El Salvador." *Boletín de Prensa* 17, no. 1 (2002).

———. "Elecciones presidenciales 99." *Boletín de Prensa* 14, no. 3 (1999).

———. "Encuesta de evaluación del año 2003." *Informe,* no. 102 (2003).

———. "Encuesta de evaluación del año 2005: Resultados de la muestra nacional." *Informe,* no. 109 (2005).

———. "Encuesta de evaluación del primer año de Francisco Flores, Asamblea Legislative, Alcaldias y post-electoral." *Informe,* no. 85 (2000).

———. "Encuesta sobre el proceso electoral de 2004." *Informe,* no. 103 (2004).

———. "Evaluacíon del país a finales de 2002 y perspectivas electorales para 2003." *Boletín de Prensa* 17, no. 4 (2002).

———. "Governabilidad y expectivas hacia las nuevas autoridadas municipales y legislativas." (1997).

———. "Los salvadoreños ante los acuerdos finales de paz." *Informe,* no. 31 (1992).

———. "Los salvadoreños evalúan el cuarto año de gobierno de Antonio Saca y opinan sobre la coyuntura político-electoral." *Boletín de Prensa* 23, no. 3 (2008).

———. "Los salvadoreños y salvadoreñas evalúan el cumplimiento de los Acuerdos de Paz." *Boletín de Prensa* 26, no. 1 (2012).

———. "Las y los salvadoreños evalúan el tercer año de gobierno de Antonio Saca." *Boletín de Prensa* 22, no. 1 (2007).

———. "Los salvadoreños frente a las elecciones presidenciales de 2004." *Boletín de Prensa* 19, no. 1 (2004).

———. "Los salvadoreños y salvadoreñas evalúan la situación del país a finales de 2007." *Boletín de Prensa* 22, no. 2 (2007).

———. *La situación de la seguridad y justicia 2009–2014: Entre expectivas de cambio, mano dura military y treguas pandilleras.* San Salvador: IUDOP, 2014.

———. "Victimización y percepción de inseguridad en El Salvador 2009." *Boletín de Prensa* 23, no. 5 (2009).

———. "Opinions and Perceptions towards Metal Mining in El Salvador." *Boletín de Prensa* 39, no. 2 (2015).

Jarstad, Anna K., and Roberto Belloni. "Introducing Hybrid Peace Governance: Impact and Prospects of Liberal Peacebuilding." *Global Governance* 18, no. 1 (2012): 1–6.

Jarstad, Anna K., and Timothy D. Sisk, eds. *From War to Democracy: Dilemmas of Peacebuilding.* New York: Cambridge University Press, 2008.

Jeong, Ho-Won. *Peacebuilding in Postconflict Societies: Strategy and Process.* Boulder: Lynne Rienner, 2005.

Johnson, Kenneth L. "Between Revolution and Democracy: Business Elites and the State in El Salvador during the 1980s." PhD dissertation, Tulane University, 1993.

Jones, Richard C. "Causes of Salvadoran Migration to the United States." *Geographical Review* 79, no. 2 (April 1989): 183–94.

Kahler, Miles. "Statebuilding after Afghanistan and Iraq." In Paris and Sisk, *Dilemmas of Statebuilding,* 287–303.

Kant, Immanuel. *To Perpetual Peace: A Philosophical Sketch.* Translated by Ted Humphrey. Indianapolis: Hackett Publishing, 2003.

Karl, Terry Lynn. "El Salvador's Negotiated Revolution." *Foreign Affairs* 71, no. 2 (Spring 1992): 147–64.

Kowalchuk, Lisa. "Can Movement Tactics Influence Media Coverage? Health-Care Struggle in the Salvadoran News." *Latin American Research Review* 44, no. 2 (2009): 109–35.

Kritz, Neil J., ed. *Transitional Justice: How Emerging Democracies Reckon with Former Regimes.* 3 vols. Washington, DC: U.S. Institute of Peace, 1995.

Krznaric, Roman. "Civil and Uncivil Actors in the Guatemalan Peace Process." *Bulletin of Latin American Research* 18, no. 1 (1999): 1–16.

Labonte, Melissa T. "From Patronage to Peacebuilding?: Elite Capture and Governance from Below in Sierra Leone." *African Affairs* 111, no. 442 (2011): 90–115.

Ladutke, Lawrence Michael. *Freedom of Expression in El Salvador: The Struggle for Human Rights and Democracy.* Jefferson, NC: McFarland, 2004.

LaFeber, Walter. *Inevitable Revolutions: The United States in Central America.* 2nd ed. New York: Norton, 1993.

Laffont, Jean-Jacques, and Jean Tirole. "The Politics of Government Decision-Making: A Theory of Regulatory Capture. *Quarterly Journal of Economics* 104, no. 4 (1991): 1089–127.

Lake, David A. "Powerful Pacifists: Democratic States and War." *American Political Science Review* 87, no. 1 (1992): 624–38.

Landolt, Patricia, Lilian Autler, and Sonia Baires. "From Hermano Lejano to Hermano Mayor: The Dialectics of Salvadoran Transnationalism." *Ethnic and Racial Studies* 22, no. 2 (1999): 290–315.

Lauria-Santiago, Aldo A. *An Agrarian Republic: Commercial Agriculture and the Politics of Peasant Communities in El Salvador, 1823–1914.* Pittsburgh: University of Pittsburgh Press, 1999.

Lawyers' Committee for Human Rights. *Improvising History: A Critical Evaluation of the United Nations Observer Mission in El Salvador.* New York: The Committee, 1995.

Layne, Christopher. "Kant or Cant: The Myth of the Democratic Peace." *International Security* 19, no. 2 (Fall 1994): 5–49.

Lederach, John Paul. *Preparing for Peace: Conflict Transformation across Cultures.* Syracuse: Syracuse University Press, 1995.

Licklider, Roy. "Obstacles to Peace Settlements." In Crocker, Hampson, and Aall, *Turbulent Peace,* 697–718.

Lindo-Fuentes, Héctor. *Weak Foundations: The Economy of El Salvador in the Nineteenth Century.* Berkley: University of California Press, 1990.

Lindo-Fuentes, Héctor, Erik Ching, and Rafael A. Lara-Martínez. *Remembering a Massacre in El Salvador: The Insurrection of 1932, Roque Dalton, and the Politics of Historical Memory.* Albuquerque: University of New Mexico Press, 2007.

López-Pintor, Rafael. "El Salvador." In *Political Finance in Post-conflict Societies,* edited by Jeff Fischer, Marcin Walecki, and Jeffrey Carlson, 49–60. Washington, DC: Center for Transitional and Post-Conflict Governance, International Foundation for Electoral Systems (IFES), May 2006.

Lowi, Theodore. *The End of Liberalism: The Second Republic of the United States.* 2nd ed. New York: Norton, 1979.

Luciak, Ilja A. *After the Revolution: Gender and Democracy in El Salvador, Nicaragua, and Guatemala.* Baltimore: Johns Hopkins University Press, 2001.

Mac Ginty, Roger. *International Peacebuilding and Local Resistance: Hybrid Forms of Peace.* Basingstoke: Palgrave Macmillan, 2011.

———. "Hybrid Peace: The Interaction between Top-Down and Bottom-Up Peace." *Security Dialogue* 41, no. 4 (2010): 391–412.

Mac Ginty, Roger, and Oliver P. Richmond, eds. *The Liberal Peace and Post-war Reconstruction: Myth or Reality?* New York: Routledge, 2009.

Mahoney, James. *The Legacies of Liberalism: Path Dependence and Political Regimes in Central America*. Baltimore: Johns Hopkins University Press, 2001.

Manning, Carrie. "Local Level Challenges to Post-conflict Peacebuilding." *International Peacekeeping* 10, no. 3 (2003): 25–43.

——. *The Making of Democrats: Elections and Party Development in Bosnia, El Salvador, and Mozambique*. New York: Palgrave Macmillan, 2008.

——. *The Politics of Peace in Mozambique: Post-conflict Democratization, 1992–2000*. Westport, CT: Praeger, 2002.

Matthews, Leah, and Erica Stahl. "Asocio public-privado en El Salvador: Análisis de impacto y recomendaciones." Fundación de Estudios para la Aplicación del Derecho. *FESPAD*. October 23, 2012. http://www.fespad.org.sv/wp-content/uploads/2013/08/asocio-publico-privado-en-el-salvador.pdf.

Mazzei, Julie M. "Finding Shame in Truth: The Importance of Public Engagement in Truth Commissions." *Human Rights Quarterly* 33, no. 2 (May 2011): 431–52.

McClintock, Cynthia. *Revolutionary Movements in Latin America: El Salvador's FMLN and Peru's Shining Path*. Washington, DC: U.S. Institute of Peace, 1998.

McIlwaine, Cathy. "Contesting Civil Society: Reflections from El Salvador." *Third World Quarterly* 19, no. 4 (1998): 651–72.

McLeod, Murdo J. *Spanish Central America: A Socioeconomic History, 1520–1720*. Berkeley: University of California Press, 1973.

Melhado, Oscar. *El Salvador: Retos económicos de fin de siglo*. San Salvador: UCA Editores, 1997.

Menjívar, Cecilia. *Fragmented Ties: Salvadoran Immigrant Networks in America*. Berkeley: University of California Press, 2000.

Menjívar, Rafael. *El Salvador: El eslabón más pequeño*. San José, Costa Rica: EDUCA, 1980.

Miller, Spring, and James Cavallaro, eds. *No Place to Hide: Gang, State, and Clandestine Violence in El Salvador*. Human Rights Program. Cambridge, MA: Harvard Law School, 2009.

Minow, Martha. *Between Vengeance and Forgiveness: Facing History after Genocide and Mass Violence*. Boston: Beacon Press, 1999.

Montes, Segundo. *El Salvador 1987: Salvadoreños refugiados en Estados Unidos*. San Salvador: Instituto de Investigaciones, UCA, 1987.

Montgomery, Tommie Sue. "Getting to Peace in El Salvador: The Roles of the United Nations Secretariat and ONUSAL." *Journal of Interamerican Studies and World Affairs* 37, no. 4 (Winter 1995): 139–72.

———. "International Missions, Observing Elections, and the Democratic Transition in El Salvador." In *Electoral Observation and Democratic Transitions in Latin America,* edited by Kevin J. Middlebrook, 115–40. Boulder: Lynne Rienner, 1998.

———, ed. *Peacemaking and Democratization in the Western Hemisphere.* Miami: North-South Center Press, 2000.

———. *Revolution in El Salvador: From Civil Strife to Civil Peace.* 2nd ed. Boulder: Westview, 1995.

———. "The United Nations and Peacemaking in El Salvador." *North-South Issues* (University of Miami: North South Center) 4, no. 3 (1995).

Moodey, Lily. "P3 Legislation in El Salvador: An Aggressive Reassertion of Neoliberal Economics?" *Council on Hemispheric Affairs,* August 7, 2013. http://www.coha.org/p3-legislation-in-el-salvador-an-aggressive-reassertion-of-neoliberal-economics/.

Moodie, Ellen. *El Salvador in the Aftermath of Peace: Crime, Uncertainty, and the Transition to Democracy.* Philadelphia: University of Pennsylvania Press, 2010.

Moore, David. "Levelling the Playing Fields and Embedding Illusions: 'Post-Conflict' Discourse and Neo-liberal 'Development' in War-Torn Africa." *Review of African Political Economy* 27, no. 83 (2000): 11–28.

Morrison, Andrew, Mayra Buvinic, and Michael Shifter. "The Violent Americas: Risk Factors, Consequences, and Policy Implications of Social and Domestic Violence." In *Crime and Violence in Latin America,* edited by Hugo Frühling and Joseph Tulchin with Heather A. Golding, 93–122. Washington, DC: Woodrow Wilson Center Press, 2003.

Mountz, Alison, Richard Wright, Ines Miyares, and Adrian J. Bailey. "Lives in Limbo: Temporary Protected Status and Immigrant Identities." *Global Networks* 2, no. 4 (2002): 335–56.

Murray, Kevin, Ellen Coletti, Jack Spence, et al. *Rescuing Reconstruction: The Debate on Post-war Economic Recovery in El Salvador.* Cambridge, MA: Hemisphere Initiatives, 1994.

Negroponte, Diana Villiers. *Seeking Peace in El Salvador: The Struggle to Reconstruct a Nation at the End of the Cold War.* New York: Palgrave Macmillan, 2012.

O'Donnell, Madalene. "Post-conflict Corruption: A Rule of Law Agenda?" In *Civil War and the Rule of Law,* edited by Agnès Hurwitz and Reyko Huang, 225–60. Boulder: Lynne Rienner, 2008.

Orozco, Manuel. *Remittances and Markets: New Players and Practices.* Washington, DC: Inter-American Dialogue, 2000.

Orr, Robert. "Building Peace in El Salvador: From Exception to Rule." In Cousens, Kumar, and Wermester, *Peacebuilding as Politics,* 153–81.

Paige, Jeffrey M. *Coffee and Power: Revolution and the Rise of Democracy in Central America*. Cambridge, MA: Harvard University Press, 1997.

Paris, Roland. *At War's End: Building Peace after Civil Conflict*. New York: Cambridge University Press, 2004.

———. "Peacebuilding and the Limits of Liberal Internationalism." *International Security* 22, no. 2 (1997): 54–89.

———. "Peacebuilding in Central America: Reproducing in the Sources of Conflict?" *International Peacekeeping* 9, no. 4 (2002): 39–68.

Paris, Roland, and Timothy D. Sisk, eds. *The Dilemmas of Statebuilding: Confronting the Contradictions of Postwar Peace Operations*. New York: Routledge, 2009.

Paus, Eva. "Exports and the Consolidation of Peace." In Boyce, *Economic Policy for Building Peace*, 247–78.

Peceny, Mark and William Stanley. "Liberal Social Reconstruction and the Resolution of Civil Wars in Central America." *International Organization* 55, no. 1 (2001): 149–82.

Peetz, Peter. "Discourses on Violence in Costa Rica, El Salvador, and Nicaragua: Laws and the Construction of Drug- and Gender-Related Violence." GIGA Working Paper 72, German Institute of Global and Area Studies, March 2008. http://www.giga-hamburg.de/dl/download.php?d=/content/publikationen /pdf/wp72_peetz.pdf.

Pelupessy, Wim. *The Limits of Economic Reform in El Salvador*. New York: Palgrave Macmillan, 1997.

Peña, Uzziel, and Tom Gibb. "El Salvador's Gang Truce: A Historic Opportunity." *NACLA Report on the Americas* 46, no.2 (Summer 2013): 12–15.

Pérez, Orlando J. "Democratic Legitimacy and Public Insecurity: Crime and Democracy in El Salvador and Guatemala." *Political Science Quarterly* 118, no. 4 (Winter 2003–4): 627–44.

———. "Gang Violence and Insecurity in Contemporary Central America." *Bulletin of Latin American Research* 32, no. 1 (March 2013): 217–34.

Perla, Héctor, Jr., Marco Mojica, and Jared Bibler. "From Guerrillas to Government: The Continued Relevance of the Central American Left." In *The New Latin American Left: Cracks in the Empire*, edited by Jeffrey R. Webber and Barry Carr, 327–56. Lanham, MD: Rowman and Littlefield, 2012.

Perry, Guillermo E., William F. Maloney, Omar S. Arias, Pablo Fajnzylber, Andrew D. Mason, and Jaime Saavedra-Chanduvi. *Informality: Exit and Exclusion*. Washington, DC: World Bank, 2007.

Petras, James. *The Left Strikes Back: Class Conflict in Latin America in the Age of Neoliberalism*. Boulder: Westview, 1999.

Platteau, Jean-Philippe. "Monitoring Elite Capture in Community-Driven Development." *Development and Change* 35, no. 2 (2004): 223–46.

Popkin, Margaret. *Peace without Justice: Obstacles to Building the Rule of Law in El Salvador.* University Park: Pennsylvania State University Press, 2000.

Pradhan, Sanjay. *Anticorruption in Transition: A Contribution to the Policy Debate.* Washington, DC: World Bank, 2000.

Pugh, Michael. "The Political Economy of Peacebuilding: A Critical Theory Perspective." *International Journal of Peace Studies* 10, no. 2 (2005): 23–42.

Pyes, Craig. "ARENA's Bid for Power." In *El Salvador: Central America in the New Cold War,* edited by Marvin E. Gettleman, Patrick Lacefield, Louis Manashe, and David Mermelstein, 165–74. New York: Grove Press, 1987.

Ray, James Lee. "Does Democracy Cause Peace?" *Annual Review of Political Science* 1, no. 1 (1998): 27–46.

Ready, Kelley. "Between Local Constituencies and Transnational Funding: Situating Salvadoran Feminism." Paper prepared for the Latin American Studies Association Conference, Miami, March 16–18, 2000.

Remmer, Karen L. "Democracy and Economic Crisis: The Latin American Experience." *World Politics* 42, no. 3 (1990): 315–35.

Richani, Nazih. "State Capacity in Postconflict Settings: Explaining Criminal Violence in El Salvador and Guatemala." *Civil Wars* 12, no. 4 (December 2010): 431–55.

Richmond, Oliver P., ed. *Palgrave Advances in Peacebuilding: Critical Developments and Approaches.* New York: Palgrave Macmillan, 2010.

———. *A Post-liberal Peace: The Infrapolitics of Peacebuilding.* Abingdon, UK: Routledge, 2011.

Rivas Pérez, Cristina. "The Dimensions of Polarization in Parliaments." In *Politicians and Politics in Latin America,* edited by Manuel Alcántara Sáez, 139–60. Boulder: Lynne Rienner, 2008.

Rivera Campos, Roberto. *La economía salvadoreña al final del siglo: Desafíos para el futuro.* San Salvador: FLACSO, 2005.

Roberts, David. *Liberal Peacebuilding and Global Governance: Beyond the Metropolis.* New York: Routledge, 2012.

———. "Statebuilding in Cambodia." In Paris and Sisk, *Dilemmas of Statebuilding,* 151–53.

Robinson, William I. *Transnational Conflicts: Central America, Social Change, and Globalization.* New York: Verso, 2003.

Salvadoreños en el Mundo. "Briefing Paper on Voting Rights for 3.3 Million Disenfranchised Salvadoran Migrants Living Overseas." http://www.2008.december18.net/web/docpapers/doc6376.pdf. Accessed April 14, 2008.

Santacruz-Giralt, María, José Miguel Cruz, Alberto Concha-Eastman, et al. *Inside the Neighborhood: Salvadoran Street Gangs' Violent Solidarity.* San

Salvador: Pan American Health Organization/Universidad Centroamericana, 2002.

Savenije, Wim, and Chris van der Borgh. "Youth Gangs, Social Exclusion and the Transformation of Violence in El Salvador." In *Armed Actors: Organized Violence and State Failure in Latin America,* edited by Kees Koonings and Dirk Kruijt, 155–71. Boulder: Lynne Rienner, 1996.

Schiff, Maurice, and Çaglar Özden. *International Migration, Remittances and the Brain Drain.* New York: Palgrave Macmillan, 2005.

Schneider, Aaron. *State-Building and Tax Regimes in Central America.* New York: Cambridge University Press, 2012.

Segovia, Alexander. "Macroeconomic Performance and Policies since 1989." In Boyce, *Economic Policy for Building Peace,* 51–72.

———. "The War Economy of the 1980s." In Boyce, *Economic Policy for Building Peace,* 31–50.

Seligson, Mitchell. "Democracy on Ice: The Multiple Challenges of Guatemala's Peace Process." In *The Third Wave of Democratization in Latin America: Advances and Setbacks,* edited by Frances Hagopian and Scott Mainwaring, 202–31. New York: Cambridge University Press, 2005.

Sending, Ole Jacob. "The Effects of Peacebuilding: Sovereignty, Patronage and Power." In Campbell, Chandler, and Sabaratnam, *Liberal Peace?,* 55–68.

Silva Ávalos, Héctor. *Infiltrados: Crónica de la corrupción en la PNC, 1992–2013.* San Salvador: UCA Editores, 2014.

Smith, William C., Carlos Acuña, and Eduardo Gamarra. *Latin American Political Economy in the Age of Neoliberal Reform.* Miami: North-South Center Press, 1994.

Smith, William C., and Roberto Patricio Korzeniewicz. *Politics, Social Change, and Economic Restructuring in Latin America.* Miami: North-South Center Press, 1997.

Snyder, Jack. *From Voting to Violence: Democratization and Nationalist Conflict.* New York: Norton, 2000.

Spalding, Rose J. "Civil Society Engagement in Trade Negotiations: CAFTA Opposition Movements in El Salvador." *Latin American Politics and Society* 49, no. 4 (2007): 85–114.

———. *Contesting Trade in Central America: Market Reform and Resistance.* Austin: University of Texas Press, 2014.

Spence, Jack. *War and Peace in Central America: Comparing Transitions toward Democracy and Social Equality in Guatemala, El Salvador, and Nicaragua.* Cambridge, MA: Hemisphere Initiatives, 2004.

Spence, Jack, David R. Dye, Mike Lanchin, and Geoff Thale, with George Vickers. *Chapúltepec: Five Years Later: El Salvador's Political Reality and Uncertain Future.* Cambridge, MA: Hemisphere Initiatives, 1997.

Spence, Jack, Mike Lanchin, and Geoff Thale. *From Elections to Earthquakes: Reform and Participation in Post-war El Salvador.* Cambridge, MA: Hemisphere Initiatives, 2001.

Spence, Jack, George Vickers, and David Dye. *The Salvadoran Peace Accords and Democratization: A Three Year Progress Report and Recommendations.* Cambridge, MA: Hemisphere Initiatives, 1995.

Stahler-Sholk, Richard. "El Salvador's Negotiated Transition: From Low-Intensity Conflict to Low-Intensity Democracy." *Journal of Interamerican Studies and World Affairs* 36, no. 4 (1994): 1–59.

Stanley, William. "Economic Migrants or Refugees from Violence? A Time-Series Analysis of Salvadoran Migration to the United States." *Latin American Research Review* 22, no. 1 (1987): 132–54.

———. *The Protection Racket State: Elite Politics, Military Extortion, and Civil War in El Salvador.* Philadelphia: Temple University Press, 1996.

Stedman, Stephen John, Donald Rothchild, and Elizabeth M. Cousens, eds. *Ending Civil Wars: The Implementation of Peace Agreements.* Boulder: Lynne Rienner, 2002.

Stigler, George J. "The Theory of Economic Regulation." *Bell Journal of Economics and Management Science* 2, no. 1 (1971): 3–21.

Teitel, Ruti G. *Transitional Justice.* New York: Oxford University Press, 2000.

Towers, Marcia, and Silvia Borzutzky. "The Socioeconomic Implications of Dollarization in El Salvador." *Latin American Politics and Society* 46, no. 3 (2004): 29–54.

United Nations. *El Salvador Agreements: The Path to Peace.* New York: United Nations Department of Public Information, 1992.

———. *The Situation in Central America: Procedures of the Establishment of a Firm and Lasting Peace and Progress in Fashioning a Region of Peace, Freedom, Democracy and Development Assessment of the Peace Process in El Salvador: Report of the Secretary General.* New York: United Nations Department of Public Information, 1997.

———. *The Situation in Central America: Progress in Fashioning a Region of Peace, Freedom, Democracy and Development.* Report of the Secretary General, August 11, 2005, A/60/218. New York: United Nations Department of Public Information, 2005.

———. *The United Nations and El Salvador, 1990–1995.* New York: United Nations Department of Public Information, 1995.

United Nations Development Programme (UNDP). *¿Cuánto cuesta la violencia a El Salvador?* San Salvador: UNDP, 2005.

———. *Informe sobre desarrollo humano, El Salvador, 2005: Una mirada al nuevo nosotros: El impacto de las migraciones.* San Salvador: UNDP, 2005.

———. *Informe sobre desarrollo humano para América Central, 2009–2010: Abrir espacios a la seguridad ciudadana y el desarrollo humano.* San Salvador: UNDP, 2009.

———. *Informe sobre desarrollo humano, El Salvador, 2007–2008: El empleo en uno de los pueblos más trabajadores del mundo.* San Salvador: UNDP, 2008.

———. *Una mirada al nuevo nostros: El impacto de las migraciones.* San Salvador: UNDP, 2005.

———. *Seguridad paz reto país: Recomendaciones para una política de seguridad ciudadana en El Salvador.* San Salvador: UNDP, 2007.

United Nations Office on Drugs and Crime (UNODC). *Crime and Development in Central America: Caught in the Crossfire.* New York: UNODC, May 2007.

———. *Transnational Organized Crime in Central America and the Caribbean: A Threat Assessment.* Vienna: UNODC, September 2012.

United States. Department of Homeland Security. *Annual Report, November 2006.* Washington, DC: Office of Immigration Statistics, Immigration Enforcement Actions, 2005.

United States. Department of State, Bureau of Western Hemispheric Affairs. *Partnership for Growth: El Salvador 2011–2015.* November 3, 2011. http://www.state.gov/p/wha/rls/fs/2011/176636.htm.

Villalobos, Joaquín. "A Democratic Revolution for El Salvador." *Foreign Policy,* no. 74 (Spring 1989): 103–22.

Wade, Christine J. "El Salvador: Contradictions of Neoliberalism and Building Sustainable Peace." *International Journal of Peace Studies* 13, no. 2 (Autumn–Winter 2008): 15–32.

———. "El Salvador: The Successful Transformation of the FMLN." In *From Soldiers to Politicians: Transforming Rebel Movements after Civil War,* edited by Jeroen de Zeeuw, 33–54. Boulder: Lynne Rienner, 2007.

———. "The Left and Neoliberalism: Postwar Politics in El Salvador." PhD dissertation, Boston University, 2003.

Wanis-St. John, Anthony, and Darren Kew. "Civil Society and Peace Negotiations: Confronting Exclusion." *International Negotiation* 13, no. 1 (2008): 11–36.

Wantchekon, Leonard. "Strategic Voting in Conditions of Political Instability: The 1994 Elections in El Salvador." *Comparative Political Studies* 32, no. 7 (1999): 810–34.

Whitfield, Teresa. *Paying the Price: Ignacio Ellacuría and the Murdered Jesuits of El Salvador.* Philadelphia: Temple University Press, 1995.

———. "The Role of the United Nations in El Salvador and Guatemala: A Preliminary Comparison." In Arnson, *Comparative Peace Processes,* 257–90.

Williams, Philip J., and Knut Walter. *Militarization and Demilitarization in El Salvador's Transition to Democracy.* Pittsburgh: University of Pittsburgh Press, 1997.

Williams, Robert G. *States and Social Evolution: Coffee and the Rise of National Governments in Central America.* Chapel Hill: University of North Carolina Press, 1994.

Wolf, Sonja. "Mara Salvatrucha: The Most Dangerous Street Gang in the Americas?" *Latin American Politics and Society* 54, no. 1 (Spring 2012): 65–99.

———. "Subverting Democracy: Elite Rule and the Limits to Political Participation in Post-war El Salvador." *Journal of Latin American Studies* 41, no. 3 (August 2009): 429–65.

Wood, Elisabeth J. *Forging Democracy from Below: Insurgent Transitions in South Africa and El Salvador.* New York: Cambridge University Press, 2000.

———. *Insurgent Collective Action and Civil War in El Salvador.* New York: Cambridge University Press, 2003.

———. "Peace Accords and Postwar Reconstruction." In Boyce, *Economic Policy for Building Peace,* 73–106.

Woodward, Susan. "Economic Priorities for Successful Peace Implementation." In Stedman, Rothchild, and Cousens, *Ending Civil Wars,* 183–214.

Wynia, Gary. *The Politics of Latin American Development.* 3rd ed. New York: Cambridge University Press, 1990.

Zablah Kuri, Arturo. *Más allá de las promesas.* San Salvador: Friedrich Ebert Stiftung, 2005.

Zamora, Rubén. "Democratic Transition or Modernization? The Case of El Salvador since 1979." In *Democratic Transitions in Central America,* edited by Jorge I. Domínguez and Marc Lindenberg, 165–79. Gainesville: University Press of Florida, 1997.

———. *El Salvador, heridas que no cierran: Los partidos políticos en la postguerra.* San Salvador: FLACSO Programa El Salvador, 1998.

———. *La izquerda partidaria salvadoreña: Entre la identidad y el poder.* San Salvador: FLACSO, 2003.

Zürcher, Christoph. "The Liberal Peace: A Tough Sell?" In Campbell, Chandler, and Sabaratnam, *Liberal Peace?,* 69–88.

Index

The names of people may refer to the individual or the administration or both. Page numbers in bold type denote pages that contain figures or tables.